张清渊

大师 掌中定乾坤

张清渊大师不论阴阳宅风水、姓名学、人相学、奇门遁甲、紫微斗数、八字、梅花心易、易经六十四卦、星相、道法学等皆娴熟精通，其独步群伦的惊天绝技－「掐指神算」更是集命理之大成，不用姓名及出生八字或其他资料，只要张大师在掌中掐指一算，即可随问随答，弹指之间拿捏来龙去脉，掌中千里遥控论乾坤是享誉国际的当代大师。张大师风水堪舆及命理咨询服务资历名扬遐尔享誉国际。

张大师从事风水堪舆及命理咨询服务，除了台湾以外足迹遍及中国大陆各省、日本、韩国、越南、泰国、菲律宾、新加坡、马来西亚、南非、东帝汶等国之政要、巨商、名流。

GRAND MASTER CHANG CHING YUAN

Grandmaster Chang is well-versed and an expert in the art of Fengshui, Science of Naming, Face Reading, Ancient Metaphysical Sciences of Qi Men Dun Jia divination, Zi Wei Dou Shu (Purple Star Astrology), Bazi (Eight Characters of Birth Time), Art of Plum Flower Calculation, Principles of the 64 Hexagrams in I-Ching, Astrology and practitioner of Taoist rites. His trademark practice of the "Finger Divination" method places him on the pedestal of the Feng Shui fraternity and he is able to predict and articulate current and future issues about any individual, even if it is the first time he has met you. Grandmaster Chang is an internationally acclaimed practitioner of the art and science of Fengshui and he has consulted in countries beyond his home country of Taiwan, such as China, Japan, Korea, Vietnam, Thailand, Philippines, Singapore, Malaysia, Africa, East Timor, etc for governments, businesses and celebrities. Amongst his clients in Taiwan, he has consulted for the top 10 wealthiest men in the country, as well as numerous millionaires and billionaires in China. His client lists include government organizations in numerous countries, commercial entities and countless celebrities.

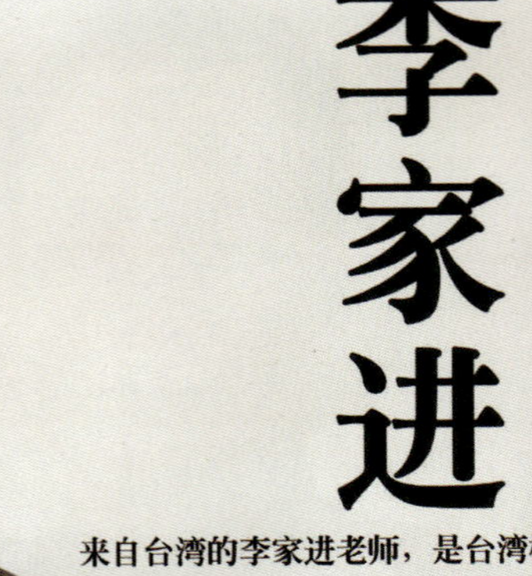

来自台湾的李家进老师，是台湾极具知名度的命理风水师父，曾在台湾知名的电视命理节目「命运好好玩」，「轻松好运气」等命理节目担任嘉宾，常以命理风水学术分析时事与解说风水知识，在台湾和新加坡更常受邀担任各大报章杂志的命理专栏作家，撰写命理风水文章以及生肖星座运程。

李家进老师，不论是紫微斗数论命，周易六爻占卜，生肖姓名学，择日学，阳宅风水鉴定都精通。为顾客论命时会用宏观与微观的角度去解析运势吉凶好坏，以及未来人生的发展方向。顾客也能够快速并且轻松的了解自身命运的得失，并能得到老师良好的建议来改善人生困境，所以不论中国，台湾与新马等地，许多顾客都变成老师的好友，并且获益良多。

MASTER LEE CHIA CHIN

Master Lee Chia-Chin is a renowned Fengshui master from Taiwan. He has appeared as a guest speaker in popular Fengshui related TV program in Taiwan, speaking about current affairs in Fengshui's perspective for many years. He has also been featured in Taiwan's Apple Daily newspaper as a regular columnist, writing about Fengshui. In addition, he is also a regular columnist in Singapore's magazine (Uweekly) and newspaper (Shin Min Daily News), sharing weekly zodiac and horoscope forecast.

Master Lee is an expert in personal life analysis, divination lot, name analysis and Fengshui. He often uses divination lot to help his customers to solve their problems and to overcome the obstacles that they faced. In addition, he also uses Fengshui theories to enhance his customers' lives and to prevent disastrous things from happening. Hence, he often received good appraisal from his customers from China, Taiwan, Singapore and Malaysia.

张瑞麟

老师 五术道法兼备

张瑞麟老师来自台湾，是国际风水易学大师张清渊的嫡传长子，深得张大师之传承，博学多闻，而且也是知名商业设计师及琉璃制作大师。

专研：民族宗教学、姓名学、紫微斗数、阴阳宅风水、择日学、易经六十四卦、正统道法学、环境设计学、琉璃美学。

瑞麟老师自幼跟随张清渊大师学习命理五术，协助大师制作传媒命理节目，制作设计开运化煞吉祥物，经营网路直播频道，执行生基园区设计工程，随张大师服务遍及中国、台湾、越南、日本、新加坡、马来西亚各地，学术精进，服务专业。瑞麟老师不仅专精风水命理学，其道法学更是造诣功深，功德无量，举凡禳解、开光、加持、化煞、安座，无一不通，在张大师的传承下，集各家所长，深得客户信任及喜爱。

MASTER CHANG JUI LING

Master Chang Jui Ling is well versed in the five arts of Chinese Metaphysics and Taoism.Master Chang Jui Ling is from Taiwan s the eldest son of Grand Master Chang Ching Yuan of International Feng Shui Easy to Learn. He inherited the erudition of Grand er Chang, is perspicacious, and is also a well-known commercial designer and Liuli coloured glaze making master.Specialized arch: Ethnic and Religious Studies, Name Studies, Ziwei Doushu, Yin-Yang House Fengshui, Selected Day Studies, I Ching 64 grams, Orthodox Taoism, Environmental Design and Liuli Aesthetics.

Master Chang Jui Ling's experience in the five techniques of numerology stems from his studies with Grand Master Chang Ching since he was a child, assisting him in the production of media numerology programs, creating and designing the mascots of ing fortune and resolving evils, and operating online live broadcast channels. Master Chang Jui Ling also helps in executing the n project of Shengji Park and serving with Grand Master Chang throughout China, Taiwan, Vietnam, Japan, Singapore, Malaysia performing academic excellence and professional service.

CONTACT : 6438 3688 / 8522 8878
ADDRESS :
1) 180 Bencoolen Street, #01-16/17 The Bencoolen Singapore 189646
2) 149 Rochor Road #05-15, Singapore 188425 Tel : 6842 5391 / 6842 5392

張家瑜

老师

运程断吉凶

专研：生肖运程预测、人相学、生肖姓名学、企业讲座、命理教学、紫微斗数

出生在风水世家，父亲是享誉国际的风水易学大师张清渊，从小耳濡目染学习五术命理，长年在新加坡玉玄门服务，将玉玄门风水命理及五路财神经营的有声有色，是命理界的后起之秀，深得客户信任及喜爱。

自从国际疫情爆发以来，经济环境剧变，一连串的隔离法规造成许多顾客无法得到命理咨询，因此家瑜老师兴起了在网络直播的念头，所以集合玉玄门大师群开播了一系列的风水命理直播，希望能说明到更多需要咨询的朋友，近期家瑜老师与时尚彩妆界合作，期待将风水命理注入时尚的世界，让更多的朋友能享受到古老文化的新视界。

Corporate Speaker

JOYCE CHANG

She has been learning Feng Shui since childhood. And being personally groomed by her father, Grand Master Chang Ching Yuan, a world-renowned Feng Shui master. She has served at YuXuanMen in Singapore for ten years.

Since the outbreak of the international epidemic, a series of quarantine regulations have prevented many customers frome receiving consultations. So, she came up with the idea of doing a live stream. Therefore, a group of masters from YuXuanMen began to broadcast a series of Zi Wei Dou Shu, Feng Shui, and Zodiac Forecast to help make a difference in prople's lives.

Recently, Joyce has cooperated with the fashion makeup industry and looks forward to injecting Feng Shui and Physiognomy into the fashion world, so that more people can enjoy the new vision of ancient culture.

CONTACT : 6438 3688 / 6369 9042
ADDRESS :
1) 180 Bencoolen Street, #01-16/17 The Bencoolen Singapore 189646
2) 149 Rochor Road #05-15, Singapore 188425 Tel : 6842 5391 / 6842 5392

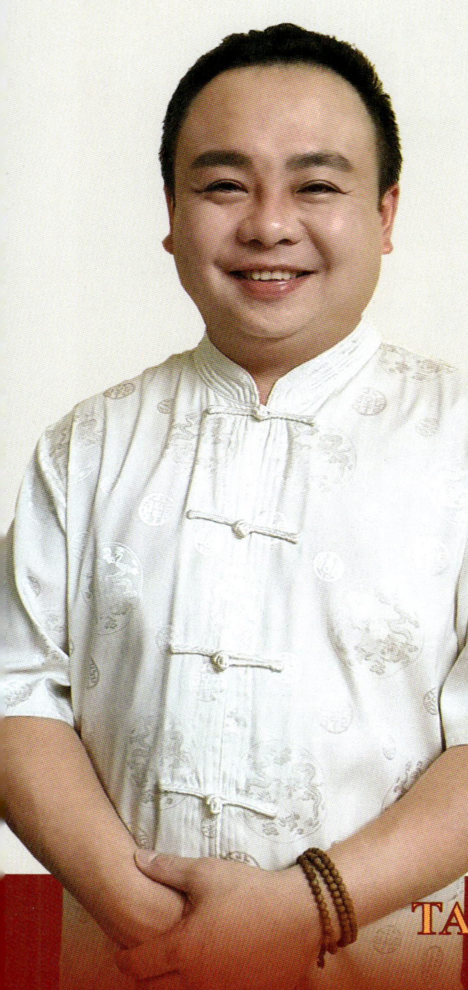

刘家良

老师

道法解灾厄

刘家良老师于2011年因九头灵狮神迹，因缘际会下结识张清渊大师，得大师点化领入道教法门，成为台湾三清宫宏圣堂六甲神坛金字门炉下弟子，宏愿道法，学以济世。

家良老师拜入张大师门下后，潜心精修五术之学，德术兼备，道法自然，精通八字学、紫微斗数、综合姓名学、易经六十四卦、阴阳宅风水堪舆、人相学、天星奇门遁甲九天玄女一二〇甲子择日秘法及正统道法学，举凡禳解、开光、加持、化煞、安座无一不通，在张大师的传承下，集各家所长，博学多才，堪称命理界的新星。

家良老师随张大师经管新加坡玉玄门事务，秉持着济世为怀的理念服务人群，为无数好友排忧解难，让客户在现实的人生中知命而掌运，创造出更多的财富，实践人生的美梦，让玉玄门专业命理团队以最优质、最专业、最热忱的精神来为大家服务，帮大众解决困难，帮助客户找到成功快捷方式，达成美满人生。

TAOIST MASTER/PRIEST
LIU JIA LIANG

Master Liu Jia-liang met Grand Master Chang Ching-yuan in 2011 by chance following the miraculous manifestation of ne-headed spiritual lion, and was initiated into Taoism by the master. Liu became a disciple of the Lioujia Divine Altar of ong Sheng Hall at the San Ching Temple in Taiwan, and made a great wish to learn the way to help the world.

After Liu became a disciple of Grand Master Chang, he devoted himself to the study of Geomancy. He then is proficient Zi, Zi Wei Dou Shu, the 64 hexagrams of the I-Ching, Yin-Yang House Feng Shui, Physiognomy, Qimen Dunjia. Under telage of Grand master Chang, Liu is known as a rising star in the field of fortune telling for his knowledge and versatility ef of evils, consecration, blessing, warding off evil spirits, and statue placement rituals at temples.

By following master Change's lead in managing the Yu Xuan Men Feng Shui in Singapore, Master Liu has been serving e with the idea of helping the world, solving the problems for countless friends, and enabling clients to know their destiny lity, so that they can create more wealth and realize their dreams in life. The Yu Xuan Men fortune telling team works the highest quality, professionalism and enthusiasm to help people solve problems, save time, reduce overspending, e wasted investment, and help customers find the quickest way to success and achieve a happy life.

四馬路

五路財神

Bugis Fortune God

新加坡五路財神座落於享有歷史盛名的四馬路上，於二〇一五年成立至今香火興旺，其正殿主祀五路財神，左右分別陪祀文財神范蠡（智慧財神）、偏財神韓信爺（賭神），壇上還有供奉媽祖、藏傳佛教之財寶天王（諸財神之首）、關聖帝君（商人守護神）、註生娘娘、偏財祖師劉海蟾（正的偏財神）、文昌帝君，福德正神（家宅社稷之神）、月下老人，所以來到四馬路五路財神無論是求正財或是求偏財、事業、考試、愛情、家庭美滿皆可如願。

- 解籤 Divination Lot / Character Analysis
- 拜斗科儀 Ritual Ceremony
- 安神入宅 Ritual Ceremony
- 流年流月運勢分析 Yearly Life Analysis
- 取名/改名 Name Selection for Companies, Individuals and New-born Babies
- 擇日 Auspicious Date Selection for Special Occasions（Marriage, Moving House, Caesarean）
- 居家/商業風水 Fengshui arrangement（Commercial / Residential）
- 祈福點燈 Wishing Lights
- 神像開光 Ritual Ceremony
- 紫微八字論命 Personal Life Analysis

紫微塔羅	卜卦	批名	北斗七星測運	面相 / 手相
Tarot Card	Divination Lot	Name Analysis	Aura Reading	Face / Palm Reading

五路財神 Bugis Fortune God / 四面觀音 Four Side Guan Yin
Tel：6438 3688 / 6369 9042
Add：180 Bencoolen Street，#01-16 / 17 The Bencoolen Singapore 189646
玉玄門命理風水
Tel：6842 5391 / 6842 5392
Add：149 Rochor Road #05-15, Singapore 188425

二〇一八年玉玄門在四馬路五路財神按奉了一尊特達靈感、尊貴靈顯的四面觀音，大家可在一年一度的觀音誕生日、觀音得道日、觀音出家日、觀音誕生日及農曆初一、十五來四馬路參拜四面觀音，轉運求福壽、納喜求財祿，讓您全年行大運、招財興旺發。

四面觀音各朝著東、西、南、北四面，每一面的觀音皆不相同，各有其深遠意義，四面觀音代表東南西北、仁義禮智、春夏秋冬、元亨利貞、福祿壽財等諸多意涵。

東方觀世音菩薩（楊柳觀音）

主消災解厄、解除疾病、平安、健康、自然自由、平等、福音、添福、家內和諧、普渡眾生。

西方觀世音菩薩（送子觀音）

主求子、求健康、祝福喜事連連、麒麟貴子、求科名、求功名、求官位、求地位、求金榜題名、求名聲顯揚、消除業障、有利懷抱希望者達成目的。

南方觀世音菩薩（持蓮觀音）

主和平和諧、所求如意、求姻緣、求婚姻、求感情、求人緣、添壽、求事業亨通、化解是非糾紛。

北方觀世音菩薩（持經觀音）

主求財、正財、橫財、求智慧開竅、求學業進步、求錢財入庫。

高雄杉林生基文化園

地灵龙气生基大法造命开运
让您改变一生的上乘风水密法

张清渊大师—最具权威之国际风水大师

现在名人、富商、高官争相种生基，以祈求旺运发财、治病、添福寿、添丁、添福贵，张清渊大师继「观音山生基文化园」後，又带领著玉玄门命理风水团队精心打造另一磅礴钜作，现已隆重登场「高雄杉林生基文化园」。

生基是人的身心靈生生不息之基礎建設

「高雄杉林生基文化园」形局多重吉砂琐镇收水纳局、雄伟厚实、紧密聚气，左右有龙虎砂拱抱，迎送有情，落脉转变而为将军挂印格，後靠有如天马飞奔而後拖贵人，天马驰坡连结成旗鼓之象，从远处鸟瞰有如祥龙献珠，又如将军挂印，水聚天心财丁两旺，其下砂有力，水口关锁严密，独得金龙禄储养龙真应水，明堂真气融结如八国城门锁正气，近案有情远朝宛如仙人上天桥步步高升之势，在如此好风水之下，能发富贵、财丁茂盛、福禄满堂、名扬四海、书勋鼎彝，并可延年益寿，您还在等什麼？赶快与我们联络吧！

180 Bencoolen St, The Bencoolen #01-16/17 Singapore189646
报名热线：+65 64383688 / 85228878 / +886 2 22723095 · 85

超渡大法會

日期：2025/04/25~27

地點：新北市板橋區光正街57號

（公館社區活動中心）

台灣報名專線：(02) 22723095•85

超渡祖先、已故親人、嬰靈 冤親債主、無主孤魂

Ritual Ceremony for Ancestors, Loved Ones, Karmic Creditors, Spirits of Infants and Pets, Wanderer Spirits

2025/04/25 星期五

第一天 科儀

0:00 ····· 启师请神（奉请神明，禀告天文）
0:30 ····· 招魂（招请要超渡的魂仪、过往亲人或宠物）
1:00 ····· 礼诵三官真经（传上天的知识为众生开智慧、升华）
2:00 ····· 午供（供养三界众神）
3:30 ····· 水忏（上卷、为众生求忏悔）
4:30 ····· 天医（奉请上古的医神治疗生前因生病往生的受度魂仪或有残缺者能使其还原）
5:30 ····· 水忏（中卷、为众生求忏悔）
6:30 ····· 水忏（下卷、为众生求忏悔）

2025/04/26 星期六

第二天 科儀

10:00 ····· 早课（礼诵消灾经为善信消灾祈福）
10:30 ····· 血湖经（为因流血意外、堕胎的婴儿、自杀或争战而往生的男女求忏悔）
11:00 ····· 血湖忏
12:00 ····· 午供（供养三界众神）
13:30 ····· 破城（帮助自杀、意外或不到60岁而往生的人，度他们离开枉死城）
15:00 ····· 破狱（帮助往生的亲人到阎王殿求忏悔破心狱往升仙界）
16:30 ····· 破血盆（为因失血而往生的人求忏悔）

2025/04/27 星期日

第三天 科儀

10:00 ····· 早课（礼诵消灾经为善信消灾祈福）
10:30 ····· 拜天公（将我们所做的法会圆满禀告上天，虔请上天给予肯定与通过）
12:00 ····· 午供（供养三界众神）
14:30 ····· 犒军（答谢护坛护法的神兵、神将庇护）
15:30 ····· 甘露施食（普施所有到法坛受度魂仪和没有被邀请的魂仪，慰其想念，济其饥渴）
16:00 ····· 法事圆满，护送魂仪往生极乐世界，敬玄谢师，送驾回銮（请神明圣驾返云宫）

Tel: +65 6842 5391, 6842 5392
149 Rochor Road #05-15,
Singapore 188425

五路財神
Bugis Fortune God

Tel: +65 6438 3688, 6369 9042
180 Bencoolen Street, #01-16/17
The Bencoolen Singapore 189646

承瑞命理风水有限公司

Tel: +65 6634 2777
10 Tampines Central 1 #04-16
Tampines 1 Singapore 529536

感恩孝思生命纪念馆

关怀尊重生命的精神，缅怀慎终追远的孝道传承，弘扬爱心孝思文化美德
打开现代人最具家庭伦理、敬老尊贤孝心，祭拜祖先的文创新视野
提供一个让您可以追念缅怀先人孝德伦纲的聚会联谊场所
祖宗牌位是代表家族血脉的延续，供奉祖先是孝敬怡亲与家庭伦理的示范。

感恩孝思生命纪念馆结合人文、信仰、科技、环保於一体

本馆位於风水宝地，交通便利，融合人文信仰、科技、传统习俗与环保理念。内部装潢采用琉璃水晶与金箔金属，营造庄严、尊贵、清静的宗教人文氛围。这里以佛、道、儒三家的礼仪供奉神明，寄托对先人的缅怀与敬意。各姓氏祖先和众生安奉於此，共享祥和祝福。馆内提供影音档案和线上追思功能，透过人文艺术呈现生命故事，让後代子孙体会传承的意义。

弥补您心中的遗憾

本馆区的服务让您免除遗憾，可以永久怀念追思先人，让祖先音容永存，让您亲情永远延续。

提供给民众最专业、最细心、最全面的服务

本馆以优质的、贴心的服务让家属安心和免除後顾之忧，专业的服务是我们一贯的信念，希望大家都能感受到永续的关怀，让我们一起走向卓越平坦的成功大道。

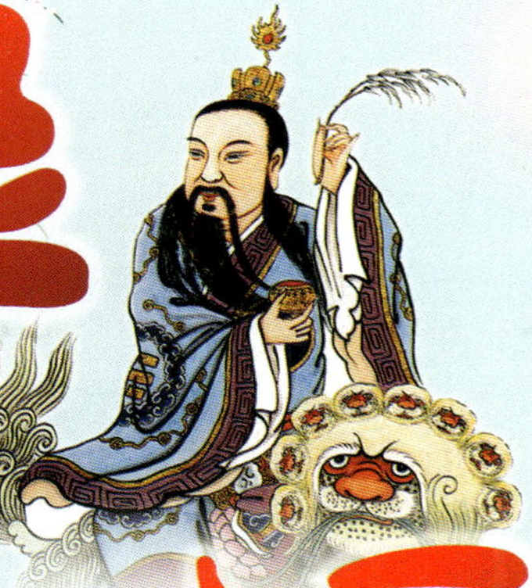

普渡

中元節

七月十五

积德尽孝

消灾改厄

LIVE

2025乙巳年線上普渡法會

法會日期：2025年9月6日（農曆七月十五）星期六

普渡項目：歷代祖先、已故親人、冤親債主、嬰靈、寵物、好兄弟、地基主

為什麼要普渡？

普渡是一種宗教儀式，基於因果循環，自然界所有事物都有其輪迴，普渡便針對於此，要為亡者助念玉玄門五路財神為發揚傳統固有化，本著眾生平等的大愛精神，以豐盛的飯菜、供品供養三界亡靈；並請高功法師誦經、召請神佛為先祖和亡靈及累世冤親債主等眾超拔追薦迴向，祈求令其業障消除，離苦得樂，往生善道。

普渡只做一次就夠了嗎？

並不是！普渡是一種功德法事，每個人或亡靈的因果業障不同，所以建議大家做普渡，就算普渡物件功德圓滿、投胎轉世，這份功德也會相互迴向、增加福報。

報名專線：(02)22723095 傳真：(02)22721846

法會現場：新北市板橋區中正路216巷148號

四马路五路财神 祈福光明灯 Wishing Light

报名专线：+65 6438 3688, 6369 9042

180 Bencoolen Street, #01-16/17 The Bencoolen Singapore 189646

四马路 五路財神 Bugis Fortune God

八大守护神光明灯 - Zodiac Guardian Wishing Light

千手千眼观世音菩萨
Thousand Arm Avalokiteshvara

鼠年生人可以选定千手观音为守护本尊。鼠年生人若能修千手观音法门，无论智慧、财富、事业、家庭等各种愿望都能心想事成。

Guardian of the Zodiac Rat

虚空藏菩萨
Akasagarbha Budhisattva

牛、虎年生人可以选定虚空藏菩萨为守护本尊。牛、虎年生人若能修虚空藏菩萨法门，能远离苦难，增强记忆力，增长福慧，增进人缘，保佑他们工作顺心，家庭和乐。

Guardian of the Zodiac Ox and Tiger

文殊菩萨
Manjushri Bodhisattva

兔年生人若能修文殊菩萨法门，可以增长智慧，增强记忆力，并能得其护佑，学业有成，事业顺利，家庭和谐，并使他们免受一切烦恼的干扰。

Guardian of the Zodiac Rabbit

普贤菩萨
Samantabhadra Bodhisattv

龙、蛇年生人可以选定普贤菩萨为守护本尊。龙、蛇年生人若能修普贤菩萨法门，可获得延年益寿，一生平稳，远离各种病痛，厄运，最快获得宵夜灭罪，成就无上菩提。

Guardian of the Zodiac Dragon and Snake

大势至菩萨
Mahasthamaprapta Bodhisattva

马年生人可以选定大势至菩萨为守护本尊。马年生人若能修大势至菩萨法门，可获得其光明力量和智慧威德，聚财守富，一生安和，在他的佛光照耀下，得到无上的信心能量。

Guardian of the Zodiac Horse

大日如来
Vairocana Bodhisattva

羊、猴年生人可以选定大日如来作为守护本尊。羊、猴年生人若能修大日如来法门，可得其威力加持开启智慧、贵人扶持、成就事业，大展宏图。

Guardian of the Zodiac Goat and Monkey

不动明王
Acala Vidyaraja

鸡年生人可以选定不动明王作为守护本尊。鸡年生人若能修不动明王法门，可得他的守护，远离罪业，一生顺逆，平安如意。

Guardian of the Zodiac Rooster

阿弥陀佛
Amitabha Buddha

狗、猪年生人可以选定阿弥陀佛为守护本尊。狗、猪年生人若能修阿弥陀佛法门，可得他的守护，消除一切灾祸业苦，一生安乐，逢凶化吉，并在临终后往生极乐世界。

Guardian of the Zodiac Dog and Pig

太岁平安灯 Tai Sui Wishing Light

祈求斗姆元君赐福岁运平和
解厄，福运亨通，光明普照
Tai Sui Wishing Light: Wish fo
protection, blessings and to overcome all obstacles.

健康如意灯 Health Wishing Light

祈求平安吉祥，身强体健，四
赐福添泰。
Health Wishing Light: Wish for protection, blessings and good

事业财利灯 Wealth Wishing Light

祈求事业发达、仕途顺遂、
财利广进、迎祥纳福。
Wealth Wishing Light: Wish fo
prosperity and success in care

文昌智慧灯 Academic Wishing Light

祈求庇佑登科及第、考试
开发潜能、增加智慧、学业
Academic Wishing Light: Wi
good exam luck, able to hav
results and to increase wisd

月老姻缘灯 Relationship Wishing Light

祈求千里姻缘一线，牵待
点盏灯，让月老帮你求得
Marriage Wishing Light: Wis
good marriage luck and able
Mr/Miss Rright soon.

药师佛光明灯 Medicine Budha Wishing Lig

祈求免于遭受疾病缠身，
灭除灾难。
Medicine Buddha Wishing Li
for all sickness to be away fr
body and to minimise the pa

强力推荐
台湾神像批发零售 Wholesale Taiwan Deity Statue

果必有因　今世种因来世果
债无不还　得生当还前生债

欠债还钱，天经地义。诺而不兑，是为失信，失信者逆於道，自有惩罚，天地间自有公平正义，物万事自有规则，这就是天道。

什麼是寿生阴债?

道教典籍《太上老君说五斗金章受生经》、《灵宝天尊说禄库受生经》和《太上元始天尊说开库钥匙妙经》详细解释了阴债的来源与影响，今生的福报并非无故而来，而是人在投生前向冥府借来的钱财及资源。这些福报让人今生拥有衣食、财运和健康等基本生活保障，因此被称为「寿生阴债」，又称「前世债」。

为什麼有人经常补财库，财运还是很糟糕?

尽管我们补了财库，为何仍不断漏财、破财呢?这是因为我们在投胎转世时，向天曹地府的库曹官借了受生禄库财。过了奈何桥後，前世的因果皆忘，因此不知有借贷受生禄库未还，导致诸事不顺、钱财不丰、感情不睦、健康不佳。

为了减轻阴债对今生的影响，玉玄门特请法师以正统道教还「欠债金」科仪替您进行交割偿还，让您今後永无拖欠之资，以了断前世因果循环。并恭请众神祈佑您常年享有嘉庆，贵人明显、事业亨通、身体健康、财源广进。这些仪式将呈上天曹库官案前验收，以此为凭，消减罪孽，解除业障。先偿还寿生阴债後，再来补财库，才能真正留住所赚来的钱财，让事业顺利、财库丰盈。

賀鳴
H.M FENGSHUI

四马路五路财神．四面观音
报名专线：+65 6438 3688 / 8522 8878
180 Bencoolen Street, #01-16/17 The Bencoolen Singapore 189646

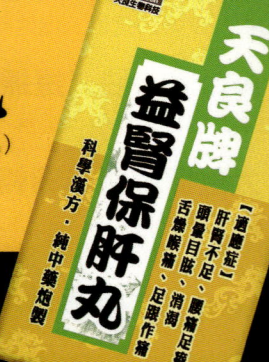

2025乙巳蛇年十二生肖開運吉祥物圖解

今年肖鼠人都適用

制化天厄、暴敗凶星
Remedy Ritual Ceremony

Suitable for all born in the year of Rat

今年肖鼠人都適用

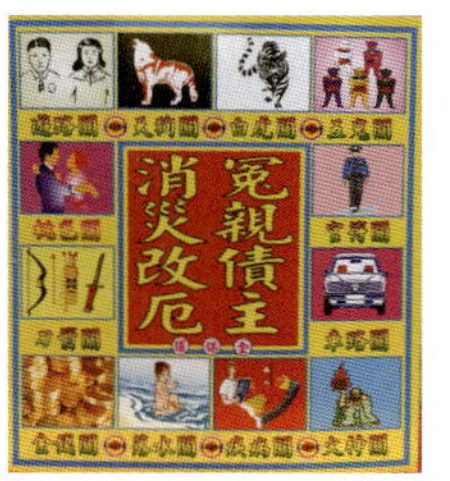

冤親債主金
Incense Paper for Karmic Creditors

今年肖鼠人都適用

千手千眼觀音菩薩本命燈
Zodiac Guardian wishing lamp

庚子年6歲

開運葫蘆
Hu Lu

戊子年18歲

琉璃魁星踢斗
Glazed Kui Xing Ta Dou

丙子年30歲

三合生肖猴鼠龍
Zodiac Benefactors (Monkey, Rat and Dragon)

甲子年42歲

黃水晶招財樹
Wealth Crystal Tree

壬子年54歲

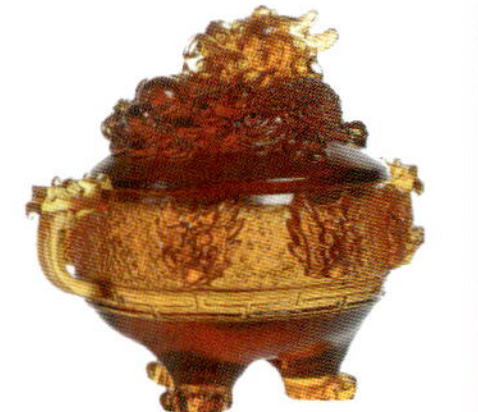

琉璃九龍聚寶盆
Nine-dragon Treasure Bowl

庚子年66歲

七彩蓮花轉運燈
Colourful Lotus Wishing Light

戊子年78歲

琉金四面觀音
Four Side Guan Yin

牛 Ox

今年肖牛人都適用

制化白虎凶星 Remedy Ritual Ceremony

Suitable for all born in the year of Ox

今年肖牛人都適用

冤親債主金
Incense Papers for Karmic Creditors

今年肖牛人都適用

虛空藏菩薩本命燈
Zodiac Guardian Wishing Light

辛丑年5歲

雷令福袋
Protective Treasure Bag

己丑年17歲

文昌智慧光明燈
Academic Wishing Light

丁丑年29歲

小桃木六帝古錢獅咬劍風鈴
Lion Head Charm

乙丑年41歲

三合生肖蛇牛雞
Zodiac Benefactors (Snake, Ox and Rooster)

癸丑年53歲

三合水晶手鍊
Zodiac Guardian Bracelet

辛丑年65歲

九品蓮花轉運燈
Ninth-grade Lotus Wishing Light

己丑年77歲

黑曜石葫蘆吊飾
Obsidian Hu Lu

今年肖虎人都適用

太歲星燈 Worship Tai Sui

Suitable for all born in the year of Tiger

今年肖虎人都適用

太歲金
Tai Sui Incense Paper

今年肖虎人都適用

虛空藏菩薩本命燈
Zodiac Guardian Wishing Light

壬寅年4歲

綠水晶文昌開運樹
Academic Crystal Tree

庚寅年16歲

琉璃玉書麒麟
Glazed Qi Lin

戊寅年28歲

黃水晶招財樹
Wealth Crystal Tree

丙寅年40歲

琉璃飛天麒麟
Glazed Qi Lin

甲寅年52歲

三合生肖虎馬狗
Zodiac Benefactors (Horse, Dog and Tiger)

壬寅年64歲

補財好運沐浴露
Wealth Body Wash

庚寅年76歲

五行水晶能量瓶
Five Element Energy Water Bottle

兔 Rabbit

今年肖兔人都適用

制化天狗、弔客凶星
Remedy Ritual Ceremony

Suitable for all born in the year of Rabbit

今年肖兔人都適用

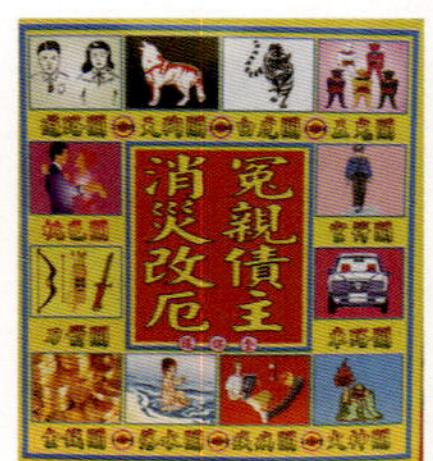

冤親債主金
Incense Paper for Karmic Creditors

今年肖兔人都適用

文殊菩薩本命燈
Zodiac Guardian Wishing Light

癸卯年3歲

補財好運沐浴露
Wealth Body Wash

辛卯年15歲

文昌智慧沐浴露
Academic Body Wash

己卯年27歲

琉璃龍龜
Glazed Dragon Turtles

丁卯年39歲

三合生肖豬兔羊
Zodiac Benefactors (Pig, Rabbit and Goat)

乙卯年51歲

琉璃龍馬奔騰
Glazed Dragon Horse

癸卯年63歲

琉璃獅咬劍文鎮
Lion Head

辛卯年75歲

琉金四面觀音
Four Side Guan Yin

龍 Dragon

今年肖龍人都適用

制化病符凶星 Remedy Ritual Ceremony

Suitable for all born in the year of Dragon

今年肖龍人都適用

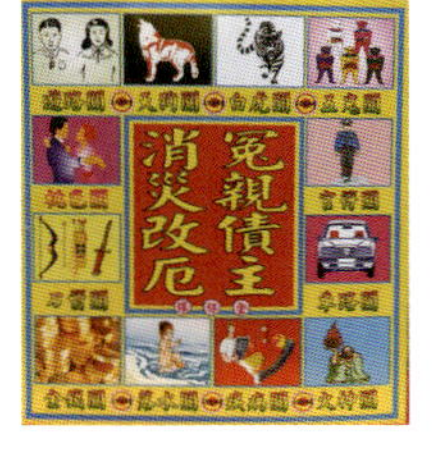

冤親債主金
Incense Papers for Karmic Creditors

今年肖龍人都適用

普賢菩薩本命燈
Zodiac Guardian Wishing Light

甲辰年2歲

開運葫蘆
Hu Lu

壬辰年14歲

琉璃蓮花童子
Lian Hua Tong Zi

庚辰年26歲

三合生肖貴人盤
Zodiac Guardian Plate

戊辰年38歲

雷令福袋
Protective Treasure Bag

丙辰年50歲

琉璃河圖龍馬
Glazed Dragon Horse

甲辰年62歲

黃水晶招財樹
Wealth Crystal Tree

壬辰年74歲

華陀除疾金
Hua Tuo Incense Paper (Prevent Sickness)

蛇 Snake

今年肖蛇人都適用

Suitable for all born in the year of Snake

太歲星燈 Worship Tai Sui

今年肖蛇人都適用

太歲金
Tai Sui Incense Paper

今年肖蛇人都適用

普賢菩薩本命燈
Zodiac Guardian
Wishing Light

乙巳年1歲

琉璃千手千眼觀音項鍊
Thousand Eyes
Guanyin necklace

癸巳年13歲

魁星踢斗隨身牌
Kui Xing Ta Dou Tablet

辛巳年25歲

八卦平安淨身手工皂
Handmade Ba Gua Soap

己巳年37歲

三合水晶手鍊
Zodiac Guardian
Bracelet

丁巳年49歲

三合生肖蛇牛雞
Zodiac Benefactors
(Snake, Ox and Rooster)

乙巳年61歲

五路財神金
Fortune God Incense
Paper

癸巳年73歲

藥師佛消災解厄燈
Medicine Buddha
Wishing Light

今年肖馬人都適用

制化桃花凶星 Remedy Ritual Ceremony

今年肖馬人都適用

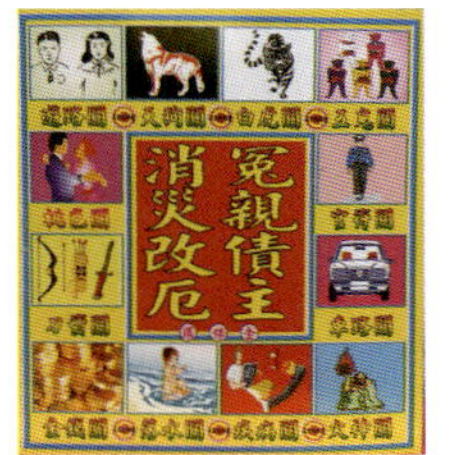

冤親債主金
Incense Paper for Karmic Creditors

今年肖馬人都適用

大勢至菩薩本命燈
Zodiac Guardian Wishing Light

今年肖馬人都適用

月老桃花旺緣燈
Marriage Wishing Light

甲午年12歲

文昌智慧沐浴露
Academic Body Wash

壬午年24歲

桃花寶袋
Love Treasure Bag

庚午年36歲

三合生肖虎馬狗
Zodiac Benefactors (Horse, Dog and Tiger)

戊午年48歲

琉璃龍鳳呈祥
Glazed Dragon-Phoenix

丙午年60歲

桃花姻緣沐浴露
Love Body Wash

甲午年72歲

五行水晶能量瓶
Five Element Energy Water Bottle

今年肖羊人都適用

制化喪門凶星 Remedy Ritual Ceremony

Suitable for all born in the year of Goat

今年肖羊人都適用

冤親債主金
Incense Papers for Karmic Creditors

今年肖羊人都適用

大日如來本命燈
Zodiac Guardian Wishing Light

今年肖羊人都適用

驅制小人金
Incense Paper (Prevent Villains)

乙未年11歲

綠水晶文昌開運樹
Academic Crystal Tree

癸未年23歲

三合生肖豬兔羊
Zodiac Benefactors (Pig, Rabbit and Goat)

辛未年35歲

琉璃獅咬劍文鎮
Lion Head

己未年47歲

九頭靈獅項鍊
Nine-headed Lion Necklace

丁未年59歲

雷令福袋
Protective Treasure Bag

乙未年71歲

琉金四面觀音
Four Side Guan Yin

猴 Monkey

今年肖猴人都適用

Suitable for all born in the year of Monkey

制化桃花及拜太歲
Remedy Ritual Ceremony, Worship Tai Sui

今年肖猴人都適用

太歲金
Tai Sui Incense Paper

今年肖猴人都適用

大日如來本命燈
Zodiac Guardian Wishing Light

今年肖猴人都適用

太歲星燈
Tai Sui Wishing Light

丙申年10歲

琉璃魁星踢斗
Glazed Kui Xing Ta Dou

甲申年22歲

桃花姻緣沐浴露
Love Body Wash

壬申年34歲

雷令福袋
Protective Treasure Bag

庚申年46歲

三合生肖猴鼠龍
Zodiac Benefactors (Monkey, Rat and Dragon)

戊申年58歲

三合水晶手鍊
Zodiac Guardian Bracelet

丙申年70歲

九品蓮花轉運燈
Ninth-grade Lotus Wishing Light

雞 Rooster

今年肖雞人都適用

制化五鬼、官符凶星 Remedy Ritual Ceremony

Suitable for all born in the year of Rooster

今年肖雞人都適用

冤親債主金
Incense Paper for Karmic Creditors

今年肖雞人都適用

不動明王本命燈
Marriage Wishing Light

今年肖雞人都適用

驅制小人金
Incense Paper (Prevent Villains)

丁酉年9歲

文昌智慧沐浴露
Academic Body Wash

乙酉年21歲

雷令福袋
Protective Treasure Bag

癸酉年33歲

龍神聖水
Dragon God Holy Water

辛酉年45歲

三合生肖蛇牛雞
Zodiac Benefactors (Snake, Ox and Rooster)

己酉年57歲

琉璃龍印寶璽
Glazed Dragon Seal

丁酉年69歲

九頭靈獅項鍊
Nine-headed Lion Necklace

今年肖狗人都適用
Suitable for all born in the year of Dog

制化死符凶星 Remedy Ritual Ceremony

今年肖狗人都適用

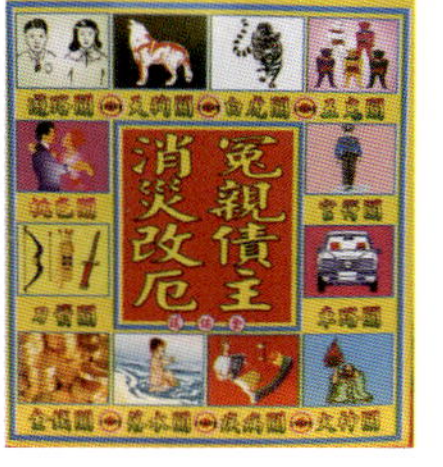

冤親債主金
Incense Papers for Karmic Creditors

今年肖狗人都適用

阿彌陀佛本命燈
Zodiac Guardian Wishing Light

今年肖狗人都適用

觀音菩薩平安健康燈
Guan Yin Wishing Light

戊戌年8歲

綠水晶文昌開運樹
Academic Crystal Tree

丙戌年20歲

魁星踢斗隨身牌
Kui Xing Ta Dou Tablet

甲戌年32歲

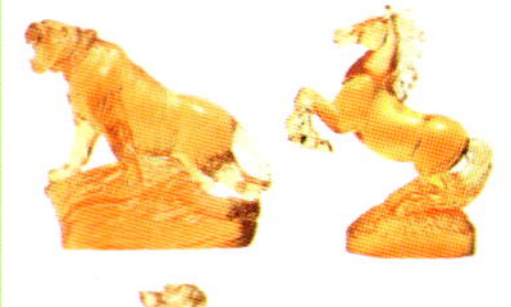

三合生肖虎馬狗
Zodiac Benefactors (Horse, Dog and Tiger)

壬戌年44歲

三合水晶手鍊
Zodiac Guardian Bracelet

庚戌年56歲

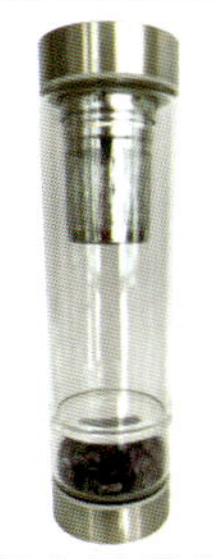

五行水晶能量瓶
Five Element Energy Water Bottle

戊戌年68歲

琉金四面觀音
Four Side Guan Yin

豬 Pig

今年肖豬人都適用

太歲星燈 Worship Tai Sui

Suitable for all born in the year of Pig

今年肖豬人都適用

太歲金
Tai Sui Incense Paper

今年肖豬人都適用

阿彌陀佛本命燈
Zodiac Guardian Wishing Light

己亥年7歲

魁星踢斗隨身牌
Kui Xing Ta Dou Tablet

丁亥年19歲

琉璃玉書麒麟
Glazed Qi Lin

乙亥年31歲

三合生肖豬兔羊
Zodiac Benefactors (Pig, Rabbit and Goat)

癸亥年43歲

驅除小人金
Incense Paper (Prevent Villains)

辛亥年55歲

八卦平安淨身手工皂
Handmade Ba Gua Soap

己亥年67歲

琉璃飛天躍馬
Glazed Flying Horse

丁亥年79歲

藥師佛消災解厄燈
Medicine Buddha Wishing Light

2025發財開運寶典

張清淵

目錄

敬神如神在

農曆諸聖神佛誕辰千秋表

誠虔則靈威

正月令

正月初一日	元始天尊萬壽
正月初一日	彌勒尊佛佛辰
正月初三日	孫天醫真人千秋
正月初六日	清水祖師佛辰
正月初八日	五殿閻羅王聖誕
正月初九日	玉皇上帝萬壽
正月十三日	關聖帝君飛昇
正月十五日	門神戶尉千秋
正月十五日	上元天官聖誕
正月十五日	臨水夫人陳靖姑千秋
正月廿二日	武德尊侯沈祖公聖誕
正月廿四日	雷都光耀大帝聖誕

二月令

二月初一日	一殿秦廣王千秋
二月初二日	濟公活佛聖誕
二月初二日	土穀尊神聖誕
二月初二日	福德正神千秋
二月初三日	文昌梓童帝君聖誕
二月初八日	三殿宋帝王千秋
二月十五日	九天玄女娘娘聖誕
二月十五日	太上老君萬壽
二月十五日	精忠岳王千秋
二月十六日	開漳聖王千秋
二月十八日	至聖先師諱辰
二月十八日	四殿五官王千秋
二月十九日	觀世音菩薩佛辰
二月廿一日	普賢菩薩佛辰
二月廿五日	三山國王千秋
二月廿六日	南宮趙真君聖誕

三月令

三月初一日	二殿楚江王千秋
三月初三日	玄天上帝萬壽
三月初六日	濟公活佛成道
三月初七日	三天主考王聖誕
三月初八日	六殿卞城王千秋
三月十五日	無極老母娘聖壽
三月十五日	保生大帝吳真人千秋
三月十五日	中路財神趙元帥聖誕
三月十六日	準提菩薩佛誕
三月十八日	南天廖將軍聖誕
三月十八日	后土皇神聖誕
三月十九日	太陽星君聖誕
三月二十日	註生娘娘千秋
三月廿三日	天上聖母聖誕
三月廿六日	鬼谷先師千秋
三月廿七日	七殿泰山王千秋
三月廿八日	蒼頡先師聖誕
三月廿八日	東嶽大帝聖誕

四月令

四月初一日	八殿都市王千秋
四月初四日	文殊菩薩佛辰
四月初八日	釋迦佛祖萬壽
四月初八日	九殿平等王千秋
四月十四日	呂純陽祖師聖誕
四月十五日	釋迦文佛得道
四月十七日	十殿轉輪王千秋
四月十八日	北極紫微帝君千秋
四月十八日	華陀神醫先師千秋
四月廿一日	李托塔天王聖誕
四月廿一日	先天朱將軍聖誕
四月廿四日	金光祖師聖誕
四月廿五日	武安尊王千秋
四月廿六日	五穀先帝千秋
四月廿六日	南鯤鯓李王爺千秋
四月廿七日	南鯤鯓范王爺千秋

五月令

五月初一日	南極長生帝君千秋
五月初五日	南天駱恩師聖誕
五月初七日	巧聖先師千秋
五月十一日	天下都城隍爺千秋
五月十三日	關平太子千秋
五月十七日	蕭府王爺千秋
五月十八日	張府天師聖誕
五月十九日	九天馬恩師聖誕

六月令

六月初三日	韋馱尊佛佛辰
六月初六日	九天李恩師聖誕
六月初七	玉皇上帝成道日
六月初十	劉海蟾祖師聖誕
六月十一日	田都元帥千秋
六月十五日	無極老母娘聖壽
六月十五日	王靈天君聖誕
六月十六日	先天王靈官聖誕
六月十八日	南鯤鯓池王爺千秋
六月十九日	觀音菩薩得道紀念
六月廿四日	關聖帝君聖誕
六月廿四日	西秦王爺千秋
六月廿四日	雷祖大帝聖誕
六月廿四日	南極大帝聖誕

七月令

七月初七日	七星娘娘千秋
七月初七日	大成魁星聖誕
七月初七日	衛房聖母聖誕
七月十三日	大勢至菩薩聖誕
七月十四日	鄭延平郡王千秋
七月十五日	中元地官聖誕
七月十八日	瑤池王母娘聖誕
七月十九日	天然古佛聖誕
七月十九日	值年太歲星君千秋
七月廿一日	普庵菩薩佛辰
七月廿三日	南客柳星君聖誕
七月廿三日	諸葛武侯千秋
七月廿三日	法主聖君千秋
七月廿五日	武德侯沈祖公千秋
七月三十日	地藏王菩薩佛辰

八月令

八月初三日	北斗星君聖誕
八月初三日	九天司命灶君千秋
八月初三日	九天朱恩師聖誕
八月初三日	姜相子牙千秋
八月初五日	雷聲普化天尊聖誕
八月初八日	瑤池大會
八月十五日	天然古佛成道
八月十五日	太陰星君聖誕
八月十五日	南宮孔恩師聖誕
八月十五日	臨水夫人林姑千秋
八月十五日	南鯤鯓朱王爺千秋
八月十八日	九天玄女娘娘千秋
八月十八日	開臺鄭國姓聖誕
八月廿二日	燃燈古佛萬壽
八月廿二日	廣澤尊王千秋
八月廿三日	桓侯張大帝聖誕
八月廿三日	邢府王爺千秋
八月廿七	至聖孔子先師聖誕
八月廿七日	中華聖母聖誕

九月令

九月初一	南斗星君聖誕
九月初九日	斗母星君聖誕
九月初九日	九皇大帝聖誕
九月初九日	中壇元帥千秋
九月初九日	酆都大帝聖誕
九月初九日	臨水夫人李姑千秋
九月十三日	天上聖母飛昇
九月十五日	孟婆尊神千秋
九月十五日	極無老母娘聖壽
九月十五日	朱聖夫子聖誕
九月十五日	南鯤鯓吳王爺千秋
九月十八日	倉聖先師千秋
九月十九日	觀音菩薩出家紀念
九月廿九日	藥師佛聖誕

十月令

十月初五日	達摩祖師佛辰
十月初十日	水仙尊王千秋
十月十二日	齊天大聖佛辰
十月十五日	下元水官大帝聖誕
十月十八日	地母至尊千秋
十月廿二日	青山靈安尊王千秋
十月廿三日	南天周倉將軍聖誕
十月廿五日	感大帝許真人千秋
十月廿七日	紫微星君聖誕

十一月令

十一月初四日	安南尊王千秋
十一月十一日	太乙救苦天尊聖誕
十一月十五日	無極老母娘聖誕
十一月十七日	阿彌陀佛佛誕
十一月十九日	九蓮菩薩佛誕
十一月廿三日	張仙大帝聖誕
十一月廿六日	廣惠聖王誕辰

十二月令

十二月初六日	普庵祖師聖誕
十二月初八日	張英濟王聖誕
十二月初八日	釋迦文佛成道
十二月十六日	福德正神千秋
十二月廿四日	送神
十二月廿五日	天神下降
十二月廿九日	華嚴菩薩佛誕
十二月廿九日	南斗北斗星下降

諸聖神佛誕辰祭拜方式

元始天尊聖誕

農曆正月初一日是元始天尊聖誕，元始天尊是道教最高神靈三清尊神之一，與靈寶天尊、道德天尊合稱「三清」，又稱玉清元始天尊。元者本也，始者初也，先天之氣也，元始天尊生於混沌之前，故名「元始」，而元始是最初的本源，為一切神仙之上，故稱「天尊」。相傳元始天尊至高無上與道同體，在天地開闢之際，向諸神現身說法演說經文，在無量劫數來臨之時，用玄妙的大道來教化眾生，稱為「開劫度人」。

祭祀方式：

供品： 壽桃、壽麵、三牲、鮮花、香燭、清茶、酒、水果五種、發糕、湯圓、紅圓、紅龜、糖果、餅乾、菜碗及應節食品。

金紙： 太極金、壽金、刈金、福金。

玉皇上帝聖誕

農曆正月初九日是玉皇上帝聖誕，俗稱天日、天公生。祂是統領三界內外十方諸神以及人間萬靈的最高神明，祂代表至高無上的天，又稱天公祖、昊天金闕玉皇大帝、玉皇大天尊、玄穹高上帝等，民間除了早晚燒香、頂禮膜拜之外，舉凡結婚、做壽時都要拜天公。農曆正月初九，為一年之初、四季之首、木氣之始，一切生命萌發，大地回春，而陽數始於一極於九，因此玉帝的誕辰是一個極尊的日子，自古歷朝都有帝王祭天的儀式，後來逐漸演變為民間祭祀玉帝，信仰深入民心。

祭祀方式：

供品： 1、祭拜天公時供桌分為頂桌和下桌，稱為「搭天臺」，是模擬上中下三界。桌旁兩側拴上一對拱形甘蔗，甘蔗兩旁則綁上高錢，象徵上界的南天門及天兵天將，祈求錢財能夠節節高升。

2、頂桌祭拜玉皇大帝，供奉三官燈座（天官、地官、水官），供奉鮮花、麵線，素三牲、五果、六齋、清茶、山珍海味：（薑、紅豆、鹽、糖）。頂桌供奉素食或水果以示對天公的尊敬。

3、下桌為供奉玉皇大帝從神所設，可準備三牲、水果五種、糖果餅乾、紅圓、米糕、發糕、紅龜等。

金紙：頂極金、天金、太極金、壽金、刈金、甲馬。

天官大帝聖誕

農曆正月十五是天官大帝聖誕，中國傳統習俗正月十五日稱上元節，也是元宵節、天官大帝聖誕。三官大帝是天官大帝、地官大帝、水官大帝的合稱，俗稱三界公，起源於人民對天、地、水的自然崇拜，三位神明主宰生老病死、命運氣數，人們為了祈求賜福，所以在上元日，張花燈拜三官，從唐宋以來，三元節都是道教的大慶日子，道經稱：「天官賜福，地官赦罪，水官解厄。」所以上元節不僅有求吉、禳災、祛邪的意義，還具有多元的民俗文化意義。

祭祀方式：

供品：清茶、鮮花、水果五種、三牲、齋菜六項、牲禮、壽桃、壽麵、發糕、湯圓、紅圓、紅龜、糖果餅乾。

金紙：頂極金、天金、太極金、壽金、刈金、甲馬。

福德正神聖誕

農曆二月初二是福德正神聖誕，福德正神又稱大伯公、土地公等等。土地公是中國民間信仰最普遍的神祇之一，祂屬於掌管土地的保護神，祭祀土地公即祭祀大地，祂是非常親近人民的神祇，如地方褓母一般。現代祭拜土地公多屬於祈福、求財、保平安、保農業收成，一般商家也供奉土地公為財神，每逢初二、十六做牙祭拜土地公，希望能庇佑生意興隆，二月初二是一年中第一次做牙，稱為「頭牙」，同時這天也是土地公的生日。

祭祀方式：

供品：三牲、水果、清香、壽桃、壽麵、春捲 (潤餅)、糖果、餅乾。

金紙：土地公金、壽金、刈金、福金。

文昌帝君聖誕

農曆二月初三日是文昌帝君聖誕，文昌帝君又稱文昌星、梓潼帝君，文昌帝君，執掌文昌府事與人間祿籍，掌管福祿、主宰功名，配上坐騎稱為祿馬，陪侍在側的神明有送祿神、書童、印童，自古以來只要是讀書人、文人、教師等都會在文昌帝君誕辰齊聚在文昌廟舉行祭典，所以想要智慧增長、學業進步、考運亨通、金榜題名、功成名就、步步高昇、工作升遷、仕途如意、加官晉祿之人，都可以祭拜文昌帝君。

祭祀方式：

供品：蔥(聰明)，蒜(精算)，芹菜(勤勞)，白蘿蔔(好彩頭)，粽子(包中)，糕點(步步高升)、壽桃、壽麵、蓮花心燈等，祭拜時要在這些供品貼上紅紙以討喜氣。

金紙：文昌智慧金、壽金、刈金、福金、文昌金衣。

太上老君聖誕

農曆二月十五日為道祖太上老君聖誕，太上老君為道教最高尊神「三清」之一，道教稱之為太上道祖、太清大帝、李老君等，據說太上老君有累世化身，伏羲時化為鬱華子，神農時化為太成子，黃帝時化為廣成子，春秋時化為老子，老子所著的《道德經》更是千古名著，說明道為宇宙萬象的真體，至道即真理是天地之根，對中華文化思想影響甚巨，張道陵天師修道時，自稱是由太上老君傳授其秘籙而創立道教，故奉老君為道教創教始祖。

祭祀方式：

供品：壽桃、壽麵、三牲、鮮花、香燭、清茶、酒、水果五種、發糕、湯圓、紅圓、紅龜、糖果、餅乾、菜碗及應節食品。

金紙：太極金、壽金、刈金、福金。

觀世音菩薩聖誕

觀世音菩薩是民間最普遍敬仰的神佛，儒釋道三教皆有供奉，是西方三聖及四大菩薩之一，其名號意為「觀察世間音聲覺悟有情」。觀世音菩薩有救苦救難、大慈大悲之心，無論世間眾生遭遇何種災難，若一心稱念觀世音菩薩名號，觀音便能尋音赴感，使其離苦得樂，故人稱「大慈大悲觀世音菩薩慈航普渡眾生」。

民間慶祝觀音誕的日子通常有三個：農曆二月十九是觀音菩薩的誕生日，農曆六月十九是觀音得道紀念日，農曆九月十九日是觀音菩薩出家紀念日。此外農曆正月廿六日，是一年一度的觀音開庫日，信眾在這個日子都會到觀音廟祈福及借庫，希望能得到觀音菩薩的保佑，使自己財運亨通、大發利市。

祭祀方式：

供品： 壽桃、壽麵、素三牲、鮮花、香燭、清茶、酒、水果五種、發糕、湯圓、紅圓、紅龜、糖果、餅乾、菜碗及應節食品。

金紙： 太極金、壽金、刈金、福金、觀音金衣。

普賢菩薩佛誕

農曆二月二十一日是普賢菩薩佛誕，普賢菩薩的來歷，一說是佛祖的第八弟子，一說是諸佛之子，普賢菩薩是漢傳佛教四大菩薩之一，象徵理德、行德與文殊菩薩的智德、正德相對應，是娑婆世界釋迦牟尼佛的左右脅侍，合稱「華嚴三聖」。民間稱為「大行普賢」，普賢菩薩也是龍、蛇年生人的守護神。

祭祀方式：

供品： 壽桃、壽麵、素三牲、水果五種、十二素齋、鮮花、清茶、清香以供之。

金紙： 太極金、壽金、刈金、福金。

中路武財神趙公明聖誕

農曆三月十五日是武財神趙公明聖誕，武財神尊稱為天官中路武財神龍虎玄壇金輪如意趙大元帥，人稱玄壇真君、玄壇元帥，武財神

手執九節神鞭，以黑虎為座騎，統領招寶、納珍、招財、利市四位仙官，合稱五路財神，專司迎祥納福，統管人世間一切金銀財寶，所以參拜供奉武財神可以讓您財源廣進、運途亨通、正財偏財皆興旺、五方財源滾滾而來。

祭祀方式：

供品：壽桃、壽麵、三牲、鮮花、香燭、清茶、酒、水果五種、發糕、湯圓、紅圓、紅龜、糖果、餅乾、菜碗及應節食品。

金紙：五路財神金、五色金、壽金、刈金、福金。

虛空藏菩薩佛誕

農曆三月十六日是虛空藏菩薩聖誕，虛空藏菩薩是大乘佛教八大菩薩之一，也是牛、虎年生人的守護神。其智慧廣大如虛空，其財富遍滿三界，能滿足信眾求智慧、財富、美名、美滿眷屬之願望。因此，虛空藏菩薩是以濟度眾生為樂的菩薩。

祭祀方式：

供品：壽桃、壽麵、素三牲、水果五種、十二素齋、鮮花、清茶、清香以供之。

金紙：太極金、壽金、刈金、福金。

註生娘娘聖誕

農曆三月二十日是註生娘娘聖誕，中國人自古以來傳宗接代的觀念根深蒂固，主司生育的註生娘娘自然香火鼎盛，註生娘娘的神像多是左手執簿本，右手持筆，象徵其記錄家家戶戶子嗣之事，註生娘娘從神為婆姊，輔佐註生娘娘保佑婦女護產安胎，或者區分所送子嗣之賢愚，註生娘娘主掌懷孕、生產，為養育之神，具授子神的屬性，所以註生娘娘為已婚不孕或受孕而求保胎之婦女的奉祀對象。

祭祀方式：

供品：壽桃、壽麵、三牲、水果五種、鮮花、清茶、清香、糖果餅乾供之。

金紙：五色金、壽金、刈金、福金。

天上聖母聖誕

農曆三月二十三日是天上聖母聖誕，俗稱媽祖娘娘，本姓林名默，生於宋太祖建隆元年，自幼茹素習道，善用道術為百姓消災解厄，深受鄉民愛戴，二十八歲時天命至，於九九重陽湄峰最高處羽化登仙。媽祖從宋朝開始就受到官方與民間的祭祀，人們對媽祖的稱呼從通玄神女而神姑、娘媽、媽祖婆，以至天上聖母，而官方封號則由夫人、聖妃、天妃以至天后，民間給予最高的崇敬。媽祖信仰傳遍海內外，更從海洋之神轉化為全能之神明，台灣的媽祖遶境活動隆重盛大至今已有一百多年歷史，因此有「三月瘋媽祖」的流傳，被稱為世界三大宗教盛事之一。

祭祀方式：

供品： 壽桃、壽麵、三牲、鮮花、香燭、清茶、酒、水果五種、發糕、湯圓、紅圓、紅龜、糖果、餅乾、菜碗及應節食品。

金紙： 五色金、壽金、刈金、福金、媽祖金衣。

文殊菩薩佛誕

農曆四月四日是文殊菩薩佛誕，文殊菩薩為佛陀釋迦牟尼的左脅侍，為華嚴三聖及四大菩薩之一，也是兔年生人的守護神。祂是佛陀的大弟子，智慧、辯才出眾，為眾菩薩之首，象徵佛陀智慧的菩薩，稱大智。文殊菩薩的本願是普利眾生，開發智慧，消除迷惑，他以慈悲和智慧為眾生指引正道，也以神通和威德為佛法護持增益。

祭祀方式：

供品： 壽桃、壽麵、素三牲、水果五種、十二素齋、鮮花、清茶、清香以供之。

金紙： 太極金、壽金、刈金、福金、金衣。

正財神范蠡聖誕

農曆四月七日是正財神范蠡聖誕，范蠡生於春秋時代，為楚國人。他是傑出的政治家、思想家和謀略家，也是一位生財有道的大商家。范蠡和文種一起輔佐越王滅吳興越，稱霸諸侯。范蠡精通經商之道，積金數萬，又能廣散錢財，范蠡十分注重商人的品德，他告誡同

行，求財應當光明正大，不能賺黑心錢，因為范蠡不求官有官做，不求財財萬貫，所以范蠡被尊為華夏商人的聖祖，人們稱他為民間財神、文財神、智慧財神、正財神。

祭祀方式：

供品：壽桃、壽麵、三牲、水果五種、菜碗、鮮花、清茶、清香、糖果餅乾以供之。

金紙：五色金、壽金、刈金、福金、財神金衣。

釋迦佛祖萬壽

農曆四月八日是釋迦佛祖萬壽，佛教於東漢時自印度傳入中國，成為民間普遍信仰的宗教之一，釋迦牟尼是佛教的創始者，生於印度迦毗羅衛國，釋迦牟尼佛也稱釋迦牟尼、如來佛、釋迦世尊、佛祖等。四月初八是浴佛節，也稱為衛塞節，是釋迦牟尼佛的誕辰，源自釋迦牟尼佛誕生後，一手指天，一手指地，說道：「天上天下，唯我獨尊。」然後有九條龍吐出清水為太子洗浴，後來，佛教徒每年為慶祝佛陀誕辰就沿用此例舉行浴佛儀式，藉此感恩佛陀慈悲的教導，祈求佛陀福澤社會，消弭災難。

祭祀方式：

供品：壽桃、壽麵、素三牲、水果五種、十二素齋、鮮花、清茶、清香以供之。

金紙：太極金、壽金、刈金、福金、金衣。

偏財祖師劉海禪師聖誕

農曆六月初十日是偏財祖師劉海禪師聖誕，俗話說：「劉海戲金蟾，步步釣金錢」傳說劉海是五代宋初時的道士，曾經在朝當官，後來辭去官職、散盡家財，一心求道，道號海蟾子，道教全真教將祂奉為北五祖之一，元世祖封其為海蟾明悟弘道真君，民間稱為劉海蟾，並尊稱為偏財神。劉海蟾師曾收服三腳咬錢金蟾，成為其腳力，幫助劉海濟世助人，濟助貧窮無數，所以被人們當做旺財瑞獸。

祭祀方式：

供品： 壽桃、壽麵、三牲、水果五種、菜碗、鮮花、清茶、清香、糖果餅乾以供之。

金紙： 五色金、壽金、刈金、福金、財神金衣。

偏財神韓信爺聖誕

農曆六月十三日是偏財神韓信爺聖誕，韓信是漢代淮陰人，著名的軍事家、戰略家、戰術家，他是西漢開國名將，漢初三傑之一，當代人們稱韓信為國士無雙、功高無二，後世評價：「言兵莫過孫武，用兵莫過韓信。」傳說他常在兵士困頓之時會設賭來激勵士兵的士氣，甚至發明了麻將、骰子等賭具，所以韓信爺以「賭」為致勝之說廣傳於民間，世人就奉拜韓信爺為賭神、偏財神，博奕業也尊崇敬奉韓信為祖師爺。

祭祀方式：

供品： 壽桃、壽麵、三牲、水果五種、菜碗、鮮花、清茶、清香、糖果餅乾以供之。

金紙： 五色金、壽金、刈金、福金、財神金衣。

關聖帝君聖誕

農曆六月廿四日是關聖帝君聖誕，關聖帝君又稱文衡聖帝、關帝爺、帝君爺、關公、關老爺、恩主公等等。關聖帝君是漢末三國時的名將關羽，由於其忠義勇武的形象，其祠廟被尊稱關帝廟，遍佈各地，為最多祠廟的中國神明之一，而歷朝帝王也都追封表彰，被尊稱為武聖，同時又受到儒道釋三教所推崇信奉。關聖帝君也是多種行業的守護神，包括讀書人的文昌神、軍警的戰神、商人的守護神，因為關老爺是正義的化身，為人尚忠義，絲毫不為錢財所動，所以被世人尊奉為商人的守護神。

祭祀方式：

供品： 壽桃、壽麵、三牲、水果五種、菜碗、鮮花、清茶、清香、糖果餅乾以供之。

金紙： 太極金、壽金、刈金、福金、關帝金衣。

魁星爺誕辰

農曆七月七日是魁星爺誕辰，魁星主文運，是文章之府，通常民間所祭拜的魁星爺左手拿著硯墨，右手握硃筆，一足踏鰲首，一腳踢著星斗以供讀書人求拜，後世依「魁」字造形，故以鬼面呈現之。自古以來盛傳魁星主文運與文昌帝君、關公、呂洞賓、朱熹合稱為五文昌，為文人仕子所崇祀。所謂獨占鰲頭乃舊時皇宮大殿台階正中之石板，有龍與鰲的浮雕，唐宋時中進士者需立於階前迎榜，為首之狀元則立於鰲頭前，故獨占鰲頭也意寓高中狀元。

祭祀方式：

供品： 供品可以用蔥(讓聰明智慧開竅)，蒜(穩操勝算)，芹菜(勤勞努力)，白蘿蔔(好彩頭)，粽子(包中)，糕點(步步高升)等。

金紙： 五色金、壽金、刈金、福金、文昌金衣、文昌智慧金。

大勢至菩薩聖誕

農曆七月十三日是大勢至菩薩聖誕，是八大菩薩之一，也是馬年生人的守護神，大勢至菩薩以智慧光普遍照一切，令眾生離三途，得無上力，能以智慧的光照亮你，讓你能用充滿智慧的眼光看清眼前的人生道路。

祭祀方式：

供品： 壽桃、壽麵、素三牲、水果五種、十二素齋、鮮花、清茶、清香以供之。

金紙： 太極金、壽金、刈金、福金、金衣。

地官大帝聖誕

農曆七月十五日是地官大帝聖誕，中國傳統習俗七月十五日稱中元節，中元節是地官生日，是地官赦罪之日，也是佛教的盂蘭盆節，民俗上會祭拜神明、祭祀祖先、家中地基主、普渡孤魂及佈施好兄弟，習俗上會在家門口點上普渡公燈，施放水燈，舉辦普渡法會。佛教信徒會在七月十五日舉行盂蘭盆會，放河燈追祭祖先，普同供養孤魂好兄弟，達到皆大歡喜，眾生平等的大愛表現。

祭祀方式：

1、**神明供品**：清茶、鮮花、水果、三牲、齋菜六項、壽桃、壽麵、發糕、湯圓、紅圓、紅龜、糖果餅乾。
神明金紙：頂極金、天金、太極金、普渡金、壽金、刈金、甲馬。

2、**祖先供品**：三牲、水果、酒、茶、六菜、糖果餅乾。
祖先金紙：刈金、大銀、小銀。

3、**地基主供品**：五味飯菜、雞腿、酒、茶。
地基主金紙：刈金、大銀、小銀。

4、**好兄弟供品**：三牲、水果、酒水、白米、罐頭、餅乾、泡麵等，還需臉盆、毛巾、牙膏、牙刷、梳子、肥皂等盥洗用品。
好兄弟金紙：刈金、大銀、小銀、更衣、往生錢。

地藏王菩薩聖誕

農曆七月三十日或七月廿九日是地藏王菩薩聖誕，也稱為地藏王節，善男信女都會在這天恭祝大願地藏王菩薩聖誕，地藏王菩薩又稱酆都大帝或幽冥教主，是娑婆界的三聖之一，也是陰間冥司主宰地獄的神靈，統帥十殿閻王，專司人間善惡，善者引渡西天，惡者則使之墜落地獄，橫死者則超生。地藏王菩薩弘願「眾生度盡，方證菩提，地獄不空，誓不成佛」，是以大孝、大願的德業度化眾生，因此深受佛道教廣為弘傳。

祭祀方式：

供品：壽桃、壽麵、素三牲、水果五種、十二素齋、鮮花、清茶、清香以供之。
金紙：太極金、壽金、刈金、福金、金衣。

月老星君

農曆八月十五日是月老星君的誕辰，月老星君又稱月下老人，簡稱月老，司職掌管人間姻緣、緣份之神。相傳每年農曆七月七日以

後，七娘媽就會將人世間未婚的男女造冊稟告天庭，再由月下老人審核載入姻緣簿，以紅線繫上夫妻的腳，使其有緣人終成眷屬，故求姻緣的男女多會敬奉月老。大家可以在農曆八月十五日前往四馬路五路財神祭拜月老，如若再恭請一份月老旺緣桃花寶袋隨身佩戴，用開運桃花手工皂來沐浴調整身心，可以提升人緣桃花，讓您在人際關係上能左右逢源，人氣強旺。

祭祀方式：

供品：紅燭一對、清香三支、粉紅色或白色百合各一朵、五種水果、糖果、餅乾、同心紅繩一份（二條）、月餅。

金紙：月老金衣、月老姻緣金、月老寶誥。

不動明王聖誕

農曆九月十三日是不動明王的誕辰，為佛教密宗五大明王主尊、八大明王首座，為鎮守中央方位的明王護法，也是雞年生人的守護神，不動明王名稱中的「不動」，是指慈悲心不變，無物可以改變撼動，「明」即為智慧光芒之意，「王」是對能操控世間萬物、現象者的尊稱。

祭祀方式：

供品：壽桃、壽麵、素三牲、水果五種、十二素齋、鮮花、清茶、清香以供之。

金紙：太極金、壽金、刈金、福金、金衣。

藥師佛聖誕

農曆九月二十九日是藥師佛的誕辰，藥師佛又稱藥師如來、藥師琉璃光佛、藥師琉璃光如來，為佛教東方淨琉璃世界之教主。藥師佛以琉璃為名，乃取琉璃之光明透徹以喻國土清靜無染，藥師如來為眾生拔苦免難，特別是貪、瞋、痴等妄念，由於眾生常受煩惱、病痛的折磨，藥師佛願力要消除這些煩惱及病痛，使眾生免於遭受疾病纏身，消減痛苦，滅除災難，健體延壽。

祭祀方式：

供品：壽桃、壽麵、素三牲、水果五種、十二素齋、鮮花、清茶、清香以供之。

金紙：太極金、壽金、刈金、福金、金衣。

水官大帝聖誕

農曆十月十五日是水官大帝的誕辰，也就是下元節，道經稱：「天官賜福，地官赦罪，水官解厄。」水官大帝職掌江河湖海水域萬靈之事，上解天災、下度生民，並考校眾生功過禍福，世人若改過遷善，就可消災解厄。厄就是災厄，生活中有許多不順遂的事情都是遇到災厄，因此把災厄化解掉，大事化小事，小事化無事，讓人們各方面都能吉祥如意，這就是解厄的意義。參加水官消災解厄補運的祈福法會，可以功德無量，好運大翻倍。

祭祀方式：

供品：清茶、鮮花、水果五種、三牲、齋菜六項、牲禮、壽桃、壽麵、發糕、湯圓、紅圓、紅龜、糖果餅乾。

金紙：頂極金、天金、太極金、壽金、刈金、甲馬。

阿彌陀佛佛誕

農曆十一月十七日是阿彌陀佛佛誕，阿彌陀佛意為無量光佛，另名無量壽佛，又稱為無量清淨佛、甘露王如來，也是狗、豬年生人的守護神。在華人地區習慣作阿彌陀佛；在大乘佛教信仰中，他是西方極樂世界的教主。大乘佛教禪宗、天台宗、賢首宗等各宗派普遍接受阿彌陀佛，而淨土宗則以一心信仰阿彌陀佛，發願往生西方極樂，為其最主要的特色。

祭祀方式：

供品：壽桃、壽麵、素三牲、水果五種、十二素齋、鮮花、清茶、清香。

金紙：太極金、壽金、刈金、福金。

◎ 乙巳年百歲年齡生肖對照表 ◎

西元	歲次	民國	日本	生肖	歲數	西元	歲次	民國	日本	生肖	歲數
1926	丙寅	十五	昭和	虎	100	1976	丙辰	六五	五一	龍	50
1927	丁卯	十六	二年	兔	99	1977	丁巳	六六	五二	蛇	49
1928	戊辰	十七	三年	龍	98	1978	戊午	六七	五三	馬	48
1929	己巳	十八	四年	蛇	97	1979	己未	六八	五四	羊	47
1930	庚午	十九	五年	馬	96	1980	庚申	六九	五五	猴	46
1931	辛未	二十	六年	羊	95	1981	辛酉	七十	五六	雞	45
1932	壬申	廿一	七年	猴	94	1982	壬戌	七一	五七	狗	44
1933	癸酉	廿二	八年	雞	93	1983	癸亥	七二	五八	豬	43
1934	甲戌	廿三	九年	狗	92	1984	甲子	七三	五九	鼠	42
1935	乙亥	廿四	十年	豬	91	1985	乙丑	七四	六十	牛	41
1936	丙子	廿五	十一	鼠	90	1986	丙寅	七五	六一	虎	40
1937	丁丑	廿六	十二	牛	89	1987	丁卯	七六	六二	兔	39
1938	戊寅	廿七	十三	虎	88	1988	戊辰	七七	六三	龍	38
1939	己卯	廿八	十四	兔	87	1989	己巳	七八	平成	蛇	37
1940	庚辰	廿九	十五	龍	86	1990	庚午	七九	二年	馬	36
1941	辛巳	三十	十六	蛇	85	1991	辛未	八十	三年	羊	35
1942	壬午	卅一	十七	馬	84	1992	壬申	八一	四年	猴	34
1943	癸未	卅二	十八	羊	83	1993	癸酉	八二	五年	雞	33
1944	甲申	卅三	十九	猴	82	1994	甲戌	八三	六年	狗	32
1945	乙酉	卅四	二十	雞	81	1995	乙亥	八四	七年	豬	31
1946	丙戌	卅五	廿一	狗	80	1996	丙子	八五	八年	鼠	30
1947	丁亥	卅六	廿二	豬	79	1997	丁丑	八六	九年	牛	29
1948	戊子	卅七	廿三	鼠	78	1998	戊寅	八七	十年	虎	28
1949	己丑	卅八	廿四	牛	77	1999	己卯	八八	十一	兔	27
1950	庚寅	卅九	廿五	虎	76	2000	庚辰	八九	十二	龍	26
1951	辛卯	四十	廿六	兔	75	2001	辛巳	九十	十三	蛇	25
1952	壬辰	四一	廿七	龍	74	2002	壬午	九一	十四	馬	24
1953	癸巳	四二	廿八	蛇	73	2003	癸未	九二	十五	羊	23
1954	甲午	四三	廿九	馬	72	2004	甲申	九三	十六	猴	22
1955	乙未	四四	三十	羊	71	2005	乙酉	九四	十七	雞	21
1956	丙申	四五	卅一	猴	70	2006	丙戌	九五	十八	狗	20
1957	丁酉	四六	卅二	雞	69	2007	丁亥	九六	十九	豬	19
1958	戊戌	四七	卅三	狗	68	2008	戊子	九七	二十	鼠	18
1959	己亥	四八	卅四	豬	67	2009	己丑	九八	廿一	牛	17
1960	庚子	四九	卅五	鼠	66	2010	庚寅	九九	廿二	虎	16
1961	辛丑	五十	卅六	牛	65	2011	辛卯	一〇〇	廿三	兔	15
1962	壬寅	五一	卅七	虎	64	2012	壬辰	一〇一	廿四	龍	14
1963	癸卯	五二	卅八	兔	63	2013	癸巳	一〇二	廿五	蛇	13
1964	甲辰	五三	卅九	龍	62	2014	甲午	一〇三	廿六	馬	12
1965	**乙巳**	**五四**	**四十**	**蛇**	**61**	2015	乙未	一〇四	廿七	羊	11
1966	丙午	五五	四一	馬	60	2016	丙申	一〇五	廿八	猴	10
1967	丁未	五六	四二	羊	59	2017	丁酉	一〇六	廿九	雞	9
1968	戊申	五七	四三	猴	58	2018	戊戌	一〇七	三十	狗	8
1969	己酉	五八	四四	雞	57	2019	己亥	一〇八	令和	豬	7
1970	庚戌	五九	四五	狗	56	2020	庚子	一〇九	二年	鼠	6
1971	辛亥	六十	四六	豬	55	2021	辛丑	一一〇	三年	牛	5
1972	壬子	六一	四七	鼠	54	2022	壬寅	一一一	四年	虎	4
1973	癸丑	六二	四八	牛	53	2023	癸卯	一一二	五年	兔	3
1974	甲寅	六三	四九	虎	52	2024	甲辰	一一三	六年	龍	2
1975	乙卯	六四	五十	兔	51	**2025**	**乙巳**	**一一四**	**七年**	**蛇**	**1**

二〇二五乙巳蛇年最強拜太歲秘法

Yi Si Year of the Snake in 2025: The Most Effective Method To Worship Tai Sui

歲次2025乙巳蛇年，值年太歲是為「吳遂星君」，俗云：「太歲當頭座，無喜便有憂。」其實，犯太歲並沒有那麼可怕，並不是所有值太歲之人都不好，甚至有人好的不得了呢！只要祭拜的方法得當，還是能夠趨吉避凶好事連連。

In 2025, Yi Si Year of the Snake, the Tai Sui of the year is "Wu Sui Xing Jun". As the saying goes, "When Tai Sui is in the head seat, if there is no joy, there will be sorrow." In fact, offending Tai Sui is not that terrible. Not all people will have ill luck. Some may even have very good luck! As long as the method of worshipping Tai Sui is proper, it can still bring good luck, avoid bad luck, and have good things happen one after another.

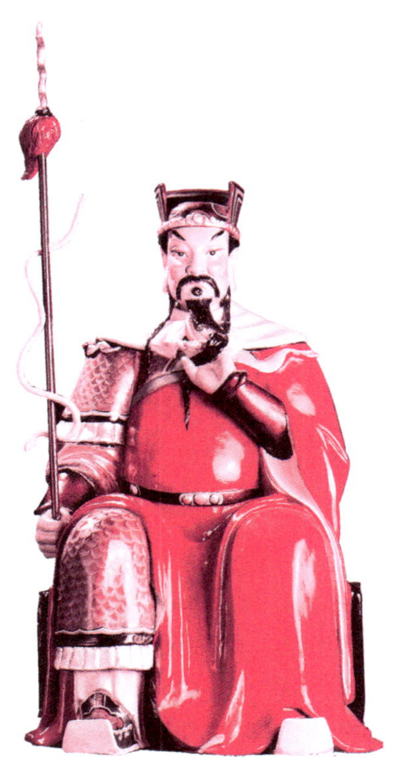

2025乙巳蛇年值年太歲為吳遂星君。
Figure: In *2025*, Yi Si Year of the Snake, the *Tai Sui* is *Wu Sui Xing Jun*.

一、二〇二五乙巳蛇年需拜太歲之生肖詳解 2025 Yi Si Year of the Snake - Detailed explanation of Zodiacs that need to worship Tai Sui Xing Jun

1、屬蛇之人為值太歲者 People born in the Year of the Snake are “Zhi Tai Sui” (Conflict with Tai Sui)

舉凡出生屬蛇之人在今年之中都為「值太歲」，其中乙巳年1965年及2025年出生之人稱為「本命年」，其他年次是稱為「太歲年」。舉凡肖蛇之人今年需拜太歲星君，尤其是1929年、1941年、1989年、2001年等生年屬蛇之人「犯太歲」特別嚴重，更需要拜太歲及安奉太歲星君。

In general, people born in the Year of the Snake are "Zhi Tai Sui" (In conflict with Tai Sui) this year. Among them, those born in 1965 and 2025 in the Yi Si Year are born in the "Zodiacal" year (Benmingnian) while the rest born in other Snake years will be considered as `Taisui" years (Taisuinian). People born in the Snake year will have to worship and enshrine Tai Sui Xing Jun to seek blessings, especially for those born in 1929, 1941, 1989 and 2001 as they are severely in conflict with Tai Sui this year.

今年肖蛇「犯太歲」特別嚴重的朋友，容易心情起伏較大，脾氣急躁，凡事總會多煩惱，半悲半喜，總有莫名其妙被羞辱造成爭執吵架等煩惱事故發生，嚴重時甚至會導致破財。

Among the people born under the sign of the Snake, those who particularly "Fan Tai Sui" (Offend Tai Sui) are prone to mood swings this year, irritable temperament, worrying about everything, and half sad, half happy. They are always inexplicably humiliated, having disputes and quarrels and other troublesome accidents. In severe cases, they can even lead to financial losses.

2、屬猴之人為刑太歲者

People born in the Year of the Monkey are "Xin Tai Sui" (Hurting Tai Sui)

今年在五行中屬於巳申相刑，所以今年屬猴之人會犯「刑太歲」。因此肖猴之人今年需拜太歲及改運制刑，尤其是1920年、1968年、1980年屬猴之人更需要特別注意，應拜太歲及禳解改運制刑。

This year in the Five Elements, the clash between Snake and Monkey (Si and Shen) results in "self-punishment", hence it is called Xin Tai Sui. As such, those who are born in the Year of the Monkey should pray to Tai Sui to prevent being punished. Among those of the Monkey genus especially those born in 1920, 1968 and 1980 will need to pay special attention and worship Tai Sui for blessings to avoid punishment.

通常犯「刑太歲」之人，較容易會有刑傷、刑事、官非、訴訟、是非、孝服及交通意外等事故發生，缺乏獨立精神，做事不能有始有終，容易敵視他人，想不開產生自殘，人際關係不和諧，小人多作亂，因不接受他人意見而遭致災厄或損失錢財。

Usually, people who commit "Xin Tai Sui" are more likely to get into criminal injuries, lawsuits, litigation, gossips, mourning and traffic accidents. They lack independence, cannot finish what they start, are easily hostile to others, and may commit self-harm due to depression. They have disharmonious interpersonal relationships, are often disrupted by villains, and suffer disasters or lose money due to not accepting other people's opinions.

3、屬豬之人為沖太歲者（今年被太歲所沖，是為歲破）
People born in the Year of the Pig are "Chong Tai Sui" (Clash with Tai Sui).This year, "Chong Tai Sui" is called Sui Po.

今年五行中屬巳亥相沖，所以肖豬之人是歲破與被太歲所沖。今年所有肖豬之人都需要拜太歲及按奉太歲星君，這些被太歲所沖的朋友衝擊最強，要特別留心。另外以1959年、1971年、2019年出生之人，比其他肖豬之人運勢更為凶險嚴重，更須去拜太歲、安太歲。

In the Five Elements this year, due to the clash of Snake and Pig (Si and Hai), those born in the Year of the Pig will clash with Tai Sui (Sui

Po). Hence it is essential for people born in the Year of the Pig to pray to Tai Sui, as the impact is most severe to this group of individuals. In particular, those born in 1959, 1971 and 2019 will have the severest impact of being negatively afflicted than other Pig genus, so they need to worship and enshrine Tai Sui.

沖太歲之「沖」有衝擊、交戰、對抗的意思。沖太歲者今年容易總是反復不停的為工作奔波勞碌，常常無功收場。健康上容易出現病痛或動手術。家庭成員容易發生不祥事件、交通意外、流血傷亡及破財等事故。懷孕者應特別小心流產的現象，人際關係容易發生爭執、口角。

The word "Chong" in "Chong Tai Sui" means to attack, fight, or confront. People who clash with Tai Sui are likely to work hard and often end up with nothing. They are more likely to suffer from illness or surgery. Family members are more likely to encounter unlucky events, traffic accidents, bloodshed, death, and financial losses. Pregnant women should be especially careful about miscarriage. Disputes and quarrels are more likely to occur in interpersonal relationships.

4、屬猴之人為破太歲者 People born in the Year of the Monkey are "Po Tai Sui" (Breaking Tai Sui)

今年五行中屬巳申相破，所以舉凡肖猴之人，皆犯「破太歲」。今年所有肖猴之人需拜太歲或點光明燈，來禳解保平安，凡1920年、1968年、1980年等出生肖猴之人犯破太歲最為嚴重。

This year, the Five Elements of the Year of the Monkey are in conflict with each other, so all people born in the Year of the Monkey will be in conflict with Tai Sui. Hence, they need to worship Tai Sui or light a bright lamp to ward off evil and ensure safety. People born in the Year of the Monkey, especially in 1920, 1968, 1980, etc. will be most seriously in conflict with Tai Sui.

破太歲有破裂的意義，通常犯破太歲之人容易無緣無故破財，不易守成，容易遭受金錢危機，甚至承受債務壓力，建議投資要謹慎，才不會造成平白的損失，不宜投資或炒股，凡事應保守謹慎為宜。

As the name implies, “Po Tai Sui” means Breaking Tai Sui. People who Po Tai Sui are prone to losing money for no reason, have difficulty maintaining their wealth, are prone to financial crises, and even debt pressure. It is recommended that they be cautious in investing to avoid unnecessary losses. They should not invest or speculate in stocks, and should be conservative and cautious in everything.

5、屬虎之人為害太歲者 People born in the Year of the Tiger is “Hai Tai Sui” (Harming Tai Sui)

今年屬寅巳相害，所以舉凡屬虎之人，今年皆犯「害太歲」。屬虎之人今年犯害太歲，應該拜太歲點光明燈來禳解保平安。同時1938年、1950年、1998年、2010年出生肖虎之人犯害太歲最為嚴重。

This year, Tiger and Snake (Yin and Si) will harm each other, so those who are born in the Year of the Tiger will “Hai Tai Sui” (Harm Tai Sui). Hence, those born in the Year of the Tiger should worship Tai Sui and light a bright lamp to seek blessings for protection. In particular, those who are born in 1938, 1950, 1998 and 2010 would be the ones who have the most serious harm.

害太歲之「害」有傷害的意思，代表兩強相爭必有一傷，注意凡事禍起內部，家人之間的相處要避免爭鬥摩擦，孕婦要注意流產現象，工作上小心人際關係不合諧及爭鬥磨擦，生意上的合作也容易發生意見不合，學生的課業容易因煩惱而停滯退步。

As the name suggests, "Hai Tai Sui” has the meaning of causing harm. It relates to when two strong people fight, one of them will be injured. Be careful that all troubles originate from within. Family

members should avoid quarrels and frictions when getting along with each other. Pregnant women should pay attention to miscarriage. At work, be careful of interpersonal disharmony and quarrels and frictions. Business cooperation is also prone to disagreements. Students' studies are likely to stagnate and regress due to worries.

二、二〇二五乙巳蛇年最有效果的拜太歲秘訣

Most effective way to worship Tai Sui in 2025 Yi Si Year of the Snake

1、安奉太歲方式 Method to Enshrine Tai Sui

太歲星君可安奉在廳堂與神佛同位，或安奉在家中清淨之處，或到寺廟及玉玄門安奉。

Tai Sui Xing Jun could be enshrined with other deities or Buddha statues in the living hall or in a clean place at home. Alternatively, you could worship Tai Sui in a temple or at Yu Xuan Men.

2、安太歲時間 Time Period to Enshrine Tai Sui

民間多在年初農曆正月十五元宵之前或擇於農曆正月初九日玉皇上帝壽辰當日來安奉太歲星君。

Most people will normally consecrate and enshrine Tai Sui Xing Jun before the Lantern Festival on the 15th day of Lunar New Year or on the birthday of the Jade Emperor on the ninth day of the first month of Lunar New Year.

3、祭拜用品 Items for Worship

祭品 Prayer Offerings：

三牲一付，香爐一個、鮮花一對、清茶三杯、酒三杯、五方仙果、湯圓三碗、糕餅五塊、面線、香燭一對、糖果、餅乾少許，齋菜六種，葷菜六種及其它應節食品皆可。

One set of meat offerings, one incense burner, two stalks of fresh flowers, three cups of tea, three cups of wine, five types of fruits, three bowls of rice dumplings, five pieces of pastry, one set of vermicelli, one pair of candles, some sweets and biscuits, six types of vegetarian dishes, six types of non-vegetarian dishes and any other festive delicacies.

香枝及金銀衣紙 Incense Sticks and Incense Papers：

玉玄門純中藥精製的微塵粒香枝及純中藥降真淨香末和太歲金、太極金、天金、尺金、壽金、元寶金、大光寶、貴人衣、轉運寶牒…等（祭祀用品、金銀衣紙，請視各地習俗備妥一套）。

Yu Xuan Men incense sticks and incense powder that are 100% made from Chinese medicinal ingredients and incense papers, Tai Sui gold, Tai Chi gold, Tian gold, Chi gold, Shou gold, Ingot gold, Large ingot, Noble clothing, Transfer treasure gold, etc. (Please prepare a set of the offerings, gold and silver clothing and incense papers according to local customs).

4、祭拜儀式 Worship Ceremony

於神桌上擺妥供品後，點燭上香，誠心默念：「吳遂太歲星君到此，鎮宅保佑闔家平安、納福招吉、消除災難或是工商倍利、五穀豐收、六畜興旺、萬事如意、財運亨通」，並可按己意，予以祈求，敬奉大吉。

After placing the offerings on the table, light the candles and incense sticks. At the same time, recite in your heart silently: “In the presence of Li Cheng Tai Sui Xing Jun, we seek your blessings to protect the family from harm and keep the family safe, attract good fortune and blessings, eliminate disasters or work issues, have bountiful harvest, ensure everything goes well and prosperous for all throughout the year.” You can seek blessings for the wishes according to your needs.

禱畢，將香枝插入香爐內，敬酒，靜待香燭燒至一半時，將金紙及書寫犯太歲者之紅紙，拱手拿起向太歲星君鞠躬三拜，開始燒化金紙，最後將酒水順時針灑繞在燒化的金紙地方三圈，安太歲的儀式即完成。

After the prayers, place the incense sticks in the incense burner. Offer a toast to Tai Sui. Wait for the incense sticks to burn halfway, then hold up the incense papers together with the red piece of paper which contains the name of the person or family member who is in conflict, offend or clash with Tai Sui and bow to Tai Sui Xing Jun thrice. Following this, burn the incense papers. Lastly, sprinkle the wine clockwise three times around the burnt incense papers and the ceremony to enshrine Tai Sui is completed.

三、歲末如何恭送太歲十二星君 How to Send Off Tai Sui at the Year End

1、送太歲星君的方式 Method to Send Off Tai Sui Xingjun

如果是在家拜太歲的朋友，應該在家中恭送太歲星君，如果您是在廟宇中拜太歲的朋友，一定要回到年初拜太歲的神壇或來四馬路五路財神送神。

For those who pray to Tai Sui at home, you should perform the "Send Off" ceremony to Tai Sui Xing Jun from home. For those who pray to Tai Sui in the temple at the beginning of the year, you should go back to the temple for the "Send Off" ceremony.

2、送太歲星君的時間 When to send off Tai Sui Xingjun

請於農曆十二月廿四日早上恭送太歲星君。

Please perform the "Send Off" ceremony on the morning of the 24th day of the 12th lunar month.

3、祭拜用品 Items for Worship

祭品 Offerings：

鮮花一對、清茶三杯、酒三杯、五方仙果、湯圓三碗、糕餅五塊、麵線、糖果、餅乾少許，或其他應節食品皆可。

Prepare two stalks of fresh flowers, three cups of tea, three cups of wine, five types of fruits, three bowls of rice dumplings, five pieces of pastries, one set of vermicelli, some sweets and biscuits, or any other festive delicacies.

香枝及金銀衣紙 Incense sticks and Incense papers：

純中藥精製的微塵粒香枝及純中藥降真淨香末和太歲金、太極金、天金、尺金、壽金、元寶金、貴人衣、雲馬、轉運寶牒，適各地習俗備妥即可等。

Incense sticks and incense powder that are 100% made from Chinese medicinal ingredients and incense papers, Tai Sui gold, Tai Chi gold, Tian gold, Chi gold, Shou gold, Ingot gold, Large ingot, Noble clothing, Transfer treasure gold, etc.

4、祭拜儀式 Worship Ceremony

步驟一 Step 1：

於神桌上擺妥供品後，點燭上香三柱。

After placing the offerings on the alter table, light up a pair of candles and three incense sticks.

步驟二 Step 2：

開始參拜恭送太歲時，每人先點上三炷香，然後宣讀送太歲疏文，以答謝太歲星君一年的照顧，或誠心默念：「本人○○○　出生於○年○月○日○時，在地址：○○○，酬謝○○太歲星君，整年鎮宅保佑闔家平安、納福招吉、消除災難或是工商倍利、五穀豐收、六畜興旺、萬事如意、財運亨通，叩謝神恩」並可按己意，予以祈求，

敬奉大吉，叩謝神恩。禱畢，將香枝插入香爐內，敬酒。

At the beginning of paying homage to “send off” Tai Sui, each person lights three incense sticks and reads the Tai Sui Shu Wen (prayer text) to thank Tai Sui Xing Jun for blessings for the past one year. Or you can sincerely recite silently: "I am ○○○ (your name), born on ○○○ (your birth date), staying at ○○○ (your address). Thank you Tai Sui Xing Jun for the blessings and protection and good fortune, eliminating disasters and work issues, ensuring bountiful harvest, making everything goes well and prosperous for the past one year”. (You can say according to your own wishes). Once done, bow three times to show your gratitude and place the incense sticks into the incense burner and offer wine.

步驟三 Step 3：

靜待香燭燒至一半時，將金紙拱手拿起向太歲星君鞠躬三拜，然後將太歲符與金紙、疏文一同燒化。最後將酒水順圓灑繞在燒化的金紙地方三圈，送太歲星君的儀式完成，即萬事大吉昌。

When the incense sticks are half burned, hold up the incense papers and bow three times to Tai Sui Xing Jun. Following this, burn the Tai Sui Talisman and Shu Wen (prayer text) together with the incense papers. Lastly, sprinkle the wine clockwise three times around the burnt incense location. This will conclude the ceremony of “Sending Off” Tai Sui Xing Jun, and everything will be auspicious.

二〇二五乙巳蛇年陽宅玄空飛星法門

2025 Yi Si Year of the Snake Flying Star Geomancy for Residence

九宮飛星論事準確、簡單、快速。九宮飛星使用觀察一間房屋的過去及現在的情況，作為即時推斷化煞及搶運的根據資料。所謂單位擺設是指宅內的開門、房間位置、神位、床位、浴廁位、廚灶位等方位。

The Nine Flying Stars (Jiugong Feixing) geomancy is accurate, simple and fast in analysing the past and present situations of a residence. It is based on observation of the conditions of a residence for real-time inference of evil spirits and enhancement of good fortune. The so-called unit furnishings refer to the position of the door, rooms, altar, bed, bathroom, toilet, kitchen, stove, etc. in the house.

當運的九星按洛書之軌跡運行，九星並沒有一定的吉凶，其吉凶是取決於哪個元運來定。由於九星的飛行軌跡，不但會受歲星太歲所影響，同時也會受流年飛星所干擾，故吉星移到的宮位就解釋為吉，反之，凶星飛到的宮位當然屬凶。

The nine stars of fortune run according to the path of Luoshu. There is no certain good or bad for the nine stars, as the flight trajectory is not only affected by the Sui Xing Tai Sui but also interfered by the flying star of the fleeting year. So the house that the lucky star moves to is interpreted as auspicious; on the contrary, the house to which the inauspicious star flies to is of course inauspicious.

玉玄門三元天星玄空陽宅心法秘錄圖

Yuxuanmen Sanyuan Tianxing Xuankong Yangzhai Secret R

Table of Flying Stars Geomancy for Residence

九星 Flying Stars	斗星 Auxiliary Stars	八卦 Ba Gua	十二地支 Twelve Earthly Branches	十二星座 Horoscope	代表意義 Definition
一白 One-White	貪狼 Flirting	坎宮 Kan Gong	子 Zi	水瓶座 Aquarius	文昌星：主事業、考試 桃花 Academic Star: Career, Exami Promotion, Romance
二黑 Two-Black	巨門 Gloomy	坤宮 Kun Gong	未、申 Wei, Shen	巨蟹座 雙子座 Cancer Gemini	病符星：主疾病、小人 陰煞、驛馬 Illness Star: Illness, Villains, G Evil Spirit, Travel
三碧 Three-Jade	祿存 Quarrels	震宮 Zhen Gong	卯 Mao	天蠍座 Scorpio	盜賊星：主賊偷、鬥爭 偏財、桃花 Theft Star: Theft, Conflict, Lon Incidental Wealth, Romance
四綠 Four-Green	文曲 Intelligence	巽宮 Xun Gong	辰、巳 Chen, Si	天秤座 處女座 Libra Virgo	桃花星：主口才、桃花 事業 Romance Star: Eloquence, Rc Intellect, Career
五黃 Five-Yellow	廉貞 Wicked	中宮 Central	中 Central		五鬼星：主投機、戰亂 強盜 Conniving Star: Investment, W Disease, Robbery
六白 Six-White	武曲 Finance	乾宮 Qian Gong	戌、亥 Xu, Hai	白羊座 雙魚座 Aries Pisces	正財星：主正財、五金 財富 Wealth Star: Wealth, Metal, Fa Fortune
七赤 Seven-Red	破軍 Ruinous	兑宮 Dui Gong	酉 You	金牛座 Taurus	是非星：主強盜、口角 破耗 Gossip Star: Robbery, Argume Damage
八白 Eight-White	左輔 Fortunate	艮宮 Gen Gong	丑、寅 Chou, Yin	魔羯座 人馬座 Capricorn Sagittarius	財福星：主偏財、財富 貴人 Fortune Star: Incidental Wealt Fame, Benefactor
九紫 Nine-Purple	右弼 Jubilation	離宮 Li Gong	午 Wu	獅子座 Leo	喜慶星：主姻緣、喜慶 血光 Joy Star: Marriage, Joy, Fire, E

二〇二五乙巳蛇年陽宅九宮飛星佈局方位

2025 Yi Si Year of the Snake Nine Flying Star Fengshui Orientation Layout for Residence

白貪狼(水) 業、人緣 reer,popularity 東南木 SE 巽宮 為流年 三煞大凶 Trible Killings Position **1** 巳為流年 太歲位 Tai Sui Position 廳/書房/臥室：凶 ving Room /Study Room/ droom：Bad 房：平 tchen：Fair 廁所：吉 Toilet：Good	六白武曲(金) 正財、升職 Wealth, Promotio 南火 S 離宮 **6** 客廳/書房/臥室：吉 Living Room /Study Room/ Bedroom：Good 廚房：吉 Kitchen：Good 廁所：凶 Toilet：Bad	八白左輔(土) 偏財 Incidental Luck 財富 Wealth 西南土 SW 坤宮 **8** 客廳/書房：吉 Living Room / Study Room： Good 臥室/廚房：平 Bedroom /Kitchen：Fair 廁所：平 Toilet：Fair
紫右弼(火) 火災 re 喜慶、血光 ilant,Accident 東木 E 震宮 流年 三煞大凶 **9** Trible illings Position 廳/廚房：凶 ving Room /Kitchen：Bad 房/臥室：凶 ıdy Room edroom ：Bad 廁所：吉 Toilet：Good	二黑巨門(土) 病符、小人 Illness, stacles CENTRAL 中宮土 **2** 客廳/書房：平 Livin g Room/Study Room：Fair 臥室/廚房：凶 Bedroom /Kitchen：Bad 廁所：凶 Toilet：Bad	四綠文曲(木) 學業、名譽 Academic, Fame 西金 W 兌宮 **4** 客廳/書房/廚房/臥室：平 Living Room / Kitchen/ Bedroom Study Room/：Fair 廁所：吉 Toilet： Good
黃廉貞(土) 難、禍害 saster 東北土 NE 艮宮 寅為流年 三煞大凶 **5** Trible Killings Position 廳：凶 ving Room：Bad 房：平 tchen：Fair 房/臥室：凶 ıdy Room edroom：Bad 廁所：吉 Toilet：Good	七赤破軍(金) 刑傷、官非 Lawsuits 北水 N 坎宮 **7** 客廳/臥室/書房：吉 Livin g Room/Bedroom/ Study Room：Good 廚房：吉 Kitchen：Good 廁所：凶 Toilet：Bad	三碧祿存(木) 是非、鬥爭 Gossips, Argument 西北金 NW 乾宮 亥為流年 歲破凶位 **3** Sui Po Position 客廳/書房/廚房：凶 Living Room/ Kitchen/ Study Room ：Bad 臥室：平 Bedroom：Fair 廁所：吉 Toilet： Good

果房間所在方位是"凶"則必須按放開運吉祥物來化解,若房間所在方位是"吉或平"是不按放開運吉祥物,但若按放開運吉祥物是可助旺增強運勢的;如果您家宅的廁所位是於家宅的前或是中央時,都是不好的方位，建議按放鎮宅吉祥物來化解。

二〇二五乙巳蛇年陽宅九宮飛星吉凶分布圖

2025 Yi Si Year of the Snake Nine Flying Star Fengshui Orientation Layout for Residence

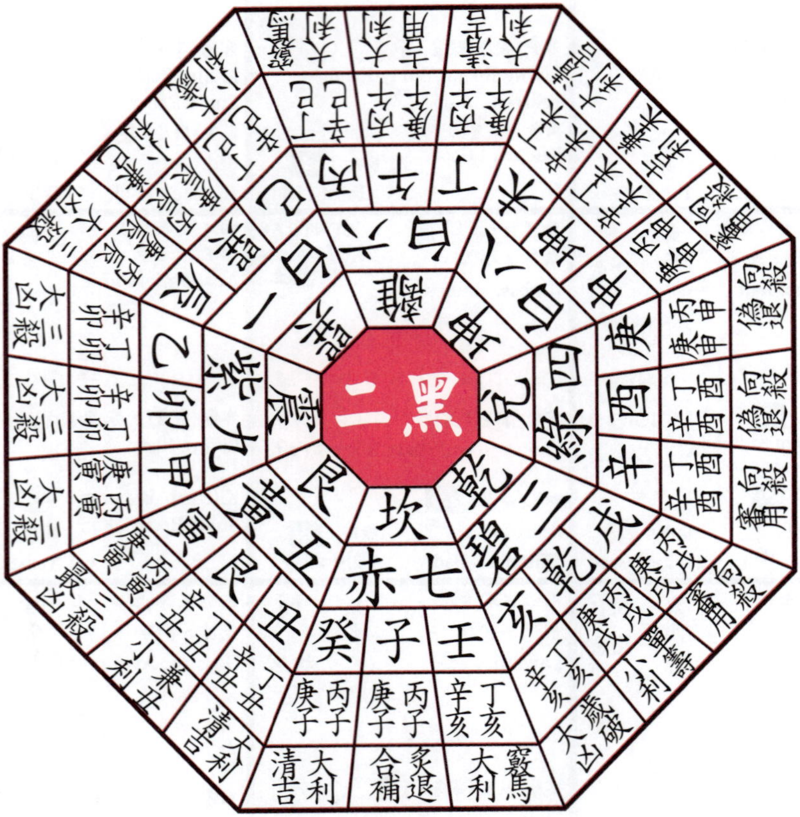

乙巳年大利南北方，不利東方

Yi Si Year is favourable for North and South, but not for East.

二〇二五乙巳蛇年陽宅九宮飛星趨吉避凶詳解

Detailed Explanation of the Nine Palace Flying Stars in Residences to seek Good Luck and Avoid Disaster in 2025 Yi Si Year of the Snake

一、文昌（催官）位 Wenchang (Academic) Position：

一白貪狼星為水，代表中男，主文昌考試、升官事業、桃花、財運。今年一白貪狼星飛入東南方巽宮，巽宮屬木，代表長女，五行是為水生木，雙星是一白貪狼星與四綠文曲星同宮。

One White Tanlang Star belongs to water element, representing the middle son, and is responsible for academic examinations, promotion, career, love, and wealth. This year, One White Star flies into the Southeast Xun Palace, which is wood element and represents the eldest daughter. In terms of the five elements, water produces wood. The double stars are One White Star and Four Green Wenqu Star in the same palace.

1、2025年陽宅在此方位吉凶各半，辰為流年三煞大凶，巳為流年太歲位。此方位如有缺角、不平、形煞，或任意興工動土修造，沒有配合天星奇門遁甲九天玄女一二〇甲子擇日秘法及玄空大卦六十四卦之卦氣卦運來做為選吉之應用，這種情形會導致宅主錢財破損，家中男是非官司纏身，學業退步，家庭不睦，桃花緋聞纏身，遭遇失竊劫財。

In 2025, the house in this direction will be half good and half bad. Chen is the Three Killings Disaster position, worst luck of the year, and Si is the Fleeting Tai Sui position of the year. If this direction has missing corner, uneven, or bad shape, or if construction is started at will, without using the Tianxing Qimen Dunjia Jiutian Xuannu 120 Jiazi secret method of choosing an auspicious date and the sixty-four hexagrams of the Xuankong Dagua as a guide

for selecting auspicious days, this situation will lead to financial losses for the owner of the house. The man in the family will be entangled in lawsuits, academic decline, family discord, romantic relationship scandals, theft and robbery.

2、今年此方位如果配置合局，能升官發財，名聲顯揚，學生金榜題名，大利文職工作，人際關係活絡，家中的中男在上半年特別興旺，農曆7月以後較差，健康方面較易產生癲癇、腦溢血、腎水腫、肝病、耳疾、足疾等方面的疾病問題，要特注意因酒色而破財婚姻失和的情事，不利生育求子。

If this position is well configured this year, you will be promoted, make money, gain fame, have your name in the list of the imperial examinations, and be successful in your studies. You will have active interpersonal relationships and it will be good for you to get a job in administrative service. The middle-aged man in the family will be particularly prosperous in the first half of the year, but will not be as good after the seventh lunar calendar month. In terms of health conditions, you will be more likely to suffer from problems such as epilepsy, cerebral hemorrhage, kidney edema, liver, ear disease and foot disease. Pay special attention to financial loss and marital discord due to alcohol and sex. It is not conducive to fertility.

二、病符位 Illness Position：

二黑巨門星為土，代表老婦，主疾病與小人、是非、陰煞、驛馬。今年二黑巨門星飛入中宮，中宮屬土，五行為土之同氣比旺，雙星是二黑巨門星與五黃廉貞星同宮。

Two Black Illness Jumen Star belongs to earth element, representing elderly women, and is responsible for illness, villains, disputes, evil spirits, and stallions. This year, the Two Black Illness Star flies into the Central Palace, which is earth element. In terms of the five elements, both are earth, which is the same energy. The double stars are the Two Black Jumen Star and the Five Yellow Lianzhen Star in the same palace.

1、2025年陽宅在此方位不利，此方位如有缺角、不平、形煞，或任意興工動土修造，沒有配合天星奇門遁甲九天玄女一二〇甲子擇日秘法及玄空大卦六十四卦之卦氣卦運來做為選吉之應用，這種情形會導致老婦多口舌是非、小人陷害、血光之災，健康方面要注意婦女病、胃病、腫瘤、精神、慢性病復發、手腳行動不便等疾病，家中容易因為陽氣不足卡到陰氣。

   In 2025, it is not favorable for the house to be in this direction. If there are missing corners, unevenness, or bad shapes in this location, or if construction is started arbitrarily, without the application of the Tianxing Qimen Dunjia Jiutian Xuannu 120 Jiazi date selection secret method and the Xuankong Dagua 64 hexagrams as the application of the hexagram qi and hexagram luck to select auspicious days, this situation will lead to the elderly women in the family facing a lot of gossips, being framed by villains, and subject to bloody disasters. In terms of health, pay attention to women's diseases, stomach diseases, tumors, mental illness, recurrence of chronic diseases, and inconvenience in movement of hands and feet. The house is prone to being blocked by Yin energy due to insufficient Yang energy.

2、若是當運且此方位配置合局，家中房地產發達，建屋工程興旺，若是失運時，雙星二五交加必損主，不利男主，易出寡婦，家中老母疾病纏身，易損家中人口，家宅容易招惹陰氣，尤其婦女會遭陰邪糾纏。

   If it is lucky and this orientation is suitable, the real estate of the family will be prosperous and the house-building project will be thriving. If it is unlucky, the combination of the Two Black and Five Yellow stars will bring harm to the owner. It will be unfavorable to the male owner, easy for a widow to appear and the elderly mother in the family will be plagued by illness. There will be losses in the

family, and the house will easily attract negative energy, especially women will be entangled by evil spirits.

三、盜賊位 Theft Position：

三碧祿存星屬木，代表長男，主小偷、孤獨、鬥爭、偏財。今年三碧祿存星飛入西北方乾宮，乾宮屬金，代表老父，五行是為金剋木，雙星是三碧祿存星與六白武曲星同宮。

Sanbi Lucun Star belongs to wood element, representing the eldest son, and is associated with thieves, loneliness, fighting, and partial wealth. This year, Sanbi Lucun Star flies into the Northwest Palace of Qian, which belongs to metal and represents the old father. In the five elements, metal restricts wood. The double star is the Sanbi Lucun Star and the Liubai Wuqu Star in the same palace.

1、2025年陽宅在此方位有流年歲破較為不利，此方位如有缺角、不平、形煞，或任意興工動土修造，沒有配合天星奇門遁甲九天玄女一二〇甲子擇日秘法及玄空大卦六十四卦之卦氣卦運來做為選吉之應用，這種情形會導致家賊失竊，長男多事，健康方面長男及老父主人易有手足、掉髮、腫瘤、肝腎的疾病，事業容易產生口角、是非、官符。

In 2025, the residence in this direction is in conflict with Tai Sui (Sui Po) and hence will have unfavorable luck. If there are missing corners, unevenness, or bad shapes in this direction, or if construction is started arbitrarily without using the secret method of selecting auspicious days according to the Tianxing Qimen Dunjia Jiutian Xuannu 120 Jiazi and the hexagram qi and hexagram luck of the sixty-four hexagrams of the Xuankong Dagua, this situation will lead to thieves stealing from the house, and the eldest son being troubled. In terms of health, the eldest son and the old father are prone to diseases of the hands and feet, hair loss, tumors, liver and kidneys. Quarrels, disputes, and legal disputes are likely to occur in the career.

2、若是當運且此方位配置合局，可升官發財，聲量大增，若是失運時，長男多是非，老父運勢遭殃，易有官司刑訟、爭執衝突，小心金屬刀傷，跌倒重傷，嚴重時肝病轉肝癌的危機。

If you are in good luck and this orientation is suitable, you can get promoted, become rich, and increase your reputation. If you are out of luck, the eldest son will have a lot of disputes, and the fortune of the old father will suffer. There will be lawsuits, disputes and conflicts. Be careful of metal knife wounds and serious injuries from falls. In severe cases, there is a risk of liver disease turning into liver cancer.

四、桃花位 Romance Position：

四綠文曲星屬木，代表長女，主文昌、科舉考試、口才、流言、文化藝術、桃花、事業。今年四綠文曲星飛入西方兌宮，兌宮屬金，代表少女，五行是為金剋木，雙星是四綠文曲星與七赤破軍星同宮。

Four Green Wenqu Star is of wood element, representing the eldest daughter, and governs academic, imperial examinations, eloquence, rumors, culture and art, romance and career. This year, Four Green Wenqu Star flies into the Western Palace of Dui, which is metal element, representing young girls. In the five elements, metal overcomes wood, and the double stars are the Four Green Wenqu Star and the Seven Red Pojun Star in the same palace.

1、2025年陽宅在此方位得利，此方位如有缺角、不平、形煞，或任意興工動土修造，沒有配合天星奇門遁甲九天玄女一二〇甲子擇日秘法及玄空大卦六十四卦之卦氣卦運來做為選吉之應用，這種情形會導致家中爭吵不和諧，家中女性易遭陰邪，刀傷之險，考試不利，是非口舌不斷，官司訴訟不斷。

In 2025, the house will benefit from this direction. If this position has missing corners, unevenness, or bad shapes, or if construction is started arbitrarily, without using the secret method of selecting auspicious days according to the Tianxing Qimen Dunjia Jiutian

Xuannu 120 Jiazi and the hexagram qi and hexagram luck of the sixty-four hexagrams of the Xuankong Dagua, this situation will lead to quarrels and disharmony in the family, and the women in the family will be prone to evil spirits, knife wounds, unfavorable examinations, constant gossips and lawsuits.

2、在此方位用之得當，女性當權強勢，財運亨通，能增強文書考運，利於靠口生財、傳播媒體、文化藝術等行業。此方位用之不得當，家中女性易有肝臟、腎臟、風邪、刀傷、不孕、頭部怪病之疾病發生，感情不順，男女關係混亂，是非口舌連連。

If this direction is used properly, women will be powerful and prosperous, and will have good luck in writing examinations, and will be good for making money through talking, media, culture and art, etc. If this direction is used improperly, women in the family will be prone to liver, kidney, evil wind, knife wounds, infertility, strange head diseases, emotional problems, chaotic relationships between man and woman, and constant gossips.

五、五黃煞 Five Yellow Disaster Position：

五黃廉貞星屬土，為五鬼星，代表投機、強盜、病毒、戰亂，是為五黃煞，主血光、脾胃、毒瘡、煙毒、癌症，並易出乩童及神經不正常之人。今年五黃廉貞星飛入東北方艮宮，艮宮屬土，代表少男，五行是為同氣比旺，雙星是五黃廉貞星與八白左輔星同宮。

Five Yellow Lianzhen Star belongs to earth element and is one of the Five Ghost Stars. It represents speculation, robbery, viruses, and war. It is the Five Yellow Evils and is responsible for blood, spleen and stomach diseases, sores, nicotine, and cancer. It is also prone to the emergence of mediums and people with mental disorders. This year, Five Yellow Lianzhen Star flies into the northeastern Gen Palace. The Gen Palace belongs to earth element and represents young boys. In terms of the five elements, both are similar in energy and prosperity. The double stars are the Five Yellow Lianzhen Star and the Eight

White Zuofu Star in the same palace.

1、2025年陽宅在此方位易遭禍患，此方位如有缺角、不平、形煞，或任意興工動土修造，沒有配合天星奇門遁甲九天玄女一二〇甲子擇日秘法及玄空大卦六十四卦之卦氣卦運來做為選吉之應用，這種情形會導致家內易有地板龜裂或崩塌之象，也容易發生無妄之災，如車禍、癌症、毒瘡、敗血症、皮膚病、胃癌、煙毒、喉肺之病，或投機、爛賭、酗酒而導致破財，尤其對家中的小兒子非常不利。

In 2025, the house in this direction is prone to disasters. If there are missing corners, unevenness, or bad shapes in this direction, or if construction is started arbitrarily without the use of the secret method of selecting auspicious days according to the Tianxing Qimen Dunjia Jiutian Xuannu 120 Jiazi and the hexagram qi and hexagram luck of the sixty-four hexagrams of the Xuankong Dagua as the application of auspiciousness, this situation will cause the floor in the house to crack or collapse, and it is also easy to have unexpected disasters, such as car accidents, cancer, acne, sepsis, skin diseases, stomach cancer, nicotine, throat and lung diseases, or speculation, gambling, alcoholism, which may lead to financial loss, especially for the youngest son in the family.

2、今年此方位如果配置合局，事業有升遷機會，學生課業進步。失運時家中小男多疾病、多凶險，小心肺部、胃部、血液等疾病，今年財運不佳，易因財物產生糾紛，要小心官司牢獄之災，家宅小心山崩、土石流，嚴重時有生命危險。

If this position is well configured this year, there will be opportunities for career advancement and students will make progress in their studies. If it is unlucky, the young boys in the family will suffer from many diseases and dangers. Be careful of lung, stomach, blood and other diseases. This year, the financial luck is not good and it is easy to have disputes over property. Be careful of lawsuits and imprisonment. Be cautious of landslides and mudslides in the house. In serious cases, there is a risk of life.

六、正財位 Positive Wealth Position：

六白武曲星為正財星屬金，代表老父，主財富、正財、武貴。今年六白武曲星飛入南方的離宮，離宮屬火，代表中女，是為火剋金，雙星是六白武曲星與九紫右弼星同宮。

Six White Wuqu Star is a positive wealth star of metal element, representing the old father, and responsible for fortune, positive wealth, and military nobility. This year, the Six White Wuqu Star flies into the Li Palace in the south of fire element. It represents the middle daughter, and fire overcomes metal. The double stars are the Six White Wuqu Star and the Nine Purple Youbi Star in the same palace.

1、2025年陽宅在此方位能得利，此方位如有缺角、不平、形煞，或任意興工動土修造，沒有配合天星奇門遁甲九天玄女一二〇甲子擇日秘法及玄空大卦六十四卦之卦氣卦運來做為選吉之應用，這種情形會導致家中男主人及少女容易破財，事業失利，家宅易有火災，父女感情失和，家宅不安寧。

In 2025, the house can benefit from this direction. If this direction is missing, uneven, or has bad shapes, or if construction is started arbitrarily, without using the secret method of selecting auspicious days according to the Tianxing Qimen Dunjia Jiutian Xuannu 120 Jiazi and the hexagram qi and hexagram luck of the sixty-four hexagrams of the Xuankong Dagua, this situation will cause the male owner and the girl in the family to lose money easily and fail in their careers. The house is prone to fire, the relationship between father and daughter is estranged, and there is no peace in the house.

2、六白武曲星是正財星，若能妥善運用此方位，會使家中男主人及小女兒從事武職大利，特別利於警察、軍人，正偏財皆興旺，家中長輩長壽，能旺丁旺財，失運時，雙星主火燒天門，男主人出事，不利長房，易有桃花劫，甚至樂極生悲，家宅發生火災，健康方面易有血液病、肺病、腦病、熱症、牙周病，家中易出叛逆子孫。

Six White Wuqu Star is a positive wealth star. If this position can

be used properly, the male owner and the little daughter in the family will benefit from engagement in military careers, especially the police and army. Both the positive and incidental wealth will be auspicious, the elders in the family will live long, and the family will be prosperous. When luck is bad, the double stars will cause riot by getting the male owner into trouble. It will be unfavorable to the eldest son who will be prone to bad relationship disasters, and even joy will turn into sorrow. Fire will occur in the house. In terms of health, there are blood diseases, lung diseases, brain diseases, fever, periodontal diseases, and rebellious children in the family.

七、是非星 Gossip Star Position：

七赤破軍星屬金，代表少女，主口舌、是非、官司、訴訟，是為是非之星。今年七赤破軍飛入北方坎宮，坎宮屬水，代表中男，五行是為金生水，雙星是七赤破軍星與一白貪狼星同宮。

Seven Red Qichi Pojun Star belongs to metal element, representing young girls, and is responsible for gossips, disputes, lawsuits, and litigation. This year, Seven Red Pojun Star flies into the northern Kan Palace, which is water element, representing the middle son. In terms of the five elements, metal produces water. The double stars are Seven Red Pojun Star and One White Tanlang Star in the same palace.

1、2025年陽宅在此方位大利，此方位如有缺角、不平、形煞，或任意興工動土修造，沒有配合天星奇門遁甲九天玄女一二〇甲子擇日秘法及玄空大卦六十四卦之卦氣卦運來做為選吉之應用，這種情形會導致家中少女、中男常有口舌是非、官司訴訟，易有舌、喉、肺、血液之病症或血光之災，小心食物中毒、感情糾紛，還須小心火災或山難土石流。

In 2025, it is very auspicious to build a house in this direction. If this direction has missing corners, is uneven, or has bad shapes, or if construction is started arbitrarily, without using the secret method of selecting auspicious days according to the Tianxing Qimen Dunjia Jiutian Xuannu 120 Jiazi and the hexagram qi and

hexagram luck of the sixty-four hexagrams of the Xuan Kong Dagua to select auspicious days, this situation will cause girls and boys in the family to often have disputes and lawsuits, and are prone to diseases of the tongue, throat, lungs, and blood, or bloody disasters. Be careful of food poisoning, emotional disputes, and also watch out for fires or landslides.

2、今年大利北方，此方位用之得當，事業升職加薪，金榜題名，大利武職如警察、軍人，今年桃花旺盛，家中喜慶臨門，失運時感情氾濫，工作遭受外放，常有是非困惑，財運不佳，人際關係失和，容易自命清高，自我欣賞，女性易有墮胎、流產、婦科疾病，家宅易有崩塌、破損、土石流災禍。

North is the most auspicious direction this year. If you use this direction properly, you will get promotion and salary increase in your career, and you will be on the list of successful candidates. It is also auspicious for military professions such as police and army. This year, you will have flourishing interpersonal relationships, and your family will have happy events. When you are unlucky, your emotions will be overflowing, and you will be demoted at work. You will often be confused, have bad financial luck, and have discord in interpersonal relationships. You will easily be self-righteous and self-admiring. Women are prone to abortion, miscarriage, and gynecological diseases. Your home is prone to collapse, damage, and landslides.

八、偏財位 Partial Wealth Position：

八白左輔星為財福星，屬土，代表少男，主偏財、貴人、財富。今年八白左輔星飛入西南方坤宮，坤宮屬土，代表老母，五行是為同氣比旺，雙星是八白左輔星與二黑巨門星同宮。

Eight White Zuofu Star is a fortune star, belonging to the earth element, representing young boys, and responsible for partial wealth, nobles and fortune. This year, Eight White Zuofu Star flies into the southwest Kun Palace, which is of earth element and represents the old mother. In terms of the five elements, both are of the same energy, and the double stars are Eight White Zuofu and Two Black Jumen in the same palace.

1、2025年陽宅在此方位小利，此方位如有缺角、不平、形煞，或任意興工動土修造，這種情形會導致家中的小兒子易受損傷，老母孤獨失偶，財運不佳，健康方面易有手腳、耳部、腸胃、骨頭、腰脊、神經系統的毛病。

In 2025, it is slightly beneficial for the house to be located in this direction. If there are missing corners, unevenness, or bad shapes in this direction, this situation will cause the youngest son in the family to be easily injured and the old mother to be lonely and widowed. The financial fortune will be bad, and the health will affect the hands, feet, ears, intestines, stomach, bones, waist, spine, and nervous system.

2、今年在此方位得利，用之得當得法，可以置業興家，旺田旺地，房地產得利，財運很好，失運時，小兒易遭受血光，出外小心犬蛇咬傷，老母易有喪夫之事，心境孤獨，易有出世的想法。

You will gain benefits from this direction this year. If you use it properly, you can build a family by investing in property, and gain profits from real estate and prosperous fields. Your fortune will be very good. When you are unlucky, your children may suffer from bloodshed, and you should be careful of dog and snake bites when going out. The old mother may lose her husband. In times of feeling lonely, may have thoughts of leaving the world.

九、喜慶貴人位 Celebrations and Nobles Position：

九紫右弼星屬火，代表中女，代表喜慶、姻緣、血光、火災、人緣、貴人及桃花。今年九紫右弼星飛入東方震宮，震宮屬木，代表長男，五行是為木生火，雙星是九紫右弼星與三碧祿存星同宮。

Jiuzi Youbi Star belongs to fire element, representing the middle daughter, and is responsible for happiness, marriage, blood, fire, popularity, nobles and romance. This year, Jiuzi Youbi Star flies into the east Zhen Palace. Zhen Palace belongs to wood element, representing the eldest son. In terms of the five elements, wood gives rise to fire. The double stars are Jiuzi Youbi and Sanbi Lucun in the same palace.

1、2025年陽宅在此方位不利，有流年三煞大凶，此方位如有缺角、不平、形煞，或任意興工動土修造，這種情形會導致家人容易發生血光之災、火燒燙傷、眼疾、心臟病、大小腸病、觸電，家中女性血崩，家中中女、長男容易惹上桃色之情事或有性別認同的問題。

   In 2025, it is unfavorable for the house to be located in this direction, as it is the disastrous Trible Killing position. If there are missing corners, unevenness, or bad shapes in this direction, this situation will cause disasters. Family members will be prone to bloody misfortune, burns, eye diseases, heart diseases, large and small intestine diseases, electric shocks, and female family members will suffer from hemorrhage. The middle daughter and eldest son in the family will be prone to engage in bad romance or gender identity problems.

2、今年在此方位用之得當得法，家門可再添光彩，事業復甦成長，能出聰明的小孩，家宅公司重新裝修或新店開幕，失運之時，感情混亂容易惹上桃色糾紛，家宅遭受火災，男性行為暴戾，健康方面要特別小心眼疾、足傷。

   If you use this direction properly this year, your family will be more glorious, your career will recover and grow, you will have smart children, your home or company will be renovated or a new store will open. When you are unlucky, your emotions will be turbulent and you will easily get into romantic disputes. Your home will suffer a fire, and men will behave violently. In terms of health, you must be especially careful about eye diseases and foot injuries.

二〇二五乙巳蛇年陽宅九宮飛星化解及加強方法

Methods to resolve and strengthen the Nine Palace Flying Stars in 2025 Yi Si Year of the Snake for Residences

1、今年一白貪狼星飛入東南方巽宮，如要化解凶災或加強運勢，可以在家宅的東南方擺放琉璃玉書麒麟、八卦盤、琉璃龍鳳杯、白水晶簇。

This year, One White Yibai Tanlang Star flies into the southeast Xun Palace. If you want to resolve disasters or strengthen your fortune, you can place a glazed Unicorn, a Bagua Plate, a glazed Dragon Phoenix Cup, and White Crystal Cluster in the southeast sector of your house.

2、今年二黑巨門星飛入中宮，如要化解凶災或加強運勢，可以在家宅的中央擺放琉金四面觀音、開運葫蘆、六帝古錢獅咬劍風鈴、桃柳檀木劍雷令福袋。

This year, Two Black Erhei Jumen Star flies into the centre of the house. If you want to resolve disasters or strengthen your fortune, you can place a Four Side Guan Yin statue, a Fortune Gourd, a Lion Head Charm and a Protective Charm in the central sector of your home.

3、今年三碧祿存星飛入西北方乾宮，如要化解凶災或加強運勢，可以在家宅的西北方擺放琉璃龍印、桃柳檀木劍雷令福袋、百福聚寶盆、琉璃龍龜。

This year, Sanbi Lucun Star flies into the northwest Qian Palace. If you want to resolve disasters or strengthen your fortune, you can place a glazed Dragon Seal, a Protective Charm, a Baifu

Cornucopia and a glazed Dragon Turtle in the northwest sector of your home.

4、今年四綠文曲星飛入西方兌宮，如要化解凶災或加強運勢，可以在家宅的西方擺放琉璃龍鳳呈祥、琉璃獅咬劍文鎮、綠水晶文昌開運樹、富貴竹。

This year, the Four Green Wenqu Star flies into the Western Palace. If you want to resolve disasters or strengthen your fortune, you can place a glazed Dragon Phoenix, a glazed Lion Head Wenzhen, an Academic Crystal Tree, and Lucky Bamboos in the west sector of your home.

5、今年五黃廉貞星飛入東北方艮宮，如要化解凶災或加強運勢，可以在家宅的東北方擺放琉璃石敢當、琉璃龍鳳杯、六帝古錢獅咬劍風鈴、琉璃魁星踢斗。

This year, the Five Yellow Lianzhen Star flies into the northeast Gen Palace. If you want to resolve disasters or strengthen your fortune, you can place a glazed Si Gan Dang, a glazed Dragon Phoenix Cup, a Lion Head Charm and a Kuixing Ta Dou in the northeast sector of your home.

6、今年六白武曲星飛入南方的離宮，如要化解凶災或加強運勢，可以在家宅的南方擺放琉璃龍鳳杯、琉璃鰲魚、琉璃九頭靈獅、綠幽靈水晶簇、納財聚寶盆。

This year, Six White Wuqu Star flies into the Li Palace in the south. If you want to avert disasters or strengthen your fortune, you can place a glazed Dragon Phoenix Cup, a glazed Ao Yu, a glazed Nine-headed Lion, Green Crystal Cluster, and a Liuli Wealth Bowl in the south sector of your home.

7、今年七赤破軍飛入北方坎宮，如要化解凶災加強運勢，可以在家宅的北方，擺放盆栽加琉璃鰲魚、琉璃龍山、紫晶洞、琉璃火焰聚寶盆、金箔葫蘆。

This year, Seven Red Pojun Star flies into the northern Kan Palace. If you want to avert disasters and strengthen your fortune, you can place potted plants, a glazed Ao Yu, a Five Element Dragon Mountain, Amethyst Cave, glazed Flame Cornucopia, and Gold Foil Gourd in the north sector of your home.

8、今年八白左輔星飛入西南方坤宮，如要化解凶災或加強運勢，可以在家宅的西南方擺放三合貴人盤、金蟾百福聚寶盆、龍銀元、琉璃五行五靈圖。

This year, Eight White Zuofu Star flies into the southwest Kun Palace. If you want to avert disasters or strengthen your fortune, you can place a Three Harmony Zodiac Benefactor Plate, a Golden Toad Treasure Bowl, Dragon Wealth Coins, and Five Elements Figure in the southwest sector of your home.

9、今年九紫右弼星飛入東方震宮，如要化解凶災或加強運勢，可以在家宅的東方擺放琉璃龍馬、琉璃龍鳳呈祥、琉金四面觀音、黃金萬兩水晶簇、富貴竹。

This year, the Jiuzi Youbi Star flies into the Zhen Palace in the east. If you want to avert disasters and strengthen your fortune, you can place a glazed Dragon Horse, a glazed Dragon Phoenix Cup, a Four Side Guan Yin statue, Gold Crystal Clusters, and Lucky Bamboos in the east sector of your home.

五路財神供奉神仙聖佛誕辰祝壽祭祀法會時間表

Bugis Fortune God Year 2025 Calendar of Deities Birthday Celebration

神佛聖號Deity	陰曆Lunar	陽曆Date	星期Day
點光明燈拜太歲法會（新加坡）	正月初三~初十	2025年1月31~2月7日	星期五~星期五
接財神（新加坡）	正月初五	2025年2月2日	星期日
玉皇上帝萬壽(拜天公)(新加坡)	正月初九	2025年2月6日	星期四
祭改禳解法會（台灣）	正月十一	2025年2月8日	星期六
安太歲、點燈法會（台灣）	正月十二	2025年2月9日	星期日
觀世音菩薩開庫日	正月廿六	2025年2月23日	星期日
福德正神千秋（接龍神）	二月初二	2025年3月1日	星期六
文昌帝君聖誕	二月初三	2025年3月2日	星期日
財寶天王聖誕	二月十二	2025年3月11日	星期二
太上道祖聖誕祝壽法會（台灣）	二月十四	2025年3月13日	星期四
太上道祖聖誕千秋	二月十五	2025年3月14日	星期五
九天玄女娘娘千秋	二月十五	2025年3月14日	星期五
觀世音菩薩誕辰	二月十九	2025年3月18日	星期二
拜龍神法會（生基）（觀音山）	二月廿一	2025年3月20日	星期四
拜龍神法會（生基）（高雄）	二月廿三	2025年3月22日	星期六
玄天上帝聖誕	三月初三	2025年3月31日	星期一
財神誕送窮迎富法會	三月十三~十五	2025年4月10~12日	星期四~星期六
武財神聖誕（趙公明）	三月十五	2025年4月12日	星期六
註生娘娘千秋	三月二十	2025年4月17日	星期四
天上聖母（媽祖）聖誕	三月廿三	2025年4月20日	星期日
超渡法會（台灣）	三月廿八~三十	2025年4月25~27日	星期五~星期日
正財神聖誕（范蠡）	四月七日	2025年5月4日	星期日
釋迦佛祖萬壽	四月八日	2025年5月5日	星期一
偏財祖師聖誕（劉海禪師）	六月初十	2025年7月4日	星期五
偏財神聖誕（韓信爺）	六月十三	2025年7月7日	星期一
觀世音菩薩得道紀念日	六月十九	2025年7月13日	星期日
關聖帝君聖誕	六月廿四	2025年7月18日	星期五
中元普渡法會（台灣）	七月十五	2025年9月6日	星期六
地藏王菩薩佛辰	七月三十	2025年9月21日	星期日
月老星君聖誕	八月十五	2025年10月6日	星期一
中壇元帥千秋	九月初九	2025年10月29日	星期三
觀世音菩薩出家紀念日	九月十九	2025年11月8日	星期六
藥師佛聖誕	九月廿九日	2025年11月18日	星期二
下元水官大帝聖誕	十月十五日	2025年12月4日	星期四
肖鼠守護神－千手觀音聖誕	二月十九	2025年3月18日	星期二
肖牛、虎守護神－虛空藏菩薩聖誕	三月十六	2025年4月13日	星期日
肖兔守護神－文殊菩薩聖誕	四月初四	2025年5月1日	星期四
肖龍、蛇守護神－普賢菩薩聖誕	二月廿一	2025年3月20日	星期四
肖馬守護神－大勢至菩薩聖誕	七月十三	2025年9月4日	星期四
肖羊、猴守護神－大日如來聖誕	四月初八	2025年5月5日	星期一
肖雞守護神－不動明王聖誕	九月十三	2025年11月2日	星期日
肖狗、豬守護神－阿彌陀佛聖誕	十一月十七	2026年1月5日	星期一
二〇二五乙巳年恭送太歲	十二月廿四	2026年2月11日	星期三

二〇二五乙巳蛇年十二生肖全年逐輪運勢

◎ 肖鼠人二〇二五年運勢詳解

Forecast for the Year 2025 for People Born in the Year of the Rat
(6、18、30、42、54、66、78歲)

肖鼠人二〇二五年運勢有紫微、龍德、玉堂貴人、天厄、暴敗入宮。今年吉星高照運勢興旺，事業蒸蒸日上，有貴人大力支持，事業及學業一飛衝天，雖有凶星禍事也能化險為夷，趨吉避凶。**肖鼠之人今年總體運勢非常好，大利事業升遷，心高氣傲反成敗局，宜至玉玄門點光明燈祈求身體健康不受災病侵擾。**

In 2025, the fortune of people born in the year of the Rat will have the blessings of auspicious stars Ziwei, Longde and Yutang Guirenbut will also come across ominous stars Tianwei (Natural calamity) and BaoBai (Violent defeat). This year, the auspicious stars will be shining brightly, your fortune will be booming and your career will be prosperous. With the support of noble people, your career and studies will soar. People born under the zodiac sign of the Rat will have very good fortune this year, with great success in career advancement. However,high-mindedness and arrogance will lead to failure. To resolve the adverse influence from the ominous stars, it is advisable to head down to Yu Xuan Men to light a Wishing Lamp for blessings on good health and protection from disasters.

今年運勢有眾多吉星拱照，帶來喜事重重，大利事業開展，工作升遷，升職加薪，財運興旺，貴人明現，學生考運亨通，能逢凶化吉，遇難呈祥，感情方面異性緣很好，凶星屬破壞力，令你事業及財運大起大落，導致功敗垂成，預防天然災害，一旦發生流行性疾病散播時要特別小心。

This year's fortune will be illuminated by many auspicious stars, bringing many happy events, great career development, job

promotion, salary increase and prosperous wealth. Noble people will appear, students will have good luck in examinations, bad luck can be turned into good luck, and disaster can turn auspicious.Interpersonal relationship will be amicable.But the ominous stars are destructive, causing fluctuations in your career and wealth, leading to failure. Be cautious of natural disasters, and be particularly careful in the event of the spread of epidemic diseases.

今年貴人高照，諸事順利，成功的秘訣在於善用貴人扶持，建議保持態度謙虛，頭腦冷靜，以免無形中得罪了貴人，學生要保持情緒平穩，自有師長提攜幫助，凡事三思而後行，決策要果決，避免暴起暴落，反而浪費大好的機運，今年健康是重點，注重飲食均衡及作息規律，有病立即就醫，以免發生憾事。

You have help from noble people this year and everything will go smoothly. The secret to success is to make good use of their support. It is recommended that you remain humble and keep a cool head to avoid offending them unintentionally. Students should keep a stable mood, as teachers will be there to support and help them. Think twice before doing anything and make decisions decisively to avoid sudden ups and downs, which will waste great opportunities. Health is the focus this year. Pay attention to a balanced diet and a regular schedule. If you are sick, seek medical attention immediately to avoid regrets.

財運 Wealth	★★★★★
事業 Career	★★★★★
感情 Relationship	★★★★
健康 Health	★★★
吉祥顏色 Lucky Color	藍色 Blue Color
吉祥數字Lucky Number	4623

歲次庚子年生人6歲（西元二〇二〇年生）
People born in Geng Zi Year are lunar 6 years old (born in 2020)

財運：小孩不論財運，父母投資小孩的學習是值得的事。

Wealth: Regardless of the child's financial luck, it is worthwhile for parents to invest in their education.

事業：小孩運勢尚可，易遭受傷病困擾，影響學習效率，多注意情緒的平穩。

Career: The child's fortune is fair, but prone to injuries and illnesses, which affect the learning efficiency. Pay more attention to emotional stability.

感情：6歲的孩子有廣泛的興趣，對外界的好奇心重，多讓他表現自己的想法。

Relationship: 6-year-old child has a wide range of interests and is very curious about the outside world. Let the child express his own ideas.

健康：健康運勢不佳，建立良好的衛生習慣以免染上流行性病毒。

Health: Health condition is poor, you should establish good hygiene habits to avoid contracting epidemic viruses.

吉祥物 Auspicious Items：

1. 今年雖有吉星降臨仍有煞星危害，宜在正月初一至正月十五期間，前往新加坡四馬路五路財神敬拜四面觀音，報名台灣玉宸齋制化災病煞星法會，點千手千眼觀音菩薩本命燈或觀音菩薩平安健康燈，供奉冤親債主金，趨吉避凶、消災解厄。

   Although there are auspicious stars befalling this year, there are still hazards from ominous stars. It is advisable to go to the Bugis Fortune God at Bencoolen Street in Singapore, between the first and fifteenth day of the first lunar month, to worship the Four Side Guan Yin. Register for the Taiwan Yu Chen Zhai puja for blessings. Light the Thousand Hands and Thousand Eyes Avalokitesvara Bodhisattva Wishing Lamp or Health Wishing Lamp, and offer the Karmic Creditors incense papers dedicated to enemies and creditors in your previous lives to seek good fortune, eliminate disasters and resolve misfortunes.

2. 在房間擺放開運葫蘆，葫蘆有收煞氣的作用，也有有行醫及助旺健康的作用，還可以避開風水上的疾厄煞氣。

   Place a good-luck Hu Lu (Gourd) in the room can absorb evil spirits, improve medical condition, boost health, and ward off diseases and disasters.

歲次戊子年生人18歲（西元二〇〇八年生）
People born in Wu Zi Year are lunar 18 years old (born in 2008)

財運：財運很好，賺到錢要好好理財，可得貴人提升財運。

Wealth: Wealth luck is very good. If you make money, you must manage it well. You have noble people to improve your wealth luck.

事業：事業運勢上升，學業精進，考運很好，應當努力學習掌握絕佳的考運。

Career: Your career fortune is on the rise, your academic performance is improving, and your examination luck is very good. You should study hard to have excellent examination performance.

感情：異性緣很好，情緒暴起暴落影響生活，小心第三者介入。

Relationship: You have good rapport with the opposite sex, but your mood swings may affect your life, so be careful about the intrusion of a third party.

健康：健康平平，宜注意氣管過敏、腸胃不適，孕婦要小心安胎，易染流行病毒。

Health: Health is average. You should pay attention to tracheal allergies and gastrointestinal discomfort. Pregnant women should be careful about miscarriage as they are susceptible to epidemic viruses.

吉祥物 Auspicious Items：

1. 今年雖有吉星降臨仍有煞星危害，宜在正月初一至正月十五期間，前往新加坡四馬路五路財神敬拜四面觀音，報名台灣玉宸齋制化災病煞星法會，點千手千眼觀音菩薩本命燈或觀音菩薩平安健康燈，供奉冤親債主金，趨吉避凶、消災解厄。

   Although there are auspicious stars coming this year, there are still dangers from ominous stars. It is advisable to go to the Bugis Fortune God at Bencoolen Street in Singapore between the first and fifteenth day of the first lunar month to worship the Four Side Guan Yin. Register for the Taiwan Yu Chen Zhai puja for blessings. Light the Thousand Hands and Thousand Eyes Avalokitesvara Bodhisattva Wishing Lamp or the Health Wishing Lamp, and offer the Karmic Creditors incense papers to seek good fortune, resolve misfortunes and eliminate disasters.

2. 學生可在書桌擺放琉璃魁星踢斗，可使學生越來越想讀書，智慧大開，工作之人可以配戴三合水晶手鍊，可增強助旺身體健康、事業興旺，還可化解意外橫災。

   Students can place a glazed Kui Xing Ta Dou on their desks to make them want to study more and broaden their wisdom. Working people can wear a Zodiac Benefactor bracelet to enhance their health, prosper their career and resolve unexpected disasters.

歲次丙子年生人30歲（西元一九九六年生）
People born in Bing Zi Year are lunar 30 years old (born in 1996)

財運：財運很好，升官加薪，貴人帶來投資機會，避免得而又失。

Wealth: Good wealth fortune, with promotion and salary increase. Noble people bring investment opportunities, and you will avoid gains and losses.

事業：工作上能掌握權柄，業務上升，適合創業或轉換跑道，可以獲得貴人幫助。

Career: You will be able to gain authority at work, your business will be on the rise. It is suitable for starting a business or changing careers, and you can get help from noble people.

感情：異性緣很好，單身之人愛情順利，已婚者婚姻和諧，須防情緒影響感情。

Relationship: Good relationships with the opposite sex. Singles will have smooth love lives and married people will have harmonious marriages. Be careful not to let your emotions affect your relationships.

健康：健康平平，注意脾胃不佳、流行病毒、身心過勞等方面的疾病。

Health: Health is average. Pay attention to diseases such as poor spleen and stomach, epidemic viruses, physical and mental overwork, etc.

吉祥物 Auspicious Items：

1. 今年雖有吉星降臨仍有煞星危害，宜在正月初一至正月十五期間，前往新加坡四馬路五路財神敬拜四面觀音，報名台灣玉宸齋制化災病煞星法會，點千手千眼觀音菩薩本命燈或武財神事業財利燈，供奉接迎貴人金、驅除小人金來消災解厄、平安健康、財源廣進。

   Although there are auspicious stars befalling this year, there are still dangers from ominous stars. It is advisable to go to the Bugis Fortune God at Bencoolen Street in Singapore, between the first and fifteenth day of the first lunar month, to worship the Four Side Guan Yin. Register for the Taiwan Yu Chen Zhai puja for blessings. Light the Thousand Hands and Thousand Eyes AvalokitesvaraBodhisattva Wishing Lamp or Wealth Wishing Lamp, and offer the Karmic Creditors incense papers to drive away villains, eliminate disasters and bring peace, health and wealth.

2. 臥室可放置琉璃三合生肖猴鼠龍或三合貴人盤，可招貴人、增強運勢、改變家運、招財進寶。

   You can place a set of Zodiac Benefactors (Monkey, Rat, Dragon) or aZodiac Benefactor Plate in the bedroom to attract noble people, change and enhance fortune and attract wealth.

歲次甲子年生人42歲（西元一九八四年生）
People born in Jia Zi Year are lunar 42 years old (born in 1984)

財運：財運很好，投資升值，薪資加碼，投資房產是不錯的選擇。

Wealth: Wealth luck is very good, investment appreciates, salary increases, and real estate is a good choice.

事業：工作運勢很好，得到貴人的幫助，應變能力強，有出色的商業頭腦。

Career: Good luck at work, getting help from noble people, have strong adaptability and excellent business acumen.

感情：感情穩定，未婚之人良緣出現，已婚之人易受異性的歡迎，小心影響婚姻。

Relationship: Relationship is stable. Good marriage will appear for singles. Married people are easily welcomed by the opposite gender, be careful about the impact on marriage.

健康：健康運勢尚可，宜注意肝膽疾病、婦科疾病、神經過敏、流行病毒。

Health: Your health is fair. You should pay attention to liver and gallbladder diseases, gynecological diseases, nervousness, and epidemic viruses.

吉祥物 Auspicious Items：

1. 今年雖有吉星降臨仍有煞星危害，宜在正月初一至正月十五期間，前往新加坡四馬路五路財神敬拜四面觀音，報名台灣玉宸齋制化災病煞星法會，點千手千眼觀音菩薩本命燈或武財神事業財利燈，供奉接迎貴人金、驅除小人金來消災解厄、平安健康、財源廣進。

   Although there are auspicious stars befalling this year, there are still dangers from ominous stars. It is advisable to go to the Bugis Fortune God at Bencoolen Street in Singapore, between the first and fifteenth day of the first lunar month, to worship the Four Side Guan Yin. Register for the Taiwan Yu Chen Zhai puja for blessings. Light the Thousand Hands and Thousand Eyes Avalokitesvara Bodhisattva Wishing Lamp or Wealth Wishing Lamp, and offer the Karmic Creditors incense papers to drive away villains, eliminate disasters and bring peace, health and wealth.

   …中或辦公室的吉祥方位擺放靈動力強大的黃水晶招財樹、龍神聖水，可以招財…創造意外財富，使用貴人顯耀沐浴露，可增強貴人運，增進人際關係。

   …werful Wealth Crystal Tree and a bottle of Dragon HolyWater in …ations at home or in the office to attract wealth and create …. Use the Benefactor Body Wash for your bath to enhance …onal relationships.

歲次壬子年生人54歲 (西元一九七二年生)
People born in Ren Zi Year are lunar 54 years old (born in 1972)

財運：財運很好，小心投資暴起暴跌，避免投資過大可以預防破財。

Wealth: Wealth luck is very good. Be careful of sudden investment fluctuations and avoid excessive investment to prevent financial losses.

事業：忙碌工作，為事業付出過人的時間，可以成為別人關鍵的貴人。

Career: Work hard and devote extraordinary time to your career, and you can become a key person to others.

感情：夫妻感情和諧，社交場合常遇異性欣賞，要懂得保持適當的距離。

Relationship: The relationship between husband and wife is harmonious. People of the opposite sex often meet in social situations and appreciate each other. They must know how to keep an appropriate distance.

健康：健康平平，宜注意心血管、眼疾、下腹部、流行病毒的疾病問題。

Health: Health is average. You should pay attention to cardiovascular, eye diseases, lower abdomen, and epidemic viral diseases.

吉祥物 Auspicious Items：

1. 今年雖有吉星降臨仍有煞星危害，宜在正月初一至正月十五期間，前往新加坡四馬路五路財神敬拜四面觀音，報名台灣玉宸齋制化災病煞星法會，點千手千眼觀音菩薩本命燈或武財神事業財利燈，供奉接迎貴人金、驅除小人金來消災解厄、平安健康、財源廣進。

   Although there are auspicious stars befalling this year, there are still dangers from ominous stars. It is advisable to go to the Bugis Fortune God at Bencoolen Street in Singapore, between the first and fifteenth day of the first lunar month, to worship the Four Side Guan Yin. Register for the Taiwan Yu Chen Zhai puja for blessings. Light the Thousand Hands and Thousand Eyes Avalokitesvara Bodhisattva Wishing Lamp or Wealth Wishing Lamp, and offer the Benefactor and Removal of Villians incense papers to drive away villains, eliminate disasters and bring peace, health and wealth.

2. 可以在家中財位擺放琉璃九龍聚寶盆，除去陰氣帶來旺財之氣，讓暴起暴跌的財運得到化解補救。

   You can place a glazed Nine-dragon Treasure Bowl in the wealth position of your home to remove negative energy and bring in good fortune, so that the sudden rise and fall of wealth can be resolved.

歲次庚子年生人66歲（西元一九六〇年生）
People born in Geng Zi Year are lunar 66 years old (born in 1960)

財運：財運不錯，理財習慣要調整，分散風險才能避免失利。

Wealth: Wealth luck is good. Financial management habits need to be adjusted and risks spread to avoid failure.

事業：工作職務升級，特別適合創業，貴人運旺盛，能為事業提供有價值的資源。

Career: The job position will be upgraded, especially suitable for starting a business. You have strong noble luck which can provide valuable resources for your career.

感情：全年人緣很好，別給伴侶壓力，體諒及安慰很重要，關係和諧才是福氣。

Relationship: You will be very popular throughout the year. Do not put pressure on your partner. It is important to be considerate and comforting. A harmonious relationship is a blessing.

健康：健康尚可，宜注意眼睛、白血球、胰臟、肝腎、流行病毒的疾病問題。

Health: Your health is acceptable. You should pay attention to diseases of the eyes, white blood cells, pancreas, liver, kidneys, and epidemic virus.

吉祥物 Auspicious Items：

1. 今年雖有吉星降臨仍有煞星危害，宜在正月初一至正月十五期間，前往新加坡四馬路五路財神敬拜四面觀音，報名台灣玉宸齋制化災病煞星法會，點千手千眼觀音菩薩本命燈或觀音菩薩平安健康燈，供奉制化供品，燒化冤親債主金，趨吉避凶、消災解厄。

   Although there are auspicious stars befalling this year, there are still dangers from ominous stars. It is advisable to go to the Bugis Fortune God at Bencoolen Street in Singapore, between the first and fifteenth day of the first lunar month, to worship the Four Side Guan Yin. Register for the TaiwanYu Chen Zhai puja. Light the Thousand Hands and Thousand Eyes Avalokitesvara Bodhisattva Wishing Lamp or the Health Wishing Lamp, and offer the Karmic Creditors incense papers to seek good fortune and eliminate disasters.

2. 可到四馬路五路財神點七彩蓮花轉運燈，讓菩薩護祐讓身心、災邪遠離、趨吉避凶。

   You can go to the Bugis Fortune God at Bencoolen Street to light the Lotus Lamp for the Bodhisattva to protect your body and mind, enhance good luck and keep away disasters and evils.

歲次戊子年生人78歲（西元一九四八年生）
People born in Wu Zi Year are lunar 78 years old (born in 1948)

財運：財運尚可，花錢要保守一點，小心詐騙偷竊損財。

Wealth: Wealth luck is fair. Be prudent with your money and be careful of fraud and theft.

事業：不要亂發脾氣，不要捲入是非糾葛，退休生活要好好安排，不要給自己壓力。

Career: Don't lose your temper, don't get involved in disputes, arrange your retirement life well, and don't put pressure on yourself.

感情：可以安排社交活動調劑生活氣氛，夫妻去旅遊也很好，別為子孫煩惱。

Relationship: You can arrange social activities to adjust the atmosphere of life. It is also good for couples to travel. Don't worry about children and grandchildren.

健康：健康不佳，要特別注意流行疾病，有病立即就醫，以免發生憾事。

Health: Health is not good. You should pay special attention to epidemic diseases and seek medical treatment immediately if you are sick to avoid regrets.

吉祥物 Auspicious Items：

1. 今年雖有吉星降臨仍有煞星危害，宜在正月初一至正月十五期間，前往新加坡四馬路五路財神敬拜四面觀音，報名台灣玉宸齋制化災病煞星法會，點千手千眼觀音菩薩本命燈或觀音菩薩平安健康燈，供奉冤親債主金，趨吉避凶、消災解厄。

   Although there are auspicious stars befalling this year, there are still dangers from ominous stars. It is advisable to go to the Bugis Fortune God at Bencoolen Street in Singapore, between the first and fifteenth day of the first lunar month, to worship the Four Side Guan Yin. Register for the Taiwan Yu Chen Zhai puja for blessings. Light the Thousand Hands and Thousand Eyes Avalokitesvara Bodhisattva Wishing Lamp or the Health Wishing Lamp, and offer the Karmic Creditors incense papers to seek good fortune and eliminate disasters.

2. 家中可擺放一尊琉金四面觀音，隨身配戴三合水晶手鍊，可助旺身體健康、闔家平安，還可化解意外橫災及小人暗害。

   You can place a glazed Four Side Guan Yin statue at home and wear a Zodiac Benefactor bracelet to help you maintain good health and family safety, and resolve unexpected disasters and evil plots.

◎ 肖牛人二〇二五年運勢詳解

Forecast for the Year 2025 for people born in the year of the Ox

(5、17、29、41、53、65、77歲)

肖牛之人二〇二五年運勢有三合、華蓋、白虎、天雄、遊奕、黃番、天哭入宮。今年吉星較少，代表個人天賦才能有所發揮，會有很好的人緣運，但是凶星眾多，主破敗損傷，易有是非小人暗害，血光橫禍，哀喪孝服之災，女性刑剋較重。**肖牛之人今年總體運勢不佳，煩惱皆因強出頭，建議至玉玄門制化白虎凶星，祈求消災解厄以保安康。**

In 2025, the fortune of people born in the year of the Ox will be influenced by Sanhe, Huagai, Baihu, Tianxiong, Youyi, Huangfan, and Tianwei entering their destiny. There are auspicious stars this year, which means that one's talents can be fully utilized, and there will be good luck in popularity. However, there are many ominous stars, which indicate there are failure and injury. It is easy to be harmed by villains, encounter bloody disasters, mourning and weeping, and women may meet heavier disaster. The fortune of people born under the zodiac sign of the Ox will generally be unfavourable this year, and their troubles will be caused by their strong will trying to stand out. It is recommended that you head to Yu Xuan Men to resolve the impact of the ominous Baihu star (White Tiger), and pray for good health and relief from disasters.

今年吉星代表人和喜悅，有很好的人緣運，但是缺乏貴人強力提攜，工作上才華展露，受到公司或上司的倚重，特別利於從事藝術、創作、設計等行業人士，學習特別利於職校學生，財運不佳小心破財，感情方面機會很多，少有適合的對象，今年白虎凶星影響巨大，主有破敗之事，不利外出遠行，要小心意外橫禍或血光之災，易有小人陷害及惡意造謠，行車外出要特別小心，不要嘗試危險的活動，如遇疾病易遭動刀之苦。

This year's auspicious stars represent people and joy. You have good luck with people, but you lack the strong support of nobles. Your talents are exposed at work and you are relied on by the company or your boss. This is especially beneficial to people engaged in art, creation, design and other industries, and it is also especially beneficial to students in vocational schools. With poor financial luck, be careful about losing money. There are many opportunities in relationships, but few suitable partners. This year, the ominous star White Tiger will have a huge influence which will lead to ruins. It is not good for traveling far away. Be careful of accidental misfortunes or bloody disasters. It is easy to be framed by malicious rumors from villains. You should be especially careful when driving and do not try dangerous activities. In case of illness, you may be vulnerable to surgery.

今年凶星強大，建議不要受外界的影響，努力在自身的發展，外出要小心車關血光，學生要小心交友不慎，而染上惡習，誤入歧途，財務處理宜保守謹慎，不宜弔喪及探病，不食喪物，一旦罹病立速就醫，勿延誤時效，孕婦須防病災，注意人身安全，避免涉入險地以防橫禍發生。

The ominous stars are strong this year. It is recommended not to be influenced by external forces.Work hard on your own development. Be careful about car accidents when going out. Students should be cautious not to make friends carelessly and pick up bad habits and go astray. Be conservative and prudent in financial management. Do not attend the wake, visit the sick or eat funeral food. If you are unwell, seek medical treatment without delay. Pregnant women must be cautious of diseases, pay attention to personal safety, and avoid dangerous places to prevent misfortunes.

財運 Wealth	★★★
事業 Career	★★★
感情 Relationship	★★★
健康 Health	★★
吉祥顏色 Lucky Color	黃色 Yellow Color
吉祥數字Lucky Number	7519

歲次辛丑年生人5歲 (西元二〇二一年生)
People born in Xin Chou Year are lunar 5 years old (born in 2021)

財運：小孩不論財運，多給予啟發性及教育性的資源。

Wealth: Regardless of wealth luck, the child should be provided with inspiring and educational resources.

事業：5歲幼兒心智快速發展，不要輕忽小孩的學習能力，打罵教育往往成為反效果。

Career: The mind of a 5-year-old child develops rapidly. Don't ignore the child's learning ability. Struggling and scolding often have the opposite effect.

感情：孩子希望大人關注，爸媽應該多花一些時間來陪伴小孩。

Relationship: The child wants adults to pay attention, and parents should spend more time with their child.

健康：健康不佳，注意氣管過敏、哮喘，小心橫禍導致血光意外之災。

Health: Health is not good, be careful of tracheal allergies and asthma, and avoid accidental bloody disasters.

吉祥物 Auspicious Items：

1. 今年犯白虎凶星，在正月初一至正月十五期間，前往新加坡四馬路五路財神敬拜四面觀音，報名台灣玉宸齋制化白虎凶星法會、點虛空藏菩薩本命燈及配戴虛空藏菩薩菩薩項鍊，燒化冤親債主金，趨吉避凶、消災解厄、學業進步，聽父母言。

   This year you will be affected by the ominous Baihu (White Tiger)star. It is advisable to go to the Bugis Fortune God at Bencoolen Street in Singapore, between the first and fifteenth day of the first lunar month, to worship the Four Side Guan Yin. Register for the Taiwan Yu Chen Zhai puja for blessings. Bodhisattva Lamp the Ksitigarbha Bodhisattva bracelet, offer the Karmic Creditors incense papers to seek good luck, eliminate disasters, make academic progress, and listen to parents' advice.

2. 本身配戴桃柳檀木劍雷令福袋，如此可以化解血光意外之災，但吉祥物需經法師持經念咒開光請神加持過後，其靈動力才有效果。

   Wearing a Protective Charm can resolve accidental blood disasters. However, the mascot has to be consecrated by a mage to recite sutras before its spiritual power can be effective.

歲次己丑年生人17歲（西元二〇〇九年生）
People born in Ji Chou Year are lunar 17 years old (born in 2009)

財運：財運不佳，小心意外破財，建議花錢要節制。

Wealth: Poor wealth luck, be careful of unexpected financial losses. You should spend money in moderation.

事業：工作壓力超大，辛苦工作，收入和付出不成正比，學生考運不佳。

Career: The work pressure is extremely high, the work is hard but the income is not proportional to the effort. Students have poor luck in examinations.

感情：機會很多，少有適合的對象，易有小人陷害及惡意造謠，導致感情失和。

Relationship: There are many opportunities to find a suitable partner, but it is easy for villains to frame you and spread malicious rumors, leading to emotional discord.

健康：健康不佳，小心意外橫禍或血光之災，行車外出要特別小心。

Health: Health is poor, be careful of accidents or bloody disasters. Be especially careful when driving.

吉祥物 Auspicious Items：

1. 今年犯白虎凶星，在正月初一至正月十五期間，前往新加坡四馬路五路財神敬拜四面觀音，報名台灣玉宸齋制化白虎凶星法會、點虛空藏菩薩本命燈及配戴虛空藏菩薩菩薩項鍊，燒化冤親債主金，消災解厄、平安健康、學業進步，聽父母言。

   This year you will be affected by the ominous White Tiger star. It is advisable to go to the Bugis Fortune God at Bencoolen Street in Singapore, between the first and fifteenth day of the first lunar month, to worship the Four Side Guan Yin. Register for the Taiwan Yu Chen Zhai puja for blessings. Light the Ksitigarbha Bodhisattva Lamp, wear the Ksitigarbha Bodhisattva bracelet, and offer the Karmic Creditors incense papers to seek good luck, eliminate disasters, make academic progress, and listen to parents' advice.

2. 可至玉玄門點文昌智慧光明燈，祭拜文昌帝君，供奉文昌智慧金，來開智慧及增加考試運。

   You can go to Yu Xuan Men to light the Wenchang Wisdom Lamp, worship Wenchang Emperor, and offer Wenchang incense papers to enhance wisdom and increase your luck in examinations.

歲次丁丑年生人29歲 (西元一九九七年生)
People born in Ding Chou Year are Lunar 29 years old (born in 1997)

財運：今年財運平平，可靠文化美術賺錢，小心意外破財。

Wealth: Your wealth this year is mediocre. You can rely on culture and art to make money, but be careful of unexpected financial losses.

事業：人緣運尚可，缺乏貴人幫助，創造力特別好，不利外出遠行。

Career: Good luck in popularity, but lacks help from noble people. Very creative. Not suitable for long distance travel.

感情：容易面臨事業與家庭的掙扎，感情機會多，易有小人陷害及惡意造謠。

Relationship: You are likely to face struggles in your career and family. There are many opportunities for relationships, but you are also prone to being framed by villains and malicious rumors.

健康：健康有隱憂，易因壓力過大而引發身體不適，小心血光外傷。

Health: There are hidden worries about health. Excessive pressure can easily cause physical discomfort. Be careful of blood trauma.

吉祥物 Auspicious Items：

1. 今年犯白虎凶星，在正月初一至正月十五期間，前往新加坡四馬路五路財神敬拜四面觀音，報名台灣玉宸齋制化白虎凶星法會、點虛空藏菩薩本命燈、月老桃花旺緣燈，供奉冤親債主金、貴人金、月老姻緣金，來禳解制化，趨吉避凶，消災解厄。

   This year you will be affected by the ominous White Tiger star. It is advisable to go to the Bugis Fortune God at Bencoolen Street in Singapore, between the first and fifteenth day of the first lunar month, to worship the Four Side Guan Yin. Register for the Taiwan Yu Chen Zhai puja for blessings. Light the Ksitigarbha Bodhisattva and Marriage Lamps and offer the Karmic Creditors, Benefactor and Marriage incense papers to seek good luck and eliminate disasters.

2. 辦公室吊掛小桃木六帝古錢獅咬劍風鈴，桌上擺放小元寶文鎮，如此在事業財運上及防小人是非方面有良好之功效。

   Hang a Lion Head Chime in the office, and place a small ingot on the table. This has a good effect on career and wealth and preventing villains and gossips.

歲次乙丑年生人41歲（西元一九八五年生）
People born in Yi Chou Year are lunar 41 years old (born in 1985)

財運：財運平平，意氣用事會導致錢財損失慘重，避免不必要的風險和支出。

Wealth: Your wealth luck is mediocre, and acting on impulse will lead to heavy losses of money. Avoid unnecessary risks and expenditures.

事業：工作多波折，缺乏動力，不要貿然改革舊制，認真努力可以得到同事的認可。

Career: There are many twists and turns at work and lack of motivation. Don't rush to reform the old system. If you work hard, you will be recognized by your colleagues.

感情：感情不平順，若是將長期積壓的情緒一次釋放，後果會變的很激烈。

Relationship: Relationships are not smooth. If the relationships that have been accumulated for a long time are released at once, the consequences will become very intense.

健康：健康平平，宜注意鼻塞、扁桃腺炎、肺癆，易有突發的血光意外之災。

Health: Health is average. You should be careful about nasal congestion, tonsillitis, and tuberculosis. Sudden blood and light accidents are easy to occur.

吉祥物 Auspicious Items：

1. 今年犯白虎凶星，在正月初一至正月十五期間，前往新加坡四馬路五路財神敬拜四面觀音，報名台灣玉宸齋制化白虎凶星法會、點虛空藏菩薩本命燈，供奉冤親債主金、接迎貴人金，趨吉避凶、消災解厄。

   This year you will be affected by the ominous White Tiger star. It is advisable to go to the Bugis Fortune God at Bencoolen Street in Singapore, between the first and fifteenth day of the first lunar month, to worship the Four Side Guan Yin. Register for the Taiwan Yu Chen Zhai puja for blessings. Light the Ksitigarbha Bodhisattva and offer the Karmic Creditors and Benefactor incense papers to seek good luck and eliminate disasters.

2. 可以在家中擺放琉璃三合生肖蛇牛雞，增加招貴人驅小人、強旺運勢、改變家運、招財進寶的無形靈動力。

   You can place the Zodiac Benefactors (Snake, Ox and Rooster) at home to increase the invisible spiritual power of attracting noble people and driving away villains, strengthening fortune, changing family fortune, and attracting wealth.

歲次癸丑年生人53歲（西元一九七三年生）
People born in Gui Chou Year are lunar 53 years old (born in 1973)

財運：財運尚可，不要投資高風險的金融產品，小心詐騙破財。

Wealth: Wealth luck is fair. Do not invest in high-risk financial products and be careful of fraud and loss of money.

事業：是非小人多，易遭他人非議，決策靈活才能應對各種挑戰。

Career: There are many villains and you are prone to criticism by others. Only by being flexible in decision-making can you cope with various challenges.

感情：家運多災多難，宜注意健康及意外橫災，避免參加高危險性的活動。

Relationship: The family will have many misfortunes, so you should pay attention to your health and unexpected disasters, and avoid participating in high-risk activities.

健康：健康平平，宜注意脾臟、胃疾、大小腸的問題，注意行車安全。

Health: Health is average. You should watch out for problems with the spleen, stomach, and large and small intestines, and pay attention to driving safety.

吉祥物 Auspicious Items：

1. 今年犯白虎凶星，在正月初一至正月十五期間，前往新加坡四馬路五路財神敬拜四面觀音，報名台灣玉宸齋制化白虎凶星法會、點虛空藏菩薩本命燈及配戴虛空藏菩薩菩薩項鍊，供奉貴人金、冤親債主金，趨吉避凶、消災解厄。

   This year you will be affected by the ominous White Tiger star. It is advisable to go to the Bugis Fortune God at Bencoolen Street in Singapore, between the first and fifteenth day of the first lunar month, to worship the Four Side Guan Yin. Register for the Taiwan Yu Chen Zhai puja for blessings. Light the Ksitigarbha Bodhisattva, wear the Ksitigarbha Bodhisattva bracelet and offer the Karmic Creditors and Benefactor incense papers to seek good luck and eliminate disasters.

2. 配戴三合水晶手鍊，可增強助旺身體健康、事業興旺之靈動力，還可化解意外橫災。

   Wearing a Zodiac Benefactor bracelet can enhance your spiritual power to boost your health and career, and can also resolve unexpected misfortunes.

歲次辛丑年生人65歲（西元一九六一年生）
People born in Xin Chou Year are lunar 65 years old (born in 1961)

財運：容易耗費大量錢財，遭遇經濟危機，不可盲目跟風或冒險投資。

Wealth: It is easy to waste a lot of money. If you encounter an economic crisis, you should not blindly follow the trend or make risky investments.

事業：工作時好時壞，不受重用，必須沉著應付，避免把禍事搞得更糟糕。

Career: Work is good and bad, and you are not given high responsibility. You must deal with it calmly to avoid making the disaster worse.

感情：面臨事業與家庭的掙扎，宜保持冷靜，控制混亂的思緒。

Relationship: When facing the struggle between career and family, it is advisable to stay calm and control chaotic thoughts.

健康：健康不佳，須防青光眼、飛蚊症、白內障，防意外之災。

Health: Poor health, need to prevent glaucoma, floaters, cataracts and accidents.

吉祥物 Auspicious Items：

1. 今年犯白虎凶星，在正月初一至正月十五期間，前往新加坡四馬路五路財神敬拜四面觀音，報名台灣玉宸齋制化白虎凶星法會、點虛空藏菩薩本命燈、藥師佛消災解厄燈，供奉冤親債主金、華佗除疾金，趨吉避凶、消災解厄。

   This year you will be affected by the ominous White Tiger star. It is advisable to go to the Bugis Fortune God at Bencoolen Street in Singapore, between the first and fifteenth day of the first lunar month, to worship the Four Side Guan Yin. Register for the Taiwan Yu Chen Zhai puja for blessings. Light the Ksitigarbha Bodhisattva and Medicine Buddha Wishing Lamps and offer the Karmic Creditors and Hua Tuo incense papers to avoid bad luck and eliminate disasters.

2. 到四馬路五路財神點九品蓮花轉運燈，可獲得觀音護祐，讓身心安穩、災邪遠離、趨吉避凶、消災解厄。

   Go to the Bugis Fortune God and light the Nine-pin Lotus Lamp, and you can receive the protection of Guan Yin to make your body and mind stable, keep away evils and eliminate disasters.

歲次己丑年生人77歲（西元一九四九年生）
People born in Ji Chou Year are lunar 77 years old (born in 1949)

財運：財運不佳，慎防財務漏洞導致破產危機。

Wealth: Poor wealth luck, be careful to prevent financial loopholes leading to bankruptcy crisis.

事業：投資不宜盲目跟從，不做沒把握的事，一旦判斷錯誤可能會人財兩失。

Career: It is not advisable to follow blindly when investing, and do not do things that you are not sure about. Once you make a wrong judgment, you may lose both life and money.

感情：家庭失和，引發沮喪、焦慮、難過的複雜情緒。

Relationship: Family discord, causing complex depression, anxiety, and sadness.

健康：健康不佳，宜注意眼睛、白血球、風濕病、糖尿病等方面的疾病。

Health: In poor health, you should pay attention to diseases of the eyes, white blood cells, rheumatism, and diabetes.

吉祥物 Auspicious Items：

1. 今年犯白虎凶星，在正月初一至正月十五期間，前往新加坡四馬路五路財神敬拜四面觀音，報名台灣玉宸齋制化白虎凶星法會、點虛空藏菩薩本命燈、藥師佛消災解厄燈，供奉冤親債主金、華佗除疾金，趨吉避凶、消災解厄。

   This year you will be affected by the ominous White Tiger star. It is advisable to go to the Bugis Fortune God at Bencoolen Street in Singapore, between the first and fifteenth day of the first lunar month, to worship the Four Side Guan Yin. Register for the Taiwan Yu Chen Zhai puja for blessings. Light the Ksitigarbha Bodhisattva and Medicine Buddha Wishing Lamps, and offer Karmic Creditors and Hua Tuo incense papers to avoid bad luck and eliminate disasters.

2. 在家中吊掛黑曜石葫蘆吊飾，葫蘆有收煞氣的作用，亦有懸壺濟世之意，有行醫及助旺健康的作用，還可以避開風水上的疾厄煞氣。

   Hang an Obsidian Hu Lu (Gourd) at home. The gourd can absorb evil spirits and has the meaning of hanging a pot to help the world. It has the function of improvinghealth, and can also avoid evil spirits and disasters.

◎ 肖虎人二〇二五年運勢詳解

Forecast for the Year 2025 for people born in the year of the Tiger (4、16、28、40、52、64、76歲)

肖虎之人二〇二五年運勢有福德、天德、福星、劫殺、捲舌、絞殺、六害、害太歲入宮。今年福星貴神高照，諸事吉慶，主登科進祿，凶星代表易有小人是非及刑獄凶災，夜間勿遠行，勿管閒事。**今年肖虎之人總體運勢很好，吉星可以減低凶星的刑剋，建議至玉玄門拜太歲及禳解改運，化解害太歲、官非、小人之災。**

The presence of auspicious stars will bring blessings to most people born under the sign of the Tiger in 2025. The auspicious stars Fude, Tiande and Fuxing will be shining brightly, and everything will be auspicious. You will be successful in education and career. Nevertheless, there are some ominous stars appearing in your fortune, such as Jiéshā, Juǎnshé, Jiǎoshā and Liùhài which represent disputes, villains and criminal imprisonment. Do not travel far at night and do not meddle with other people's business. People born in the year of the Tiger have good overall fortune this year. Auspicious stars can reduce the negative influence of ominous stars. It is recommended to go to Yu Xuan Men to worship Tai Sui and to resolve disasters, legal disputes and villains.

今年福氣貴人齊臨，工作運勢非常好，有貴人扶持又有錢賺，學生智慧大開，考運亨通，感情緣份美滿，貴人星帶來良好的人際關係，凶星主有招盜賊或殺傷之事，災禍往往起於內部，家人相處易有摩擦爭吵，孕婦要注意流產現象，工作上如果失去貴人，會導致人際關係不合諧，生意上的合作也容易發生意見不合，學生的課業容易因煩惱而停滯，嚴重時深陷小人是非及刑獄凶災。

This year, blessings and noble people will come to you. Your work luck will be very good. You will have the support of noble people and you will make money. Students will be intelligent, examinations

will be successful, and your relationship will be happy. The noble star will bring you good interpersonal relationships. The ominous star will attract thieves or murderers. Disasters often originate from within. It is easy for family members to have frictions and quarrels when getting along. Pregnant women should pay attention to the phenomenon of miscarriage. If you lose nobles at work, it will lead to disharmony in interpersonal relationships. Disagreements may easily occur in business cooperation. Students' academic performance may easily be affected by problems. Troubled and stagnant, in severe cases, one is trapped in villains' wrong-doings and prison disaster.

今年好運勝過壞運，工作方面如要更進一步，必須先將人際關係處理好，避免爭鬥摩擦，得失成敗都掌握在自己的手中，建議修身養性，奉公守法，勿聽讒言，靜而後動，做好帳務管理，預防錢財暗中損失，遇到困難要懂得求助，自有貴人來助。

Good luck outweighs bad luck this year. If you want to go further at work, you must first handle your interpersonal relationships well and avoid fights and frictions. Success or failure is all in your own hands. It is recommended to cultivate your character and abide by the law. Do not listen to slander, be quiet before taking action, and do manage your accounts well to prevent secret losses of money.Know how to ask for help when encountering difficulties, and there will be noble people to assist you.

財運 Wealth	★★★★
事業 Career	★★★★
感情 Relationship	★★★
健康 Health	★★★
吉祥顏色 Lucky Color	綠色 Green Color
吉祥數字Lucky Number	6834

歲次壬寅年生人4歲 (西元二〇二二年生)
People born in Ren Yin Year are lunar 4 years old (born in 2022)

財運：小孩不論財運，可以幫小孩購買儲蓄保險。

Wealth: Regardless of your child's financial luck, you can help the child buy savings insurance.

事業：小孩智慧大開，學習快速，學校學習易有適應問題。

Career: The child is very smart, learns quickly, and has difficulty adapting to school.

感情：四歲小孩出現反抗情緒，父母盡可能不要讓自己情緒上來，以擁抱取代責罰。

Relationship: When a four-year-old child shows signs of rebellion, parents should try their best not to let emotions rise and use hugs instead of punishments.

健康：健康很好，宜注意跌倒或碰撞造成血光意外之災的情況。

Health: Health is very good, but be careful about accidents caused by falls or collisions.

吉祥物 Auspicious Items：

1. 今年犯害太歲，在正月初一至正月十五期間前往新加坡四馬路五路財神來敬拜四面觀音，點太歲星燈、虛空藏菩薩本命燈、文昌智慧光明燈，供奉太歲金、文昌智慧金來禳解制化、平安健康、學業進步，聽父母言。

   This year, because of the clash with Tai Sui, it is advisable to go to the Bugis Fortune God at Bencoolen Street in Singapore, between the first and fifteenth day of the first lunar month, to worship the Four Side Guan Yin. Light the Tai Sui, Ksitigarbha Bodhisattva and Wenchang Wishing Lamps, and offer the Tai Sui and Wenchang incense papers to avoid disasters and ill health, make academic progress, and listen to parents' advice.

2. 書桌上可擺放綠水晶文昌開運樹，可使學童越來越想讀書而思想敏捷，以促進頭腦精明學富五車之功。

   A Crystal Academic Tree can be placed on the desk to make the child wants to study and think more quickly, so as to promote a smart mind and acquire rich knowledge.

歲次庚寅年生人16歲（西元二〇一〇年生）
People born in Geng Yin Year are lunar 16 years old (born in 2010)

財運：財運一般，容易被詐騙或遭受偷竊而損失錢財。

Wealth: Average wealth luck, easy to be defrauded or get stolen and lose money.

事業：讀書運勢很好，考運興旺，注意課業壓力過大而導致行為叛逆，有貴人幫助。

Career: You will have good luck in studying and in taking examinations. Be careful about rebellious behaviour caused by excessive academic pressure. You will have help from noble people.

感情：感情運勢強旺，容易陷入熱戀，感情基礎尚未成熟，小心影響學業。

Relationship: The relationship luck is strong, and it is easy to fall in love. The emotional foundation is not yet mature, so it may affect studies.

健康：健康不佳，容易染上流行性病毒，易有跌倒撞傷的血光之災。

Health: In poor health, you are easily infected with epidemic viruses, and you are prone to bloody accidents such as falls and bruises.

吉祥物 Auspicious Items：

1. 今年犯害太歲，在正月初一至正月十五期間前往新加坡四馬路五路財神來敬拜四面觀音，點太歲星燈、虛空藏菩薩本命燈、文昌智慧光明燈，供奉太歲金、文昌智慧金來禳解制化、平安健康、學業進步。

   This year, because you are affected by the clash with Tai Sui, it is advisable to go to the Bugis Fortune God at Bencoolen Street in Singapore, between the first and fifteenth day of the first lunar month, to worship the Four Side Guan Yin. Light the Tai Sui, Ksitigarbha Bodhisattva and Wenchang Wishing Lamps, and offer the Tai Sui and Wenchang incense papers to avoid disasters and ill health, and enhance academic progress.

2. 書桌上可擺放琉璃玉書麒麟，沐浴時使用文昌智慧沐浴露來助旺文昌氣運，助使學生讀書專心、頭腦敏捷、考運亨通。

   Place a glazed Qi Lin (Unicorn) on the desk, and use Academic Body Wash to bathe can enhance wisdom, improve concentration on studies, be quick-thinking and achieve academic excellence.

歲次戊寅年生人28歲 (西元一九九八年生)
People born in Wu Yin Year are lunar 28 years old (born in 1998)

財運：財運尚可，跟對貴人會為您帶來財運，易受他人拖累而破財。

Wealth: Your wealth luck is fair, and being with noble person will bring you wealth, but you will easily be dragged down by others and lose your money.

事業：貴人運勢強旺，事業蒸蒸日上，人際關係容易出現摩擦及意見不合。

Career: Have strong noble luck and prosperous career. Friction and disagreements are prone to occur in interpersonal relationships.

感情：交友機會多，心情冷熱兩極，太神秘會讓感情熱度轉淡，停滯不前。

Relationship: There are many opportunities to make friends, and the mood is both hot and cold. Being too mysterious will make the relationship fade and stagnate.

健康：健康平平，宜注意消化系統等疾病，孕婦要小心安胎、流產、開刀的問題。

Health: Health is average. You should pay attention to digestive system and other diseases. Pregnant women should be careful about pregnancy, miscarriage, and surgery issues.

吉祥物 Auspicious Items：

1. 今年犯害太歲，在正月初一至正月十五期間前往新加坡四馬路五路財神來敬拜四面觀音，點太歲星燈、虛空藏菩薩本命燈、月老桃花旺緣燈，供奉貴人金、太歲金、月老姻緣金來禳解制化，趨吉避凶，消災解厄，催旺財運。

   This year, because you are affected by the clash with Tai Sui, it is advisable to go to the Bugis Fortune God at Bencoolen Street in Singapore, between the first and fifteenth day of the first lunar month, to worship the Four Side Guan Yin. Light the Tai Sui, Ksitigarbha Bodhisattva and Marriage Wishing Lamps, and offer the Benefactor, Tai Sui and Marriage incense papers to avoid disasters and bring good luck and prosperity.

2. 在家中及辦公室的吉祥方位擺放靈動力強大的黃水晶招財樹及龍神聖水，可求事業順遂，升官發達、招財進寶。

   Place a powerful Crystal Wealth Tree and a bottle of Dragon Holy Water in auspicious locations at home and in the office can enhance smooth career, job advancement and prosperity.

歲次丙寅年生人40歲（西元一九八六年生）
People born in Bing Yin Year are lunar 40 years old (born in 1986)

財運：財運非常好，投資獲利，正財收穫豐盛，妥善規畫投資理財，偏財也會有好成果。

Wealth: Wealth luck is very good, investments are profitable, and the regular income is plentiful. If you plan your investments and financial management properly, the side income will also have good results.

事業：工作忙碌，業務獲得同事支援，有升官加爵的機會，小心有心人背地中傷。

Career: Busy at work, with support from colleagues in business and opportunities for promotion and title. Beware of backbiting by malicious people.

感情：感情平順，單身者能遇上不錯的對象，做出重要的決定前，要先跟伴侶達成共識。

Relationship: Relationships are smooth. Singles can meet a good partner. Before making important decisions, they must first reach a consensus with their partner.

健康：健康很好，不要讓身體過度疲勞，宜注意消化性潰瘍、胃食道逆流。

Health: Health is very good but do not let your body be overtired. You should pay attention to peptic ulcers and gastroesophageal reflux.

吉祥物 Auspicious Items：

1. 今年犯害太歲，在正月初一至正月十五期間前往新加坡四馬路五路財神來敬拜四面觀音，點太歲星燈、虛空藏菩薩本命燈，供奉貴人金、太歲金來禳解制化，趨吉避凶，消災解厄，催旺財運。

   This year, because you are affected by the clash with Tai Sui, it is advisable to go to the Bugis Fortune God at Bencoolen Street in Singapore, between the first and fifteenth day of the first lunar month, to worship the Four Side Guan Yin. Light the Tai Sui, Ksitigarbha Bodhisattva Wishing Lamps, and offer the Benefactor and Tai Sui incense papers to avoid disasters, and bring good luck and prosperity.

2. 擺設琉璃飛天麒麟可以改變各種運程，如健康運、夫妻運、子女運、家宅及事業運、財運、開智慧增強貴人運、讀書運等。

   You can display a glazed Flying Unicorn to change various fortunes, such as health, husband and wife, children, home, career and wealth, opening up wisdom and enhancing noble luck, studies, etc.

歲次甲寅年生人52歲 (西元一九七四年生)
People born in Jia Yin Year are lunar 52 years old (born in 1974)

財運：財運很好，會有大財進出，但須注意是非官訟而導致破財。

Wealth: Wealth luck is very good, and you will have a lot of money coming in and out, but you must be careful not to lose money due to legal litigation.

事業：工作上有福氣，有升官加薪的機運，可得貴人臨門一腳的助力，需注意口舌是非。

Career: You are lucky at work and have the opportunity to get promotion and salary increase. You may get help from noble person, but you need to be careful about gossips and verbal disputes.

感情：感情誘惑多，須特別留意感情誘惑陷阱，當心捲入三角戀情。

Relationship: There are many emotional temptations. You must pay special attention to the emotional temptation traps and be careful of being involved in a love triangle.

健康：健康很好，宜注意肝膽之疾、婦女隱疾、神經過敏，福星眾多可化解病災。

Health: Health is very good. You should pay attention to liver and gallbladder diseases, hidden diseases of women, and nervousness. There are many lucky stars this year to resolve diseases.

吉祥物 Auspicious Items：

1. 今年犯害太歲，在正月初一至正月十五期間前往新加坡四馬路五路財神來敬拜四面觀音，點太歲星燈、虛空藏菩薩本命燈及配戴虛空藏菩薩項鍊，供奉貴人金、太歲金，趨吉避凶，消災解厄，催旺財運。

   This year, because you are affected by the clash with Tai Sui, it is advisable to go to the Bugis Fortune God at Bencoolen Street in Singapore, between the first and fifteenth day of the first lunar month, to worship the Four Side Guan Yin. Light the Tai Sui, Ksitigarbha Bodhisattva Wishing Lamps, and wear the Ksitigarbha Bodhisattva bracelet. Offer the Benefactor and Tai Sui incense papers to avoid disasters and bring good luck and prosperity.

2. 可以在家中擺放琉璃三合生肖虎馬狗，增加招貴人驅小人、強旺運勢、改變家運、招財進寶的無形靈動力。

   You can place a set of Benefactor Zodiacs (Tiger, Horse and Dog) at home to increase the invisible spiritual power of attracting noble people and driving away villains, strengthening luck, changing family fortune, and attracting wealth.

歲次壬寅年生人64歲（西元一九六二年生）
People born in Ren Yin Year are lunar 64 years old (born in 1962)

財運：財運很好，有貴人在背後指點，提供準確建議能夠賺不少錢。

Wealth: Wealth luck is very good. You can make a lot of money with noble people to guide you and provide accurate advice.

事業：工作運勢很好，做事有始有終，人際關係和諧，注意小人多作亂。

Career: Good luck at work, things will start and end, and interpersonal relationships will be harmonious. Be careful that villains tend to cause trouble.

感情：感情容易聚少離多或夫妻半途無緣，要更用心感情的維繫。

Relationship: Relationship tend to get together less, or couples may not get along halfway, so pay more attention to the maintenance of relationship.

健康：健康很好，宜注意眼睛、白血球、風濕、肝旺、敗腎等方面疾病。

Health: Health is very good. Pay attention to eye, white blood cell, rheumatism, liver disease, kidney failure and other diseases.

吉祥物 Auspicious Items：

1. 今年犯害太歲，在正月初一至正月十五期間前往新加坡四馬路五路財神來敬拜四面觀音，點太歲星燈、虛空藏菩薩本命燈、藥師佛消災解厄燈，供奉貴人金、太歲金、華佗除疾金來禳解制化、趨吉避凶、消災解厄。

   This year, because you are affected by the clash with Tai Sui, it is advisable to go to the Bugis Fortune God at Bencoolen Street in Singapore, between the first and fifteenth day of the first lunar month, to worship the Four Side Guan Yin. Light the Tai Sui,Ksitigarbha Bodhisattva and Medicine Buddha Wishing Lamps, and offer the Benefactor, Tai Sui and Hua Tuo incense papers to resolve disasters, and turn bad luck into good luck.

2. 建議用補財好運沐浴露來沐浴，可淨旺磁場能量，保佑全家平安吉祥。

   Recommend to use the Wealth Body Wash for bathing, which can purify and strengthen the magnetic field energy, and bless the family with safety and auspiciousness.

歲次庚寅年生人76歲 (西元一九五〇年生)
People born in Geng Yin Year are lunar 76 years old (born in 1950)

財運：財運不錯，要把握住關鍵時刻，見好就收可以保住財氣。

Wealth: Wealth luck is good. You must seize the critical moment and settle when things are good to keep your wealth.

事業：年事已高，在家安享清福就好，適當運動可保健康，過度操勞小心意外發生。

Career: As you age, you can enjoy peace and quiet at home. Proper exercise can protect your health. Be careful of accidents caused by overwork.

感情：多陪陪老伴，子女很孝順，夫妻可以多參加旅遊活動。

Relationship: Spend more time with your wife, your children will be filial, and the couple can participate in more travel activities.

健康：身體健康尚可，宜注意肝膽、血壓疾病，開刀時小心併發症，福星可化解病災。

Health: The body is in good health, but you should pay attention to liver, gallbladder, and blood pressure diseases, be careful of complications during surgery. Lucky stars can resolve the disease.

吉祥物 Auspicious Items：

1. 今年犯害太歲，在正月初一至正月十五期間前往新加坡四馬路五路財神來敬拜四面觀音，點太歲星燈、虛空藏菩薩本命燈及藥師佛消災解厄燈，供奉貴人金、太歲金、華佗除疾金來禳解制化、趨吉避凶、消災解厄。

   This year, because you are affected by the clash with Tai Sui, it is advisable to go to the Bugis Fortune God at Bencoolen Street in Singapore, between the first and fifteenth day of the first lunar month, to worship the Four Side Guan Yin. Light the Tai Sui, Ksitigarbha Bodhisattva and Medicine Buddha Wishing Lamps, and offer the Benefactor, Tai Sui and Hua Tuo incense papers to resolve disasters, and turn bad luck into good luck.

2. 隨身攜帶五行水晶能量瓶，讓您產生磁場共振效應，直接吸收良好的能量來源，達到五行相生，開運旺財的目標。

   Carry a five-element Energy Water Bottle with you will generate a magnetic field resonance effect, directly absorbing good energy sources, and achieving the goal of mutual generation of the five elements, bringing good luck and wealth.

◎ 肖兔人二〇二五年運勢詳解

Forecast for the Year 2025 for people born in the year of the Rabbit

（3、15、27、39、51、63、75歲）

肖兔之人二〇二五年運勢有祿勳、天狗、弔客、天殺、空亡、吞陷星入宮。今年有名利之星降臨，工作事業帶來升職加薪，凶星主破財耗損，被人侵吞錢財，血光意外，官非爭訟，留心家中易發生哭泣及服喪之事。**肖兔之人在今年的總體運勢不佳，易有破財、傷病、喪事臨門，宜至玉玄門補財庫及制化天狗、弔客來化煞增福，添加財運。**

People born under the zodiac sign of the Rabbit will be besieged by misfortunes due to the line-up of ominous stars in 2025. There will be obstacles and disasters from Tengu, Diaoke, Tiansha, Kongwang and Tunxian descending upon you. On the bright side, the star of fame and wealth Luxun enters your fortune, and your career will bring you promotion and salary increase. However, the ominous stars will lead to loss of money, embezzlement, bloody accidents and legal disputes. Be careful that weeping and mourning are likely to occur at home. People born under the zodiac sign of the Rabbit will have poor overall fortune this year, as they are prone to financial losses, injuries and bereavement in the family. It is advisable to go to Yu Xuan Men for blessings to replenish the treasury, resolve the impact of ominous stars Tengu and Diaoke, to ward off disasters, and enhance good luck andwealth.

今年吉星有祿勳入宮，代表工作上受賞識提攜，聲望提高，有升職加薪的現象，但是今年凶星眾多，災喪之星強大，家中易發生喪事及哭泣自殘之事，工作上是非交加，小人官非暗害，財運大好大壞，易有破財之險，例如突如其來的意外開支，投資失誤及詐騙事件而招致損財，出外要小心意外災難，空亡星會使運勢減半，努力白費，感情上多困擾焦慮，情緒起伏不定。

This year, the auspicious star Luxunwill come, which means that you will be appreciated and supported at work, your reputation

will be improved, and you will be promoted and have increase in salary. However, there are many ominous stars this year, and their destroyingpower is strong. Funerals, weeping and self-mutilation are likely to occur at home. At work, gossips are intertwined, villains and legal issues are not undermined, the fortune is at extreme good and bad, and it is easy to be in danger of losing money, such as sudden unexpected expenses, investment mistakes and fraud incidents. Be careful of unexpected disasters when going out. The ominous Kongwangstar will cut your fortune in half, rendering efforts in vain, with fluctuating emotional distress and anxiety.

今年整體運勢凶多吉少，雖利於名利發展，但是破耗凶星更為強大，建議謹言慎行，不要意氣用事及逞強好鬥，小心詐騙手段而破財，注意行車人身安全，勿入喪家及探病，以免為人擔煞，女性須防產厄及婦科病，多關心家人的身體健康，預防家中發生哭泣及服喪之事。

The overall fortune this year is more likely to be bad than good. Although it is good for the development of fame and fortune, the evil star of loss is more powerful. It is recommended that you be careful in what you say and do, don't be impulsive and aggressive, and be careful of losing money through fraud. Pay attention to personal safety when driving, and don't visit the sick or enter a funeral home so as not to take over the disaster. Women must avoid complications during childbirth and gynecological diseases, pay more attention to the health of family members, and prevent crying and mourning at home.

財運 Wealth	★★★
事業 Career	★★
感情 Relationship	★★
健康 Health	★★
吉祥顏色 Lucky Color	綠色 Green Color
吉祥數字Lucky Number	1349

歲次癸卯年生人3歲（西元二〇二三年生）
People born in Gui Mao Year are lunar 3 years old (born in 2023)

財運：幼兒不論財運，父母可以幫小孩儲蓄教育基金。

Wealth: Regardless of the financial luck of the child, parents can help save for education funds.

事業：情緒不穩，常常哭鬧不休，父母多點耐心，不要老用責備及處罰來應對。

Career: The child is emotionally unstable, often crying. Parents should be more patient and don't always respond with blame and punishment.

感情：小孩非常需要父母的關愛，可以多安排一些有教育意義的出遊行程。

Relationship: The child needs the love of parents very much. You can arrange more educational outings.

健康：雖有天狗入宮，但健康運勢尚可，宜注意消化、排泄系統、流行性感冒等疾病。

Health: Although the ominous Tengu star is present, the health fortune is still good. Pay attention to diseases such as indigestion, excretory system, and influenza.

吉祥物 Auspicious Items：

1. 犯天狗、弔客煞星，在正月初一至十五期間，前往新加坡四馬路五路財神來敬拜四面觀音，報名台灣玉宸齋制化天狗、弔客法會，點文殊菩薩本命燈，供奉冤親債主金，來趨吉避凶、消解病災。

   To resolve the negative impact of ominous stars Tengu and Diaoke, it is advisable to go to the Bugis Fortune God at Bencoolen Street in Singapore, between the first and fifteenth day of the first lunar month, to worship the Four Side Guan Yin. Register for the Taiwan Yu Chen Zhai puja for blessings. Light the Manjushri Bodhisattva Wishing Lamp and offer the Karmic Creditors incense papers for good luck toeliminate diseases and disasters.

2. 建議用補財好運沐浴露來沐浴，可淨旺磁場能量，保佑全家平安吉祥。

   It is recommended to use Wealth Body Wash for bathing, which can purify and strengthen the magnetic field energy and bless the family with safety and auspiciousness.

歲次辛卯年生人15歲 (西元二〇一一年生)
People born in Xin Mao Year are lunar 15 years old (born in 2011)

財運：財運不佳，容易為了興趣嗜好多花錢。

Wealth: Poor luck in finance, you will easily spend too much money on hobbies.

事業：考運不佳，情緒煩躁，學習阻礙多，特別注意英文、數學、國文等學科的退步。

Career: Poor luck in examinations, irritable mood, and many obstacles in learning. Pay special attention to regression in English, Mathematics, Chinese and other subjects.

感情：有心儀的對象出現，情緒變化起伏，是非煩惱不斷，建議先以課業為優先。

Relationship: Someone you like appears, relationship fluctuates, and worries about gossips continue. It is recommended to give priority to schoolwork.

健康：抵抗力稍弱，宜注意鼻塞、扁桃腺炎、腎臟、肺部氣管等方面的問題。

Health: Immunity is slightly weak. You should pay attention to problems such as nasal congestion, tonsillitis, kidneys, lungs and trachea.

吉祥物 Auspicious Items：

1.犯天狗、弔客煞星，在正月初一至十五期間，前往新加坡四馬路五路財神來敬拜四面觀音，報名台灣玉宸齋制化天狗、弔客法會，點文殊菩薩本命燈，供奉冤親債主金，來趨吉避凶、消解病災。

   To resolve the negative impact of ominous stars Tengu and Diaoke, it is advisable to go to the Bugis Fortune God at Bencoolen Street in Singapore, between the first and fifteenth day of the first lunar month, to worship the Four Side Guan Yin. Register for the Taiwan Yu Chen Zhai puja for blessings. Light the Manjushri Bodhisattva Wishing Lamp and offer the Karmic Creditors incense papers for good luck to eliminate diseases and disasters.

2. 建議用文昌智慧沐浴露來沐浴，至四馬路五路財神點文昌智慧光明燈，燒化文昌智慧金，來開智慧，促進學業進步，增強考試運。

   It is recommended to use Wisdom Body Wash to bathe.Head down to Bugis Fortune God at Bencoolen Street to light the Wisdom WishingLamp, and burn the Wenchangincense papers to unlock wisdom, promote academic progress, and enhance examination luck.

歲次己卯年生人27歲（西元一九九九年生）
People born in Ji Mao Year are lunar 27 years old (born in 1999)

財運：財運不佳，錢財左手進右手出，生活物品損壞大破財。

Wealth: Poor wealth luck, money enters the left hand and comes out from the right. Daily items are damaged, incurring money lost.

事業：工作運勢不佳，壓力加大，慎防對手搶奪績效成果，計畫停滯難行。

Career: Poor luck at work with increased pressure. Beware of rivals snatching performance results, plans stagnant and difficult to implement.

感情：健康狀況不佳，注意氣管、肛門疾病，留心長輩健康，以免喪事臨門。

Relationship: Relationships are not going well, quarrels cause emotional rifts, competitors appear, and relationships face a time of choice.

健康：健康問題多，會有疾病纏身，婦女須注意子宮卵巢流產方面的問題。

Health: In poor health, be cautious of diseases of the trachea and anus. Pay attention to the health of your elders to avoid bereavement.

吉祥物 Auspicious Items：

1. 犯天狗、弔客煞星，在正月初一至十五期間，前往新加坡四馬路五路財神來敬拜四面觀音，報名台灣玉宸齋制化天狗、弔客法會，點文殊菩薩本命燈或武財神事業財利燈，供奉冤親債主金、五路財神金，來趨吉避凶、消解病災，催旺財運。

   To resolve the negative impact of ominous stars Tengu and Diaoke, it is advisable to go to the Bugis Fortune God at Bencoolen Street in Singapore, between the first and fifteenth day of the first lunar month, to worship the Four Side Guan Yin. Register for the Taiwan Yu Chen Zhai puja for blessings. Light the Manjushri Bodhisattva Wishing Lamp and offer the Karmic Creditors incense papers for good luck to eliminate diseases and disasters and enhance prosperity.

2. 在家中貴人方位擺放一對琉璃小龍龜，象徵時時進財、日日進財，又能守得住財，使用桃花寶袋、開運桃花手工皂可增強異性桃花，增強人緣桃花。

   Place a pair of glazed Dragon Turtles at the Noble location at home, which symbolize making money from time to time every day, and keeping the money. Carry a Love Charm and use the Handmade Cupid Soap to enhance your interpersonal relationship and popularitywith the opposite sex.

歲次丁卯年生人39歲（西元一九八七年生）
People born in Ding Mao Year are lunar 39 years old (born in 1987)

財運：財運起伏，有暴發的錢財，小心意外禍事導致金錢和財物的損失。

Wealth: Wealth luck is mediocre. Beware of financial loss because of paperwork and contracts. It is best not to invest in the stock market.

事業：工作有升遷機會，小心大環境變化造成公司裁員或倒閉，要預備轉業的出路。

Career: There are opportunities for promotion at work. Be careful of company layoffs or bankruptcy due to changes in the general environment, and prepare for a career change.

感情：感情平平，未婚者缺乏機會，已婚者困擾焦慮，夫妻常為小孩意見不合爭吵。

Relationship: Relationships are mediocre. Singles lack opportunities. Married people are troubled and anxious. Couples often quarrel over children.

健康：健康平平，宜注意青光眼、乾眼症，留心長輩健康，以免有喪事臨門。

Health: Health is average. You should be cautious of glaucoma and dry eye syndrome, and pay attention to the health of your elders to avoid any bereavement.

吉祥物 Auspicious Items：

1. 犯天狗、弔客煞星，在正月初一至十五期間，前往新加坡四馬路五路財神來敬拜四面觀音，報名台灣玉宸齋制化天狗、弔客法會，點文殊菩薩本命燈、武財神事業財利燈、月老桃花旺緣燈供奉冤親債主金、五路財神金、月老旺緣金，來趨吉避凶，消解病災，催旺財運，化解爛桃花。

   To resolve the assault of ominous stars Tengu and Diaoke, it is advisable to go to the Bugis Fortune God at Bencoolen Street in Singapore, between the first and fifteenth day of the first lunar month, to worship the Four Side Guan Yin. Register for the Taiwan Yu Chen Zhai puja for blessings. Light the Manjushri Bodhisattva, Wealth and Marriage Wishing Lamps and offer the Karmic Creditors, Wealth and Marriage incense papers to eliminate diseases, disasters and bad romance and enhance prosperity.

2. 想要增強財運可以在手上戴一串三合水晶手鏈或在家中擺放琉璃三合生肖豬兔羊吉祥物，可助其勇往直前，貴人明顯，辦公效率提高，業績上揚之效。

   If you want to boost your wealth, you can wear a Zodiac Benefactor bracelet or place a set of the glazed Zodiac Benefactors (Pig, Rabbit and Goat) at home which can help you move forward bravely, make nobles appear, and improve office efficiency and performance.

歲次乙卯年生人51歲（西元一九七五年生）
People born in Yi Mao Year are lunar 51 years old (born in 1975)

財運：財運一般，有加薪機會，小心詐騙損財投資失利。

Wealth: Wealth luck is average. There is a chance for salary increase. Be careful of fraud and investment failure.

事業：事業運起伏，有升遷機會，同事競爭激烈，小心小人暗害，遭受責罰。

Career: Career fortune fluctuates. There are opportunities for promotion. Competition among colleagues is fierce, be careful of being back-stabbed by villains and suffer punishment.

感情：對伴侶感情冷淡，積壓已久的問題突然爆發，嚴重時導致婚姻失和。

Relationship: Feeling indifferent to your partner, long-standing problems suddenly erupt, leading to marital discord in severe cases.

健康：健康平平，宜注意口乾舌燥、胃寒、下痢，今年勿探病送喪。

Health: Your health is average. You should pay attention to dry mouth, cold stomach and diarrhea. Do not visit the sick or attend funeral this year.

吉祥物 Auspicious Items：

1. 犯天狗、弔客煞星，在正月初一至十五期間，前往新加坡四馬路五路財神來敬拜四面觀音，報名台灣玉宸齋制化天狗、弔客法會，點文殊菩薩本命燈，供奉冤親債主金，來趨吉避凶、消解病災。

   To resolve the assault of ominous stars Tengu and Diaoke, it is advisable to go to the Bugis Fortune God at Bencoolen Street in Singapore, between the first and fifteenth day of the first lunar month, to worship the Four Side Guan Yin. Register for the Taiwan Yu Chen Zhai puja for blessings. Light the Manjushri Bodhisattva Wishing Lamp and offer the Karmic Creditors incense papers for good luck to eliminate diseases and disasters.

2. 在家中或辦公室的旺氣位，擺放琉璃龍馬奔騰，可制小人且增加貴人，龍馬是莫測高深、深藏不露、轉危為安、以少勝多的最佳致勝利器。

   Place a glazed Dragon Horse at the Prosperous location at home or in the office can control villains and increase nobles. The Dragon Horse is unpredictable, its power is hidden deeply, turning danger into safety, defeating more with less and the best weapon for victory.

歲次癸卯年生人63歲（西元一九六三年生）
People born in Gui Mao Year are lunar 63 years old (born in 1963)

財運：有小財進帳，小心因為意外血光之災或家人傷災而耗費錢財。

Wealth: Small fortunes will come into your account, but be careful not to waste money due to unexpected bloody disasters or family injuries.

事業：工作繁忙，有接受獎賞機會，要注意職業災害及小人陷害。

Career: Busy at work, there are opportunities to receive rewards, but beware of occupational disasters and villains.

感情：家庭運勢平平，避免小事而引起爭端糾紛，可以規畫全家出國旅行。

Relationship: The family fortune is average. Avoid disputes caused by trivial matters, and you can plan a family trip abroad.

健康：健康尚可，須注意提防肺部、心頭鬱悶等疾病，今年勿探病送喪。

Health: Your health is acceptable, but you need to pay attention to problems such as lung disease and depression. Do not visit the sick or attend funeral this year.

吉祥物 Auspicious Items：

1. 犯天狗、弔客煞星，在正月初一至十五期間，前往新加坡四馬路五路財神來敬拜四面觀音，報名台灣玉宸齋制化天狗、弔客法會，點文殊菩薩本命燈，供奉冤親債主金，來趨吉避凶、消解病災。

   To resolve the assault of ominous stars Tengu and Diaoke, it is advisable to go to the Bugis Fortune God at Bencoolen Street in Singapore, between the first and fifteenth day of the first lunar month, to worship the Four Side Guan Yin. Register for the Taiwan Yu Chen Zhai puja for blessings. Light the Manjushri Bodhisattva Wishing Lamp and offer the Karmic Creditors incense papers for good luck to eliminate diseases and disasters.

2. 桌上擺放琉璃獅咬劍文鎮或小元寶文鎮，具有化解小人、口舌是非及旺財的功能，但吉祥物要經法師請神、加持、開光及玉宸齋特製淨香末來淨旺，以加強它的靈動力，讓它效應更神速。

   Placing a glazed Lion Head Chime or Lucky Ingot on the table has the function of resolving villains, verbal disputes and increasing wealth. However, the mascot hasto be consecrated by a mage to recite sutras, with Yu Chen Zhai's pure incense powder, before its spiritual power can be rapid and effective.

歲次辛卯年生人75歲（西元一九五一年生）
People born in Xin Mao Year are lunar 75 years old (born in 1951)

財運：財運不佳，投資失利，小心詐騙或借貸而破財。

Wealth: Poor financial luck, investment failure, beware of fraud or loss of money due to loans.

事業：工作出現漏洞產生危機，退休之人家中多煩事，可以多與朋友聚餐，抒解心情。

Career: There are loopholes in work and crises occur. Retired people have many troubles at home. They can have more dinners with friends to relieve their mood.

感情：家中多是非衝突，哭鬧不休，精神多焦慮，情緒起伏大。

Relationship: There are many conflicts and disputes at home, non-stop hue and cry, lots of anxiety, and high emotional fluctuations.

健康：健康不佳，注意氣管哮喘、攝護腺、肺癌等，勿探病，有病請立即就醫。

Health: In poor health, pay attention to tracheal asthma, prostate, lung cancer, etc. Do not visit the sick. If you are unwell, seek medical treatment immediately.

吉祥物 Auspicious Items：

1. 犯天狗、弔客煞星，在正月初一至十五期間，前往新加坡四馬路五路財神來敬拜四面觀音，報名台灣玉宸齋制化天狗、弔客法會，點文殊菩薩本命燈，供奉冤親債主金、華佗除疾金來趨吉避凶、消解病災。

   To resolve the assault of ominous stars Tengu and Diaoke, it is advisable to go to the Bugis Fortune God at Bencoolen Street in Singapore, between the first and fifteenth day of the first lunar month, to worship the Four Side Guan Yin. Register for the Taiwan Yu Chen Zhai puja for blessings. Light the Manjushri Bodhisattva Wishing Lamp and offer the Karmic Creditors and Hua Tuo incense papers for good luck to eliminate diseases and disasters.

2. 家中放置琉金四面觀音或配戴平安健康琉璃吊飾，可以招貴人防小人，並可以減輕天狗、弔客的沖煞，保佑全年健康平安。

   Place a Four Side Guan Yin statue at home or wear a Health Pendant to attract noble people and guard against villains, mitigate the disasters of Tengu and Diaoke, and enhance health and safety throughout the year.

◎ 肖龍人二〇二五年運勢詳解

Forecast for the Year 2025 for people born in the year of the Dragon (2、14、26、38、50、62、74歲)

肖龍之人二〇二五年運勢逢天喜、病符、陌越、歲煞、流年三煞、羊刃、寡宿、囚獄入宮。今年吉星代表人際關係融洽，異性緣很好，但是凶星眾多，主多疾病、損人、瘟疫、橫禍、刑罰牢獄之災。**肖龍之人今年總體運勢凶中有吉，感情人緣是亮點，注意健康狀況，建議到玉玄門點光明燈祭化病符、孤寡煞為佳。**

In 2025, the fortune of people born in the Year of the Dragon will be guarded by Bingfu, Moyue, Suisha, Liunian Sansha, Yangren, Guasu and Qiuyu stars. This year's auspicious star Tianxi represent harmonious interpersonal relationships and good compatibility with the opposite gender. However, there are many ominous stars, which indicate the likelihood of bringing diseases, harm, plagues, misfortunes, punishments and imprisonment. The overall fortune of people born under the sign of the Dragon this year is there is good in misfortune. Love and relationships are the highlights. Pay attention to your health. It is recommended that you head down to Yu Xuan Men to light a wishing lamp to resolve illness and loneliness from Bingfu and Guasha stars.

今年天喜星降臨主有喜慶之事，未婚者異性緣佳，感情機會多，已婚者求子機緣增大，事業上人際關係活絡，但是身心受困，阻力波折不斷，缺乏貴人力挺，今年病符代表抵抗力弱或疾病纏身，財運一波三折難有進展，小心是非不斷，人事不和，血光橫禍時有，嚴重時官司、牢獄纏身，今年雖然人緣不錯，如不化解寡宿煞氣，反而孤單憂慮，家庭身心都會陷入危機破裂，女性更應注意。

The arrival of the auspicious star Tianxi this year brings joy. Singles have good luck with the opposite gender and have many opportunities for relationships. Married people have greater chances of seeking children and have active interpersonal relationships in their careers. However, they

are physically and mentally trapped, with constant obstacles and twists and turns, and lack of support from noble people. This year's Bingfu star represents weak resistance or illness. The various ominous stars will present difficulties in making progress in financial fortunes, with constant disputes, personal disharmony, bloody disasters, and in serious cases, lawsuits and imprisonment. Although the popularity luck is good this year, if the negative influences from the ominous stars are not resolved, you will instead end up lonely, your family will be in crisis physically and mentally, and women should pay more attention to this.

今年事業感情上應該要催旺貴人運，化解孤寡煞氣，讓好人緣能夠發揮效力，財運方面建議補強財庫，讓財運反弱轉強，最重要的還是健康狀態，一定要注意身心保健，提升自己的免疫力，有病就立即就醫，多安排一些運動及休閒娛樂來調劑身心，勿入病人家，勿食喪家食物，出外行車留心意外血光之災，孕婦更要注意安胎事宜。

This year, in terms of career and relationship, you should boost your luck to have the presence of noble people, and mitigate the negative influence of loneliness. In terms of financial luck, you should strengthen the treasury so that financial luck can turn from weak to strong. The most important thing is your health. You must pay attention to your health physically and mentally, improve your immunity, and seek medical treatment immediately if you are sick. Arrange more exercises and leisure entertainment to recuperate your body and mind. Do not visit the sick, do not eat food from a bereaved home, be careful of accidental blood disasters when driving, and pregnant women should pay more attention to pregnancy wellbeing.

財運 Wealth	★★
事業 Career	★★★
感情 Relationship	★★★
健康 Health	★
吉祥顏色 Lucky Color	黃色 Yellow Color
吉祥數字Lucky Number	2067

歲次甲辰年生人2歲（西元二〇二四年生）
People born in Jia Chen Year are 2 years old (born in 2024)

財運：小孩不論財運，今年免疫力稍弱，病災讓父母多花錢財。

Wealth: Regardless of wealth luck, the child will have a weak immunity this year, and illness may cause parents to spend more money.

事業：小孩哭鬧時父母可以試著先轉移孩子的注意力，適度告知及給予選擇權。

Career: When a child cries, parents can try to divert the child's attention first, inform him appropriately and give him a choice.

感情：二歲的孩子最需要被重視和有人關心他・此時要著重生活常規的建立。

Relationship: A two-year-old child needs the most attention and someone to care about. At this time, you should focus on establishing daily routines.

健康：健康運勢不佳，宜注意流行性病毒、血液疾病、腸病毒、眼疾等方面的疾病。

Health: Health condition is bad. Pay attention to epidemic viruses, blood diseases, enteroviruses, eye and other diseases.

吉祥物 Auspicious Items：

1. 今年犯病符，在正月初一至十五期間，前往新加坡四馬路五路財神敬拜四面觀音，報名台灣玉宸齋制化病符法會，點普賢菩薩本命燈、觀音平安健康燈、藥師佛消災解厄燈，供奉冤親債主金、華陀除疾金來消災解厄，趨吉避凶，平安健康。

   This year, to contain the negative influence of Bingfu star (Sickly Amulet), it is advisable to head down to the Bugis Fortune God in Singapore, between the first and fifteenth day of the first lunar month, to pray to the Four Side Guan Yin. Register for the Taiwan Yu Chen Zhai puja for blessings. Light the Samantabhadra, Guan Yin and Medicine Buddha Wishing Lamps and offer the Karmic Creditors and Hua Tuo incense papers to resolve disasters and misfortunes, seek good luck and ensure good health.

2. 在臥房擺放開運葫蘆，葫蘆有收煞氣和助旺健康的作用，可避開風水的疾厄煞氣。

   Place a good-luck Hu Lu (Gourd) in the bedroom. The gourd has the effect of absorbing evil spirits and negative energy and promoting health.

歲次壬辰年生人14歲 (西元二〇一二年生)
People born in Ren Chen Year are 14 years old (born in 2012)

財運：財運平平，因意外之災導致父母破財。

Wealth: The wealth luck is mediocre, and parents will spend money due to unexpected disasters.

事業：成績及考運一般，易因環境適應不良造成情緒不穩，儘量不要涉足不良場所。

Career: Average grades and examination luck, easy to be emotionally unstable due to poor adaptation to the environment. Try not to get involved in bad places.

感情：情感易受波動，易交不良的損友導致行為偏差，父母要多花時間關懷。

Relationship: Relationship is susceptible to fluctuations, and bad friends often lead to behavioral deviations. Parents should spend more time caring for them.

健康：病符入宮，但是健康運勢尚可，宜注意腸胃不適，嘔吐腹瀉的疾病。

Health: The illness star appears in your fortune, but your health condition is still good. You should pay attention to gastrointestinal discomfort, vomiting and diarrhea.

吉祥物 Auspicious Items：

1. 今年犯病符，在正月初一至十五期間，前往新加坡四馬路五路財神敬拜四面觀音，報名台灣玉宸齋制化病符法會，點普賢菩薩本命燈、文昌智慧光明燈，供奉冤親債主金、華陀除疾金、文昌智慧金來消災解厄，祈求身體健康、學業精進。

   This year, to contain the negative influence of Bingfu star (Sickly Amulet), it is advisable to head down to the Bugis Fortune God in Singapore, between the first and fifteenth day of the first lunar month, to pray to the Four Side Guan Yin. Register for the Taiwan Yu Chen Zhai puja for blessings. Light the Samantabhadra Bodhisattva and Wenchang Wishing Lamps and offer the Karmic Creditors and Hua Tuo incense papers to eliminate disasters and resolve misfortunes, ensure good health and academic improvement.

2. 小孩房間擺放琉璃蓮花童子，可讓小孩專心讀書，學業進步，避免交到壞朋友。

   Place a glazed Lian Hua Tong Zi in a child's room can help him concentrate on studying, improve academically, and avoid making bad friends.

歲次庚辰年生人26歲（西元二〇〇〇年生）
People born in Geng Chen Year are 26 years old (born in 2000)

財運：財運不佳，易受人設計陷害而破耗損財。

Wealth: Poor financial luck, easy to be framed by others and lose money.

事業：大環境形勢不利，容易招來企圖不良之人，合作時易被欺瞞陷害。

Career: The general environment is unfavorable. It is easy to attract people with bad intentions, and to be deceived and framed when co-operating.

感情：感情上矛盾不斷，想要另找情緒出口，如不好好處理反而受到傷害。

Relationship: Emotional conflicts continue, and you want to find another outlet for your relationship. If you don't handle well, you will get hurt.

健康：健康不佳，宜注意眼睛、胰臟病、肝旺、腎臟病問題，孕婦尤須注意安胎流產。

Health: Health condition is unfavorable. You should pay attention to eye, pancreatic disease, liver and kidney diseases. Pregnant women should especially pay attention to miscarriage.

吉祥物 Auspicious Items：

1. 今年犯病符，在正月初一至十五期間，前往新加坡四馬路五路財神敬拜四面觀音，報名台灣玉宸齋制化病符煞星法會，點普賢菩薩本命燈、觀音平安健康燈、藥師佛消災解厄燈，供奉冤親債主金、華陀除疾金來消災解厄，以祈求平安消災解厄，趨吉避凶，身體健康。

   This year, to contain the negative influence of Bingfu star (Sickly Amulet), it is advisable to head down to the Bugis Fortune God in Singapore, between the first and fifteenth day of the first lunar month, to pray to the Four Side Guan Yin. Register for the Taiwan Yu Chen Zhai puja for blessings. Light the Samantabhadra Bodhisattva, Guan Yin and Medicine Buddha Wishing Lamps and offer the Karmic Creditors and Hua Tuo incense papers to eliminate disasters and resolve misfortunes, ensure good health and prosperity.

2. 臥室可放置琉璃三合生肖猴鼠龍或三合貴人盤，可招貴人、增強運勢、改變家運、招財進寶。

   Put a set of Zodiac Benefactors (Monkey, Rat and Dragon) or a Noble Plate in the bedroom, which can attract noble people and enhance good fortune.

歲次戊辰年生人38歲（西元一九八八年生）
People born in Wu Chen Year are 38 years old (born in 1988)

財運：財氣很差，不宜投資高風險產品，避免意外破財。

Wealth: Wealth luck is very poor. It is not suitable to invest in high-risk products to avoid unexpected financial losses.

事業：工作環境暗潮洶湧，只要專注自己的責任範圍就能避開破耗的危機。

Career: The work environment is undercurrent and surging. As long as you focus on your own scope of responsibility, you can avoid the crisis of depletion.

感情：感情起伏，分離厄運降臨，身心受困，阻力波折不斷。

Relationship: Relationships are ups and downs. Separation and misfortune come, causing physical and mental difficulties. Resistance and twists and turns are constant.

健康：健康不佳，注意肝膽、皮膚疾病，婦女尤須注意子宮卵巢流產的問題。

Health: Health condition is unfavourable. Pay attention to liver, gallbladder and skin diseases. Women should especially pay attention to the problem of uterine and ovarian miscarriage.

吉祥物 Auspicious Items：

1. 今年犯病符，在正月初一至十五期間，前往新加坡四馬路五路財神敬拜四面觀音，報名台灣玉宸齋制化病符法會，點普賢菩薩本命燈、觀音平安健康燈、藥師佛消災解厄燈，供奉冤親債主金、華陀除疾金來消災解厄，以祈求消災解厄，趨吉避凶，平安健康。

   This year, to contain the negative influence of Bingfu star (Sickly Amulet), head down to the Bugis Fortune God in Singapore, between the first and fifteenth day of the first lunar month, to pray to the Four Side Guan Yin. Register for the Taiwan Yu Chen Zhai puja for blessings. Light the Samantabhadra Bodhisattva, Guan Yin and Medicine Buddha Wishing Lamps and offer the Karmic Creditors and Hua Tuo incense papers to eliminate disasters and resolve misfortunes, ensure good luck and good health.

2. 隨身配戴桃柳檀木劍雷令福袋能斬妖除小人、化煞辟邪，點五路財神燈、祭拜五路財神金可使您補足財庫，財運大開。

   Carry a Protective Charm with you to ward off evil spirits and villains. Light a Wealth Wishing Lamp to help you replenish your treasury and your fortune will flourish.

歲次丙辰年生人50歲（西元一九七六年生）
People born in Bing Chen Year are 50 years old (born in 1976)

財運：今年財運平平，大環境對你不利，只能有小財入庫。

Wealth: Your wealth luck is mediocre this year. The general environment is not good for you, so you can only make small fortunes.

事業：事業運勢一般，人際關係活絡，缺乏貴人相助，儘量以靜制動，保留競爭力。

Career: The career fortune is average, interpersonal relationships are active, and there is lack of help from noble people. Try to be quiet and retain competitiveness.

感情：家中成員風波較多，易有喜事臨門，盡量多吸收正面能量，才能趨吉避凶。

Relationship: Although there are turmoils among family members, happy events are easy to happen. Try to absorb as much positive energy as possible, so as to seek good luck and avoid bad luck.

健康：健康不佳，宜注意脾胃、腳腿浮腫、肝旺，因菸酒而引起的疾病。

Health: Health condition is not favourable. You should pay attention to swollen spleen and stomach, edema of legs and feet, liver disease, and diseases caused by tobacco and alcohol.

吉祥物 Auspicious Items：

1. 今年犯病符，在正月初一至十五期間，前往新加坡四馬路五路財神敬拜四面觀音，報名台灣玉宸齋制化病符法會，點普賢菩薩本命燈、觀音平安健康燈、藥師佛消災解厄燈，供奉冤親債主金、華陀除疾金來消災解厄，以祈求消災解厄，趨吉避凶，平安健康。

   This year, to contain the negative influence of Bingfu star (Sickly Amulet), it is advisable to head down to the Bugis Fortune God in Singapore, between the first and fifteenth day of the first lunar month, to pray to the Four Side Guan Yin. Register for the Taiwan Yu Chen Zhai puja for blessings. Light the Samantabhadra Bodhisattva, Guan Yin and Medicine Buddha Wishing Lamps and offer the Karmic Creditors and Hua Tuo incense papers to eliminate disasters and resolve misfortunes, ensure good luck and good health.

2. 擺放琉璃河圖龍馬，可制小人增貴人，龍馬能轉危為安、以少勝多的最佳致勝利器。

   Display a Dragon Horse can control villains and increase nobles. The Dragon Horse can turn danger into safety and it is the best weapon to win more with less.

歲次甲辰年生人62歲 (西元一九六四年生)
People born in Jia Chen Year are 62 years old (born in 1964)

財運：財運尚可，難聚大財，不要投機走險以免大破財。

Wealth: Wealth luck is fair, but it is difficult to make a big fortune. Do not speculate and take risks to avoid losing money.

事業：事業運平平，人緣尚可，缺乏貴人幫助，要用平常心來面對危機與困難。

Career: Career fortune is mediocre, your popularity is acceptable, but you lack the help of noble people. You should face crises and difficulties with a normal mind.

感情：容易意見不合，建議多忍讓，增加彼此間的關懷，以免感情生變。

Relationship: It is easy to disagree. It is recommended to be more tolerant and increase care for each other to avoid changes in feelings.

健康：健康尚可，宜注意肝膽、骨骼酸痛、神經過敏、車禍骨折等方面的疾病問題。

Health: Health is acceptable, but you should pay attention to diseases such as liver and gallbladder, bone pain, nervousness, car accident fractures, etc.

吉祥物 Auspicious Items：

1. 今年犯病符，在正月初一至十五期間，前往新加坡四馬路五路財神敬拜四面觀音，報名台灣玉宸齋制化病符法會，點普賢菩薩本命燈、觀音平安健康燈、藥師佛消災解厄燈，供奉冤親債主金、華陀除疾金來消災解厄，以祈求消災解厄，趨吉避凶，平安健康。

   This year, to contain the negative influence of Bingfu star (Sickly Amulet), it is advisable to head down to the Bugis Fortune God in Singapore between the first and fifteenth day of the first lunar month, to pray to the Four Side Guan Yin. Register for the Taiwan Yu Chen Zhai puja for blessings. Light the Samantabhadra, Guan Yin and Medicine Buddha Wishing Lamps and offer the Karmic Creditors and Hua Tuo incense papers to eliminate disasters and resolve misfortunes, seek good luck and ensure good health.

2. 在家中及辦公室的吉祥方位擺放靈動力強大的黃水晶招財樹及龍神聖水，可求事業順利、升官發達、招財進寶。

   Place a powerful Wealth Crystal Tree and a bottle of Dragon Holy Water in the auspicious locations at home and in the office to wish for smooth career, promotion and wealth.

歲次壬辰年生人74歲（西元一九五二年生）
People born in Ren Chen Year are 74 years old (born in 1952)

財運：財運平平，易因朋友陷害而耗費錢財，理財一定要謹慎。

Wealth: Wealth luck is mediocre, and you can easily waste money due to being framed by friends. You must be careful in managing your finances.

事業：事業運勢不佳，容易遭周遭親人拖累或朋友扯後腿，凡事謹慎為宜。

Career: Poor career luck, you may easily be dragged down by relatives or friends around you. It is advisable to be cautious in everything.

感情：家中吵鬧不安寧，夫妻要彼此多關注對方的健康及心情，易有喜事臨門。

Relationship: Noisy and unrest at home, husband and wife should pay more attention to each other's health and mood, as happy events are likely to come.

健康：健康不佳，宜注意血液循環、心臟、腎臟問題，勿探病小心意外血光之災。

Health: Health condition is unfavourable. You should pay attention to blood circulation, heart, and kidney problems. Do not visit sick people, and be careful of accidental blood injuries.

吉祥物 Auspicious Items：

1. 今年犯病符，在正月初一至十五期間，前往新加坡四馬路五路財神敬拜四面觀音，報名台灣玉宸齋制化病符法會，點普賢菩薩本命燈、觀音平安健康燈、藥師佛消災解厄燈，供奉冤親債主金、華陀除疾金來消災解厄，以祈求消災解厄，趨吉避凶，平安健康。

   This year, to contain the negative influence of Bingfu star (Sickly Amulet), head down to the Bugis Fortune God in Singapore, between the first and fifteenth day of the first lunar month, to pray to the Four Side Guan Yin. Register for the Taiwan Yu Chen Zhai puja for blessings. Light the Samantabhadra, Guan Yin and Medicine Buddha Wishing Lamps and offer the Karmic Creditors and Divine Pardon Hua Tuo incense papers to eliminate disasters and resolve misfortunes, seek good luck and ensure good health.

2. 家中擺放琉璃龍龜，可添加載福、載壽、載寶、滿載而歸、歸庫之靈動力。

   Place a glazed Dragon Turtle at home can enhance the spiritual power of increasing blessings, longevity, bringing home a full load of treasure, and returning money to the treasury.

◎ 肖蛇人二〇二五年運勢詳解

Forecast for the Year 2025 for people born in the year of the Snake

（1、13、25、37、49、61、73歲）

肖蛇人二〇二五年運勢逢八座、天解、解神、歲駕、太歲、伏屍、血刃、劍鋒、指背、浮沉坐守。今年犯太歲加上凶星諸多，要更加警惕人身安全，身體健康，意外橫災，工作財運艱難險阻，還好有解厄吉星入宮，能減低凶星的危害。**肖蛇之人今年總體運勢好壞參半，需拜太歲星君及改運制刑以祈求身體健康，運事順利，凡事謹慎小心才能逢凶化吉。**

Clashing with Tai Sui in year 2025, the fortune of people born under the Snake zodiac will definitely be in low luck with the assembly of various inauspicious stars, namely Fushi, Xueren, Jianfeng, Zhibei and Fuchen. You need to be more vigilant about your personal safety and health. Unexpected disasters, work and financial fortune are difficult and dangerous. Fortunately, there are auspicious stars Tianjie, Jieshen and Suijia to mitigate the negative impact and harm. People born under the zodiac sign of the Snake will have mixed fortunes this year. They need to pray to Tai Sui to change their fortunes to resolve the disasters and to have good health. They must be cautious in everything so that they can turn bad luck into good luck.

今年行運吉星利於工作上的升遷，能展現領導能力，利於升學考試，選舉競爭，今年凶星主有不測橫災，血光橫禍，易招人嫉妒誹謗，背後惡意中傷，多是非紛擾，恐有水厄，不宜遠行，全年運勢載浮載沉，小心尖刀利器刑罰械鬥之災，女性需防產厄，今年幸有吉星來化解災厄，能減輕凶煞的危害。

This year's auspicious stars are good for promotion at work and can demonstrate leadership skills, which is conducive for college entrance examinations and election competitions. The ominous stars are likely to cause unexpected and bloody disasters. It is easy to attract jealousy and malicious slander behind the scenes and many disputes. As there is possible

water disaster, it is not advisable to travel far. The fortune throughout the year is fluctuating. Be careful of sharp knives and weapons, torture and violence. Women need to prevent birth disasters. Fortunately, there are auspicious stars this year to reduce the harm from ominous stars.

今年太歲入宮，吉星無法完全化解凶星的干擾，建議拜太歲星君及禳解改運制刑，今年財運不佳可以補財庫催旺財氣，家宅有關動土興造之事都應避開，避免遠行旅遊，感情運不佳忌嫁娶，容易因為感情失利而造成情緒低落，一定要特別注意健康況，才能趨吉避凶。

Tai Sui enters your fortune this year, and the auspicious stars cannot completely resolve the interference of the ominous stars. It is recommended to pray to Tai Sui for changes in luck and resolve disasters. For the poor financial luck this year, you can replenish your treasury and boost your wealth. You should avoid anything related to construction or travelling to far distances. Avoid getting married because you do not have good fortune in love, as you may easily become depressed due to a failed relationship. Pay special attention to your health in order to have good luck and avoid bad luck.

財運 Wealth	★
事業 Career	★★
感情 Relationship	★★★
健康 Health	★
吉祥顏色 Lucky Color	紅色 Red Color
吉祥數字Lucky Number	3728

歲次乙巳年生人1歲（西元二〇二五年生）
People born in Yi Si Year are 1 year old (born in 2025)

今年各月份出生新生兒之運勢 Forecast For Monthly Born Babies

正月生 Lunar 1st Month	新春之時，陽氣將盛，活躍起來，四出有路，有貴人相助，白手起家。 In the New Year, Yang will be strong and active, there will be opportunities in all directions, there will be help from noble people, and one will start from scratch.
二月生 Lunar 2nd Month	驚蟄之時，眠中驚醒，作事猶豫，特立獨行，祿薄福輕，煩事不斷。 During the period of Jingzhe, one wakes up from sleep, hesitates in doing things, acts independently, has little salary and light fortune, and has constant troubles.
三月生 Lunar 3rd Month	清明之時，聰敏巧能，能成大事，多勞多功，謀事順利，福祿雙全。 During the Qingming period, one will be smart and skillful, able to accomplish great things. One works harder and achieve more, plans will go smoothly, and will have both good fortune and wealth.
四月生 Lunar 4th Month	立夏之時，威鎮四方，秉性聰敏，地位權貴，天降之福，一帆風順。 At the beginning of Summer, one is powerful in all directions, has a smart personality, a powerful status, and is blessed by heaven, and everything goes smoothly.
五月生 Lunar 5th Month	芒種之時，膽識過人，觀察敏銳，一生平安，家運隆昌，多得貴人相助。 During the Grain season, one has extraordinary courage and keen observation; a peaceful life and a prosperous family with help from noble people.
六月生 Lunar 6th Month	小暑之時，萬事如意，有天賜之福，夫妻相榮，子孫顯貴，德才兼備。 During the period of Xiaoshu, everything goes well, with blessings from heaven, a happy couple, prominent children and grandchildren, and both virtuous and talented.
七月生 Lunar 7th Month	立秋之時，凡事如願，智勇雙全，功業成就，受人敬仰，白手成家。 At the beginning of Autumn, everything goes as planned, one is both wise and brave, achieves success in career, respected by others, and build a family from scratch.

八月生 Lunar 8th Month	白露之時，忠厚傳家，靈機應變，才華洋溢，建功立業，生活幸福。 During the period of White Dew, one will be loyal to the family, resourceful, talented, successful, and live a happy life.
九月生 Lunar 9th Month	寒露之時，秉性純良，忠誠守信，責任感強，踏實穩重，刻苦耐勞。 In the Cold Dew, one is pure in nature, loyal and trustworthy, has a strong sense of responsibility, is firm, steady and hard-working.
十月生 Lunar 10th Month	立冬之時，不能吃苦耐勞，遇事怕難，保守固執，缺乏創新冒險精神。 At the beginning of winter, he can't bear hardships and stand hard work, afraid of difficulties, conservative and stubborn, and lacks the spirit of innovation and adventure.
十一月生 Lunar 11th Month	大雪之時，心直口快，好打不平，財運起伏，工作能力強，出外得利。 During Heavy Snow, one is outspoken, like to fight for justice, has ups and downs in fortune, has strong working ability, and gain benefits when travelling.
十二月生 Lunar 12th Month	小寒之時，歲寒冰凍，一生幸福，衣祿豐富，財路亨通，快樂富貴。 In the period of Xiaohan, when the year is cold and frozen, one has a happy life, rich clothing and wealth, happy and prosperous.
吉祥物 Auspicious Items	1. 今年犯太歲，在正月初一至十五期間，前往新加坡四馬路五路財神敬拜四面觀音、太歲星君，點太歲星燈、普賢菩薩本命燈，供奉太歲金來消災解厄，以祈求消災解厄，趨吉避凶，平安健康。 This year, to resolve the clash with Tai Sui, it is advisable to go to the Bugis Fortune God at Bencoolen Street in Singapore, between the first and fifteenth day of the first lunar month, to worship the Four Side Guan Yin and Tai Sui. Light the Tai Sui and Samantabhadra Bodhisattva Wishing Lamps, and offer the Tai Sui incense papers to seek good luck, eliminate disasters and have good health. 2. 新生兒若是受到驚嚇或啼哭不止，可用琉璃千手千眼觀音項鍊置放於枕頭下，便可收安神定魄之效。 If the newborn is frightened or cries incessantly, You can place a glazed Thousand Hands and Thousand Eyes Guan Yin necklace under his pillow to calm the mind and soul.

歲次癸巳年生人13歲（西元二〇一三年生）
People born in Kui Si Year are 13 years old (born in 2013)

財運：財運平平，為才藝及興趣多花費不少錢。

Wealth: Your wealth luck is mediocre, and you will spend a lot of money on your talents and hobbies.

事業：學業及考運還可以，在團體中能展現領導能力，小心尖刀利器械鬥之災。

Career: Academic and examination luck are good, and leadership skills can be demonstrated in a group. Be careful of fighting with sharp knives and instruments.

感情：人際關係平平，心情較為起伏，會反抗父母安排，父母應該多給鼓勵支持。

Relationship: Interpersonal relationships are mediocre, moods are fluctuating, and will resist parental arrangements. Parents should give more encouragement and support.

健康：健康運勢尚可，須注意肺部、耳朵、筋骨受傷，還須防橫災及意外傷害。

Health: Your health is fair, but you must pay attention to injuries to the lungs, ears, muscles and bones, and beware of disasters and accidental injuries.

吉祥物 Auspicious Items：

1. 今年犯太歲，在正月初一至十五期間，前往新加坡四馬路五路財神敬拜四面觀音、太歲星君，點太歲星燈、普賢菩薩本命燈、文昌智慧光明燈，供奉太歲金、文昌智慧金來消災解厄，開啟智慧及增強考試、讀書運。

   This year, to resolve the clash with Tai Sui, it is advisable to go to the Bugis Fortune God at Bencoolen Street in Singapore, between the first and fifteenth day of the first lunar month, to worship the Four Side Guan Yin and Tai Sui. Light the Tai Sui, Samantabhadra Bodhisattva and Wenchang Wishing Lamps, and offer the Tai Sui and Wenchang incense papers to eliminate disasters, unlock wisdom and enhance luck in examinations.

2. 書桌上可擺放琉璃玉書麒麟或魁星踢斗隨身牌可使學童思想敏捷，頭腦精明，學識精進。

   Placing a glazed Qilin (Unicorn) or Kui Xing Ta Dou on the desk can help students think quickly, have a sharp mind and advanced in knowledge.

歲次辛巳年生人25歲 (西元二〇〇一年生)
People born in Xin Si Year are 25 years old (born in 2001)

財運：財運不佳，理財要謹慎，容易意外損財或是疾病損財。

Wealth: Wealth luck is not favourable. You should be cautious in financial management. It is easy to lose money unexpectedly or due to illness.

事業：犯太歲特別嚴重，需拜太歲以保平安，容易遭受到血光意外之災。

Career: The clash with Tai Sui is particularly serious. You need to pray to Tai Sui to ensure safety as you are prone to accidental bloody disasters.

感情：感情不太穩定，情緒陷入低潮，易走極端行為，試著轉移焦點到別的興趣上。

Relationship: Relationship is not stable. The mood is at a low ebb, and it is easy to go to extreme behaviors. Try to shift the focus to other interests.

健康：犯太歲嚴重，健康不佳，宜注意扁桃腺炎、氣管、腎臟症狀。

Health: Seriously clashing with Tai Sui, your health is poor. You should pay attention to tonsillitis, trachea, and kidney symptoms.

吉祥物 Auspicious Items：

1. 今年犯太歲，在正月初一至十五期間，前往新加坡四馬路五路財神敬拜四面觀音、太歲星君，點太歲星燈、普賢菩薩本命燈、武財神事業財利燈，供奉太歲金、五路財神金來消災解厄，催旺運勢，收得招財進寶之效。

   This year, to resolve the clash with Tai Sui, it is advisable to go to the Bugis Fortune God at Bencoolen Street in Singapore, between the first and fifteenth day of the first lunar month, to worship the Four Side Guan Yin and Tai Sui. Light the Tai Sui, Samantabhadra Bodhisattva and Wealth Wishing Lamps, and offer the Tai Sui and Wealth incense papers to ward off disasters and misfortunes, boost your fortune, and bring in wealth and treasure.

2. 使用八卦平安淨身手工皂可驅除邪氣、鎮定安神、淨身除穢。

   Using the Bagua Purifying Soap can drive off evil spirits, calm the mind, and purify the body to remove impurities.

歲次己巳年生人37歲（西元一九八九年生）
People born in Ji Si Year are 37 years old (born in 1989)

財運：財運不佳，做大額投資或購買較貴重物品時易損失錢財。

Wealth: Poor wealth luck, easy to lose money when making large investments or buying more valuable items.

事業：缺乏獨立精神，做事常有始無終，容易遭受他人敵視，小人多作亂。

Career: Lacking independent spirit, often starting things but not finishing them, easily subjected to hostility from others, and prone to chaos caused by villains.

感情：感情運勢不佳，易出現競爭的對手，嚴重會導致分離，今年不利嫁娶。

Relationship: Relationship fortune is not good, and prone to rivals, which may lead to separation. This year is not good for getting married.

健康：犯太歲嚴重健康不佳，注意氣管、口腔、脾胃、皮膚、意外橫禍等方面的問題。

Health: Clashing with Tai Sui will lead to serious poor health. Pay attention to problems in the trachea, mouth, spleen and stomach, skin, accidents, etc.

吉祥物 Auspicious Items：

1. 今年犯太歲，在正月初一至十五期間，前往新加坡四馬路五路財神敬拜四面觀音、太歲星君，點太歲星燈、普賢菩薩本命燈、武財神事業財利燈，供奉太歲金、五路財神金來消災解厄，催旺運勢，收得招財進寶之效。

   This year, to resolve your clash with Tai Sui, it is advisable to go to the Bugis Fortune God at Bencoolen Street in Singapore, between the first and fifteenth day of the first lunar month, to worship the Four Side Guan Yin and Tai Sui. Light the Tai Sui, Samantabhadra Bodhisattva and Wealth Wishing Lamps, and offer the Tai Sui and Wealth incense papers to dispel disasters, and have the effect of attracting wealth and treasure.

2. 想要增強財運可以在手上戴一串三合水晶手鍊，可招貴人、增強運勢、招財進寶。

   If you want to enhance your wealth, you can wear a Zodiac Benefactor bracelet, which can attract noble people, enhance your fortune, and attract wealth.

歲次丁巳年生人49歲 (西元一九七七年生)
People born in Ding Si Year are 49 years old (born in 1977)

財運：財運尚可，容易引起帳目糾紛，慎防劫財，不適合進行大額投資。

Wealth: The wealth luck is fair, but it is easy to cause accounting disputes. Be careful to prevent money robberies. It is not suitable for large investments.

事業：工作運勢上升，能展現領導能力，還能得到長輩上司的照顧。

Career: Your fortune at work will increase, you will be able to demonstrate leadership skills, and you will be cared for by your senior bosses.

感情：感情穩定，夫妻感情較為和諧，煩憂之事可以化解，外出旅遊可以調和感情。

Relationship: Relationship is stable. The relationship between husband and wife is relatively harmonious, worries can be resolved, and traveling can harmonize the relationship.

健康：健康不錯，宜注意眼睛、白血球、肝旺、濕氣、陰虧、敗腎等方面的疾病。

Health: Your health is good. You should pay attention to diseases of the eyes, white blood cells, liver, moisture, yin deficiency, kidney failure, etc.

吉祥物 Auspicious Items：

1. 今年犯太歲，在正月初一至十五期間，前往新加坡四馬路五路財神敬拜四面觀音、太歲星君，點太歲星燈、普賢菩薩本命燈、武財神事業財利燈，供奉太歲金、五路財神金來消災解厄，催旺運勢，收得招財進寶之效。

   This year, to resolve your clash with Tai Sui, it is advisable to go to the Bugis Fortune God at Bencoolen Street in Singapore, between the first and fifteenth day of the first lunar month, to worship the Four Side Guan Yin and Tai Sui. Light the Tai Sui, Samantabhadra Bodhisattva and Wealth Wishing Lamps, and offer the Tai Sui and Wealth incense papers to eliminate disasters, and have the effect of attracting wealth and treasure.

2. 可以在家中擺放琉璃三合生肖蛇牛雞，增加招貴人驅小人、強旺運勢、改變家運、招財進寶的無形靈動力。

   You can place a set of the Zodiac Benefactors (Snake, Cow and Rooster) at home to increase the invisible spiritual power of attracting noble people and drive away villains, strengthening and changing fortune, and attracting wealth.

歲次乙巳年生人61歲（西元一九六五年生）
People born in Yi Si year are 61 years old (born in 1965)

財運：財運一般，小心金錢轉出外地投資而破財。

Wealth: Wealth luck is average. Be careful of losing money by transferring money out of town for investment.

事業：工作運勢不錯，容易由內部產生矛盾，凡事總會多煩惱，半悲半喜。

Career: Work fortune is good, but internal conflicts are likely to arise. Everything will be troublesome and you will feel partially happy and sad.

感情：常因壓力而造成感情的衝突，應當心平氣和讓伴侶瞭解自己煩惱。

Relationship: Emotional conflicts are often caused by stress. You should calmly let your partner understand your worries.

健康：健康狀況不佳，疾病容易由內而外轉變，注意車禍及交通事故。

Health: In poor health, diseases can easily change from the inside out. Pay attention to car accidents and traffic mishaps.

吉祥物 Auspicious Items：

1. 今年犯太歲，在正月初一至十五期間，前往新加坡四馬路五路財神敬拜四面觀音、太歲星君，點太歲星燈、普賢菩薩本命燈、武財神事業財利燈，供奉太歲金、五路財神金來消災解厄，催旺運勢，收得招財進寶之效。

   This year, to resolve the clash with Tai Sui, it is advisable to go to the Bugis Fortune God at Bencoolen Street in Singapore, between the first and fifteenth day of the first lunar month, to worship the Four Side Guan Yin and Tai Sui. Light the Tai Sui, Samantabhadra Bodhisattva and Wealth Wishing Lamps, and offer the Tai Sui and Wealth incense papers to ward off disasters, and have the effect of attracting wealth and treasure.

2. 可配戴桃柳檀木劍雷令福袋，在事業、財運、健康方面有好效果。

   You can wear a Protective Charm, which has good effects on career, wealth and health.

歲次癸巳年生人73歲 (西元一九五三年生)
People born in Gui Si Year are 73 years old (born in 1953)

財運：財運尚可，可以持續積蓄財富，會有意外小財。

Wealth: Wealth luck is fair, you can continue to accumulate wealth, and you will have unexpected small fortunes.

事業：事業運勢平平，儘量打團體戰，小心意外橫災，退休之人要放寬心胸。

Career: Career fortune is average. Try to work as a team and be careful of unexpected disasters. Retirees should be open-minded.

感情：家中偶有是非紛擾，只要順其自然，理性排解糾紛，自能排憂解難。

Relationship: There are occasional disputes at home. Let nature take its course and resolve disputes rationally, you will be able to solve your problems.

健康：健康運勢尚可，須注意提防胸腔肺部、咳嗽、心頭鬱悶、腸道等疾病。

Health: Your health condition is fair, but you must pay attention to chest, lung, cough, depression, intestinal and other diseases.

吉祥物 Auspicious Items：

1. 今年犯太歲，在正月初一至十五期間，前往新加坡四馬路五路財神敬拜四面觀音、太歲星君，點太歲星燈、普賢菩薩本命燈、藥師佛消災解厄燈，供奉太歲金、華陀除疾金來消災解厄，禳解制化保平安。

   This year, to resolve the clash with Tai Sui, it is advisable to go to the Bugis Fortune God at Bencoolen Street in Singapore, between the first and fifteenth day of the first lunar month, to worship the Four Side Guan Yin and Tai Sui. Light the Tai Sui, Samantabhadra Bodhisattva and Hua Tuo Wishing Lamps, and offer the Tai Sui and Hua Tuo incense papers to eliminate disasters for safety and good health.

2. 可到四馬路五路財神點七彩蓮花轉運燈，讓菩薩護祐讓身心、災邪遠離、趨吉避凶。

   Head down to Bugis Fortune God to light a Lotus Lamp and let the Bodhisattva protect your body and mind, keep away disasters and evils, and boost good luck.

◎ 肖馬人二〇二五年運勢詳解

Forecast for the Year 2025 for people born in the year of the Horse

（12、24、36、48、60、72歲）

肖馬之人二〇二五年運勢有太陽、歲殿、文昌、天廚、桃花、咸池、紅豔、天空、晦氣、流霞星諸星照臨。今年太陽星高照，男性喜事連連，女性小心禍事纏身，多得貴人，事業學業表現出色，桃花非常旺盛，小心爛桃花敗身破財。**肖馬之人今年總體運勢極佳，事業財運好事成雙，但是桃花運易氾濫成災，建議到玉玄門祭化桃花煞，讓運勢喜上加喜，好上加好。**

In 2025, people born in the Year of the Horse can expect to enjoy a relatively good year due to the presence of strong auspicious stars, namely Taiyang, Suidian, Wenchang and Tianchu. The other stars which may appear in your fortune include Taohua, Xianchi, Hongyan, Tiankong, Huiqi and Liuxia. The Sun (Taiyang) is shining brightly this year, and men will have many happy events, but women should be careful of troubles. Thanks to the help of noble people, career and academic performance will be outstanding, and relationships will be very prosperous. Be careful of bad romance that will ruin your life and wealth. People born in the Year of the Horse will have excellent overall fortunes this year, and good things will come in pairs in terms of career and wealth, but bad romance can easily become a disaster. It is recommended to go to Yu Xuan Men for blessings to resolve the influence of romance star Taohua so that your fortune will be even better.

今年太陽星高照，整個運勢會動起來，事業能在動中得利，較為勞碌奔波，利於升官加薪、政治、公益、公眾等事業發展，財運方面非常興旺，可靠貴人得財，享天降之祿，得天賜之福，感情方面眾多桃花星齊臨，能廣結人緣，異性緣特別出眾，易有桃花氾濫導致損財，今年凶星代表處事天馬行空，倒楣禍事突發，注意小人是非、血光意外、產厄血崩、開刀骨折之災，不過今年有眾多吉星來化解，能逢凶化吉。

As the sun shines brightly this year, the whole fortune will be in motion. The career will benefit from the motion, and you will be busier, which will give rise to promotion and salary increase, politics, charity, public and other career development. Your financial fortune will be very prosperous, and you can rely on noble people to get wealth and enjoy the blessings from heaven. In terms of relationships, many peach blossom stars are present, which can make you popular, and your compatibility with the opposite sex is particularly outstanding. It is easy to have excessive romantic relationships flooding in that lead to financial losses. This year, the evil star represents your unrestrained thinking and unfortunate things will happen suddenly. Be careful of gossips with villains, bloody accidents, postpartum hemorrhage, and fractures during surgery. Nevertheless, this year there are many lucky stars to resolve the disasters.

今年好運上升，可以全力衝刺事業、學業，建議凡事腳踏實地，謙虛待人，不要好大喜功，虛浮不實，只聽好話，盡量避免出入聲色場所留戀酒色，今年文昌星旺盛，所以考生最好能祭拜文昌帝君來助旺文昌氣運，庇佑學業精進，金榜題名。

Good luck will rise this year, and you can go all out to pursue your career and studies. It is recommended that you be down-to-earth in everything, be humble to others, don't be too grandiose about your achievements and only listen to good things. Try to avoid going to sensual places and lingering on wine and sex. Wenchang (Wisdom star) is strong this year, so it is best for candidates to take advantage of the opportunity to pay homage to Emperor Wenchang to boost your luck and get your name on the list of successful candidates.

財運 Wealth	★★★★
事業 Career	★★★★★
感情 Relationship	★★★★
健康 Health	★★★★
吉祥顏色 Lucky Color	紅色 Red Color
吉祥數字Lucky Number	8215

歲次甲午年生人12歲（西元二〇一四年生）
People born in Jai Wu Year are 12 years old (Born in 2014)

財運： 財運很好，有領獎學金或中獎的機運，避免在網路世界亂消費。

Wealth: Very good wealth luck. There is a chance of receiving a scholarship or winning a lottery. Avoid spending randomly in the online world.

事業： 學業考運很好，比賽易得好成績，凡事腳踏實地，努力充實，不要眼高手低。

Career: Good luck in academic examinations, easy to get good results in competitions. Be down-to-earth in everything, work hard and don't be too high-minded.

感情： 人際關係非常好，學校活動忙碌，小心感情太旺盛導致心情及學業大亂。

Relationship: The interpersonal relationship is very good, and the school activities are busy. Be careful that too strong relationship will cause chaos in mood and studies.

健康： 健康很好，宜注意骨骼酸痛、神經過敏的疾病，保持飲食均衡，睡眠充足。

Health: Health condition is very good. You should pay attention to bone pain and nervousness, maintain a balanced diet, and get enough sleep.

吉祥物 Auspicious Items：

1. 今年犯桃花煞，在正月初一至正月十五期間，前往新加坡四馬路五路財神敬拜四面觀音，報名台灣玉宸齋制化桃花法會，點大勢至菩薩本命燈、文昌智慧光明燈，燒化文昌智慧金、貴人金，來消災解厄，開啟智慧及增強考試、讀書運。

   This year, the impact of ominous Sangmen star is serious. It is advisable to head down to Bugis Fortune God between the first and fifteenth day of the first lunar month to pray to the Four Side Guan Yin. Burn the Karmic Creditors, Academic and Benefactors incense papers, and light the Zodiac Guardian and Academic wishing lamps to dispel the disasters.

2. 隨身攜帶魁星踢斗隨身牌，使用文昌智慧沐浴露來沐浴，可助旺文昌氣運，使學業精進進步。

   Carry the Kui Xing Ta Dou portable card with you and use the Wisdom Body Wash to bathe, which can help enhance wisdom and improve studies.

歲次壬午年生人24歲 (西元二〇〇二年生)
People born in Ren Wu Year are 24 years old (Born in 2002)

財運：財運很好，有加薪機會，貴人能夠增強你的財運。

Wealth: The wealth luck is very good. There are opportunities for salary increases, and noble people can enhance your wealth luck.

事業：讀書運很好，能在動中得利，不要好高騖遠，可以得到貴人幫助，職務上升。

Career: Good luck in studying, you can benefit from work. Don't be too ambitious, you can get help from noble people, and your position will rise.

感情：桃花旺盛，異性緣特別好，過度放縱情慾，小心爛桃花敗身破財。

Relationship: Relationship luck is strong, and you are particularly good with the opposite gender. If you over indulge in lust, beware of bad romance that will ruin your life and fortune.

健康：健康很好，注意心氣不足、腸胃病、心臟病，孕婦要注意流產現象。

Health: Health is very good. Pay attention to insufficient heart energy, gastrointestinal problems, and heart disease. Pregnant women should pay attention to miscarriage.

吉祥物 Auspicious Items：

1. 今年犯桃花煞，在正月初一至正月十五期間，前往新加坡四馬路五路財神敬拜四面觀音，報名台灣玉宸齋制化桃花法會，點大勢至菩薩本命燈、月老桃花旺緣燈，供奉月老姻緣金、貴人金，以獲得神明護祐讓身心安定財運亨通。

   This year, to resolve the disaster from Taohua, it is advisable to go to Bugis Fortune God at Bencoolen Street in Singapore, between the first and fifteenth day of the first lunar month, to worship the Four Side Guan Yin. Register for the Taiwan Yu Chen Zhai puja for blessings to resolve disasters. Light the Mahasthamaprapta Bodhisattva and Marriage Wishing Lamps, and offer the Marriage and Benefactor incense papers to seek protection, make your body and mind stable and prosperous.

2. 使用桃花寶袋、開運桃花手工皂、桃花沐浴露可增強異性桃花、增強人緣桃花，化解爛桃花，增添正派的桃花運勢。

   Use a Love Charm, Handmade Cupid Soap and Love Body Wash to resolve bad romance and boost interpersonal relationship.

歲次庚午年生人36歲（西元一九九〇年生）
People born in Geng Wu Year are 36 years old (Born in 1990)

財運：財運不錯，常有意外之事花錢損財，或因爛桃花而損失財物。

Wealth: Good fortune, but unexpected events often lead to loss of money, or loss of property due to bad romance.

事業：事業有虛浮空忙的現象，精神壓力較重，貴人運好，應該善用人際關係的幫助。

Career: There is a tendency for you to be busy but superficial in your career, and you are under a lot of mental stress. However, you have good luck with noble people, so you should make good use of the help of your interpersonal relationships.

感情：喜事臨門，利於結婚生子，真心誠懇自能感動對方，小心感情出現變數。

Relationship: Happy event is coming, good for marriage and childbirth. Being sincere can impress the other person, but beware of changes in your relationship.

健康：健康平平，要多注意肝膽、解毒功能、皮膚等方面的疾病，孕婦要注意安胎。

Health: Health is average. Pay more attention to liver and gallbladder, detoxification function, skin and other diseases. Pregnant women should pay attention to miscarriage.

吉祥物 Auspicious Items：

1. 今年犯桃花煞，在正月初一至正月十五期間，前往新加坡四馬路五路財神敬拜四面觀音，報名台灣玉宸齋制化桃花法會，點大勢至菩薩本命燈、月老桃花旺緣燈，供奉月老姻緣金、貴人金，以獲得神明護祐讓身心安定。

   This year, to resolve the disaster from Taohua, it is advisable to go to Bugis Fortune God at Bencoolen Street in Singapore, between the first and fifteenth day of the first lunar month, to worship the Four Side Guan Yin. Register for the Taiwan Yu Chen Zhai puja for blessings to resolve disasters. Light the Mahasthamaprapta Bodhisattva and Marriage Wishing Lamps, and offer the Marriage and Benefactor incense papers to seek protection and make your body and mind stable.

2. 臥室可放置三合琉璃虎馬狗生肖，隨身可以配戴三合水晶手鍊，如此可招貴人、增強運勢、招財進寶。

   Put a set of Zodiac Benefactors (Tiger, Horse and Dog) in the bedroom, and wear a Zodiac Benefactor bracelet to attract noble people, enhance good luck, and attract wealth.

歲次戊午年生人48歲 (西元一九七八年生)
People born in Wu Wu Year are 48 years old (Born in 1978)

財運：財運非常好，有多個管道進財，財來財去，守不住財。

Wealth: Wealth luck is very good. There are many ways to make money. Money comes and goes, but cannot keep it.

事業：利於政治家、建築師、律師等行業，工作很順，幻想虛浮反讓事業失敗。

Career: It is good for politicians, architects, lawyers and other industries. The work will be smooth, but illusions will make the career fail.

感情：桃花運旺盛異性緣佳，未婚之人有喜事臨門，感情生活多采多姿，若心存兒戲反生是非禍端。

Relationship: With good relationship luck, you will have compatibility with the opposite gender. If you are single, you will have happy events and a colorful love life. However, if you have a child's play in your heart, you will end up with troubles.

健康：健康平平，宜注意肝膽、解毒功能、皮膚疾病，要注意做定期的健康檢查。

Health: Health is average. You should pay attention to liver and gallbladder, detoxification function, and skin diseases. Take note of regular health check-ups.

吉祥物 Auspicious Items：

1. 今年犯桃花煞，在正月初一至正月十五期間，前往新加坡四馬路五路財神敬拜四面觀音，報名台灣玉宸齋制化桃花法會，點大勢至菩薩本命燈、月老桃花旺緣燈，供奉月老姻緣金、貴人金，以獲得神明護祐讓身心安定，財源廣進。

   This year, to resolve the disaster from Taohua, it is advisable to go to Bugis Fortune God at Bencoolen Street in Singapore, between the first and fifteenth day of the first lunar month, to worship the Four Side Guan Yin. Register for the Taiwan Yu Chen Zhai puja for blessings to resolve disasters. Light the Mahasthamaprapta Bodhisattva and Marriage Wishing Lamps, and offer the Marriage and Benefactor incense papers to seek protection and make your body and mind stable and prosperous.

2. 置放琉璃納財寶盆於家中財位，來催旺財氣，在臥室擺放琉璃龍鳳呈祥，來助您招得人緣，祈求覓得良緣，婚姻幸福美滿，斬除不良桃花纏身。

   Place a Wealth Bowl in the Wealth sector of your home to boost your wealth luck. Place a Dragon Phoenix Cup in the bedroom to help you attract good interpersonal relationship, happy marriage, and get rid of bad romance.

歲次丙午年生人60歲（西元一九六六年生）
People born in Bing Wu Year are 60 years old (Born in 1966)

財運：財運很好，可以增資與開創新業，要預防錢財左進右出。

Wealth: Wealth luck is very good. You can increase investment and start a new business but be careful of money going in and out.

事業：事業能升官加薪，忌操心操勞，心浮氣躁，多開發外地客源會有意外的收穫。

Career: You can get a promotion and a raise in your career, but avoid worrying too much and being impatient. Developing more foreign customers will bring unexpected gains.

感情：家運和諧平順，家中易有喜事臨門，不要進出聲色場所，以免造成婚姻破裂。

Relationship: Family fortune is harmonious and smooth, and happy events are likely to happen at home. Do not visit sensual places to avoid breaking up the marriage.

健康：健康狀況小有問題，宜注意脾胃不佳、腳腿浮腫、肝旺及濕熱等方面的疾病。

Health: If you have minor health problems, you should pay attention to diseases such as poor spleen and stomach, swollen legs and feet, liver deficiency, dampness and heat, etc.

吉祥物 Auspicious Items：

1. 今年犯桃花煞，在正月初一至正月十五期間，前往新加坡四馬路五路財神敬拜四面觀音，報名台灣玉宸齋制化桃花法會，點大勢至菩薩本命燈、月老桃花旺緣燈、藥師佛消災解厄燈，供奉月老姻緣金、華陀除疾金，以獲得神明護祐讓身心安定。

   This year, to resolve the negative impact from Taohua, it is advisable to go to the Bugis Fortune God at Bencoolen Street in Singapore, between the first and fifteenth day of the first lunar month, to worship the Four Side Guan Yin. Register for the Taiwan Yu Chen Zhai puja for blessings. Light the Mahasthamaprapta Bodhisattva, Marriage and Medicine Buddha Wishing Lamps and offer the Marriage and Hua Tuo incense papers for blessings to bring peace of mind and body.

2. 臥室擺放琉璃龍鳳呈祥，使用開運桃花手工皂或桃花沐浴露來沐浴，來助您招得人緣，婚姻幸福美滿，斬除不良桃花纏身。

   Placing a glazed Dragon Phoenix in the bedroom can bring good luck, and using Handmade Cupid Soap or Love Body Wash to bathe can help attract popularity, have a happy marriage, and get rid of bad romance.

歲次甲午年生人72歲 (西元一九五四年生)
People born in Jia Wu Year are 72 years old (Born in 1954)

財運：財運很好，有爆發進財的機會，但是太貪心、太急切反而會破財。

Wealth: Wealth luck is very good, and there are opportunities to make a fortune, but being too greedy and eager will lead to loss of money.

事業：運勢不錯，退休之人可多參加一些公益活動，不要太過胡思亂想讓自己煩心。

Career: Your fortune is good. Retired people can participate in more charity activities and don't let your imagination run wild and make yourself upset.

感情：夫妻感情和諧，家中易有喜事臨門，女性感情較為起伏，要注意災厄及橫禍。

Relationship: The relationship between husband and wife is harmonious, and happy events are likely to happen at home. Women's emotions are more ups and downs, so be careful about disasters and misfortunes.

健康：健康平平，宜注意肝膽、骨骼酸痛、神經過敏疾病，有病要立即就醫。

Health: Health is average. You should pay attention to liver, gallbladder, bone pain, and nervousness. If you are sick, seek medical attention immediately.

吉祥物 Auspicious Items：

1. 今年犯桃花煞，在正月初一至正月十五期間，前往新加坡四馬路五路財神敬拜四面觀音，報名台灣玉宸齋制化桃花法會，點大勢至菩薩本命燈、觀音平安健康燈，供奉華佗除疾金、貴人金，以獲得神明護祐讓身心安定。

   This year, to resolve the negative impact from Taohua, it is advisable to go to Bugis Fortune God at Bencoolen Street in Singapore, between the first and fifteenth day of the first lunar month, to worship the Four Side Guan Yin. Register for the Taiwan Yu Chen Zhai puja for blessings. Light the Mahasthamaprapta Bodhisattva and Guan Yin Wishing Lamps and offer the Hua Tuo and Benefactor incense papers to bring peace of mind and body.

2. 隨身攜帶五行水晶能量瓶，讓你的飲用水產生磁場共振效應，直接吸收良好的能量來源，達到五行相生，開運旺財的目標。

   Carry a five-element crystal Energy Water Bottle to make your drinking water produce a magnetic field resonance effect. It will directly absorb good energy sources, and achieve the goal of mutual generation of the five elements and bring good luck and wealth.

◎ 肖羊人二〇二五年運勢詳解

Forecast for the Year 2025 for people born in the year of the Goat

（11、23、35、47、59、71歲）

肖羊之人二〇二五年運勢有喪門、地喪、地雌、擎天、豹尾、飛廉、天殺、大殺坐守。今年運勢動靜急速轉變，缺乏吉星轉運，凶星特主家中易有死喪哭泣之事，要特別注意血光、刑傷、小人、是非、盜賊及飛來橫禍，男性要注意刑剋之災。**今年肖羊之人的總體運勢不佳，如要避免小人是非及災喪臨門，建議至玉玄門制化喪門凶星以保人宅平安。**

In 2025, a line up of ominous stars spells misfortunes for people born under the zodiac sign of the Goat. This year's fortune changes rapidly with the presence of ominous stars which include Sangmen, Desàng, Decí, Qíngtiān, Bàowěi, Fēilián, Tiānshā and Dàsha. There is a lack of lucky stars. The ominous stars are prone to bring death and weeping in the family. Pay special attention to blood injuries, villains, disputes, thieves and unexpected disasters. Men should pay attention to the disasters that can be overcome by punishment. The overall fortune of people born under the sign of the Goat is not good. If you want to avoid villains, disasters and bereavements, it is recommended to go to Yu Xuan Men for blessings to control the evil stars and keep people and home safe.

今年缺乏吉神轉運，事業起伏不定，注意職業的變動，財運不佳，容易破財損失物件，學生考運平平，要加倍努力，否則成績不理想。今年凶星眾多，如喪門、地雌、地喪皆主死喪哭泣、盜竊劫財之事，不可輕忽大意。飛廉主小人中傷，口舌糾紛，流言蜚語毀謗。大殺、擎天主易有血光、刑傷、暴力傷害、飛來橫禍，較會有交通意外，男性要別注意刑傷，懷孕者留心產厄，逢豹尾則不利嫁娶及興造動工等事。

With the absence of lucky stars this year, your career will be fluctuating. Be careful about career changes. Financial luck is not good. It is easy to lose

money and lose things. Students will have mediocre luck in examinations. You need to work harder, otherwise your grades will be unsatisfactory. There are many unlucky stars this year, such as Sangmen, Desàng and Decí, which are all about death, mourning, crying, theft and robbery. Don't take it lightly. Fēilián is about slander by villains and verbal disputes. Dàsha and Qingtian are about blood, criminal injury, violent injury and sudden misfortunes. There is a high probability of traffic accidents. Men should pay attention to criminal injuries. Pregnant women should pay attention to childbirth. The presence of Bàowěi means it is not good for marriage and construction.

今年災喪特別嚴重，勿探病、弔喪、勿食喪家食物以免受災殃，有病立即就醫，否則小病拖成大病，還要特別注意血光意外之災，行車要注意交通意外，最好能至玉玄門化解口舌小人、血光之災及喪門凶星。

Disasters and bereavements are particularly serious this year. To avoid disasters, do not visit the sick, pay condolences, or eat food from the bereaved family. Seek medical attention immediately if you are sick, otherwise a minor illness will turn into a serious one. Pay special attention to blood accidents. Be careful of traffic accidents when driving. It is advisable to visit Yu Xuan Men to resolve the negative impact of the ominous stars which will bring disputes, bloody injuries, death and mourning.

財運 Wealth	★
事業 Career	★★
感情 Relationship	★★
健康 Health	★
吉祥顏色 Lucky Color	黃色 Yellow Color
吉祥數字Lucky Number	7530

歲次乙未年生人11歲（西元二〇一五年生）
People born in Yi Wei Year are 11 years old (Born in 2015)

財運：小孩不論財運，易有盜竊、劫財、刑傷之事而破財。

Wealth: Regardless of the child's financial luck, it is easy to lose money due to theft, robbery, or safety.

事業：成績退步，考運不佳，容易沉迷電子產品或社交網路，忽略了學校的課業。

Career: Performance decline, poor luck in examinations, easy addiction to electronic products or social networks, and neglect of schoolwork.

感情：人際關係錯亂，容易交到壞朋友，為了迎合別人的眼光，而放棄了自己的價值。

Relationship: Interpersonal relationships are disordered. It is easy to make bad friends, and you give up your own value in order to please others.

健康：健康不好，宜注意眼睛、腦神經的問題，還要注意交通意外及人身安全。

Health: Health condition is not good. You should pay attention to problems with your eyes and brain nerves, as well as traffic accidents and personal safety.

吉祥物 Auspicious Items：

1. 今年犯喪門煞星嚴重，在正月初一至正月十五期間，前往新加坡四馬路五路財神敬拜四面觀音，報名台灣玉宸齋制化喪門法會，點大日如來本命燈、文昌智慧光明燈，供奉冤親債主金、文昌智慧金，來禳解制化保平安，增強讀書運勢。

   This year, you will be seriously affected by the mourning star Sangmen. It is advisable to go to the Bugis Fortune God at Bencoolen Street in Singapore, between the first and fifteenth day of the first lunar month, to pray to the Four Side Guan Yin. Register for the Taiwan Yu Chen Zhai puja to resolve disasters. Light the Vairocana Tathagata and Wenchang Wishing Lamps, and offer the Karmic Creditors and Wenchang incense papers to eliminate disasters, ensure safety and enhance academic progress.

2. 書桌上可擺放綠水晶文昌開運樹及琉璃魁星踢斗，可使學童思想敏捷，學業進步，智慧大開。

   Placing an Academic Crystal Tree and a Kui Xing Da Tou on the desk can make schoolchildren think quickly, improve academic results and expand their wisdom.

歲次癸未年生人23歲（西元二〇〇三年生）
People born in Gui Wei Year are 23 years old (Born in 2003)

財運：財運平平，在娛樂吃喝方面消費較多，小心被公司減薪。

Wealth: Wealth luck is mediocre. You spend more on entertainment, food and drink. Be careful about your salary being cut by the company.

事業：不論學生考試或是升等評鑑都表現不佳，易受小人陷害困擾，事業起伏不定。

Career: Poor performance in both student examinations and promotion evaluations. Easy to be framed by villains and career fluctuating.

感情：感情困難重重，表面堅強內心受苦，愛情突然變調，應該保持樂觀脫離悲傷。

Relationship: There are a lot of difficulties in relationships. You may be strong on the outside but suffering on the inside. Love may change suddenly. You should stay optimistic and stay away from sadness.

健康：健康平平，注意肝功能、胃病、經血不調，車禍血光之災，女性要注意安胎。

Health: Health is average. Pay attention to liver function, stomach problem, irregular menstrual blood, and blood injuries in car accidents. Women should pay attention to miscarriage.

吉祥物 Auspicious Items：

1. 今年犯喪門煞星嚴重，在正月初一至正月十五期間，前往新加坡四馬路五路財神敬拜四面觀音，報名台灣玉宸齋制化喪門法會，點大日如來本命燈、文昌智慧光明燈，供奉冤親債主金、文昌智慧金、驅制小人金，可以獲得菩薩護祐，減少小人是非。

   This year, you will be seriously affected by the mourning star Sangmen. It is advisable to go to the Bugis Fortune God at Bencoolen Street in Singapore, between the first and fifteenth day of the first lunar month, to pray to the Four Side Guan Yin. Register for the Taiwan Yu Chen Zhai puja to resolve disasters from the ominous star. Light the Vairocana Tathagata and Wenchang Wishing Lamps, and offer the Karmic Creditors and Wengchang incense papers to eliminate disasters and villain disputes.

2. 臥室可放置琉璃三合生肖豬兔羊吉祥物，如此可招貴人、增強運勢、改變家運、招財進寶。

   Placing a set of Zodiac Benefactors (Pig, Rabbit and Goat) in the bedroom can attract noble people, enhance fortune, change family fortune, and attract wealth.

歲次辛未年生人35歲（西元一九九一年生）
People born in Xin Wei Year are 35 years old (Born in 1991)

財運：財運不佳，求財困難阻礙，須防暗中消耗破財，貿然投資小心大破財。

Wealth: Poor wealth luck, difficulty in seeking wealth. Beware of secretly spending and losing money, and be careful of making rash investments and losing money.

事業：工作不順，小心公司裁員而失業，缺乏貴人幫助，常遭小人暗害。

Career: Work is not doing well. You may lose your job due to company layoffs. You lack the help of noble people, and you are often back-stabbed by villains.

感情：常常意見不合爭吵不休，婚姻遇到瓶頸，勿沈溺酒色，留戀聲色場所。

Relationship: You often have disagreements and quarrels, and your marriage encounters bottlenecks. Do not indulge in passion or alcohol, or be obsessed in sensual places.

健康：健康較差，宜注意性功能及婦科方面的疾病，女性要注意安胎問題。

Health: Poor health, you should pay attention to sexual function and gynecological diseases. Women should pay attention to miscarriage issues.

吉祥物 Auspicious Items：

1. 今年犯喪門煞星嚴重，在正月初一至正月十五期間，前往新加坡四馬路五路財神敬拜四面觀音，報名台灣玉宸齋制化喪門法會，點大日如來本命燈、武財神事業財利燈，供奉冤親債主金、五路財神金、驅制小人金，可以獲得菩薩護祐，減少小人是非。

   This year, you will be seriously affected by the mourning star Sangmen. It is advisable to go to the Bugis Fortune God at Bencoolen Street in Singapore, between the first and fifteenth day of the first lunar month, to pray to the Four Side Guan Yin. Register for the Taiwan Yu Chen Zhai puja for blessings. Light the Vairocana Tathagata and Wealth Wishing Lamps, and offer the Karmic Creditors and Wealth incense papers to eliminate disasters and villain disputes.

2. 桌上擺放琉璃獅咬劍文鎮，具有化解小人是非及旺財的靈動力，能化解破財及事業不順的危機。

   Placing a Lion Head Charm on the table has the spiritual power to eliminate villain disputes and resolve the crisis of losing money and career failure.

歲次己未年生人47歲（西元一九七九年生）
People born in Ji Wei Year are 47 years old (Born in 1979)

財運：財運不佳，容易被詐騙而破財，或投資誤判形勢而大破財。

Wealth: Poor wealth luck, easy to be defrauded and lose money, or misjudge the situation in investment resulting in big loss of money.

事業：事業阻礙重重，易受小人是非的干擾傷害，小心飛來橫禍而遭受傷害。

Career: There are many obstacles in career, and you are easily disturbed by villains. Be careful of misfortune and harm.

感情：感情不佳，要多體諒伴侶，不要將負面情緒隨意爆發，造成難以收拾的後果。

Relationship: If your relationship is not good, you should be more considerate of your partner and don't explode your negative emotions at will, causing consequences that are difficult to deal with.

健康：災喪特別嚴重，勿探病、弔喪以免受災殃，有病立即就醫，否則小病拖成大病。

Health: Disasters and bereavements are particularly serious. Do not visit the sick or pay condolences to avoid disasters. Seek medical attention immediately if you are unwell, otherwise a minor illness will turn into a serious one.

吉祥物 Auspicious Items：

1. 今年犯喪門煞星嚴重，在正月初一至正月十五期間，前往新加坡四馬路五路財神敬拜四面觀音，報名台灣玉宸齋制化喪門法會，點大日如來本命燈、武財神事業財利燈，供奉冤親債主金、五路財神金、驅制小人金，可以獲得菩薩護祐，減少小人是非。

   This year, you will be seriously affected by the mourning star Sangmen. It is advisable to go to the Bugis Fortune God at Bencoolen Street in Singapore, between the first and fifteenth day of the first lunar month, to pray to the Four Side Guan Yin. Register for the Taiwan Yu Chen Zhai puja for blessings. Light the Vairocana Tathagata and Wealth Wishing Lamps, and offer the Karmic Creditors and Wealth incense papers to eliminate disasters and villain disputes.

2. 可以隨身配戴九頭靈獅項鍊，如此可助己身元神光采、健康平安，發揮押煞制小人的無形能量。

   You can wear the Nine-headed Lion necklace at all times, which can help you to have a radiant spirit, be healthy and safe, and exert the invisible energy to ward off evil and resolve villains.

歲次丁未年生人59歲 (西元一九六七年生)
People born in Ding Wei Year are 59 years old (Born in 1967)

財運：財運平平，不宜投資金額過大造成資金周轉不靈，投機事業難聚財。

Wealth: Wealth luck is mediocre. It is not suitable to invest too much, which will lead to poor capital turnover, and it is difficult to accumulate wealth through speculation.

事業：工作能提升知名度，提防小人暗害及意外血光之災，小心工作環境出現轉變。

Career: Work can enhance your reputation. Beware of back-stabbing by villains and accidental bloody disasters, and be careful of changes in the work environment.

感情：感情平淡，多陪伴家人，夫妻間多營造親密的氣氛，以免出現溝通的障礙。

Relationship: Relationship is flat. Spend more time with your family, and create an intimate atmosphere between husband and wife to avoid communication barriers.

健康：健康平平，宜注意呼吸系統、扁桃腺炎、攝護腺疾病，不要太過操勞積勞成疾。

Health: Health is average. You should pay attention to respiratory system, tonsillitis, and prostate diseases. Don't overwork yourself and get sick.

吉祥物 Auspicious Items：

1. 今年犯喪門煞星嚴重，在正月初一至正月十五期間，前往新加坡四馬路五路財神敬拜四面觀音，報名台灣玉宸齋制化喪門法會，點大日如來本命燈、觀音菩薩平安健康燈，供奉冤親債主金、五路財神金、驅制小人金，可以獲得菩薩護祐，減少小人是非。

   This year, you will be seriously affected by the mourning star Sangmen. It is advisable to go to the Bugis Fortune God at Bencoolen Street in Singapore, between the first and fifteenth day of the first lunar month, to pray to the Four Side Guan Yin. Register for the Taiwan Yu Chen Zhai puja for blessings. Light the Vairocana Tathagata and Wealth Wishing Lamps, and offer the Karmic Creditors and Wealth incense papers to eliminate disasters and villain disputes.

2. 隨身配戴桃柳檀木劍雷令福袋或綠眼貔貅戒指能除小人化煞辟邪，可以獲得神明護祐讓身心安定。

   Carrying a Protective Charm or wearing a Green Pixiu Ring can ward off villains and evil spirits, and be blessed with stabilized body and mind.

歲次乙未年生人71歲（西元一九五五年生）
People born in Yi Wei Year are 71 years old (Born in 1955)

財運：財運平平，投資後續力不足，見好就收，慎防詐騙而破財。

Wealth: Wealth luck is mediocre, and the follow-up ability of investment is insufficient. Just accept it when it is good, and be careful to avoid fraud and loss of money.

事業：事業運勢平平，不宜遠行，小人是非纏身，退休之人好好安享天倫之樂。

Career: Your career fortune is mediocre, and it is not suitable to travel far. You will be troubled by villain disputes. Retired people will enjoy the happiness of their family.

感情：家庭和樂，平時與子孫多關懷交流，注意家人出入安全及健康狀況。

Relationship: Have a harmonious family, care for and communicate with your children and grandchildren more often, and pay attention to the safety and health of your family members when they go out.

健康：健康不佳，宜注意肝、腎、眼睛、白血球之疾，勿入喪家，不要去探病。

Health: Poor health, you should pay attention to diseases of the liver, kidneys, eyes, and white blood cells. Do not go to funeral home or visit sick people.

吉祥物 Auspicious Items：

1. 今年犯喪門煞星嚴重，在正月初一至正月十五期間，前往新加坡四馬路五路財神敬拜四面觀音，報名台灣玉宸齋制化喪門法會，點大日如來本命燈、藥師佛消災解厄燈，供奉冤親債主金、華佗除疾金、驅制小人金，可以獲得菩薩護祐，減少小人是非。

   This year, you will be seriously affected by the mourning star Sangmen. It is advisable to go to the Bugis Fortune God at Bencoolen Street in Singapore, between the first and fifteenth day of the first lunar month, to pray to the Four Side Guan Yin. Register for the Taiwan Yu Chen Zhai for blessings. Light the Vairocana Tathagata and Medicine Buddha Wishing Lamps, and offer the Karmic Creditors and Hua Tuo incense papers to eliminate disasters and villain disputes.

2. 家中可擺放一尊琉金四面觀音，可助旺家運平安、家和萬事興，置於汽車上還可化解意外橫災及小人暗害。

   You can place a Four Face Guan Yin statute at home to enhance prosperity and peace and harmony to your family. Displaying it in your car can also help to resolve unexpected disasters, harm and evil plots from villains.

◎ 肖猴人二〇二五年運勢詳解

Forecast for the Year 2025 for people born in the year of the Monkey
（10、22、34、46、58、70歲）

肖猴之人二〇二五年運勢有太陰、天乙貴人、歲合、貫索、勾神、孤辰、亡神、歲刑、刑太歲、破太歲等星坐守。今年太陰吉星高照，主陰盛陽衰，喜事臨門，有最吉貴人，事業上升，財運亨通，學業進步，凶星會造成事業阻礙、官司、小人是非、刑剋之事，要預防急症或突發災厄。**今年肖猴之人的總體運勢吉中藏凶，好運多過壞運，宜至玉玄門拜太歲星君化解刑太歲、破太歲，制桃花、孤寡煞以保平安。**

A mediocre year awaits people born in the Year of the Monkey. In 2025, you have auspicious stars Taiyin, Tianyi Nobleman and Suihe descending upon your fortune. However, besides Xing Tai Sui and Po Tai Sui, you have ominous stars Guansuo, Goushen, Guchen, Wangshen and Suixing which may pop in for annoying stopover bringing discord and tension. This year, the auspicious star Taiyin shines brightly, which means that Yin is strong and Yang is weak. (Yin – representing female, passive, negative principle in nature, the moon and Yang – representing male, active, positive principle in nature, the sun). The auspicious stars will bring happy events at home. There will be the most auspicious nobleman, career will rise, wealth will be prosperous, and academic progress will be made. But the ominous stars will cause career obstacles, lawsuits, villain disputes, and punishments. Be careful of emergencies or sudden disasters. This year, the overall fortune of people born in the Year of the Monkey is good but with hidden dangers. Nevertheless, good luck outweighs bad luck. It is advisable to go to Yu Xuan Men to worship Tai Sui Xing Jun to resolve Xing Tai Sui and Po Tai Sui to ensure safety, and overcome bad interpersonal relationships and loneliness.

今年行運吉神有太陰、歲合、天乙貴人守護，事業多貴人，能升官進財，利於交友、合伙，可以投資房地產或流行時尚產業，還能減

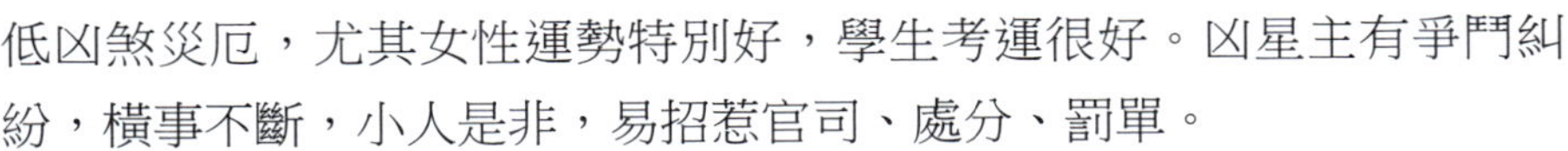
低凶煞災厄，尤其女性運勢特別好，學生考運很好。凶星主有爭鬥糾紛，橫事不斷，小人是非，易招惹官司、處分、罰單。

This year, the lucky stars Taiyin, Suihe, and Tianyi protect you. You will have many noble people in your career, and you will be promoted and make money. It is good for making friends and forming partnerships. You can invest in real estate or fashion industries, and you can reduce bad luck and disasters. Women will have particularly good luck. Students will have good grades in examinations. However, the ominous stars will bring disputes, constant troubles, and villains. It is easy to get involved in lawsuits, penalties, and fines.

今年總體運勢吉中藏凶，建議不要與親友產生借貸關係，接納貴人的意見，不要惡性競爭及意氣用事，注重團體和諧，避免單打獨鬥，保持情緒的平穩，今年是成家立業的好時機，需防感情傷害及桃色糾紛導致人財兩失。

The overall fortune this year is good but contains hidden dangers. It is recommended that you stay away from loan relationships with relatives and friends. Accept the opinions of noble people, do not engage in vicious competition or act on impulse, focus on group harmony, avoid fighting alone, and maintain stability. This is a good time to start a family and build a career, but you need to guard against emotional harm and romantic affairs that may lead to loss of both life and finance.

財運 Wealth	★★★
事業 Career	★★★
感情 Relationship	★★★
健康 Health	★★★
吉祥顏色 Lucky Color	金色 Gold Color
吉祥數字Lucky Number	1780

歲次丙申年生人10歲 (西元二〇一六年生)
People born in Bing Shen Year are 10 years old (Born in 2016)

財運：小孩不論財運，家長可以多提供教具或才藝課程。

Wealth: Regardless of the child's wealth, parents can provide more teaching aids or talent courses.

事業：今年學業進步，考運不錯，養成正確的讀書習慣是一輩子的財富。

Career: There is academic progress this year and good examination luck. Developing the right study habits is a lifetime wealth.

感情：人際關係互動良好，能得到師長的提攜，家長要多陪伴學童。

Relationship: Interpersonal relationships are good, teachers can support, parents should spend more time with their children.

健康：身體健康很好，注意便秘、消化不良、流行性感冒。

Health: Physical health is very good, pay attention to constipation, indigestion and influenza.

吉祥物 Auspicious Items：

1. 今年犯桃花、刑太歲、破太歲等煞星，在正月初一至正月十五期間，前往新加坡四馬路五路財神敬拜四面觀音，報名台灣玉宸齋制化桃花、刑太歲、破太歲法會，點太歲星燈、大日如來本命燈、文昌智慧光明燈，燒化太歲金、冤親債主金、文昌智慧金可以獲得菩薩護祐。

   This year you are affected by Xing Tai Sui, Po Tai Sui and the romance star. It is advisable to go to the Bugis Fortune God at Bencoolen Street in Singapore, between the first and fifteenth day of the first lunar month, to worship the Four Side Guan Yin. Register for the Taiwan Yu Chen Zhai puja to resolve the negative influence. Light the Tai Sui, Buddha Vairocana and Wenchang Wishing Lamps, and offer the Tai Sui, Karmic Creditors and Wenchang incense papers for protection.

2. 可以掛魁星踢斗畫或是在書桌上擺放琉璃魁星踢斗來助旺文昌氣運，助使學童讀書專心、頭腦敏捷，讓考運亨通、金榜題名。

   You can hang a painting of Kui Xing Ta Dou or display a liuli Kui Xing Ta Dou on the desk to help boost Wenchang luck. It will help students study with concentration and agility, and make them have good luck and excel in examinations.

甲申年生人22歲 (西元二〇〇四年生)
People born in Jia Shen Year are 22 years old (Born in 2004)

財運：財運很好，工作或投資都大有收穫，可以投資房地產或流行時尚產業。

Wealth: Good wealth luck, work or investment will be very rewarding. You can invest in real estate or fashion industry.

事業：學生的考運很旺，努力認真自能進步成功，職場上有貴人相助，容易無意間得罪他人。

Career: Students have good luck in examinations, and they can make progress and succeed if they work hard. There are noble people to help in the workplace, but it is easy to offend others unintentionally.

感情：桃花運很好，在無意間與異性擦出火花，不要太放縱情慾，好好享受愛情的浪漫美好。

Relationship: Good luck in relationship. Sparks with the opposite sex unintentionally, don't indulge in lust too much, enjoy the romance and beauty of love.

健康：健康很好，宜注意耳部、尿道感染、風流病等方面的問題。

Health: Good health, pay attention to ear, urinary tract infection, venereal disease and other problems.

吉祥物 Auspicious Items：

1. 今年犯桃花、刑太歲、破太歲等煞星，在正月初一至正月十五期間，前往新加坡四馬路五路財神敬拜四面觀音，報名台灣玉宸齋制化桃花、刑太歲、破太歲法會，點太歲星燈、大日如來本命燈、觀音菩薩平安健康燈，燒化太歲金、冤親債主金、月老姻緣金可以獲得菩薩護祐。

   This year you are affected by Xing Tai Sui, Po Tai Sui and the romance star. It is advisable to go to the Bugis Fortune God at Bencoolen Street in Singapore, between the first and fifteenth day of the first lunar month, to worship the Four Side Guan Yin. Register for the Taiwan Yu Chen Zhai puja to resolve the negative influence. Light the Tai Sui, Buddha Vairocana and Guan Yin Wishing Lamps, and offer the Tai Sui, Karmic Creditors and Wenchang incense papers for protection.

2. 可使用開運桃花手工皂、桃花姻緣沐浴露來沐浴也可以提升人緣桃花，讓您在人際關係上能左右逢源，增添桃花運勢。

   You can use the Handmade Cupid Soap and Love Body Wash to bathe to enhance your popularity, so that you can get along well with others and boost your interpersonal relationships.

歲次壬申年生人34歲（西元一九九二年生）
People born in Ren Shen Year are 34 years old (Born in 1992)

財運：財運尚可，小心無緣無故破財守不住財，一旦資金凍結將面臨債務壓力。

Wealth: Wealth luck is fair, but be careful of losing money for no reason and not being able to keep it. Once the funds are frozen, you will face debt pressure.

事業：工作壓力加大，易有人事糾紛阻礙，小心官司或被小人陷害，可能被禍事牽連。

Career: Work pressure increases, and there are personnel disputes and obstacles. Be careful of lawsuits or being framed by villains, or you may be involved in disasters.

感情：桃花運旺盛異性緣佳，感情生活多采多姿，若心存兒戲反生是非禍端。

Relationship: Relationship luck is strong and popularity with opposite gender is good. Relationship life is colorful, but if you take it lightly, it will cause trouble.

健康：健康狀況多，須注意提防脾胃不佳、腳腿浮腫、肝旺，注意橫禍及血光之災。

Health: There are many health conditions. You must pay attention to poor spleen and stomach, swollen legs and feet, and liver hyperactivity. Pay special attention to sudden and bloody disasters.

吉祥物 Auspicious Items：

1. 今年犯桃花、刑太歲、破太歲等煞星，在正月初一至正月十五期間，前往新加坡四馬路五路財神敬拜四面觀音，報名台灣玉宸齋制化桃花、刑太歲、破太歲法會，點太歲星燈、大日如來本命燈、觀音菩薩平安健康燈，燒化太歲金、冤親債主金、月老姻緣金可以獲得菩薩護祐。

   This year you are affected by Xing Tai Sui, Po Tai Sui and the romance star. It is advisable to go to the Bugis Fortune God at Bencoolen Street in Singapore, between the first and fifteenth day of the first lunar month, to worship the Four Side Guan Yin. Register for the Taiwan Yu Chen Zhai puja to resolve the negative influence. Light the Tai Sui, Buddha Vairocana and Guan Yin Wishing Lamps, and offer the Tai Sui, Karmic Creditors and Marriage incense papers for protection.

2. 隨身配戴桃柳檀木劍雷令福袋能斬妖除小人化煞辟邪，其壓煞功能是不管清明掃墓或是探病送喪、出差旅遊或見有普渡、車禍、病喪諸事等，皆不怕鬼魅纏身之擾。

   Wear a Protective Charm which can kill demons, get rid of villains and ward off evil spirits. It has the functions of suppressing evil spirits, no matter whether you are sweeping graves during the Qingming Festival, visiting the sick and sending off the dead, traveling on business, attending a general salvation, car accidents, illness and funerals, etc., you don't have to worry about being troubled by ghosts.

歲次庚申年生人46歲 (西元一九八〇年生)
People born in Geng Shen Year are 46 years old (Born in 1980)

財運：財運不佳，要注意文書契約的簽訂，小心漏稅及罰單而導致破財。

Wealth: Wealth luck is not good. Be careful when signing documents and contracts. Be careful of tax evasion and fines that may lead to financial loss.

事業：工作上困擾阻礙多，注意飛來橫禍，人際關係出現失和，會陷入危險的境地。

Career: There are many troubles and obstacles at work. Watch out for unexpected disasters. There will be discord in interpersonal relationships, and you will fall into a dangerous situation.

感情：感情有阻礙，已婚者要謹慎處理婚姻冷淡，小心第三者介入婚姻導致家庭失和。

Relationship: There are obstacles in relationships. Married people should be handle with caution the coldness of marriage. Be careful of third parties intervening in marriage and causing family discord.

健康：健康不佳，易引起脾胃不佳、胃食道逆流、哮喘病、神經痛、骨頭酸痛疾病。

Health: Poor health, which can easily cause diseases such as poor spleen and stomach, gastroesophageal reflux, asthma, neuralgia, bone pain, etc.

吉祥物 Auspicious Items：

1. 今年犯桃花、刑太歲、破太歲等煞星，在正月初一至正月十五期間，前往新加坡四馬路五路財神敬拜四面觀音，報名台灣玉宸齋制化桃花、刑太歲、破太歲法會，點太歲星燈、大日如來本命燈、觀音菩薩平安健康燈，燒化太歲金、冤親債主金、月老姻緣金可以獲得菩薩護祐。

   This year you are affected by Xing Tai Sui, Po Tai Sui and the romance star. It is advisable to go to the Bugis Fortune God at Bencoolen Street in Singapore, between the first and fifteenth day of the first lunar month, to worship the Four Side Guan Yin. Register for the Taiwan Yu Chen Zhai puja to resolve the negative influence. Light the Tai Sui, Buddha Vairocana and Guan Yin Wishing Lamps, and offer the Tai Sui, Karmic Creditors and Marriage incense papers for protection.

2. 臥室可放置琉璃三合生肖猴鼠龍或三合貴人盤，可招貴人、增強運勢、改變家運、招財進寶。

   You can place a set of liuli Zodiac Benefactors (Monkey, Rat and Dragon) or a Zodiac Benefactor Plate in the bedroom to attract noble people, enhance fortune, change family fortune, and attract wealth.

歲次戊申年生人58歲（西元一九六八年生）
People born in Wu Shen Year are 58 years old (Born in 1968)

財運：有小財進帳，小心錢財因糾紛而破財，行車注意安全以免傷身及破財。

Wealth: Small money will come in, but be careful of losing money due to disputes. Pay attention to driving safety to avoid injury and loss of money.

事業：工作起伏，推行新方案時缺乏執行力，提防橫禍官非之災，能得貴人資助。

Career: Work will be fluctuating, and you will lack execution when implementing new plans. Beware of disasters such as legal troubles, and you will get help from noble people.

感情：桃花運旺盛，需防感情傷害及桃色糾紛導致人財兩失，千萬不要放縱情慾。

Relationship: Romance luck is strong, but you need to prevent emotional hurt and romantic disputes that may lead to loss of both life and money. Don't indulge in lust.

健康：健康平平，宜注意心臟、血壓、頭部、眼睛、血液循環等方面的疾病。

Health: Health is average, but you should pay attention to diseases of the heart, blood pressure, head, eyes, and blood circulation.

吉祥物 Auspicious Items：

1. 今年犯桃花、刑太歲、破太歲等煞星，在正月初一至正月十五期間，前往新加坡四馬路五路財神敬拜四面觀音，報名台灣玉宸齋制化桃花、刑太歲、破太歲法會，點太歲星燈、大日如來本命燈、觀音菩薩平安健康燈，燒化太歲金、冤親債主金、月老姻緣金可以獲得菩薩護祐。

   This year you are affected by Xing Tai Sui, Po Tai Sui and the romance star. It is advisable to go to the Bugis Fortune God at Bencoolen Street in Singapore, between the first and fifteenth day of the first lunar month, to worship the Four Side Guan Yin. Register for the Taiwan Yu Chen Zhai puja to resolve the negative influence. Light the Tai Sui, Buddha Vairocana and Guan Yin Wishing Lamps, and offer the Tai Sui, Karmic Creditors and Marriage incense papers for protection.

2. 可以配戴三合水晶手鍊，可增強助旺身體健康、事業興旺，還可化解意外橫災。

   You can wear a Zodiac Benefactor Bracelet to enhance health, advance career and resolve unexpected disasters.

歲次丙申年生人70歲（西元一九五六年生）
People born in Bing Shen Year are 70 years old (Born in 1956)

財運：財運很好，適合投資房地產資訊及時尚產業，勿聽信流言及小道消息。

Wealth: Good Wealth luck, suitable for investment in real estate information and fashion industry. Do not listen to rumors and gossips.

事業：事業運很好，決策不要優柔寡斷，加強抗壓性，小心官非纏身，有貴人相助。

Career: Good career luck, don't be indecisive in decision-making, strengthen stress resistance, be careful of legal troubles, there are noble people to help.

感情：保持樂觀風格，生活充滿幽默感，避免多愁善感的情緒，凡事以和諧為優先。

Relationship: Maintain an optimistic style, life is full of humor, avoid sentimentality, and give priority to harmony in everything.

健康：健康尚可，宜注意肝膽疾病、脾胃不佳、風濕症，小心意外事故造成身體受傷。

Health: Your health is fair, but you should pay attention to liver and gallbladder diseases, poor spleen and stomach, rheumatism, and be careful of physical injuries caused by accidents.

吉祥物 Auspicious Items：

1. 今年犯桃花、刑太歲、破太歲等煞星，在正月初一至正月十五期間，前往新加坡四馬路五路財神敬拜四面觀音，報名台灣玉宸齋制化桃花、刑太歲、破太歲法會，點太歲星燈、大日如來本命燈、觀音菩薩平安健康燈，燒化太歲金、冤親債主金、月老姻緣金可以獲得菩薩護祐。

   This year you are affected by Xing Tai Sui, Po Tai Sui and the romance star. It is advisable to go to the Bugis Fortune God at Bencoolen Street in Singapore, between the first and fifteenth day of the first lunar month, to worship the Four Side Guan Yin. Register for the Taiwan Yu Chen Zhai puja to resolve the negative influence. Light the Tai Sui, Buddha Vairocana and Guan Yin Wishing Lamps, and offer the Tai Sui, Karmic Creditors and Marriage incense papers for protection.

2. 到四馬路五路財神點九品蓮花轉運燈，可獲得觀音護祐，讓身心安穩、災邪遠離、趨吉避凶、消災解厄。

   Go to the Bugis Fortune God to light the Lotus Fortune Lamp for blessings from Guan Yin to bring you peace of mind and body, keep away evil and disasters, and help you have good fortune.

◎ 肖雞人二〇二五年年運勢詳解

Forecast for the Year 2025 for people born in the year of the Rooster

（9、21、33、45、57、69歲）

肖雞之人二〇二五年運勢有三台、三合、將星、金匱、地解、飛符、五鬼、官符、破碎、的煞、年符、孤虛等星坐守。今年吉星代表升官仕進，事業上受到重用，財運可儲積財富，有貴人暗助，但是今年凶星眾多，浮沉不定，須防小人暗害，虛耗失財、疾病纏身、官非流血、喪服哭泣之災。**今年肖雞之人的總體運勢吉凶各半，宜至玉玄門制五鬼、官符以保平安，消災解厄。**

The battle between the lucky stars and ominous stars meant that people born in the Year of the Rooster will encounter promotion and accumulation of wealth but will also meet with misfortunes and obstacles in 2025. This year, you will be guarded by the lucky stars Santai, Sanhe, Jiangxing, Jinkui and Dijie but will also be attacked by ominous stars Feifu, Wugui, Guanfu, Posui, Desha, Nianfu and Guxu. The lucky stars represent advancement and being valued in your career. You can accumulate wealth with the help of nobles. However, there are many ominous stars this year, and your fortune will be unpredictable. You must be careful of hidden harm from villains, loss of wealth, illness, official disputes, and mourning. This year the overall fortune of people born in the Year of the Rooster is half good and half bad. It is advisable to go to Yu Xuan Men to appease Wugui (Five Ghosts) and Guanfu (Official Talisman) to ensure safety and eliminate disasters.

今年吉星代表事業上能獲得更多的機會，能展現出掌控力、決斷力，特別需要展現出管理的能力，非常利於文職晉升，財運方面有財帛星相助，可以激發出理財、管理的潛質，讓財富有多方面的進帳，學生考運尚可，感情婚姻不順利，心境常有孤獨空虛之感，精神壓力倍增，凶星方面特別多官司訴訟的困擾，須防小人暗害，合約糾紛，破財失業，流血意外的危機，健康上要注意腫瘤、毒品、惡疾纏身，今年雖有地解能解厄化凶，化險爲夷，卻難以化凶為吉。

This year, the lucky stars represent more opportunities in career, and you can show control and decisiveness, especially management ability, which is very conducive to promotion in civil service. In terms of wealth, there is help from the wealth star, which can stimulate the potential of financial management, so that wealth can be earned in many aspects. Students' examination luck is fair. However, relationship and marriage are not smooth. You often feel lonely and empty, and your mental pressure is doubled. In terms of ominous stars, there are many troubles in lawsuits. You must guard against the danger of villains, contract disputes, financial loss and unemployment, and bloody accidents. On health conditions, you must pay attention to tumors, drugs, and serious diseases. Although there is a Dijie star this year that can resolve disasters and turn dangers into safety, it is difficult to turn disasters into good fortune.

今年運勢吉凶相伴，心情起伏不定，建議低潮時多找些朋友傾訴，勿鑽牛角尖，奮鬥時儘量展現自己的能力，提升工作及學習效率，可以補財庫及催旺貴人運，勿貪不義之財，家宅、辦公室不可隨意興工動土，避免因精神壓力過大而走向極端，多注意突發疾病及血光橫禍，有病立即就醫，絕對不可以碰觸毒品，女性需防產厄或婦科病。

This year's fortune will be mixed with good and bad, and your mood will be unstable. It is recommended that you find more friends to talk to when you are down, and do not get stuck in a dead end. When struggling, try your best to show your abilities and improve your work and study efficiency. This can replenish your treasury and boost your fortune. Do not be greedy for ill-gotten gains. Do not start construction in your home or office at will. Avoid going to extremes due to excessive mental stress. Pay more attention to sudden illnesses and bloody disasters. See a doctor immediately if you are sick. Never touch drugs. Women need to prevent childbirth or gynecological diseases.

財運 Wealth	★★★
事業 Career	★★★
感情 Relationship	★
健康 Health	★★
吉祥顏色 Lucky Color	白色 White Color
吉祥數字Lucky Number	5786

歲次丁酉年生人9歲（西元二〇一七年生）
People born in Ding You Year are 9 years old (Born in 2017)

財運：小孩不論財運，可以從小培養適當的興趣。

Wealth: Regardless of wealth luck, children can develop appropriate interests from an early age.

事業：學業有進步，考運尚可，在學校常發生是非糾紛，容易花太多時間在電玩及上網。

Career: Academic progress is good, examination luck is fair, but disputes often occur at school, and they tend to spend too much time on video games and the Internet.

感情：新的課業活動充滿新鮮感，人際關係容易發生問題，常觸犯班規，家長要多關心瞭解。

Relationship: New academic activities are full of freshness, interpersonal relationships are prone to problems, and they often violate class rules. Parents should pay more attention to them.

健康：健康平平，易有耳鼻喉病或流行性感冒，多運動強身，維持健康的飲食習慣。

Health: Health is average, prone to ear, nose and throat diseases or influenza, and should exercise more to keep fit and maintain healthy eating habits.

吉祥物 Auspicious Items：

1. 今年犯五鬼、官符煞星，在正月初一至正月十五期間，前往四馬路五路財神敬拜四面觀音，報名台灣玉宸齋制化五鬼、官符法會，點不動明王本命燈、觀音菩薩平安健康燈、文昌智慧光明燈，燒化冤親債主金、華陀除疾金、文昌智慧金，可以獲得眾神護祐讓平安健康，學業進步。

   This year, with the presence of Sifu ominous star, it is advisable to head down to Bugis Fortune God between the first and fifteenth day of the first lunar month, to pray to the Four Side Guan Yin. Participate in the ritual ceremony, light the Zodiac Guardian, Health and Academic wishing lamps and burn the Karmic Creditors, Huatuo and Academic incense papers for good health and progress in studies.

2. 沖涼時使用文昌智慧沐浴露，可增強讀書運勢，祭拜文昌帝君以求開智慧及增強考試運。

   Put an Academic Crystal Tree and a bottle of Holy Water on the study desk to make the child more keen to study and acquire quick thinking, so as to promote the mind to be smart and achieve academic excellance.

歲次乙酉年生人21歲 (西元二〇〇五年生)
People born in Yi You Year are 21 years old (Born in 2005)

財運：財運尚可，需謹慎理財，易受偷竊損財，小心看管財物。

Wealth: Wealth luck is fair, but you need to be careful with your finances. You may suffer from theft and loss of belongings, so be careful with your property.

事業：工作上難有貴人相助，容易誤踩長官上司的地雷，學生考運平平，健康會影響課業學習。

Career: It is difficult to get help from noble people at work, and it is easy to step on the landmines of superiors. Students have average examination luck, and health will affect their studies.

感情：感情運勢不佳，心境常有孤獨空虛，不要被虛假的外表所欺騙。

Relationship: Relationship luck is not good, and you often feel lonely and empty. Don't be deceived by false appearances.

健康：健康會有小毛病，宜注意便秘、風濕酸痛、眼睛結膜炎、乾眼症等方面問題。

Health: There will be minor health problems, and you should pay attention to problems such as constipation, rheumatism, conjunctivitis, and dry eyes.

吉祥物 Auspicious Items：

1. 今年犯五鬼、官符煞星，在正月初一至正月十五期間，前往四馬路五路財神敬拜四面觀音，報名台灣玉宸齋制化五鬼、官符法會，點不動明王本命燈、觀音菩薩平安健康燈、文昌智慧光明燈，燒化冤親債主金、華陀除疾金、驅制小人金，可以獲得眾神護祐讓平安健康，減少小人是非。

   This year, to contain the negative influences of Wugui and Guanfu ominous stars, head down to the Bugis Fortune God in Singapore, between the first and fifteenth day of the first lunar month, to pray to the Four Side Guan Yin. Register for the Taiwan Yu Chen Zhai puja for blessings. Light the Bodhisattva Acala, Guan Yin and Wenchang Wishing Lamps and offer the Karmic Creditors, Hua Tuo and Prevent Villains incense papers for safety and health and reduce villains and disputes.

2. 書桌上可擺放綠水晶文昌開運樹，來助旺文昌氣運，工作者可配戴桃柳檀木劍雷令福袋，減少事業及財運上遇小人是非之效。

   You can display an Academic Crystal Tree on the desk to help boost Wenchang luck. Working people can carry a Protective Charm to reduce the chances of encountering villains and troubles in career and wealth.

歲次癸酉年生人33歲（西元一九九三年生）
People born in Gui You Year are 33 years old (Born in 1993)

財運：正財運不錯，有意外之錢財，不要為人背書借貸造成負債。

Wealth: Good wealth luck, there will be unexpected money. Don't endorse others to borrow money and cause debt.

事業：工作在穩定中繼續發展，能夠一展長才，仍有危機潛伏，小心小人記恨暗害。

Career: Work continues to develop in a stable manner. You can show your talents, but there are still potential crises. Be careful of villains who hold grudges and secretly harm you.

感情：愛情機運尚可，有邂逅異性的良機，太過急進強求反而失去機會。

Relationship: Relationship luck is fair. There is a good opportunity to meet the opposite gender, but being too aggressive and forceful will lose the opportunity.

健康：健康平平，須注意提防肝火虛旺、眼睛酸痛、筋骨酸痛，注意行車安全。

Health: Health is average. You need to be careful to prevent liver fire, eye pain, muscle and bone pain, and pay attention to driving safety.

吉祥物 Auspicious Items：

1. 今年犯五鬼、官符煞星，在正月初一至正月十五期間，前往四馬路五路財神敬拜四面觀音，報名台灣玉宸齋制化五鬼、官符法會，點不動明王本命燈、觀音菩薩平安健康燈、武財神事業財利燈，燒化冤親債主金、貴人金、驅制小人金，可以獲得眾神護祐讓平安健康，減少小人是非。

   This year, to contain the negative influences of Wugui and Guanfu ominous stars, head down to the Bugis Fortune God in Singapore, between the first and fifteenth day of the first lunar month, to pray to the Four Side Guan Yin. Register for the Taiwan Yu Chen Zhai puja for blessings. Light the Bodhisattva Acala, Guan Yin and Wealth Wishing Lamps and offer the Karmic Creditors, Benefactor and Prevent Villains incense papers for safety and health and reduce villains and disputes.

2. 在家中及辦公室的吉祥方位擺放靈動力強大的黃水晶招財樹及龍神聖水，可求事業順遂，升官發達、招財進寶。

   Place a Citrine Tree and a bottle of powerful Holy Water in auspicious locations at home and in the office for success and promotion in your career, and enhance wealth.

歲次辛酉年生人45歲 (西元一九八一年生)
People born in Xin You Year are 45 years old (Born in 1981)

財運：財運不佳，易有破財之事，要仔細分析消息來源以免誤判或被陷害。

Wealth: Wealth luck is not good, and it is easy to lose money. Analyze carefully the source of information to avoid misjudgment or being framed.

事業：同事合夥之間多是非小人，注意文書契約的簽訂以免招來官符及爭訟。

Career: There are many villains among colleagues and partners. Pay attention to the signing of documents and contracts to avoid lawsuits and disputes.

感情：工作忙碌易引發另一半的埋怨或是感情變得疏遠，建議要挪出時間多陪伴家人，未婚者桃花缺缺。

Relationship: Being busy at work can easily lead to complaints from your partner or alienation in your relationship. It is recommended to spend more time with your family. For unmarried people, romance is lacking.

健康：今年健康方面有點狀況，男性宜注意關節障礙、腸胃不佳等問題，女性需注意經水不調、心血虧虛、腰酸膝軟等症狀。

Health: There are some problems in health this year. Men should pay attention to joint disorders, poor gastrointestinal problems, etc. Women should pay attention to symptoms such as irregular menstruation, deficiency of heart blood, back pain and weak knees.

吉祥物 Auspicious Items：

1. 今年犯五鬼、官符煞星，在正月初一至正月十五期間，前往四馬路五路財神敬拜四面觀音，報名台灣玉宸齋制化五鬼、官符法會，點不動明王本命燈、觀音菩薩平安健康燈、武財神事業財利燈，燒化冤親債主金、貴人金、驅制小人金，可以獲得眾神護祐讓平安健康，減少小人是非。

   This year, to contain the negative influences of Wugui and Guanfu ominous stars, head down to the Bugis Fortune God in Singapore, between the first and fifteenth day of the first lunar month, to pray to the Four Side Guan Yin. Register for the Taiwan Yu Chen Zhai puja for blessings. Light the Bodhisattva Acala, Guan Yin and Wealth Wishing Lamps and offer the Karmic Creditors, Benefactor and Prevent Villains incense papers for safety and health, and reduce villains and disputes.

2. 可以在家中擺放琉璃三合生肖蛇牛雞，增加招貴人驅小人、強旺運勢、改變家運、招財進寶的無形靈動力。

   You can place a set of liuli Zodiac Benefactors (Snake, Ox and Rooster) at home to attract nobles and get rid of villains, strengthen your fortune, change your family fortune, and attract wealth with their invisible spiritual power.

歲次己酉年生人57歲（西元一九六九年生）
People born in Ji Jou Year are 57 years old (Born in 1969)

財運：財運不佳，投資運不佳，衝動投資小心大破財。

Wealth: Bad wealth and investment luck, be careful of big losses if you make impulsive investments.

事業：文件要仔細看，以免因為文書錯誤而受罰，嚴重時會惹上官司糾紛或行事罰款。

Career: Read documents carefully to avoid being punished for clerical errors. In serious cases, you may get into lawsuits or fines.

感情：未婚者桃花不佳，已婚者感情較多事端，處理不好甚至有破裂的現象。

Relationship: Unmarried people have bad luck with relationship, and married people have more problems with their relationship. If not handled properly, there may even be a breakup.

健康：今年健康狀況不佳，宜注意口腔、腸胃病，要預防惡疾腫瘤突發。

Health: This year's health is not good. Pay attention to oral and gastrointestinal diseases, and prevent the sudden onset of malignant diseases and tumors.

吉祥物 Auspicious Items：

1. 今年犯五鬼、官符煞星，在正月初一至正月十五期間，前往四馬路五路財神敬拜四面觀音，報名台灣玉宸齋制化五鬼、官符法會，點不動明王本命燈、觀音菩薩平安健康燈、武財神事業財利燈，燒化冤親債主金、貴人金、驅制小人金，可以獲得眾神護祐讓平安健康，減少小人是非。

   This year, to contain the negative influences of Wugui and Guanfu ominous stars, head down to the Bugis Fortune God in Singapore, between the first and fifteenth day of the first lunar month, to pray to the Four Side Guan Yin. Register for the Taiwan Yu Chen Zhai puja for blessings. Light the Bodhisattva Acala, Guan Yin and Wealth Wishing Lamps and offer the Karmic Creditors, Benefactor and Prevent Villains incense papers for safety and health, and reduce villains and disputes.

2. 辦公室擺琉璃龍印寶璽可掌權柄，壓制小人，避免因蓋章、擔保、契合約不合，引起無謂財損是非。

   Placing a liuli Dragon Seal in your office can help you gain power, suppress villains, and avoid unnecessary financial losses and disputes caused by inconsistent seals, guarantees, and contracts.

歲次丁酉年生人69歲（西元一九五七年生）
People born in Ding You Year are 69 years old (Born in 1957)

財運： 財運不錯，易有偷竊貪瀆的事件纏身要小心提防。

Wealth: Good wealth luck, but you may be involved in theft and corruption, so be careful.

事業： 事業能小幅成長，要力求穩健成長，注意員工或下屬的管理問題。

Career: Your career can grow slightly, but you should strive for steady growth and pay attention to the management of employees or subordinates.

感情： 家中的是非瑣事較多，不要用情緒來處理事情，小心意外血光之災。

Relationship: There are many trivial issues at home, so don't use emotions to handle matters, and be careful of unexpected bloody disasters.

健康： 健康尚可，宜注意支氣管、扁桃腺炎、攝護腺之症，要小心突發性惡疾纏身。

Health: Your health is fair, but you should pay attention to bronchitis, tonsillitis, and prostate diseases, and be careful of sudden serious diseases.

吉祥物 Auspicious Items：

1. 今年犯五鬼、官符煞星，在正月初一至正月十五期間，前往四馬路五路財神敬拜四面觀音，報名台灣玉宸齋制化五鬼、官符法會，點不動明王本命燈、觀音菩薩平安健康燈、武財神事業財利燈，燒化冤親債主金、貴人金、驅制小人金，可以獲得眾神護祐讓平安健康，減少小人是非。

   This year, to contain the negative influences of Wugui and Guanfu ominous stars, head down to the Bugis Fortune God in Singapore, between the first and fifteenth day of the first lunar month, to pray to the Four Side Guan Yin. Register for the Taiwan Yu Chen Zhai puja for blessings. Light the Bodhisattva Acala, Guan Yin and Wealth Wishing Lamps and offer the Karmic Creditors, Benefactor and Prevent Villains incense papers for safety and health, and reduce villains and disputes.

2. 隨身配戴九頭靈獅項鍊，桌上擺琉璃獅咬劍文鎮，具有化解口舌是非並可減輕五鬼及官符的沖煞。

   Wear a 9-headed Lion Necklace and place a Lion Head Charm on the table to resolve gossips and reduce the negative impact of the Wugui and Guanfu ominous stars.

◎ 肖狗人二〇二五年運勢詳解

Forecast for the Year 2025 for people born in the year of the Dog

（8、20、32、44、56、68歲）

肖狗之人二〇二五年運勢有歲枝德、月德、紅鸞、扳鞍、死符、小耗、飛刃、唐符。今年行運吉星可謂是福祿雙全，能減輕流年災煞使您救危濟弱，當環境變遷時利於向外發展，事業宜文宜武，感情紅鸞星動喜事將近，凶星要注意劫難災傷，小人病災，哭泣喪事。**今年肖狗之人的總體運勢不錯，能得到貴人提拔得到功名利祿，宜至玉玄門祭改死符及點光明燈禳解災病以保安康。**

In 2025, an auspicious year could be expected for people born in the Year of the Dog. The presence of auspicious stars Suizhide, Yuede, Hongluan and Banan can bring you both blessings and fortune, which can reduce the disasters of the year from ominous stars Sifu, Xiaohao, Feiren and Tangfu. When the environment changes from the current state of your life, it is beneficial to develop outward. Your career is suitable for both civil and military affairs. When the Hongluan star moves in your relationship, happy events are approaching. Pay attention to ominous stars bringing disasters, injuries, illnesses, villains, and funeral weeping. This year, the overall fortune of people born in the Year of the Dog is good. You can be promoted by nobles and gain fame and fortune. It is advisable to go to Yu Xuan Men to negate the eruption from Sifu (Death Doomed Talisman) and light the Wishing Lamp to ward off disasters and diseases.

今年有福德之星守命，所以會帶來一整年的福氣，功名仕途順利，在學業或事業上可獲得眷顧，，特別利於工作上向外發展，能適應環境變動，外派得利，要自己積極主動，更有機會上位，能得貴人扶持，工作文職武職皆宜，利於考試增強聲量，今年紅鸞星動主家有喜事臨門，未婚之人要把握良機。凶星代表爭鬥、官非、病災、横禍，行事多耗時間不聚財，賺錢沒有效益，口舌之爭導致人際關係出現問題，尤其要嚴防突來急症，嚴重時家中易有喪事降臨。

In 2025, the star of fortune guards your life, so it will bring you blessings for the whole year. Your career will be smooth, and you will be favored in your studies or career. It is especially beneficial for you to develop outward in your work, adapt to changes in the environment, and benefit from being sent abroad. You must be proactive to have a better chance of getting promoted and supported by nobles. You are suitable for both civil and military jobs, and it is beneficial to take examinations to enhance your reputation. This year, the approaching Hongluan star moves in, and there will be happy events in your family. Singles should seize the opportunity. The ominous stars represent fighting, legal disputes, illnesses, disasters, and misfortunes. You will spend a lot of time doing things but it does not accumulate wealth. You will not be able to make money effectively. Disputes will lead to problems in interpersonal relationships. You must be especially careful to prevent sudden emergency. In serious cases, there will be death in your family.

今年運勢多福壽，適合外出工作，建議外出時避免無謂的交際應酬，凡事以靜制動，審慎小心，要增強抗煞力，避免感染流行性疾病，勿入喪家及探病，以免為人擔煞，別去陰地以免沾惹上邪祟陰煞之物，還要注意行車安全及健康狀況，有病就立即就醫，不要小病拖成大病。

This is a good year for you to go out to work. It is recommended that you avoid unnecessary social activities when going out, be calm and cautious in everything, strengthen your ability to resist shocks, and avoid being infected with epidemic diseases. Do not enter funeral homes or visit the sick so as not to bring bad luck to yourself, and do not go to cemeteries to avoid getting in contact with evil spirits. Also, pay attention to driving safety and your health condition. If you are sick, seek medical attention immediately, and do not let a minor illness develop into a major one.

財運 Wealth	★★★
事業 Career	★★★★
感情 Relationship	★★★★
健康 Health	★★
吉祥顏色 Lucky Color	紅色 Red Color
吉祥數字Lucky Number	2059

歲次戊戌年生人8歲（西元二〇一八年生）
People born in Wu Xu Year are 8 years old (Born in 2018)

財運：父母會為小孩花費不少金錢，切莫養成小孩奢侈浪費的價值觀。

Wealth: Parents will spend a lot of money on their children, so don't let them develop extravagant and wasteful values.

事業：學習狀況持平，情緒起伏較大，要多聽聽學童的心聲，不要過度擔憂。

Career: The learning situation is average, but the mood fluctuates greatly. You should listen more to the students' voices and don't worry too much.

感情：小孩鬧脾氣是因為在學習環境中遭受挫折或是人際關係出現狀況的投射。

Relationship: Children's temper is caused by setbacks in the learning environment or the projection of interpersonal relationship situations.

健康：健康狀態不佳，宜注意頭部撞傷、眼睛感染、腸病毒之病症。

Health: The health condition is not good, so you should pay attention to head injuries, eye infections, and enterovirus diseases.

吉祥物 Auspicious Items：

1. 今年犯死符煞星，在正月初一至正月十五期間，前往四馬路五路財神敬拜四面觀音，參加制化死符法會，點阿彌陀佛本命燈、觀音菩薩平安健康燈、文昌智慧光明燈，燒化冤親債主金、華陀除疾金、文昌智慧金，可以獲得眾神護祐讓平安健康，學業進步。

   This year you will be assaulted by the evil star Sifu (Death Doomed Talisman). It is advisable to go to the Bugis Fortune God at Bencoolen Street in Singapore, between the first and fifteenth day of the first lunar month, to worship the Four Side Guan Yin. Register for the Taiwan Yu Chen Zhai puja for blessings. Light the Buddha Amitabha, Guan Yin and Wenchang Wishing Lamps, and offer the Karmic Creditors, Hua Tuo and Wenchang incense papers to seek protection and health, and enhance academic progress.

2. 書桌上擺綠水晶文昌開運樹及龍神聖水，可使學子讀書而思想敏捷，以促進頭腦精明學富五車之功。

   Placing an Academic Tree and a bottle of Holy Water on the desk can help students study and think quickly, thereby promoting a sharp mind and becoming knowledgeable.

歲次丙戌年生人20歲（西元二〇〇六年生）
People born in Bing Xu Year are 20 years old (Born in 2006)

財運：財運尚可，上半年財運較佳，下半年容易損耗破財。

Wealth: Fair, better in the first half of the year, easy to lose money in the second half.

事業：考運很好，特別利於工作上向外發展，能適應環境變動。

Career: Good luck in examinations, especially good for career development, able to adapt to changes in the environment.

感情：愛情運勢很旺，三分鐘熱度是感情最大的障礙，免得失去時後悔莫及。

Relationship: Relationship luck is very strong. Three minutes of passion is the biggest obstacle to a relationship; don't regret it when you lose it.

健康：健康狀況一般，宜注意膀胱、尿道結石、便秘等病症，孕婦要注意安胎。

Health: Health is average, but you should pay attention to bladder, urethral stones, constipation and other diseases. Pregnant women should pay attention to fetal protection.

吉祥物 Auspicious Items：

1. 今年犯死符煞星，在正月初一至正月十五期間，前往四馬路五路財神敬拜四面觀音，參加制化死符法會，點阿彌陀佛本命燈、觀音菩薩平安健康燈、文昌智慧光明燈，燒化冤親債主金、華陀除疾金、文昌智慧金，可以獲得眾神護祐讓平安健康，學業進步。

   This year you will be assaulted by the evil star Sifu. It is advisable to go to the Bugis Fortune God at Bencoolen Street in Singapore, between the first and fifteenth day of the first lunar month, to worship the Four Side Guan Yin. Register for the Taiwan Yu Chen Zhai puja for blessings. Light the Buddha Amitabha, Guan Yin and Wenchang Wishing Lamps, and offer the Karmic Creditors, Hua Tuo and Wenchang incense papers to seek protection and health, and enhance academic progress.

2. 可配帶魁星踢斗隨身牌及魁星勝利平安符來助旺文昌氣運，助使學生讀書專心、頭腦敏捷、讓考運亨通、金榜題名。

   Wearing the Kui Xing Ta Dou and the Kui Xing Victory Amulet can help students boost their Wenchang luck, concentrate on their studies, be quick-witted, and have good luck in examinations and achieve academic excellence.

歲次甲戌年生人32歲（西元一九九四年生）
People born in Jia Xu Year are 32 years old (Born in 1994)

財運：財運一般，行事多耗時間不聚財。

Wealth: Average wealth luck, things take a lot of time and do not bring in any wealth.

事業：外派工作得利，積極主動有機會上位，能得貴人扶持，工作文職武職皆宜。

Career: Outsourcing work will benefit you. Being active and proactive will give you a chance to get promoted. You will get support from nobles, and you are suitable for both civil and military jobs.

感情：今年紅鸞星動主家有喜事臨門，未婚之人要把握良機。

Relationship: The romance star is moving this year, which means there will be happy events in your family. Unmarried people should seize the opportunity.

健康：今年健康不錯，宜注意腎臟結石、流行病毒，孕婦要小心安胎的問題。

Health: Good health this year, but you should pay attention to kidney stones and epidemic viruses, and pregnant women should be careful about the problem of keeping the fetus.

吉祥物 Auspicious Items：

1. 今年犯死符煞星，在正月初一至正月十五期間，前往四馬路五路財神敬拜四面觀音，參加制化死符法會，點阿彌陀佛本命燈、觀音菩薩平安健康燈、武財神事業財利燈，燒化冤親債主金、華陀除疾金、本命財庫補運錢，來開運消災解厄、趨吉避凶、平安健康。

   This year you will be assaulted by the evil star Sifu. It is advisable to go to the Bugis Fortune God at Bencoolen Street in Singapore, between the first and fifteenth day of the first lunar month, to worship the Four Side Guan Yin. Register for the Taiwan Yu Chen Zhai puja for blessings. Light the Buddha Amitabha, Guan Yin and Wealth Wishing Lamps, and offer the Karmic Creditors, Hua Tuo and Zodiac Benefactor incense papers to eliminate disasters and have good luck, protection and health.

2. 可以在家中擺放琉璃三合生肖虎馬狗，增加招貴人驅小人、強旺運勢、改變家運、招財進寶的無形靈動力。

   You can place a set of liuli Zodiac Benefactors (Tiger, Horse and Dog) at home to attract nobles and get rid of villains, strengthen your fortune, change your family fortune, and attract wealth with their invisible spiritual power.

歲次壬戌年生人44歲 (西元一九八二年生)
People born in Ren Xu Year are 44 years old (Born in 1982)

財運：財運不穩定，無故破財，橫財切勿強求，以免人財兩失。

Wealth: Wealth luck is unstable, you will lose money for no reason. Don't force yourself to make unexpected fortune, so as not to lose both money and life.

事業：事業遇上麻煩阻礙多，績效易退難進，職場暗潮洶湧，不要掉以輕心。

Career: There are many troubles and obstacles in your career. Performance is easy to decline but difficult to advance. The workplace is turbulent, don't take it lightly.

感情：桃花運旺盛，不要太放縱情慾，未婚之人調整自己的愛情觀，姻緣自然會浮出水面。

Relationship: You have a strong romance luck, don't indulge in lust too much. Unmarried people should adjust their relationship view, and marriage will naturally surface.

健康：今年健康問題多，宜注意腫瘤、花柳病、脾胃不佳、肝旺及濕熱等症。

Health: There are many health problems this year. You should pay attention to tumors, syphilis, poor spleen and stomach, liver hyperactivity and damp heat.

吉祥物 Auspicious Items：

1. 今年犯死符煞星，在正月初一至正月十五期間，前往四馬路五路財神敬拜四面觀音，參加制化死符法會，點阿彌陀佛本命燈、觀音菩薩平安健康燈、武財神事業財利燈，燒化冤親債主金、華陀除疾金、本命財庫補運錢，來開運消災解厄、趨吉避凶、平安健康。

   This year you will be assaulted by the evil star Sifu. It is advisable to go to the Bugis Fortune God at Bencoolen Street in Singapore, between the first and fifteenth day of the first lunar month, to worship the Four Side Guan Yin. Register for the Taiwan Yu Chen Zhai puja for blessings. Light the Buddha Amitabha, Guan Yin and Wealth Wishing Lamps, and offer the Karmic Creditors, Hua Tuo and Zodiac Benefactor incense papers to eliminate disasters and have good luck, protection and health.

2. 配戴朱砂項鍊或三合水晶手鍊，家中可擺放一尊琉金四面觀音，可以助旺家運平安、家和萬事興，還可化解意外橫災及小人暗害。

   Wearing a cinnabar necklace or a zodiac benefactor bracelet and placing a Four Side Guan Yin statue at home can help bring good fortune, peace and prosperity to the family, and can also resolve unexpected disasters and harm from villains.

歲次庚戌年生人56歲（西元一九七〇年生）
People born in Geng Xu Year are 56 years old (Born in 1970)

財運：財運不佳，量入為出以免入不敷出，小心意外破財。

Wealth: Wealth luck is not good, spend within your means to avoid spending more than you earn, and be careful of unexpected financial losses.

事業：工作上是非小人多，職場上明爭暗鬥嚴重，利於向外發展。

Career: There are many villains at work, and the workplace is full of open and secret struggles. It is beneficial to develop outward.

感情：桃花中暗藏爛桃花，已婚要謹言慎行，盡量不要出入是非場所及聲色場所。

Relationship: There is a hidden bad romance among your relationships. Married people should be careful in words and deeds, and try not to go to places of gossip and entertainment.

健康：健康不佳，宜注意胃下垂、氣管及肺線炎，勿入喪家，勿食喪家食物。

Health: Poor health, you should pay attention to gastroptosis, trachea and pneumonia. Do not enter funeral home, and do not eat funeral food.

吉祥物 Auspicious Items：

1. 今年犯死符煞星，在正月初一至正月十五期間，前往四馬路五路財神敬拜四面觀音，參加制化死符法會，點阿彌陀佛本命燈、觀音菩薩平安健康燈、武財神事業財利燈，燒化冤親債主金、華陀除疾金、貴人金，來開運消災解厄、趨吉避凶、平安健康。

   This year you will be assaulted by the ominous star Sifu. It is advisable to go to the Bugis Fortune God at Bencoolen Street in Singapore, between the first and fifteenth day of the first lunar month, to worship the Four Side Guan Yin. Register for the Taiwan Yu Chen Zhai puja for blessings. Light the Buddha Amitabha, Guan Yin and Wealth Wishing Lamps, and offer the Karmic Creditors, Hua Tuo and Benefactor incense papers to eliminate disasters and have good luck, protection and health.

2. 隨身攜帶五行水晶能量瓶，讓您產生磁場共振效應，直接吸收良好的能量來源，達到五行相生，開運旺財的目標。

   Carrying an Energy Water Bottle with you will generate a magnetic field resonance effect, directly absorbing good energy sources, and achieving the goal of mutual generation of the Five Elements, and bringing you good luck and wealth.

歲次戊戌年生人68歲 (西元一九五八年生)
People born in Wu Xu Year are 68 years old (Born in 1958)

財運：財運不佳，放縱感情或酒色容易導致破財，甚至惹上官司、刑罰。

Wealth: Bad wealth luck. Indulgence in passion or alcohol can easily lead to financial ruin, or even lead to lawsuits and penalties.

事業：今年要以靜制動，等待出擊良機，不要固執主觀。

Career: This year, you should be calm and wait for the right opportunity to strike. Don't be stubborn.

感情：夫妻相處多摩擦，為子女教育爭吵在所難免，彼此應該多體諒。

Relationship: There will be a lot of friction between husband and wife. It is inevitable to quarrel over the education of children. You should be more considerate of each other.

健康：健康不佳，宜注意腦神經、眼壓過高、心血管方面的疾病。

Health: Poor health. Pay attention to diseases of the brain nerves, high intraocular pressure, and cardiovascular diseases.

吉祥物 Auspicious Items：

1. 今年犯死符煞星，在正月初一至正月十五期間，前往四馬路五路財神敬拜四面觀音，參加制化死符法會，點阿彌陀佛本命燈、觀音菩薩平安健康燈、藥師佛消災解厄燈，燒化冤親債主金、接迎貴人金、華陀除疾金來消災解厄、平安健康、財源廣進。

   This year you will be assaulted by the evil star Sifu. It is advisable to go to the Bugis Fortune God at Bencoolen Street in Singapore, between the first and fifteenth day of the first lunar month, to worship the Four Side Guan Yin. Register for the Taiwan Yu Chen Zhai puja for blessings. Light the Buddha Amitabha, Guan Yin and Wealth Wishing Lamps, and offer the Karmic Creditors, Hua Tuo and Benefactor incense papers to eliminate disasters and have good luck, protection and health.

2. 家中放置琉金四面觀音或配戴平安健康琉璃吊飾，可以招貴人防小人，並可以減輕死符的沖煞，保佑全年健康平安。

   Placing a Four Face Guan Yin statute at home or wearing a Health Pendant can attract noble people and prevent villains, and also reduce the impact of Sifu, blessing you with health and safety throughout the year.

◎ 肖豬人二〇二五年運勢詳解

Forecast for the Year 2025 for people born in the year of the Pig

（7、19、31、43、55、67、79歲）

肖豬之人二〇二五年運勢有國印、驛馬、歲破、大耗、月空、闌干、披頭等星入宮。今年正沖太歲，運程反覆，煩惱是非多，工作上能得授權，環境易有異動改變，適合奔波遠行，須防禍事阻礙，小人暗中破壞，易有破財危機，家運失和，要特別留意長輩的健康狀態。**肖豬之人今年總體運勢不佳，雖然運勢反覆，工作還是有所進展，建議至玉玄門拜太歲星君及點光明燈自可消災解厄、趨吉避凶。**

The luck of people born in the Year of the Pig takes a nosedive this year with ominous stars Sui Po, Da Hao, Yue Kong, Lu Gan, and Pi Tou in their fortune. In 2025, they will be in conflict with Tai Sui, so their fortunes will fluctuate, and they will have many troubles and disputes. With auspicious stars Guoyin and Ji Ma, they will be authorized at work, and their environment will change easily. It is suitable for traveling far away, but they must be careful of disasters and obstacles, and villains will secretly sabotage them. They may suffer financial crises and family discord, and they should pay special attention to the health of their elders. People born in the Year of the Pig will have an unfavourable overall fortune this year. Although their fortunes fluctuate, they will still make progress at work. It is recommended that they go to Yu Xuan Men to worship Tai Sui Xing Jun and light a Wishing Lamp to eliminate disasters and avoid misfortunes.

今年歲破、大耗等煞星入宮，代表煩惱是非多，運勢反反覆覆，事業上易產生異動變化，較為奔波勞碌，越動越有機會，利於外務及外勤人員，也利於遠鄉發展，財運易有大破財的現象，小心投資誤判，負債纏身，今年壓力持續加大，容易影響您的身心健康、人際關係、工作品質，因為旅遊運不錯，可以藉由旅遊調劑一下生活的壓力，披頭主孝服之事，要特別留意父母長輩的健康狀況，今年煞忌星多不利婚嫁。

This year, evil stars such as Sui Po and Da Hao enter your fate, which means there will be many troubles and disputes, and your fortune will be

subject to fluctuations. There will be changes in your career, and you will be busy and hard-working. The more you move, the more opportunities you will have. It is good for foreign affairs and field personnel, and also for development in remote areas. You may suffer a great loss of wealth. Be careful of investment misjudgments and debts. The pressure will continue to increase this year, which may easily affect your physical and mental health, interpersonal relationship, and work quality. Because your travel fortune is good, you can use travel to relieve the pressure of life. Pi Tou indicates mourning, so you should pay special attention to the health of your parents and elders. This year, the evil stars are not favorable for marriage.

今年雖然運勢多阻礙，對自己的言行或外界事務要格外小心仔細，可以避免不利的事情發生，建議沉潛備戰，多累積生存技能，面對困局時要懂得靈活變通，絕不意氣用事，適當的抒解釋放壓力，避免精神疾病纏身，交友要謹慎，識人不明傷害最大，夫妻要互相體諒包容以防半途無緣，家中長輩如有不適，請立即就醫，以免造成不可挽回的遺憾。

Although there are many obstacles in your fortune this year, be extra careful about your words and deeds or external affairs to avoid adverse events. It is recommended that you stay low and prepare for battle. Accumulate more survival skills and be flexible when facing difficulties. Never act on impulse, release stress appropriately, and avoid mental illness. Be cautious in making friends as knowing the wrong person can cause the greatest harm. Couples should be considerate and tolerant of each other to avoid being separated halfway. If the elders in your family are unwell, please seek medical attention immediately to avoid irreparable regrets.

財運 Wealth	★
事業 Career	★★
感情 Relationship	★★
健康 Health	★
吉祥顏色 Lucky Color	黑色 Black Color
吉祥數字Lucky Number	9158

歲次己亥年生人7歲（西元二〇一九年生）
People born in Ji Hai Year are 7 years old (Born in 2019)

財運：小孩不論財運，父母容易因孩子生病或意外災厄而破財。

Wealth: Regardless of the children's wealth luck, parents are likely to spend money due to the children's illness or accidental disaster.

事業：學業會有學習障礙，要耐心的協助小孩克服難關，享受學習的樂趣。

Career: There will be learning difficulties in school, so you should patiently help your children overcome difficulties and enjoy the fun of learning.

感情：多陪伴孩子及多參與親子互動可收到良好成效。

Relationship: Spending more time with your children and participating in parent-child interactions will achieve good results.

健康：健康運勢不佳，宜注意外傷、胃病，平時在飲食及生活習慣要特別注意。

Health: Health is not good, pay attention to external injuries and stomach problems, and pay special attention to diet and living habits.

吉祥物 Auspicious Items：

1. 今年犯歲破，宜在正月初一至正月十五期間，可至四馬路五路財神來敬拜四面觀音、太歲星君，供奉太歲金、文昌智慧金，點太歲星燈、阿彌陀佛本命燈、文昌智慧燈禳解歲破，還來開運消災解厄、趨吉避凶、開啟智慧，學業精進、平安健康。

   Due to the clash with Tai Sui this year, it is advisable to go to the Bugis Fortune God at Bencoolen Street in Singapore, between the first and fifteenth day of the first lunar month, to worship the Four Side Guan Yin. Light the Tai Sui, Wenchang and Buddha Amitabha Wishing Lamps, and offer the Tai Sui and Wenchang incense papers to ward off disasters, bring good luck, enhance wisdom, progress in studies, and have safety and health.

2. 隨身攜帶魁星踢斗隨身牌，使用文昌智慧沐浴露來沐浴，可助旺文昌氣運，使學業精進進步。

   Carry a Kui Xing Tao Dou Amulet with you and use Wenchang Body Wash to bathe can help boost your Wenchang luck and make academic progress.

歲次丁亥年生人19歲(西元二〇〇七年生)
People born in Ding Hai Year are 19 years old (Born in 2007)

財運：財運不錯，打工賺錢還算順利，有錢的話先存起來別亂花。

Wealth: Good wealth luck, making money from part-time jobs is quite smooth. If you have money, save it first and don't spend it carelessly.

事業：學業有進步，考運不錯，工作之人能夠得到不錯的學習經驗。

Career: Academic progress, good examination luck, working people can get good learning experience.

感情：感情生活平穩，可以給對方一些驚喜，更能使感情增溫。

Relationship: Love life is stable. You can give the other party some surprises, and it can also warm up the relationship.

健康：健康很好，宜注意眼睛、肝旺、濕氣、陰虧等疾病，小心意外的血光之災。

Health: Health is very good. You should pay attention to diseases such as eyes, liver, dampness, and yin deficiency, and be careful of unexpected blood disasters.

吉祥物 Auspicious Items：

1. 今年犯歲破，宜在正月初一至正月十五期間，可至四馬路五路財神來敬拜四面觀音、太歲星君，供奉太歲金、文昌智慧金、貴人金，點太歲星燈、阿彌陀佛本命燈、文昌智慧燈禳解歲破，還來開運消災解厄、趨吉避凶、開啟智慧，學業精進、平安健康。

   Due to the clash with Tai Sui this year, it is advisable to go to the Bugis Fortune God at Bencoolen Street in Singapore, between the first and fifteenth day of the first lunar month, to worship the Four Side Guan Yin. Light the Tai Sui, Buddha Amitabha and Wenchang Wishing Lamps, and offer the Tai Sui, Wenchang and Benefactor incense papers to ward off disasters, bring good luck, enhance wisdom, progress in studies, and have safety and health.

2. 書桌上可擺放琉璃玉書麒麟或魁星踏斗可使學童思想敏捷，頭腦精明，學識精進。

   Place a liuli Qi Lin (Unicorn) or Kui Xing Ta Dou on the study desk can help students think quickly, have sharp mind, and improve their knowledge.

歲次乙亥年生人31歲（西元一九九五年生）
People born in Yi Hai Year are 31 years old (Born in 1995)

財運：今年財運不錯，小有進財，偏財運不佳，出外財運佳。

Wealth: This year's wealth luck is not bad, with some income. Incidental wealth luck is not good, but the wealth luck is good when you travel.

事業：事業上產生異動變化，較為奔波勞碌，要堅守崗位，切莫失去自信心。

Career: There will be changes in your career, and you will be busy. You must stick to your position and don't lose your confidence.

感情：愛情出現曙光或是轉機，好好把握時機，用心經營感情。

Relationship: There will be a glimmer of hope or a turnaround in relationship. Seize the opportunity and manage your relationship carefully.

健康：健康一般，應注意陰虧、糖尿病、濕氣之疾，少吃生冷食物以免病從口入。

Health: Health is average, but you should pay attention to diseases such as Yin deficiency, diabetes, and dampness, and eat less raw and cold food to avoid diseases from the mouth.

吉祥物 Auspicious Items：

1. 今年犯歲破，宜在正月初一至正月十五期間，可至四馬路五路財神來敬拜四面觀音、太歲星君，供奉太歲金、驅除小人金、貴人金，點太歲星燈、阿彌陀佛本命燈、武財神事業財利燈來消災解厄、平安健康、財源廣進。

   Due to the clash with Tai Sui this year, it is advisable to go to the Bugis Fortune God at Bencoolen Street in Singapore, between the first and fifteenth day of the first lunar month, to worship the Four Side Guan Yin. Light the Tai Sui, Buddha Amitabha and Wealth Wishing Lamps, and offer the Tai Sui, Prevent Villains and Benefactor incense papers to ward off disasters, have safety and health and bring good luck and wealth.

2. 臥室可放置琉璃三合生肖豬兔羊吉祥物，如此可招貴人、增強運勢、改變家運、招財進寶。

   You can place a set of liuli Zodiac Benefactors (Pig, Rabbit and Goat) in the bedroom. This can attract noble people, improve luck, change family fortune, and attract wealth.

歲次癸亥年生人43歲（西元一九八三年生）
People born in Gui Hai Year are 43 years old (Born in 1983)

財運：財運易有大破財的現象，小心投資誤判，負債纏身。

Wealth: Wealth luck has a phenomenon of great loss of money. Be careful of investment misjudgment leading to debt.

事業：越動越有機會，利於外務及外勤人員，也利於遠鄉發展。

Career: The more you move, the more opportunities you will have, conducive to foreign affairs and field personnel, and also good for development in remote areas.

感情：感情平平，所有的煩惱必須冷靜處理，今年不利婚嫁。

Relationship: Relationship is average. All troubles must be handled calmly. This year is not favorable for marriage.

健康：健康尚可，宜注意腸道、肺部或內耳不平衡，特別留意父母長輩的健康狀況。

Health: Health is fair. Pay attention to intestinal, lung or inner ear imbalances. Pay special attention to the health of parents and elders.

吉祥物 Auspicious Items：

1. 今年犯歲破，宜在正月初一至正月十五期間，可至四馬路五路財神來敬拜四面觀音、太歲星君，供奉太歲金、驅除小人金、貴人金，點太歲星燈、阿彌陀佛本命燈、武財神事業財利燈來消災解厄、平安健康、財源廣進。

   Due to the clash with Tai Sui this year, it is advisable to go to the Bugis Fortune God at Bencoolen Street in Singapore, between the first and fifteenth day of the first lunar month, to worship the Four Side Guan Yin. Light the Tai Sui, Buddha Amitabha and Wealth Wishing Lamps, and offer the Tai Sui, Prevent Villains and Benefactor incense papers to ward off disasters, have safety and health, and bring good luck and wealth.

2. 隨身配戴桃柳檀木劍雷令福袋或綠眼貔貅戒指能除小人化煞辟邪，可以獲得神明護祐讓身心安定。

   Wearing a Protective Charm or a Pixiu Ring can drive away villains and evil spirits, and can gain the protection of gods and bring peace of mind and body.

歲次辛亥年生人55歲（西元一九七一年生）
People born in Xin Hai Year are 55 years old (Born in 1971)

財運：財運不佳，投資失利，小心將錯就錯造成負債累累。

Wealth: Bad wealth luck, investment failure, be careful not to make mistakes and get into debt.

事業：運勢起伏反覆，工作上奔波勞碌到頭來卻總以徒勞無功收場。

Career: Ups and downs in fortune, hard work at work always ends in vain.

感情：婚姻感情多爭執口角，相爭無好話，尖銳的語言反而釀成無法收拾的局面。

Relationship: There are many arguments in marriage and relationship. No good words in arguments, sharp words will lead to an unmanageable situation.

健康：健康不佳，宜注意鼻塞、扁桃腺炎、攝護腺、氣管、肺癆、吐血等疾病。

Health: Poor health, pay attention to nasal congestion, tonsillitis, prostate, trachea, tuberculosis, vomiting blood and other diseases.

吉祥物 Auspicious Items：

1. 今年犯歲破，宜在正月初一至正月十五期間，可至四馬路五路財神來敬拜四面觀音、太歲星君，供奉太歲金、驅除小人金、貴人金，點太歲星燈、阿彌陀佛本命燈、武財神事業財利燈來消災解厄、平安健康、財源廣進。

   Due to the clash with Tai Sui this year, it is advisable to go to the Bugis Fortune God at Bencoolen Street in Singapore, between the first and fifteenth day of the first lunar month, to worship the Four Side Guan Yin. Light the Tai Sui, Buddha Amitabha and Wealth Wishing Lamps, and offer the Tai Sui, Prevent Villains and Benefactor incense papers to ward off disasters, have safety and health and bring good luck and wealth.

2. 可使用八卦平安淨身手工皂可驅除邪氣、鎮定安神、淨身除穢。

   You can use the Handmade Ba Gua Soap to drive away evil spirits, calm the mind, and cleanse the body.

歲次己亥年生人67歲（西元一九五九年生）
People born in Ji Hai Year are 67 years old (Born in 1959)

財運：財運不佳，有破財的現象，不要輕信小道消息盲目投資，以免血本無歸。

Wealth: Wealth luck is not good, there is a phenomenon of losing money. Do not believe in gossips and invest blindly, so as not to lose all your money.

事業：工作上阻礙重重，煩惱壓力很大，是非不斷，要忍耐不公平的對待。

Career: There are many obstacles in work, great troubles and pressure, constant disputes, and you must endure unfair treatment.

感情：愛情煩惱多，不要太嘮叨伴侶，否則家中是非不斷影響夫妻感情。

Relationship: Love brings many troubles. Do not nag your partner too much, otherwise the family disputes will continue to affect the relationship between husband and wife.

健康：健康運勢不佳，宜注意氣喘、支氣管炎、脾臟、腸胃等症狀，小心飛來橫禍。

Health: Health luck is not good. You should pay attention to asthma, bronchitis, spleen, stomach and other symptoms, and be careful of unexpected disasters.

吉祥物 Auspicious Items：

1. 今年犯歲破，宜在正月初一至正月十五期間，可至四馬路五路財神來敬拜四面觀音、太歲星君，供奉太歲金、驅除小人金、貴人金，點太歲星燈、阿彌陀佛本命燈、武財神事業財利燈來消災解厄、平安健康、財源廣進。

   Due to the clash with Tai Sui this year, it is advisable to go to the Bugis Fortune God at Bencoolen Street in Singapore, between the first and fifteenth day of the first lunar month, to worship the Four Side Guan Yin. Light the Tai Sui, Buddha Amitabha and Wealth Wishing Lamps, and offer the Tai Sui, Prevent Villains and Benefactor incense papers to ward off disasters, have safety and health and bring good luck and wealth.

2. 可在辦公室放置琉璃精製之飛天躍馬，在事業上平步青雲，讓財富的累積，更如飛馬騰雲，扶搖直上。

   You can place a Flying Horse in your office to help you get ahead in your career and accumulate wealth like a flying horse soaring into the sky.

歲次丁亥年生人79歲 (西元一九四七年生)
People born in Ding Hai Year are 79 years old (Born in 1947)

財運：財運一般，進財機會小有，如果三心兩意恐會讓錢財得而又失。

Wealth: Wealth luck is average, with a small chance of making money. However, if you are indecisive, you may gain and lose the money.

事業：事業運不錯，遠行外出可獲得更多有利的機會，下半年要小心意外的禍事。

Career: Career luck is good. You can get more favorable opportunities by traveling afar. Be careful of unexpected misfortunes in the second half of the year.

感情：夫老妻可享受清福，不要誤信饞言導致彼此無謂的爭執。

Relationship: The couple can enjoy a peaceful life. Don't believe in rumors and cause unnecessary disputes.

健康：健康尚可，宜注意眼睛、白血球、風濕、肝旺、腎臟病、糖尿病等疾病。

Health: Health is fair, but you should pay attention to diseases such as eyes, white blood cells, rheumatism, liver hyperactivity, kidney disease, diabetes, etc.

吉祥物 Auspicious Items：

1. 今年犯歲破，宜在正月初一至正月十五期間，可至四馬路五路財神來敬拜四面觀音、太歲星君，供奉太歲金、華陀除疾金、貴人金，點太歲星燈、阿彌陀佛本命燈、藥師佛消災解厄燈來消災解厄、平安健康、財源廣進。

   Due to the clash with Tai Sui this year, it is advisable to go to the Bugis Fortune God at Bencoolen Street in Singapore, between the first and fifteenth day of the first lunar month, to worship the Four Side Guan Yin. Light the Tai Sui, Buddha Amitabha and Medicine Buddha Wishing Lamps, and offer the Tai Sui, Hua Tuo and Benefactor incense papers to ward off disasters, have safety and health and bring good luck and wealth.

2. 可到四馬路五路財神點七彩蓮花轉運燈，讓菩薩護祐讓身心、災邪遠離、趨吉避凶。

   You can go to the Bugis Fortune God to light up the Lotus Lamp and seek the Bodhisattva's blessings to protect your body and mind, avoid disasters, and have good fortune.

接財神的重要吉日

Auspicious dates to welcome the arrival of the God of Fortune

吉日節慶 Auspicious Event	農曆日期 Lunar Calendar	西曆日期 Date
春節 Lunar New Year	農曆正月初一 1st Day of 1st Month	2025年1月29日 29/01/2025
立春 Beginning of Spring	農曆正月初六（癸卯日） 6th Day of 1th Month	2025年2月3日（癸卯日） 03/02/2025
天公聖誕（玉皇上帝） Heavenly Jade Emperor's Anniversary	農曆正月初九 9th Day of 1st Month	2025年2月6日 06/02/2025
觀音開庫日 Goddess of Mercy's Treasury Day	農曆正月廿六 26th Day of 1st Month	2025年2月23日 23/02/2025
大伯公聖誕（福德正神） God of Earth' s Anniversary	農曆二月初二 2th Day of 2nd Month	2025年3月1日 01/03/2025
趙公明聖誕（武財神） Warrior God of Wealth's Anniversary	農曆三月十五 15th Day of 3rd Month	2025年4月12日 12/04/2025
紫微大帝聖誕 Zi Wei Da Di's Anniversary	農曆四月十八 18th Day of 4th Month	2025年5月15日 15/05/2025
九皇大帝聖誕 Nine Emperors' Anniversary	農曆九月初九 9th Day of 9th Month	2025年10月29日 29/10/2025

玉玄門網路頻道系列

好運來開講直播
張清淵大師
李家進老師
每週四晚上
09：00開播

【好運來開講】

【大師修心思維】

【好運來開講】

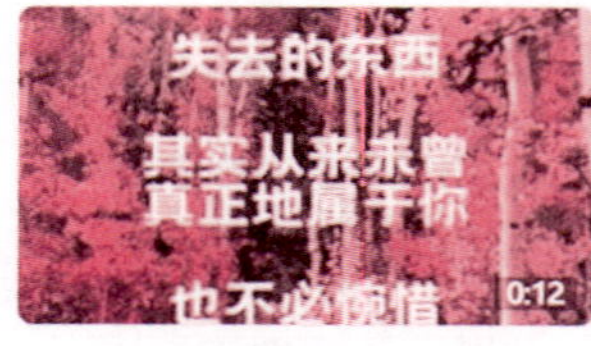

【好運來開講系列短片】

【李老師私房話】

【大師神測字】

【好運來開講直播】

每個星期四 21：00～22：00張清淵大師及李家進老師張家瑜老師主講直播

【好運來開講系列短片】

每週一/三/五/日更新·與您分享關於命理、風水等大家最喜歡的話題

【好運來開講】【張大師修心思維】【張大師神測字】【李老師私房話】

歡迎加入！請記得幫我們公開分享+讚+追蹤！歡迎直播中和我們互動唷！

張清淵-易經五術生活研究網

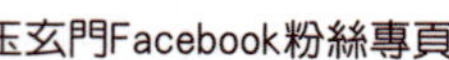
玉玄門Facebook粉絲專頁

玉玄門IG粉絲專頁

玉玄門youtube頻道專頁

玉玄門抖音- TikTok專頁

玉玄門WHATS APP客服帳號

玉玄門官方網站

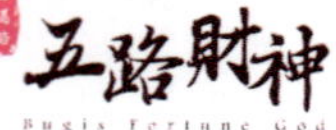

二〇二五年除夕敬神祭祖的最佳吉時

今年農曆十二月二十九日是除夕，除夕意為「舊歲至除夕而除，明旦且換新歲」。由於其為一年的終點和另一年的即將開始，因此民間最為重視，也是全家團圓的日子，而這天的拜拜稱為「辭歲」，目的是要感謝眾神及祖先一整年來的照顧與庇祐，所以除夕拜拜豐盛的酒菜絕對少不了，同時也要秉持著感恩惜福的心情來祭拜，而祭拜時愈虔誠，獲得的福蔭也愈多。

中國人敬神同時祭祖，會把祭祖當做敬神來看待，因為拜年是感恩尊敬父母長輩，在新舊交替的時刻，更該感恩和尊敬的是祖先、天地，所以傳統文化中除夕最重要的就是敬神祭祖。

一、2025年除夕敬神祭祖吉時

除夕農曆12月29日（西元2025年1月28日）正沖2011、1951年出生肖兔之人。

除夕吉時	吉星降臨	正沖生肖	開運顏色
01：00 至 03：00	三合、進祿	1955年出生肖羊	紅色、紫色、粉紅 桃紅、橘紅
07：00 至 09：00	六合、武曲	1958年出生肖狗	綠色、青色、茶綠 墨綠、草綠
09：00 至 11：00	三合、長生、帝旺	1959年出生肖豬	綠色、青色、茶綠 墨綠、草綠

除夕吉時	吉星降臨	正沖生肖	開運顏色
11：00 至 13：00	喜神、進貴	1960年出生肖鼠	白色、米白、乳黃 銀色、金黃
13：00 至 15：00	天德、進貴 天赦、寶光	1961年出生肖牛	白色、米白、乳黃 銀色、金黃
17：00 至 19：00	長生、福星、大進	1963年出生肖兔	紅色、紫色、粉紅 桃紅、橘紅
21：00 至 23：00	天官、貴人、驛馬	1965年出生肖蛇	黃色、咖啡、茶色 土褐、土黃

【拜拜小貼士】

1. 祭拜過神明的供品，可以再用來祭拜地基主或祖先。
2. 祭拜地基主，拜的方向是廚房面向客廳或屋宅後門向屋內祭拜。
3. 拜祖先時要先讓祖先用過餐，子孫才能食用，所以一般都是在吃飯以前就要拜好。而祭拜時，碗要疊放，有幾個碗就要有幾雙筷子，筷頭朝祖先牌位，筷尾朝向供品方向。

二〇二五年送神的最佳時辰，大掃除有哪些好日子？

俗謂「送神早，接神晚」，每年終時，即農曆十二月廿四日，都要祭拜送神，廿四日至除夕其間都可打掃家宅，以祈除舊佈新，正月初一開始就不許打掃，以保留家中財氣不流失，至正月初五的破五節為止。

一、送神的祭拜供品

鮮花、酒水、五方仙果、湯圓、糕餅、麵線、糖果、餅乾或其他應節食品皆可。送神紙錢，五色金或三色金亦可備太歲金、太歲貴人衣、雲馬（主要燒給神明駕駛的神馬、兵將使用的鎧甲和頭盔等）、玉宸齋純中藥精製的香枝及淨香末來祭拜。（祭祀用品、金銀紙錢，請視各地習俗備妥一套或到四馬路五路財神購買）

二、送送神及清理神龕（又稱清塵）的禁忌

所謂送神，只是將太歲星君、十二神煞以及家中的九天司命灶王爺或舉行有關祈福科儀時，所請降來的神明及神兵神將送返天庭而家神是帶玉旨天命來，祂可隨時往返天地間來上稟天庭，所以是不用送的，送神後就可清塵了，此時可將神尊及神桌所有東西做清潔，但香爐不能移動，只要用乾淨布擦拭，再將爐內半節香腳清除，香爐中的香灰不能倒出，若將灰都倒出再安爐回去，那就要重來安爐儀式，詳情可洽詢玉玄門命理風水或四馬路五路財神。

三、2025年送神日的最佳送神時辰

農曆12月24日（西元2025年1月23日），正沖2006年出生肖狗之人

最佳時辰	最佳送神生肖	正沖生肖	開運顏色
01：00 至 03：00	鼠、牛、虎、蛇 馬、雞、豬	1955年出生肖羊	黃色、茶色 土褐、土黃
05：00 至 07：00	虎、兔、龍、蛇 馬、狗、豬	1957年出生肖雞	綠色、青色 碧綠、草青
07：00 至 09：00	鼠、牛、虎、兔 龍、羊、猴、雞	1958年出生肖狗	黑色、藍色 灰白、水青
09：00 至 11：00	鼠、牛、兔、蛇 馬、羊、猴、雞	1959年出生肖豬	黑色、藍色 灰白、水青
11：00 至 13：00	虎、蛇、馬、羊 雞、狗、豬	1960年出生肖鼠	紅色、紫色 粉紅、桃紅
13：00 至 15：00	兔、蛇、馬、羊 雞、狗、豬	1961年出生肖牛	紅色、紫色 粉紅、桃紅

四、2025年大掃除的最佳時間

收工日必須視各種行業的營業狀況而定，通常收工日會在農曆12月24日送神以後，開始大掃除時來訂定收工的日期。以下列出今年大掃除的最佳時間有：

農曆	西曆
12月24日	2025年1月23日
12月25日	2025年1月24日
12月26日	2025年1月25日
12月28日	2025年1月27日
12月29日	2025年1月28日

2025乙巳蛇年新春開工開市最佳吉日

新春開市，通常指的是各行業開張的日子，多數的商家都會選擇良辰吉日來舉行開工儀式，討個好彩頭，祈求新的一年能得到財神的保佑而生意興隆、財源廣進。一般會選在正月初五財神日或破五節來開市，並且接迎財神破五窮，張清淵大師在此特為各位朋友列出2025乙巳蛇年新春開工最佳吉日，提供給您做為參考。若新春開工（開市）有人遇到當日正沖生肖之人，宜參照開運顏色的服飾來穿著，即可化解減輕其被沖煞之煞氣，而且這樣與神明的感應力也較強。

2025乙巳蛇年新春開工開市最佳吉日

<table>
<tr><th>開市吉日</th><th>開市吉時</th><th>吉祥生肖</th><th>正沖生肖</th><th>開運顏色</th></tr>
<tr><td rowspan="3">農曆
正月初九
（西元2月6日）</td><td rowspan="2">05：00
至
07：00</td><td rowspan="2">鼠、虎、兔、龍
馬、羊、雞、狗
豬</td><td>日沖：
2020年肖鼠</td><td>朱色、紅色</td></tr>
<tr><td>時沖：
2005年肖雞</td><td>金色、白色</td></tr>
<tr><td>11：00
至
13：00</td><td>牛、虎、蛇、馬
羊、狗</td><td>時沖：
2008年肖鼠</td><td>綠色、青色</td></tr>
<tr><td rowspan="3">農曆
正月十二日
（西元2月9日）</td><td rowspan="2">09：00
至
11：00</td><td rowspan="2">鼠、牛、龍、蛇
馬、羊、猴、雞</td><td>日沖：
2023年肖兔</td><td>黃色、茶色</td></tr>
<tr><td>時沖：
1983年肖豬</td><td>金色、白色</td></tr>
<tr><td>11：00
至
13：00</td><td>牛、虎、兔、蛇
馬、羊、猴、狗
豬</td><td>時沖：
1984年肖鼠</td><td>黃色、茶色</td></tr>
</table>

開市吉日	開市吉時	吉祥生肖	正沖生肖	開運顏色
農曆 正月十八日 （西元2月15日）	05：00 至 07：00	鼠、虎、兔、龍、馬、羊、猴、狗、豬	日沖： 1969年肖雞	朱色、紅色
			時沖： 1993年肖雞	黃色、茶色
	07：00 至 09：00	鼠、牛、虎、兔、龍、羊、狗、雞	時沖： 1994年肖狗	綠色、青色
	09：00 至 11：00	牛、虎、蛇、馬、羊、猴、雞	時沖： 1995年肖豬	綠色、青色
農曆 二月廿九日 （西元2月26日）	05：00 至 07：00	虎、兔、龍、馬、羊、雞、狗、豬	日沖： 1980年肖猴	黑色、藍色
			時沖： 2005年肖雞	金色、白色
	07：00 至 09：00	鼠、虎、兔、龍、蛇、猴、雞、豬	時沖： 2006年肖狗	朱色、紅色
	11：00 至 13：00	牛、虎、蛇、馬、羊、狗	時沖： 2008年肖鼠	綠色、青色

2025年接財神方位、吉時、怎麼拜

財神喜淨不喜髒，在新春除夕晚上接財神前先用玉玄門八卦淨身手工皂沖涼，將身體穢氣消除掉，並將家中所有燈火開亮，有供奉神明、祖先者，當接財神的吉時到，就點燃以純中藥精製零污染的玉玄門上等妙貢香，然後向家中的神明稟報，家中無神明的人，可向貴人方位與旺方拜拜即可。

若在財神位及生門位擺放龍神聖水及五個龍銀元，可增強求吉效果，讓您今年十二個月份，無論在求神、求財喜、求貴人、事業等都可諸事吉祥及財氣興旺。

一、接2025年農曆正月初一拜拜接財神的吉祥方位

吉祥方位（凡事迎之）	喜神	東南方
	休門	東南方
	財神	正北方
	生門	正南方
	開門	正東方
煞神方位（凡事避之）	五鬼	正南方
	死門	正北方
	日殺	正北方

一、2025年農曆正月初一拜拜接財神的吉祥方位

1、焚香開門取卯時大吉，巳時次吉，出行找親朋好友可以在卯時向東南喜神方出行，之後再轉向自己要前往的方向，焚香關門取申時大吉，酉時次吉。

2、若家中有人遇到當日正沖生肖之人，宜參照開運顏色的服飾來穿著，即可化解減輕其被沖煞之煞氣，而且這樣與神明的感應力也較強。

3、農曆正月初一（國曆2025年1月29日），正沖2012年出生肖龍之人，可以穿戴純白、金黃、銀白色系衣飾來開運化煞。

最佳時辰	最適合生肖	正沖生肖	開運顏色	吉祥方位
03：00 至 05：00	牛、虎、兔、龍 馬、羊、狗、豬	1968年 出生肖猴	紅色、紫色、粉紅 桃紅、橘紅、朱紅	東南方、正北方 正南方、正東方
05：00 至 07：00	鼠、虎、兔、龍 羊、猴、狗、豬	1969年 出生肖雞	紅色、紫色、粉紅 桃紅、橘紅、朱紅	東南方、正北方 正南方、正東方
09：00 至 11：00	牛、蛇、馬、羊 猴、雞、豬	1971年 出生肖豬	黃色、咖啡、茶色 土褐、土黃、棕色	東南方、正北方 正南方、正東方
13：00 至 15：00	鼠、兔、蛇、馬 羊、猴、豬	1973年 出生肖牛	黑色、藍色、灰白 淺藍、水藍、深藍	東南方、正北方 正南方、正東方
15：00 至 17：00	鼠、牛、龍、蛇 羊、猴、雞、狗	1974年 出生肖虎	純白、金黃、乳黃 銀白、米白、花白	東南方、正北方 正南方、正東方
17：00 至 19：00	牛、虎、龍、蛇 馬、猴、雞、狗	1975年 出生肖兔	純白、金黃、乳黃 銀白、米白、花白	東南方、正北方 正南方、正東方

挑良辰吉日存錢，讓您財源滾滾一路發

想要在2025年鴻運當頭、財源廣進、財富源源不絕、生生不息的朋友，可以運用今年的三個吉祥節日來存錢開財運哦！第一個是正月初五迎財神日；第二個是立春存款；第三個是觀音開庫日。

1、初五迎財神送窮出門興旺發

正月初五，一般來說是各行各業開張的日子，只要在這天選一個吉利的時辰開張就能得到財神的保佑，正月初五也是為玄壇真君武財神趙公明下凡巡視人間的日子，也有人在這天祭拜商財神（正財神）范蠡，祈求正財興旺，因此商家都會迎接財神並舉行「團拜」。尤其是做生意的人可在新春期間前往四馬路五路財神來祭拜五路財神、商財神，祈求正財興旺。大家可運用正月初五迎財神日來存款贏得財運，招財聚財的好方法。

2、立春存款代表好的開始就是奠定了成功的基礎

第一個是立春存款，代表好的開始，通常華人的習俗會在立春日存錢，「春」在閩南語有存錢的意思，立春是二十四節氣中的第一個節氣，「立」是開始的意思，「春」就是動，表示寒冷的冬天快要結束了，大地萬物開始有生機，春天即將降臨大地了，一年之計在於春，好的開始就是奠定了成功的基礎，所以選用立春日存錢是非常吉祥的開運象徵。

3、觀音開庫日引財入庫的最佳時機

農曆正月廿六日，是為觀音開庫日。民間認為觀音是最仁慈、最可信、最無私的神明，只要向觀音菩薩上香求借，都可得償所願。因此，大家都在這日子到觀音廟或四馬路五路財神來祈福及借庫，祈望能得到觀音菩薩的保佑，使自己財運亨通、大發利市。所以，大家可

在觀音開庫日來存款，是引財入庫的好吉時。玉玄門命理風水，在新加坡四馬路五路財神供奉了一尊特達靈感尊貴靈顯的四面觀音，歡迎大家可在一年一度的觀音開庫日來四馬路四面觀音借庫轉運及迎新祈福，讓您虎年行大運、招財興旺發。

2025最佳銀行存款吉日

立春	農曆正月初六（西元2025年2月3日）
正月初五迎財神	農曆正月初五（西元2025年2月2日）
觀音開庫日	農曆正月廿六（西元2025年2月23日）

2025十二生肖最佳銀行存款數位

鼠	168	龍	468	猴	268
牛	88	蛇	736	雞	756
虎	358	馬	99	狗	666
兔	368	羊	558	豬	618

註：如果來不及到銀行存款之人，可將新鈔放入家內聚寶盆中或財位上，讓您正財偏財皆興旺，五方財源滾滾而來，財源廣進運途亨通，不會輸給去銀行存款的效果，也省去了手續跟時間。如果家中沒聚寶盆者，也可直接當日來我們四馬路五路財神奉請五路財神聚寶盆回家更好，一舉兩得，聚財納寶，金銀財寶滿廳堂，當日需備妥存款數位，由我們老師當場開光加持，放入聚寶盆內，效果更佳。

二〇二五乙巳蛇年生肖禳解一覽表

生肖	出生年次	祭改名稱	點燈獻金	全年運勢
鼠 千手千眼觀音菩薩	2020 2008 1996 1984 1972 1960 1948 1936 1924	制天厄暴敗 紫微星拱照	千手千眼觀音本命燈 月老姻緣燈 太歲金 制桃花金	紫微、龍德、玉堂貴人、天厄、暴敗 今年吉星高照運勢興旺，事業蒸蒸日上，有貴人大力支持，事業及學業一飛衝天，雖有凶星禍事也能化險為夷，趨吉避凶。 今年總體運勢非常好，大利事業升遷，心高氣傲反成敗局，宜至玉玄門點光明燈祈求身體健康不受災病侵擾。
牛 虛空藏菩薩	2021 2009 1997 1985 1973 1961 1949 1937 1925	制白虎	虛空藏菩薩本命燈 藥師佛燈 華陀除疾金 五路財神金	三合、華蓋、白虎、天雄、遊奕、黃番、天哭 今年吉星較少，代表個人才能有所發揮，會有很好的人緣運，但是凶星眾多，主破敗損傷，易有是非小人暗害，血光橫禍，哀喪孝服之災，女性刑剋較重。 今年總體運勢不佳，煩惱皆因強出頭，建議至玉玄門制化白虎凶星，祈求消災解厄以保安康。
虎 虛空藏菩薩	2022 2010 1998 1986 1974 1962 1950 1938 1926	制小人官非 害太歲 吉星照臨	虛空藏菩薩本命燈 藥師佛燈 華陀除疾金 官符消災金	福德、天德、福星、劫殺、捲舌、絞殺、害太歲 今年福星貴神高照，諸事吉慶，主登科進祿，凶星代表易有小人是非及刑獄凶災，夜間勿遠行，勿管閒事，工作方面必須先將人際關係處理好，避免爭鬥摩擦，得失成敗都掌握在自己的手中，建議修身養性，奉公守法。 今年總體運勢很好，吉星可以減低凶星的刑剋，建議至玉玄門拜太歲及禳解改運，化解害太歲、官非、小人之災。
兔 文殊菩薩	2023 2011 1999 1987 1975 1963 1951 1939 1927	制弔客 制天狗	文殊菩薩本命燈 事業財利燈 文昌智慧金 接迎貴人金	祿勳、天狗、弔客、天殺、空亡、吞陷星 今年有名利之星降臨，工作事業帶來升職加薪，凶星主破財耗損，被人侵吞財錢財，血光意外，官非爭訟，留心家中易發生哭泣及服喪之事。 今年的總體運勢不佳，破財、傷病、喪事臨門，建議謹言慎行，不要意氣用事及逞強好鬥，小心詐騙手段而破財，注意行車人身安全，勿入喪家及探病，宜至玉玄門補財庫及制化天狗、弔客來化煞增福，添加財運。
龍 普賢菩薩	2012 2000 1988 1976 1964 1952 1940 1928 1916	化孤寡煞 制流年三煞 制病符	普賢菩薩本命燈 太歲星燈 驅除小人金 冤親債主金	天喜、病符、陌越、歲煞、流年三煞、羊刃、寡宿囚獄 今年吉星代表人際關係融洽，異性緣很好，但是凶星眾多，主多疾病、損人、瘟疫、橫禍、刑罰牢獄之災，今年最重要的還是健康狀態，一定要注意身心保健，有病就立即就醫，勿入病人家，出外行車留心意外血光之災。 今年總體運勢凶中有吉，感情人緣是亮點，注意健康狀況，建議到玉玄門點光明燈祭化病符、孤寡煞為佳。
蛇 普賢菩薩	2013 2001 1989 1977 1965 1953 1941 1929 1917	制小人刑煞 太歲當頭	普賢菩薩本命燈 事業財利燈 驅除小人金 冤親債主金	八座、天解、解神、歲駕、太歲、伏屍、血刃、劍鋒、指背、浮沉 今年犯太歲加上凶星諸多，要更加警惕人身安全，身體健康，意外橫災，工作財運艱難險阻，還好有解厄吉星入宮，能減低凶星的危害。 今年總體運勢好壞參半，需拜太歲星君及改運制刑以祈求身體健康，運事順利，凡事謹慎小心才能逢凶化吉。

Zodiac That Need To Worship 'Tai Sui' For the Year 2025
(Those that are highlighted)

生肖	出生年次	祭改名稱	點燈獻金	全年運勢
馬 大勢至菩薩	2014 2002 1990 1978 1966 1954 1942 1930 1918	化桃花煞 太陽高照	大勢至菩薩本命燈 太歲星燈 太歲金 驅除小人金	太陽、歲殿、文昌、天廚、桃花、咸池、紅豔、天空、晦氣、流霞 今年太陽星高照，男性喜事連連，女性小心禍事纏身，多得貴人，事業學業表現出色，桃花非常旺盛，小心爛桃花敗身破財。 今年總體運勢極佳，事業財運好事成雙，但是桃花運易氾濫成災，建議到玉玄門祭化桃花煞，讓運勢喜上加喜，好上加好。
羊 大日如來	2015 2003 1991 1979 1967 1955 1943 1931 1919	制喪門	大日如來本命燈 事業財利燈 冤親債主金 驅除小人金	喪門、地喪、地雌、擎天、飛廉、天殺、大殺 今年運勢動靜急速轉變，缺乏吉星轉運，凶星特主家中易有死喪哭泣之事，要特別注意血光、刑傷、小人、是非、盜賊及飛來橫禍，男性要注意刑剋之災。 今年肖羊之人的總體運勢不佳，如要避免小人是非及災喪臨門，建議至玉玄門制化喪門凶星以保人宅平安。
猴 大日如來	2016 2004 1992 1980 1968 1956 1944 1932 1920	化孤寡煞 制刑太歲 制桃花 破太歲	大日如來本命燈 藥師佛燈 華陀除疾金 官符消災金	太陰、天乙貴人、歲合、貫索、勾神、孤辰、亡神、歲刑、刑太歲、破太歲 今年太陰吉星高照，主陰盛陽衰，喜事臨門，有最吉貴人，事業上升，財運亨通，學業進步，凶星會造成事業阻礙、官司、小人非、刑剋之事，要預防急症或突發災厄。 今年總體運勢吉中藏凶，好運多過壞運，宜至玉玄門拜太歲星君化解刑太歲、破太歲，制桃花、孤寡煞以保平安。
雞 不動明王	2017 2005 1993 1981 1969 1957 1945 1933 1921	制五鬼 制官符	不動明王本命燈 太歲星燈 太歲金 本命財庫補運錢	三台、三合、將星、金匱、地解、飛符、五鬼、官符、破碎、的煞、年符、孤虛 今年吉星代表升官仕進，事業上受到重用，財運可儲積財富，有貴人暗助，但是今年凶星眾多，浮沉不定，須防小人暗害，虛耗失財、疾病纏身、官非流血、喪服哭泣之災。 今年總體運勢吉凶各半，宜至玉玄門制五鬼、官符以保平安，消災解厄。
狗 阿彌陀佛	2018 2006 1994 1982 1970 1958 1946 1934 1922	制死符	阿彌陀佛本命燈 觀音平安燈 驅除小人金 貴人接迎金	歲枝德、月德、紅鸞、扳鞍、死符、小耗、飛刃、唐符 今年行運吉星可謂是福祿雙全，能減輕流年災煞使您救危濟弱，當環境變遷時利於向外發展，事業宜文宜武，感情紅鸞星動喜事將近，凶星要注意劫難災傷，小人病災，哭泣喪事。 今年總體運勢不錯，能得到貴人提拔得到功名利祿，宜至玉玄門祭改死符及點光明燈禳解災病以保安康。
豬 阿彌陀佛	2019 2007 1995 1983 1971 1959 1947 1935 1923	沖太歲	阿彌陀佛本命燈 觀音平安燈 冤親債主金 貴人接迎金	國印、驛馬、歲破、大耗、月空、闌干、披頭 今年正沖太歲，運程反覆，煩惱是非多，工作上能得授權，環境易有異動改變，適合奔波遠行，須防禍事阻礙，小人暗中破壞，易有破財危機，家運失和，要特別留意長輩的健康狀態。 今年總體運勢不佳，雖然運勢反覆，工作還是有所進展，建議至玉玄門拜太歲星君及點光明燈自可消災解厄、趨吉避凶。

西元二〇二六年	星期	丙午太歲		幸運生肖	開運顏色	忌諱顏色	正財方位	偏財方位	文昌方位	正沖生肖	正沖生肖開運顏色	吉祥數字	貴人方位	煞方
2月10	星期二	十二月廿三	乙卯	庚戌年—狗 56歲	綠條紋	土黃色	正東	正中	正南	己酉年—雞 57歲	純白色	07 48	正北 西南	西
11	星期三	廿四	丙辰	辛酉年—雞 45歲	金蔥色	草綠色	東南	正西	西南	庚戌年—狗 56歲	藍灰色	49 02	西北 正西	南
12	星期四	廿五	丁巳	壬申年—猴 34歲	雪白色	墨綠色	正南	正西	正西	辛亥年—豬 55歲	靛藍色	25 16	西北 正西	東
13	星期五	廿六	戊午	癸未年—羊 23歲	深咖啡	寶藍色	東南	正北	西南	壬子年—鼠 54歲	紅藍色	35 40	正東 東南	北
14	星期六	廿七	己未	甲午年—馬 12 72歲	稻草黃	深黑色	正南	正北	正西	癸丑年—牛 53歲	薰衣紫	50 12	正北 西南	西
15	星期日	廿八	庚申	乙巳年—蛇 61歲	粉紫色	銀白色	西南	正東	西北	甲寅年—虎 52歲	翠玉綠	37 29	東北 西南	南
16	星期一	廿九	辛酉	丙辰年—龍 50歲	深紫色	金黃色	正西	正東	正北	乙卯年—兔 51歲	翡翠綠	05 32	正南 東北	東
17	星期二	一月初一	壬戌	丁卯年—兔 40歲	草綠色	淺棕色	西北	正南	東北	丙辰年—龍 51歲	金黃色	27 16	正東 東南	北
18	星期三	初二	癸亥	戊寅年—虎 29歲	淺綠色	黃褐色	正北	正南	正東	丁巳年—蛇 50歲	銀白色	28 47	正東 東南	西
19	星期四	初三	甲子	己丑年—牛 18 78歲	水藍色	紫紅色	東北	正中	東南	戊午年—馬 49歲	淡咖啡	23 36	東北 西南	南
20	星期五	初四	乙丑	庚子年—鼠 67歲	深藍色	朱紅色	正東	正中	正南	己未年—羊 48歲	香檳黃	42 16	正北 西南	東
21	星期六	初五	丙寅	辛亥年—豬 56歲	墨綠色	寶藍色	東南	正西	西南	庚申年—猴 47歲	橘紅色	10 13	西北 正西	北
22	星期日	初六	丁卯	壬戌年—狗 45歲	咖啡色	藍灰色	正南	正西	正南	辛酉年—雞 46歲	粉紅色	34 29	西北 正西	西
23	星期一	初七	戊辰	癸酉年—雞 34歲	粉紅色	銀白色	東南	正北	西南	壬戌年—狗 45歲	嫩綠色	11 21	東北 西南	南
24	星期二	初八	己巳	甲申年—猴 23 83歲	橘紅色	粉金色	正南	正北	正西	癸亥年—豬 44歲	孔雀綠	01 40	正北 西南	東

西元（二〇二六年）	星期	太歲乙巳（農曆）	干支	幸運生肖	開運顏色	忌諱顏色	正財方位	偏財方位	文昌方位	正沖生肖	正沖生肖開運顏色	吉祥數字	貴人方位	煞方
1月26	星期一	十二月初八	庚子	乙丑年－牛 41歲	銀白色	嫩綠色	西南	正東	西北	甲午年－馬 12歲	金白色	28 23	東北 西南	南
27	星期二	初九	辛丑	丙子年－鼠 30歲	乳白色	孔雀綠	正西	正東	正北	乙未年－羊 11歲	淺灰色	47 36	正南 東北	東
28	星期三	初十	壬寅	丁亥年－豬 19 79歲	道奇藍	山茶紅	西北	正南	東北	丙申年－猴 10 70歲	深黃色	06 19	正東 東南	北
29	星期四	十一	癸卯	戊戌年－狗 68歲	蔚藍色	粉紅色	正北	正南	正東	丁酉年－雞 9 69歲	鵝黃色	09 37	正東 東南	西
30	星期五	十二	甲辰	己酉年－雞 57歲	土黃色	水藍色	東北	正中	東南	戊戌年－狗 8 68歲	朱紅色	30 12	東北 西南	南
31	星期六	十三	乙巳	庚申年－猴 46歲	淺棕色	靛藍色	正東	正中	正南	己亥年－豬 7 67歲	蜜桃紅	43 16	正北 西南	東
2月1	星期日	十四	丙午	辛未年－羊 35歲	綠圖騰	淡咖啡	東南	正西	西南	庚子年－鼠 6 66歲	金蔥色	40 19	西北 正西	北
2	星期一	十五	丁未	壬午年－馬 24歲	碧綠色	香檳黃	正南	正西	正西	辛丑年－牛 5 65歲	金黃色	34 13	西北 正西	西
3	星期二	十六	戊申	癸巳年－蛇 13 73歲	金條紋	淺綠色	東南	正南	西南	壬寅年－虎 4 64歲	深藍色	44 10	東北 西南	南
4	星期三	十七	己酉	甲辰年－龍 62歲	乳白色	青綠色	正南	正北	正西	癸卯年－兔 3 63歲	天藍色	08 02	正北 西南	東
5	星期四	十八	庚戌	乙卯年－兔 51歲	淺藍色	亮紅色	西南	正東	正西	甲辰年－龍 2 62歲	鮮黃色	11 29	東北 西南	北
6	星期五	十九	辛亥	丙寅年－虎 40歲	深黑色	淺紫色	正西	正東	正北	乙巳年－蛇 1 61歲	深咖啡	21 37	正南 東北	西
7	星期六	二十	壬子	丁丑年－牛 29歲	鮮紅色	金黃色	西北	正南	東北	丙午年－馬 60歲	墨綠色	45 26	正東 東南	南
8	星期日	廿一	癸丑	戊子年－鼠 18 78歲	深紫色	雪白色	正北	正南	正東	丁未年－羊 59歲	綠條紋	27 35	正東 東南	東
9	星期一	廿二	甲寅	己亥年－豬 67歲	楓綠色	咖啡色	東北	正中	東南	戊申年－猴 58歲	金黃色	46 28	東北 西南	北

西元二〇二六年	太歲乙巳		幸運生肖	開運顏色	忌諱顏色	正財方位	偏財方位	文昌方位	正沖生肖	正沖生肖開運顏色	吉祥數字	貴人方位	煞方
1月11	星期日	十一月廿三	乙酉	庚辰年─龍 26歲	青碧綠	焦糖色	正東	正中	正南	己卯年─兔 27歲	雪白色	46 19	正北 西南	東
12	星期一	廿四	丙戌	辛卯年─兔 15 75歲	金白色	青綠色	東南	正西	西南	庚辰年─龍 26歲	深黑色	33 27	西北 正西	北
13	星期二	廿五	丁亥	壬寅年─虎 64歲	乳黃色	嫩綠色	正南	正西	正西	辛巳年─蛇 25歲	淺藍色	26 42	西北 正西	西
14	星期三	廿六	戊子	癸丑年─牛 53歲	淺黃色	淺土色	東南	正北	西南	壬午年─馬 24歲	深栗紫	31 34	東北 西南	南
15	星期四	廿七	己丑	甲子年─鼠 42歲	咖啡色	深藍色	正南	正北	正西	癸未年─羊 23歲	亮紅色	07 16	正北 西南	東
16	星期五	廿八	庚寅	乙亥年─豬 31歲	深藍色	金白色	西南	正東	西北	甲申年─猴 22歲	亮綠色	47 28	東北 西南	北
17	星期六	廿九	辛卯	丙戌年─狗 20 80歲	紅紫色	金黃色	正西	正東	正北	乙酉年─雞 21歲	楓綠色	11 07	正南 東北	西
18	星期日	三十	壬辰	丁酉年─雞 69歲	墨綠色	深褐色	西北	正南	東北	丙戌年─狗 20歲	乳黃色	42 19	正東 東南	南
19	星期一	十二月初一	癸巳	戊申年─猴 58歲	粉綠色	咖啡色	正北	正南	正東	丁亥年─豬 19歲	檸檬黃	35 29	正東 東南	東
20	星期二	初二	甲午	己未年─羊 47歲	藍灰色	粉紫色	東北	正中	東南	戊子年─鼠 18 78歲	深黃色	38 41	東北 西南	北
21	星期三	初三	乙未	庚午年─馬 36歲	深黑色	橘紅色	正東	正中	正南	己丑年─牛 17歲	香檳黃	05 18	正北 西南	西
22	星期四	初四	丙申	辛巳年─蛇 25歲	淡咖啡	水藍色	東南	正西	西南	庚寅年─虎 16歲	橘紅色	20 29	西北 正西	南
23	星期五	初五	丁酉	壬辰年─龍 14 74歲	土黃色	灰白色	正南	正西	正西	辛卯年─兔 15 75歲	桃紅色	21 35	西北 正西	東
24	星期六	初六	戊戌	癸卯年─兔 63歲	朱紅色	金白色	東南	正北	西南	壬辰年─龍 14歲	草綠色	04 49	東北 西南	北
25	星期日	初七	己亥	甲寅年─虎 52歲	粉紅色	金黃色	正南	正北	正西	癸巳年─蛇 13歲	碧綠色	32 11	正北 西南	西

西元二〇二六年	星期	太歲乙巳	干支	幸運生肖	開運顏色	忌諱顏色	正財方位	偏財方位	文昌方位	正沖生肖	正沖生肖開運顏色	吉祥數字	貴人方位	煞方
12月27	星期六	十一月初八	庚午	乙未年—羊 71歲	金黃色	草地綠	西南	正東	西北	甲子年—鼠 42歲	道奇藍	10 40	東北 西南	北
28	星期日	初九	辛未	丙午年—馬 60歲	乳白色	檸檬綠	正西	正東	正北	乙丑年—牛 41歲	蔚藍色	13 42	正南 東北	西
29	星期一	初十	壬申	丁巳年—蛇 49歲	銀白色	紫紅色	西北	正南	東北	丙寅年—虎 40歲	深咖啡	21 15	正東 東南	南
30	星期二	十一	癸酉	戊辰年—龍 38歲	水藍色	棗紅色	正北	正南	正東	丁卯年—兔 39歲	深棕色	06 26	正東 東南	東
31	星期三	十二	甲戌	己卯年—兔 27歲	可可色	淡藍色	東北	正中	東南	戊辰年—龍 38歲	棗紅色	28 43	東北 西南	北
1月1	星期四	十三	乙亥	庚寅年—虎 16 76歲	鵝黃色	丈青色	正東	正中	西南	己巳年—蛇 37歲	豔紅色	21 35	正北 西南	西
2	星期五	十四	丙子	辛丑年—牛 65歲	橄欖綠	深褐色	東南	正西	西南	庚午年—馬 36歲	暗金色	30 42	西北 正西	南
3	星期六	十五	丁丑	壬子年—鼠 54歲	粉綠色	咖啡色	正南	正西	正西	辛未年—羊 35歲	金黃色	07 35	西北 正西	東
4	星期日	十六	戊寅	癸亥年—豬 43歲	亮金色	水綠色	東南	正北	西南	壬申年—猴 34歲	天藍色	45 36	東北 西南	北
5	星期一	十七	己卯	甲戌年—狗 32歲	灰白色	楓綠色	正南	正北	正西	癸酉年—雞 33歲	湖水藍	29 14	正北 西南	西
6	星期二	十八	庚辰	乙酉年—雞 21 81歲	藍條紋	桃紅色	西南	正東	西北	甲戌年—狗 32歲	米黃色	01 03	東北 西南	南
7	星期三	十九	辛巳	丙申年—猴 70歲	寶藍色	火紅色	正西	正東	正北	乙亥年—豬 31歲	深棕色	19 31	正南 東北	東
8	星期四	二十	壬午	丁未年—羊 59歲	葡萄紫	金黃色	西北	正南	東北	丙子年—鼠 30歲	淺綠色	28 12	正東 東南	北
9	星期五	廿一	癸未	戊午年—馬 48歲	深紅色	純白色	正北	正南	正東	丁丑年—牛 29歲	草青色	19 43	正東 東南	西
10	星期六	廿二	甲申	己巳年—蛇 37歲	青翠色	咖啡色	東北	正中	東南	戊寅年—虎 28歲	銀白色	02 13	東北 西南	南

二〇二五年 西元		太歲 乙巳		幸運生肖	開運顏色	忌諱顏色	正財方位	偏財方位	文昌方位	正沖生肖	正沖生肖開運顏色	吉祥數字	貴人方位	煞方
12月12	星期五	十月廿三	乙卯	庚戌年—狗 56歲	綠條紋	土黃色	正東	正中	正南	己酉年—雞 57歲	純白色	12 35	正北 西南	西
13	星期六	廿四	丙辰	辛酉年—雞 45歲	金蔥色	草綠色	東南	正西	西南	庚戌年—狗 56歲	藍灰色	35 39	西北 正西	南
14	星期日	廿五	丁巳	壬申年—猴 34歲	雪白色	墨綠色	正南	正西	正西	辛亥年—豬 55歲	靛藍色	11 28	西北 正西	東
15	星期一	廿六	戊午	癸未年—羊 23歲	深咖啡	寶藍色	東南	正北	西南	壬子年—鼠 54歲	紅藍色	01 31	正東 東南	北
16	星期二	廿七	己未	甲午年—馬 12 72歲	稻草黃	深黑色	正南	正北	正西	癸丑年—牛 53歲	薰衣紫	38 47	正北 西南	西
17	星期三	廿八	庚申	乙巳年—蛇 61歲	粉紫色	銀白色	西南	正東	西北	甲寅年—虎 52歲	翠玉綠	16 40	東北 西南	南
18	星期四	廿九	辛酉	丙辰年—龍 50歲	深紫色	金黃色	正西	正東	正北	乙卯年—兔 51歲	翡翠綠	02 29	正南 東北	東
19	星期五	三十	壬戌	丁卯年—兔 39歲	草綠色	淺棕色	西北	正南	東北	丙辰年—龍 50歲	金黃色	09 33	正東 東南	北
20	星期六	十一月初一	癸亥	戊寅年—虎 28歲	淺綠色	黃褐色	正北	正南	正東	丁巳年—蛇 49歲	銀白色	14 17	正東 東南	西
21	星期日	初二	甲子	己丑年—牛 17 77歲	水藍色	紫紅色	東北	正中	東南	戊午年—馬 48歲	淡咖啡	09 14	東北 西南	南
22	星期一	初三	乙丑	庚子年—鼠 66歲	深藍色	朱紅色	正東	正中	正南	己未年—羊 47歲	香檳黃	01 49	正北 西南	東
23	星期二	初四	丙寅	辛亥年—豬 55歲	墨綠色	寶藍色	東南	正西	西南	庚申年—猴 46歲	橋紅色	07 18	西北 正西	北
24	星期三	初五	丁卯	壬戌年—狗 44歲	咖啡色	藍灰色	正南	正西	正南	辛酉年—雞 45歲	粉紅色	12 20	西北 正西	西
25	星期四	初六	戊辰	癸酉年—雞 33歲	粉紅色	銀白色	東南	正北	西南	壬戌年—狗 44歲	嫩綠色	06 27	東北 西南	南
26	星期五	初七	己巳	甲申年—猴 22 82歲	橋紅色	粉金色	正南	正北	正西	癸亥年—豬 43歲	孔雀綠	15 20	正北 西南	東

二〇二五年 西元	星期	太歲乙巳	太歲乙巳	幸運生肖	開運顏色	忌諱顏色	正財方位	偏財方位	文昌方位	正沖生肖	正沖生肖開運顏色	吉祥數字	貴人方位	煞方
11月27	星期四	十月初八	庚子	乙丑年—牛 41歲	銀白色	嫩綠色	西南	正東	西北	甲午年—馬 12歲	金白色	09 08	東北 西南	南
28	星期五	初九	辛丑	丙子年—鼠 30歲	乳白色	孔雀綠	正西	正東	正北	乙未年—羊 11歲	淺灰色	37 34	正南 東北	東
29	星期六	初十	壬寅	丁亥年—豬 19 79歲	道奇藍	山茶紅	西北	正南	東北	丙申年—猴 10 70歲	深黃色	03 34	正東 東南	北
30	星期日	十一	癸卯	戊戌年—狗 68歲	蔚藍色	粉紅色	正北	正南	正東	丁酉年—雞 9 69歲	鵝黃色	35 04	正東 東南	西
12月1	星期一	十二	甲辰	己酉年—雞 57歲	土黃色	水藍色	東北	正中	東南	戊戌年—狗 8 68歲	朱紅色	16 27	東北 西南	南
2	星期二	十三	乙巳	庚申年—猴 46歲	淺棕色	靛藍色	正東	正中	正南	己亥年—豬 7 67歲	蜜桃紅	02 12	正北 西南	東
3	星期三	十四	丙午	辛未年—羊 35歲	綠圖騰	淡咖啡	東南	正西	西南	庚子年—鼠 6 66歲	金蔥色	47 37	西北 正西	北
4	星期四	十五	丁未	壬午年—馬 24歲	碧綠色	香檳黃	正南	正西	正西	辛丑年—牛 5 65歲	金黃色	35 17	西北 正西	西
5	星期五	十六	戊申	癸巳年—蛇 13 73歲	金條紋	淺綠色	東南	正南	西南	壬寅年—虎 4 64歲	深藍色	03 07	東北 西南	南
6	星期六	十七	己酉	甲辰年—龍 62歲	乳白色	青綠色	正南	正北	正西	癸卯年—兔 3 63歲	天藍色	08 37	正北 西南	東
7	星期日	十八	庚戌	乙卯年—兔 51歲	淺藍色	亮紅色	西南	正東	正西	甲辰年—龍 2 62歲	鮮黃色	11 18	東北 西南	北
8	星期一	十九	辛亥	丙寅年—虎 40歲	深黑色	淺紫色	正西	正東	正北	乙巳年—蛇 1 61歲	深咖啡	24 34	正南 東北	西
9	星期二	二十	壬子	丁丑年—牛 29歲	鮮紅色	金黃色	西北	正南	東北	丙午年—馬 60歲	墨綠色	05 33	正東 東南	南
10	星期三	廿一	癸丑	戊子年—鼠 18 78歲	深紫色	雪白色	正北	正南	正東	丁未年—羊 59歲	綠條紋	26 24	正東 東南	東
11	星期四	廿二	甲寅	己亥年—豬 67歲	楓綠色	咖啡色	東北	正中	東南	戊申年—猴 58歲	金黃色	02 18	東北 西南	北

二〇二五年 西元	太歲 乙巳		幸運生肖	開運顏色	忌諱顏色	正財方位	偏財方位	文昌方位	正沖生肖	正沖生肖開運顏色	吉祥數字	貴人方位	煞方
11月 12	星期三	九月 廿三	乙酉	庚辰年—龍 26歲	青碧綠	焦糖色	正東	正中	正南	己卯年—兔 27歲	雪白色	13 17	正北 西南	東
13	星期四	廿四	丙戌	辛卯年—兔 15 75歲	金白色	青綠色	東南	正西	西南	庚辰年—龍 26歲	深黑色	08 04	西北 正西	北
14	星期五	廿五	丁亥	壬寅年—虎 64歲	乳黃色	嫩綠色	正南	正西	正西	辛巳年—蛇 25歲	淺藍色	13 37	西北 正西	西
15	星期六	廿六	戊子	癸丑年—牛 53歲	淺黃色	淺土色	東南	正北	西南	壬午年—馬 24歲	深栗紫	20 05	東北 西南	南
16	星期日	廿七	己丑	甲子年—鼠 42歲	咖啡色	深藍色	正南	正北	正西	癸未年—羊 23歲	亮紅色	11 19	正北 西南	東
17	星期一	廿八	庚寅	乙亥年—豬 31歲	深藍色	金白色	西南	正東	西北	甲申年—猴 22歲	亮綠色	14 36	東北 西南	北
18	星期二	廿九	辛卯	丙戌年—狗 20 80歲	紅紫色	金黃色	正西	正東	正北	乙酉年—雞 21歲	楓綠色	03 31	正南 東北	西
19	星期三	三十	壬辰	丁酉年—雞 69歲	墨綠色	深褐色	西北	正南	東北	丙戌年—狗 20歲	乳黃色	37 39	正東 東南	南
20	星期四	十月 初一	癸巳	戊申年—猴 58歲	粉綠色	咖啡色	正北	正南	正東	丁亥年—豬 19歲	檸檬黃	40 38	正東 東南	東
21	星期五	初二	甲午	己未年—羊 47歲	藍灰色	粉紫色	東北	正中	東南	戊子年—鼠 18 78歲	深黃色	32 17	東北 西南	北
22	星期六	初三	乙未	庚午年—馬 36歲	深黑色	橘紅色	正東	正中	正南	己丑年—牛 17歲	香檳黃	13 26	正北 西南	西
23	星期日	初四	丙申	辛巳年—蛇 25歲	淡咖啡	水藍色	東南	正西	西南	庚寅年—虎 16歲	橘紅色	08 14	西北 正西	南
24	星期一	初五	丁酉	壬辰年—龍 14 74歲	土黃色	灰白色	正南	正西	正西	辛卯年—兔 15 75歲	桃紅色	15 04	西北 正西	東
25	星期二	初六	戊戌	癸卯年—兔 63歲	朱紅色	金白色	東南	正北	西南	壬辰年—龍 14歲	草綠色	03 11	東北 西南	北
26	星期三	初七	己亥	甲寅年—虎 52歲	粉紅色	金黃色	正南	正北	正西	癸巳年—蛇 13歲	碧綠色	11 20	正北 西南	西

二〇二五年西元	星期	太歲乙巳		幸運生肖	開運顏色	忌諱顏色	正財方位	偏財方位	文昌方位	正沖生肖	正沖生肖開運顏色	吉祥數字	貴人方位	煞方
10月28	星期二	九月初八	庚午	乙未年—羊 71歲	金黃色	草地綠	西南	正東	西北	甲子年—鼠 42歲	道奇藍	10 11	東北 西南	北
29	星期三	初九	辛未	丙午年—馬 60歲	乳白色	檸檬綠	正西	正東	正北	乙丑年—牛 41歲	蔚藍色	01 06	正南 東北	西
30	星期四	初十	壬申	丁巳年—蛇 49歲	銀白色	紫紅色	西北	正南	東北	丙寅年—虎 40歲	深咖啡	25 35	正東 東南	南
31	星期五	十一	癸酉	戊辰年—龍 38歲	水藍色	棗紅色	正北	正南	正東	丁卯年—兔 39歲	深棕色	15 45	正東 東南	東
11月1	星期六	十二	甲戌	己卯年—兔 27歲	可可色	淡藍色	東北	正中	東南	戊辰年—龍 38歲	棗紅色	01 23	東北 西南	北
2	星期日	十三	乙亥	庚寅年—虎 16 76歲	鵝黃色	丈青色	正東	正中	西南	己巳年—蛇 37歲	豔紅色	21 33	正北 西南	西
3	星期一	十四	丙子	辛丑年—牛 65歲	橄欖綠	深褐色	東南	正西	西南	庚午年—馬 36歲	暗金色	39 41	西北 正西	南
4	星期二	十五	丁丑	壬子年—鼠 54歲	粉綠色	咖啡色	正南	正西	正西	辛未年—羊 35歲	金黃色	02 29	西北 正西	東
5	星期三	十六	戊寅	癸亥年—豬 43歲	亮金色	水綠色	東南	正北	西南	壬申年—猴 34歲	天藍色	03 47	東北 西南	北
6	星期四	十七	己卯	甲戌年—狗 32歲	灰白色	楓綠色	正南	正北	正西	癸酉年—雞 33歲	湖水藍	28 39	正北 西南	西
7	星期五	十八	庚辰	乙酉年—雞 21 81歲	藍條紋	桃紅色	西南	正東	西北	甲戌年—狗 32歲	米黃色	09 08	東北 西南	南
8	星期六	十九	辛巳	丙申年—猴 70歲	寶藍色	火紅色	正西	正東	正北	乙亥年—豬 31歲	深棕色	17 39	正南 東北	東
9	星期日	二十	壬午	丁未年—羊 59歲	葡萄紫	金黃色	西北	正南	東北	丙子年—鼠 30歲	淺綠色	44 55	正東 東南	北
10	星期一	廿一	癸未	戊午年—馬 48歲	深紅色	純白色	正北	正南	正東	丁丑年—牛 29歲	草青色	33 22	正東 東南	西
11	星期二	廿二	甲申	己巳年—蛇 37歲	青翠色	咖啡色	東北	正中	東南	戊寅年—虎 28歲	銀白色	11 37	東北 西南	南

西元二〇二五年		太歲乙巳		幸運生肖	開運顏色	忌諱顏色	正財方位	偏財方位	文昌方位	正沖生肖	正沖生肖開運顏色	吉祥數字	貴人方位	煞方
10月13	星期一	八月廿二	乙卯	庚戌年—狗 56歲	綠條紋	土黃色	正東	正中	正南	己酉年—雞 57歲	純白色	14 26	正北 西南	西
14	星期二	廿三	丙辰	辛酉年—雞 45歲	金蔥色	草綠色	東南	正西	西南	庚戌年—狗 56歲	藍灰色	19 16	西北 正西	南
15	星期三	廿四	丁巳	壬申年—猴 34歲	雪白色	墨綠色	正南	正西	正西	辛亥年—豬 55歲	靛藍色	46 34	西北 正西	東
16	星期四	廿五	戊午	癸未年—羊 23歲	深咖啡	寶藍色	東南	正北	西南	壬子年—鼠 54歲	紅藍色	27 02	正東 東南	北
17	星期五	廿六	己未	甲午年—馬 12 72歲	稻草黃	深黑色	正南	正北	正西	癸丑年—牛 53歲	薰衣紫	30 41	正北 西南	西
18	星期六	廿七	庚申	乙巳年—蛇 61歲	粉紫色	銀白色	西南	正東	西北	甲寅年—虎 52歲	翠玉綠	08 21	東北 西南	南
19	星期日	廿八	辛酉	丙辰年—龍 50歲	深紫色	金黃色	正西	正東	正北	乙卯年—兔 51歲	翡翠綠	27 49	正南 東北	東
20	星期一	廿九	壬戌	丁卯年—兔 39歲	草綠色	淺棕色	西北	正南	東北	丙辰年—龍 50歲	金黃色	21 33	正東 東南	北
21	星期二	九月初一	癸亥	戊寅年—虎 28歲	淺綠色	黃褐色	正北	正南	正東	丁巳年—蛇 49歲	銀白色	39 41	正東 東南	西
22	星期三	初二	甲子	己丑年—牛 17 77歲	水藍色	紫紅色	東北	正中	東南	戊午年—馬 48歲	淡咖啡	01 29	東北 西南	南
23	星期四	初三	乙丑	庚子年—鼠 66歲	深藍色	朱紅色	正東	正中	正南	己未年—羊 47歲	香檳黃	34 36	正北 西南	東
24	星期五	初四	丙寅	辛亥年—豬 55歲	墨綠色	寶藍色	東南	正西	西南	庚申年—猴 46歲	橘紅色	18 24	西北 正西	北
25	星期六	初五	丁卯	壬戌年—狗 44歲	咖啡色	藍灰色	正南	正西	正南	辛酉年—雞 45歲	粉紅色	33 39	西北 正西	西
26	星期日	初六	戊辰	癸酉年—雞 33歲	粉紅色	銀白色	東南	正北	西南	壬戌年—狗 44歲	嫩綠色	03 34	東北 西南	南
27	星期一	初七	己巳	甲申年—猴 22 82歲	橘紅色	粉金色	正南	正北	正西	癸亥年—豬 43歲	孔雀綠	28 39	正北 西南	東

西元二〇二五年	星期	太歲乙巳		幸運生肖	開運顏色	忌諱顏色	正財方位	偏財方位	文昌方位	正沖生肖	正沖生肖開運顏色	吉祥數字	貴人方位	煞方
9月28	星期日	八月初七	庚子	乙丑年—牛 41歲	銀白色	嫩綠色	西南	正東	西北	甲午年—馬 12歲	金白色	16 18	東北 西南	南
29	星期一	初八	辛丑	丙子年—鼠 30歲	乳白色	孔雀綠	正西	正東	正北	乙未年—羊 11歲	淺灰色	14 39	正南 東北	東
30	星期二	初九	壬寅	丁亥年—豬 19 79歲	道奇藍	山茶紅	西北	正南	東北	丙申年—猴 10 70歲	深黃色	17 25	正東 東南	北
10月1	星期三	初十	癸卯	戊戌年—狗 68歲	蔚藍色	粉紅色	正北	正南	正東	丁酉年—雞 9 69歲	鵝黃色	32 41	正東 東南	西
2	星期四	十一	甲辰	己酉年—雞 57歲	土黃色	水藍色	東北	正中	東南	戊戌年—狗 8 68歲	朱紅色	04 12	東北 西南	南
3	星期五	十二	乙巳	庚申年—猴 46歲	淺棕色	靛藍色	正東	正中	正南	己亥年—豬 7 67歲	蜜桃紅	08 24	正北 西南	東
4	星期六	十三	丙午	辛未年—羊 35歲	綠圖騰	淡咖啡	東南	正西	西南	庚子年—鼠 6 66歲	金蔥色	17 19	西北 正西	北
5	星期日	十四	丁未	壬午年—馬 24歲	碧綠色	香檳黃	正南	正西	正西	辛丑年—牛 5 65歲	金黃色	24 31	西北 正西	西
6	星期一	十五	戊申	癸巳年—蛇 13 73歲	金條紋	淺綠色	東南	正南	西南	壬寅年—虎 4 64歲	深藍色	05 39	東北 西南	南
7	星期二	十六	己酉	甲辰年—龍 62歲	乳白色	青綠色	正南	正北	正西	癸卯年—兔 3 63歲	天藍色	26 33	正北 西南	東
8	星期三	十七	庚戌	乙卯年—兔 51歲	淺藍色	亮紅色	西南	正東	正西	甲辰年—龍 2 62歲	鮮黃色	13 14	東北 西南	北
9	星期四	十八	辛亥	丙寅年—虎 40歲	深黑色	淺紫色	正西	正東	正北	乙巳年—蛇 1 61歲	深咖啡	15 37	正南 東北	西
10	星期五	十九	壬子	丁丑年—牛 29歲	鮮紅色	金黃色	西北	正南	東北	丙午年—馬 60歲	墨綠色	03 11	正東 東南	南
11	星期六	二十	癸丑	戊子年—鼠 18 78歲	深紫色	雪白色	正北	正南	正東	丁未年—羊 59歲	綠條紋	18 21	正東 東南	東
12	星期日	廿一	甲寅	己亥年—豬 67歲	楓綠色	咖啡色	東北	正中	東南	戊申年—猴 58歲	金黃色	05 40	東北 西南	北

西元二〇二五年		太歲乙巳		幸運生肖	開運顏色	忌諱顏色	正財方位	偏財方位	文昌方位	正沖生肖	正沖生肖開運顏色	吉祥數字	貴人方位	煞方
9月13	星期六	七月廿二	乙酉	庚辰年—龍 26歲	青碧綠	焦糖色	正東	正中	正南	己卯年—兔 27歲	雪白色	45 35	正北西南	東
14	星期日	廿三	丙戌	辛卯年—兔 15 75歲	金白色	青綠色	東南	正西	西南	庚辰年—龍 26歲	深黑色	15 21	西北正西	北
15	星期一	廿四	丁亥	壬寅年—虎 64歲	乳黃色	嫩綠色	正南	正西	正西	辛巳年—蛇 25歲	淺藍色	23 13	西北正西	西
16	星期二	廿五	戊子	癸丑年—牛 53歲	淺黃色	淺土色	東南	正北	西南	壬午年—馬 24歲	深栗紫	17 48	東北西南	南
17	星期三	廿六	己丑	甲子年—鼠 42歲	咖啡色	深藍色	正南	正北	正西	癸未年—羊 23歲	亮紅色	26 46	正北西南	東
18	星期四	廿七	庚寅	乙亥年—豬 31歲	深藍色	金白色	西南	正東	西北	甲申年—猴 22歲	亮綠色	47 01	東北西南	北
19	星期五	廿八	辛卯	丙戌年—狗 20 80歲	紅紫色	金黃色	正西	正東	正北	乙酉年—雞 21歲	楓綠色	11 18	正南東北	西
20	星期六	廿九	壬辰	丁酉年—雞 69歲	墨綠色	深褐色	西北	正南	東北	丙戌年—狗 20歲	乳黃色	03 31	正東東南	南
21	星期日	三十	癸巳	戊申年—猴 58歲	粉綠色	咖啡色	正北	正南	正東	丁亥年—豬 19歲	檸檬黃	23 42	正東東南	東
22	星期一	八月初一	甲午	己未年—羊 47歲	藍灰色	粉紫色	東北	正中	東南	戊子年—鼠 18 78歲	深黃色	31 36	東北西南	北
23	星期二	初二	乙未	庚午年—馬 36歲	深黑色	橘紅色	正東	正中	正南	己丑年—牛 17歲	香檳黃	11 41	正北西南	西
24	星期三	初三	丙申	辛巳年—蛇 25歲	淡咖啡	水藍色	東南	正西	西南	庚寅年—虎 16歲	橘紅色	16 17	西北正西	南
25	星期四	初四	丁酉	壬辰年—龍 14 74歲	土黃色	灰白色	正南	正西	正西	辛卯年—兔 15 75歲	桃紅色	19 27	西北正西	東
26	星期五	初五	戊戌	癸卯年—兔 63歲	朱紅色	金白色	東南	正北	西南	壬辰年—龍 14歲	草綠色	25 18	東北西南	北
27	星期六	初六	己亥	甲寅年—虎 52歲	粉紅色	金黃色	正南	正北	正西	癸巳年—蛇 13歲	碧綠色	06 22	正北西南	西

西元二〇二五年		太歲乙巳		幸運生肖	開運顏色	忌諱顏色	正財方位	偏財方位	文昌方位	正沖生肖	正沖生肖開運顏色	吉祥數字	貴人方位	煞方
8月29	星期五	七月初七	庚午	乙未年—羊 71歲	金黃色	草地綠	西南	正東	西北	甲子年—鼠 42歲	道奇藍	29 34	東北 西南	北
30	星期六	初八	辛未	丙午年—馬 60歲	乳白色	檸檬綠	正西	正東	正北	乙丑年—牛 41歲	蔚藍色	01 36	正南 東北	西
31	星期日	初九	壬申	丁巳年—蛇 49歲	銀白色	紫紅色	西北	正南	東北	丙寅年—虎 40歲	深咖啡	05 40	正東 東南	南
9月1	星期一	初十	癸酉	戊辰年—龍 38歲	水藍色	棗紅色	正北	正南	正東	丁卯年—兔 39歲	深棕色	38 47	正東 東南	東
2	星期二	十一	甲戌	己卯年—兔 27歲	可可色	淡藍色	東北	正中	東南	戊辰年—龍 38歲	棗紅色	18 25	東北 西南	北
3	星期三	十二	乙亥	庚寅年—虎 16 76歲	鵝黃色	丈青色	正東	正中	西南	己巳年—蛇 37歲	豔紅色	06 22	正北 西南	西
4	星期四	十三	丙子	辛丑年—牛 65歲	橄欖綠	深褐色	東南	正西	西南	庚午年—馬 36歲	暗金色	03 27	西北 正西	南
5	星期五	十四	丁丑	壬子年—鼠 54歲	粉綠色	咖啡色	正南	正西	正西	辛未年—羊 35歲	金黃色	15 26	西北 正西	東
6	星期六	十五	戊寅	癸亥年—豬 43歲	亮金色	水綠色	東南	正北	西南	壬申年—猴 34歲	天藍色	23 26	東北 西南	北
7	星期日	十六	己卯	甲戌年—狗 32歲	灰白色	楓綠色	正南	正北	正西	癸酉年—雞 33歲	湖水藍	15 28	正北 西南	西
8	星期一	十七	庚辰	乙酉年—雞 21 81歲	藍條紋	桃紅色	西南	正東	西北	甲戌年—狗 32歲	米黃色	19 25	東北 西南	南
9	星期二	十八	辛巳	丙申年—猴 70歲	寶藍色	火紅色	正西	正東	正北	乙亥年—豬 31歲	深棕色	45 26	正南 東北	東
10	星期三	十九	壬午	丁未年—羊 59歲	葡萄紫	金黃色	西北	正南	東北	丙子年—鼠 30歲	淺綠色	37 26	正東 東南	北
11	星期四	二十	癸未	戊午年—馬 48歲	深紅色	純白色	正北	正南	正東	丁丑年—牛 29歲	草青色	10 20	正東 東南	西
12	星期五	廿一	甲申	己巳年—蛇 37歲	青翠色	咖啡色	東北	正中	東南	戊寅年—虎 28歲	銀白色	09 37	東北 西南	南

二〇二五年西元		太歲乙巳		幸運生肖	開運顏色	忌諱顏色	正財方位	偏財方位	文昌方位	正沖生肖	正沖生肖開運顏色	吉祥數字	貴人方位	煞方
8月14	星期四	閏六月廿一	乙卯	庚戌年—狗 56歲	綠條紋	土黃色	正東	正中	正南	己酉年—雞 57歲	純白色	12 37	正北 西南	西
15	星期五	廿二	丙辰	辛酉年—雞 45歲	金蔥色	草綠色	東南	正西	西南	庚戌年—狗 56歲	藍灰色	17 20	西北 正西	南
16	星期六	廿三	丁巳	壬申年—猴 34歲	雪白色	墨綠色	正南	正西	正西	辛亥年—豬 55歲	靛藍色	25 34	西北 正西	東
17	星期日	廿四	戊午	癸未年—羊 23歲	深咖啡	寶藍色	東南	正北	西南	壬子年—鼠 54歲	紅藍色	09 01	正東 東南	北
18	星期一	廿五	己未	甲午年—馬 12 72歲	稻草黃	深黑色	正南	正北	正西	癸丑年—牛 53歲	薰衣紫	04 29	正北 西南	西
19	星期二	廿六	庚申	乙巳年—蛇 61歲	粉紫色	銀白色	西南	正東	西北	甲寅年—虎 52歲	翠玉綠	15 38	東北 西南	南
20	星期三	廿七	辛酉	丙辰年—龍 50歲	深紫色	金黃色	正西	正東	正北	乙卯年—兔 51歲	翡翠綠	33 20	正南 東北	東
21	星期四	廿八	壬戌	丁卯年—兔 39歲	草綠色	淺棕色	西北	正南	東北	丙辰年—龍 50歲	金黃色	30 15	正東 東南	北
22	星期五	廿九	癸亥	戊寅年—虎 28歲	淺綠色	黃褐色	正北	正南	正東	丁巳年—蛇 49歲	銀白色	07 53	正東 東南	西
23	星期六	七月初一	甲子	己丑年—牛 17 77歲	水藍色	紫紅色	東北	正中	東南	戊午年—馬 48歲	淡咖啡	08 27	東北 西南	南
24	星期日	初二	乙丑	庚子年—鼠 66歲	深藍色	朱紅色	正東	正中	正南	己未年—羊 47歲	香檳黃	21 31	正北 西南	東
25	星期一	初三	丙寅	辛亥年—豬 55歲	墨綠色	寶藍色	東南	正西	西南	庚申年—猴 46歲	橘紅色	03 59	西北 正西	北
26	星期二	初四	丁卯	壬戌年—狗 44歲	咖啡色	藍灰色	正南	正西	正南	辛酉年—雞 45歲	粉紅色	04 43	西北 正西	西
27	星期三	初五	戊辰	癸酉年—雞 33歲	粉紅色	銀白色	東南	正北	西南	壬戌年—狗 44歲	嫩綠色	26 18	東北 西南	南
28	星期四	初六	己巳	甲申年—猴 22 82歲	橘紅色	粉金色	正南	正北	正西	癸亥年—豬 43歲	孔雀綠	19 32	正北 西南	東

西元二〇二五年		太歲乙巳		幸運生肖	開運顏色	忌諱顏色	正財方位	偏財方位	文昌方位	正沖生肖	正沖生肖開運顏色	吉祥數字	貴人方位	煞方
7月30	星期三	閏六月初六	庚子	乙丑年—牛 41歲	銀白色	嫩綠色	西南	正東	西北	甲午年—馬 12歲	金白色	14 39	東北 西南	南
31	星期四	初七	辛丑	丙子年—鼠 30歲	乳白色	孔雀綠	正西	正東	正北	乙未年—羊 11 71歲	淺灰色	08 37	正南 東北	東
8月1	星期五	初八	壬寅	丁亥年—豬 19 79歲	道奇藍	山茶紅	西北	正南	東北	丙申年—猴 10 70歲	深黃色	11 29	正東 東南	北
2	星期六	初九	癸卯	戊戌年—狗 68歲	蔚藍色	粉紅色	正北	正南	正東	丁酉年—雞 9 69歲	鵝黃色	23 26	正東 東南	西
3	星期日	初十	甲辰	己酉年—雞 57歲	土黃色	水藍色	東北	正中	東南	戊戌年—狗 68歲	朱紅色	07 28	東北 西南	南
4	星期一	十一	乙巳	庚申年—猴 46歲	淺棕色	靛藍色	正東	正中	正南	己亥年—豬 67歲	蜜桃紅	13 05	正北 西南	東
5	星期二	十二	丙午	辛未年—羊 35歲	綠圖騰	淡咖啡	東南	正西	西南	庚子年—鼠 66歲	金蔥色	35 18	西北 正西	北
6	星期三	十三	丁未	壬午年—馬 24歲	碧綠色	香檳黃	正南	正西	正西	辛丑年—牛 65歲	金黃色	11 04	西北 正西	西
7	星期四	十四	戊申	癸巳年—蛇 13 73歲	金條紋	淺綠色	東南	正南	西南	壬寅年—虎 64歲	深藍色	13 48	東北 西南	南
8	星期五	十五	己酉	甲辰年—龍 62歲	乳白色	青綠色	正南	正北	正西	癸卯年—兔 3 63歲	天藍色	06 22	正北 西南	東
9	星期六	十六	庚戌	乙卯年—兔 51歲	淺藍色	亮紅色	西南	正東	正西	甲辰年—龍 2 62歲	鮮黃色	16 35	東北 西南	北
10	星期日	十七	辛亥	丙寅年—虎 40歲	深黑色	淺紫色	正西	正東	正北	乙巳年—蛇 1 61歲	深咖啡	27 41	正南 東北	西
11	星期一	十八	壬子	丁丑年—牛 29歲	鮮紅色	金黃色	西北	正南	東北	丙午年—馬 60歲	墨綠色	14 36	正東 東南	南
12	星期二	十九	癸丑	戊子年—鼠 18 78歲	深紫色	雪白色	正北	正南	正東	丁未年—羊 59歲	綠條紋	18 31	正東 東南	東
13	星期三	二十	甲寅	己亥年—豬 67歲	楓綠色	咖啡色	東北	正中	東南	戊申年—猴 58歲	金黃色	02 38	東北 西南	北

西元二〇二五年		太歲乙巳		幸運生肖	開運顏色	忌諱顏色	正財方位	偏財方位	文昌方位	正沖生肖	正沖生肖開運顏色	吉祥數字	貴人方位	煞方
7月15	星期二	六月廿一	乙酉	庚辰年—龍 26歲	青碧綠	焦糖色	正東	正中	正南	己卯年—兔 27歲	雪白色	05 22	正北 西南	東
16	星期三	廿二	丙戌	辛卯年—兔 15 75歲	金白色	青綠色	東南	正西	西南	庚辰年—龍 26歲	深黑色	16 35	西北 正西	北
17	星期四	廿三	丁亥	壬寅年—虎 64歲	乳黃色	嫩綠色	正南	正西	正西	辛巳年—蛇 25歲	淺藍色	20 32	西北 正西	西
18	星期五	六月廿四	戊子	癸丑年—牛 53歲	淺黃色	淺土色	東南	正北	西南	壬午年—馬 24歲	深栗紫	13 31	東北 西南	南
19	星期六	廿五	己丑	甲子年—鼠 42歲	咖啡色	深藍色	正南	正北	正西	癸未年—羊 23歲	亮紅色	33 38	正北 西南	東
20	星期日	廿六	庚寅	乙亥年—豬 31歲	深藍色	金白色	西南	正東	西北	甲申年—猴 22歲	亮綠色	49 55	東北 西南	北
21	星期一	廿七	辛卯	丙戌年—狗 20 80歲	紅紫色	金黃色	正西	正東	正北	乙酉年—雞 21歲	楓綠色	09 54	正南 東北	西
22	星期二	廿八	壬辰	丁酉年—雞 69歲	墨綠色	深褐色	西北	正南	東北	丙戌年—狗 20歲	乳黃色	11 18	正東 東南	南
23	星期三	廿九	癸巳	戊申年—猴 58歲	粉綠色	咖啡色	正北	正南	正東	丁亥年—豬 19 79歲	檸檬黃	27 28	正東 東南	東
24	星期四	三十	甲午	己未年—羊 47歲	藍灰色	粉紫色	東北	正中	東南	戊子年—鼠 78 18歲	深黃色	06 29	東北 西南	北
25	星期五	閏六月初一	乙未	庚午年—馬 36歲	深黑色	橘紅色	正東	正中	正南	己丑年—牛 17歲	香檳黃	10 25	正北 西南	西
26	星期六	初二	丙申	辛巳年—蛇 25歲	淡咖啡	水藍色	東南	正西	西南	庚寅年—虎 16 76歲	橘紅色	08 11	西北 正西	南
27	星期日	初三	丁酉	壬辰年—龍 14 74歲	土黃色	灰白色	正南	正西	正西	辛卯年—兔 15 75歲	桃紅色	19 34	西北 正西	東
28	星期一	初四	戊戌	癸卯年—兔 63歲	朱紅色	金白色	東南	正北	西南	壬辰年—龍 14歲	草綠色	13 06	東北 西南	北
29	星期二	初五	己亥	甲寅年—虎 52歲	粉紅色	金黃色	正南	正北	正西	癸巳年—蛇 13歲	碧綠色	20 32	正北 西南	西

西元二〇二五年	6月30	7月1	2	3	4	5	6	7	8	9	10	11	12	13	14
	星期一	星期二	星期三	星期四	星期五	星期六	星期日	星期一	星期二	星期三	星期四	星期五	星期六	星期日	星期一
太歲乙巳	六月初六	初七	初八	初九	初十	十一	十二	十三	十四	十五	十六	十七	十八	十九	二十
	庚午	辛未	壬申	癸酉	甲戌	乙亥	丙子	丁丑	戊寅	己卯	庚辰	辛巳	壬午	癸未	甲申
幸運生肖	乙未年—羊 71歲	丙午年—馬 60歲	丁巳年—蛇 49歲	戊辰年—龍 38歲	己卯年—兔 27歲	庚寅年—虎 16 76歲	辛丑年—牛 65歲	壬子年—鼠 54歲	癸亥年—豬 43歲	甲戌年—狗 32歲	乙酉年—雞 21 81歲	丙申年—猴 70歲	丁未年—羊 59歲	戊午年—馬 48歲	己巳年—蛇 37歲
開運顏色	金黃色	乳白色	銀白色	水藍色	可可色	鵝黃色	橄欖綠	粉綠色	亮金色	灰白色	藍條紋	寶藍色	葡萄紫	深紅色	青翠色
忌諱顏色	草地綠	檸檬綠	紫紅色	棗紅色	淡藍色	丈青色	深褐色	咖啡色	水綠色	楓綠色	桃紅色	火紅色	金黃色	純白色	咖啡色
正財方位	西南	正西	西北	正北	東北	正東	東南	正南	東南	正南	西南	正西	西北	正北	東北
偏財方位	正東	正東	正南	正南	正中	正中	正西	正西	正北	正北	正東	正東	正南	正南	正中
文昌方位	西北	正北	東北	正東	東南	西南	西南	正西	西南	正西	西北	正北	東北	正東	東南
正沖生肖	甲子年—鼠 42歲	乙丑年—牛 41歲	丙寅年—虎 40歲	丁卯年—兔 39歲	戊辰年—龍 38歲	己巳年—蛇 37歲	庚午年—馬 36歲	辛未年—羊 35歲	壬申年—猴 34歲	癸酉年—雞 33歲	甲戌年—狗 32歲	乙亥年—豬 31歲	丙子年—鼠 30歲	丁丑年—牛 29歲	戊寅年—虎 28歲
正沖生肖開運顏色	道奇藍	蔚藍色	深咖啡	深棕色	棗紅色	豔紅色	暗金色	金黃色	天藍色	湖水藍	米黃色	深棕色	淺綠色	草青色	銀白色
吉祥數字	13 51	02 37	31 35	25 40	04 32	19 25	05 14	44 03	16 30	05 18	06 37	16 38	03 16	24 47	38 39
貴人方位	東北 西南	正南 東北	正東 東南	正東 東南	東北 西南	正北 西南	西北 正西	西北 正西	東北 西南	正北 西南	東北 西南	正南 東北	正東 東南	正東 東南	東北 西南
煞方	北	西	南	東	北	西	南	東	北	西	南	東	北	西	南

西元二〇二五年	星期	太歲乙巳		幸運生肖	開運顏色	忌諱顏色	正財方位	偏財方位	文昌方位	正沖生肖	正沖生肖開運顏色	吉祥數字	貴人方位	煞方
6月15	星期日	五月二十	乙卯	庚戌年—狗 56歲	綠條紋	土黃色	正東	正中	正南	己酉年—雞 57歲	純白色	06 23	正北 西南	西
16	星期一	廿一	丙辰	辛酉年—雞 45歲	金蔥色	草綠色	東南	正西	西南	庚戌年—狗 56歲	藍灰色	07 28	西北 正西	南
17	星期二	廿二	丁巳	壬申年—猴 34歲	雪白色	墨綠色	正南	正西	正西	辛亥年—豬 55歲	靛藍色	08 36	西北 正西	東
18	星期三	廿三	戊午	癸未年—羊 23歲	深咖啡	寶藍色	東南	正北	西南	壬子年—鼠 54歲	紅藍色	03 18	正東 東南	北
19	星期四	廿四	己未	甲午年—馬 12 72歲	稻草黃	深黑色	正南	正北	正西	癸丑年—牛 53歲	薰衣紫	19 34	正北 西南	西
20	星期五	廿五	庚申	乙巳年—蛇 61歲	粉紫色	銀白色	西南	正東	西北	甲寅年—虎 52歲	翠玉綠	29 33	東北 西南	南
21	星期六	廿六	辛酉	丙辰年—龍 50歲	深紫色	金黃色	正西	正東	正北	乙卯年—兔 51歲	翡翠綠	23 35	正南 東北	東
22	星期日	廿七	壬戌	丁卯年—兔 39歲	草綠色	淺棕色	西北	正南	東北	丙辰年—龍 50歲	金黃色	13 36	正東 東南	北
23	星期一	廿八	癸亥	戊寅年—虎 28歲	淺綠色	黃褐色	正北	正南	正東	丁巳年—蛇 49歲	銀白色	09 17	正東 東南	西
24	星期二	廿九	甲子	己丑年—牛 17 77歲	水藍色	紫紅色	東北	正中	東南	戊午年—馬 48歲	淡咖啡	25 33	東北 西南	南
25	星期三	六月初一	乙丑	庚子年—鼠 66歲	深藍色	朱紅色	正東	正中	正南	己未年—羊 47歲	香檳黃	42 01	正北 西南	東
26	星期四	初二	丙寅	辛亥年—豬 55歲	墨綠色	寶藍色	東南	正西	西南	庚申年—猴 46歲	橘紅色	29 36	西北 正西	北
27	星期五	初三	丁卯	壬戌年—狗 44歲	咖啡色	藍灰色	正南	正西	正南	辛酉年—雞 45歲	粉紅色	14 28	西北 正西	西
28	星期六	初四	戊辰	癸酉年—雞 33歲	粉紅色	銀白色	東南	正北	西南	壬戌年—狗 44歲	嫩綠色	30 41	東北 西南	南
29	星期日	初五	己巳	甲申年—猴 22 82歲	橘紅色	粉金色	正南	正北	正西	癸亥年—豬 43歲	孔雀綠	12 49	正北 西南	東

西元二〇二五年		太歲乙巳		幸運生肖	開運顏色	忌諱顏色	正財方位	偏財方位	文昌方位	正沖生肖	正沖生肖開運顏色	吉祥數字	貴人方位	煞方
5月31	星期六	五月初五	庚子	乙丑年—牛 41歲	銀白色	嫩綠色	西南	正東	西北	甲午年—馬 12歲	金白色	16 30	東北 西南	南
6月1	星期日	初六	辛丑	丙子年—鼠 30歲	乳白色	孔雀綠	正西	正東	正北	乙未年—羊 11歲	淺灰色	17 31	正南 東北	東
2	星期一	初七	壬寅	丁亥年—豬 19 79歲	道奇藍	山茶紅	西北	正南	東北	丙申年—猴 10 70歲	深黃色	03 37	正東 東南	北
3	星期二	初八	癸卯	戊戌年—狗 68歲	蔚藍色	粉紅色	正北	正南	正東	丁酉年—雞 69歲	鵝黃色	02 16	正東 東南	西
4	星期三	初九	甲辰	己酉年—雞 57歲	土黃色	水藍色	東北	正中	東南	戊戌年—狗 68歲	朱紅色	29 33	東北 西南	南
5	星期四	初十	乙巳	庚申年—猴 46歲	淺棕色	靛藍色	正東	正中	正南	己亥年—豬 67歲	蜜桃紅	09 22	正北 西南	東
6	星期五	十一	丙午	辛未年—羊 35歲	綠圖騰	淡咖啡	東南	正西	西南	庚子年—鼠 66歲	金蔥色	23 43	西北 正西	北
7	星期六	十二	丁未	壬午年—馬 24歲	碧綠色	香檳黃	正南	正西	正西	辛丑年—牛 65歲	金黃色	13 18	西北 正西	西
8	星期日	十三	戊申	癸巳年—蛇 13 73歲	金條紋	淺綠色	東南	正南	西南	壬寅年—虎 64歲	深藍色	03 08	東北 西南	南
9	星期一	十四	己酉	甲辰年—龍 62歲	乳白色	青綠色	正南	正北	正西	癸卯年—兔 63歲	天藍色	14 44	正北 西南	東
10	星期二	十五	庚戌	乙卯年—兔 51歲	淺藍色	亮紅色	西南	正東	正西	甲辰年—龍 62歲	鮮黃色	07 32	東北 西南	北
11	星期三	十六	辛亥	丙寅年—虎 40歲	深黑色	淺紫色	正西	正東	正北	乙巳年—蛇 61歲	深咖啡	05 39	正南 東北	西
12	星期四	十七	壬子	丁丑年—牛 29歲	鮮紅色	金黃色	西北	正南	東北	丙午年—馬 60歲	墨綠色	04 27	正東 東南	南
13	星期五	十八	癸丑	戊子年—鼠 18 78歲	深紫色	雪白色	正北	正南	正東	丁未年—羊 59歲	綠條紋	08 14	正東 東南	東
14	星期六	十九	甲寅	己亥年—豬 67歲	楓綠色	咖啡色	東北	正中	東南	戊申年—猴 58歲	金黃色	13 17	東北 西南	北

二〇二五年 西元		太歲 乙巳		幸運生肖	開運顏色	忌諱顏色	正財方位	偏財方位	文昌方位	正沖生肖	正沖生肖開運顏色	吉祥數字	貴人方位	煞方
5月16	星期五	四月十九	乙酉	庚辰年—龍 26歲	青碧綠	焦糖色	正東	正中	正南	己卯年—兔 27歲	雪白色	07 39	正北 西南	東
17	星期六	二十	丙戌	辛卯年—兔 15 75歲	金白色	青綠色	東南	正西	西南	庚辰年—龍 26歲	深黑色	19 24	西北 正西	北
18	星期日	廿一	丁亥	壬寅年—虎 64歲	乳黃色	嫩綠色	正南	正西	正西	辛巳年—蛇 25歲	淺藍色	33 38	西北 正西	西
19	星期一	廿二	戊子	癸丑年—牛 53歲	淺黃色	淺土色	東南	正北	西南	壬午年—馬 24歲	深栗紫	03 08	東北 西南	南
20	星期二	廿三	己丑	甲子年—鼠 42歲	咖啡色	深藍色	正南	正北	正西	癸未年—羊 23歲	亮紅色	01 26	正北 西南	東
21	星期三	廿四	庚寅	乙亥年—豬 31歲	深藍色	金白色	西南	正東	西北	甲申年—猴 22歲	亮綠色	11 30	東北 西南	北
22	星期四	廿五	辛卯	丙戌年—狗 20 80歲	紅紫色	金黃色	正西	正東	正北	乙酉年—雞 21歲	楓綠色	07 41	正南 東北	西
23	星期五	廿六	壬辰	丁酉年—雞 69歲	墨綠色	深褐色	西北	正南	東北	丙戌年—狗 20歲	乳黃色	18 32	正東 東南	南
24	星期六	廿七	癸巳	戊申年—猴 58歲	粉綠色	咖啡色	正北	正南	正東	丁亥年—豬 19歲	檸檬黃	04 34	正東 東南	東
25	星期日	廿八	甲午	己未年—羊 47歲	藍灰色	粉紫色	東北	正中	東南	戊子年—鼠 18 78歲	深黃色	25 05	東北 西南	北
26	星期一	廿九	乙未	庚午年—馬 36歲	深黑色	橘紅色	正東	正中	正南	己丑年—牛 17歲	香檳黃	14 36	正北 西南	西
27	星期二	五月初一	丙申	辛巳年—蛇 25歲	淡咖啡	水藍色	東南	正西	西南	庚寅年—虎 16 76歲	橘紅色	06 29	西北 正西	南
28	星期三	初二	丁酉	壬辰年—龍 14 74歲	土黃色	灰白色	正南	正西	正西	辛卯年—兔 15 75歲	桃紅色	15 27	西北 正西	東
29	星期四	初三	戊戌	癸卯年—兔 63歲	朱紅色	金白色	東南	正北	西南	壬辰年—龍 14歲	草綠色	30 40	東北 西南	北
30	星期五	初四	己亥	甲寅年—虎 52歲	粉紅色	金黃色	正南	正北	正西	癸巳年—蛇 13歲	碧綠色	10 25	正北 西南	西

二〇二五年西元		太歲乙巳		幸運生肖	開運顏色	忌諱顏色	正財方位	偏財方位	文昌方位	正沖生肖	正沖生肖開運顏色	吉祥數字	貴人方位	煞方
5月1	星期四	四月初四	庚午	乙未年—羊 71歲	金黃色	草地綠	西南	正東	西北	甲子年—鼠 42歲	道奇藍	04 34	東北 西南	北
2	星期五	初五	辛未	丙午年—馬 60歲	乳白色	檸檬綠	正西	正東	正北	乙丑年—牛 41歲	蔚藍色	05 25	正南 東北	西
3	星期六	初六	壬申	丁巳年—蛇 49歲	銀白色	紫紅色	西北	正南	東北	丙寅年—虎 40歲	深咖啡	10 30	正東 東南	南
4	星期日	初七	癸酉	戊辰年—龍 38歲	水藍色	棗紅色	正北	正南	正東	丁卯年—兔 39歲	深棕色	12 31	正東 東南	東
5	星期一	初八	甲戌	己卯年—兔 27歲	可可色	淡藍色	東北	正中	東南	戊辰年—龍 38歲	棗紅色	31 36	東北 西南	北
6	星期二	初九	乙亥	庚寅年—虎 16 76歲	鵝黃色	丈青色	正東	正中	西南	己巳年—蛇 37歲	豔紅色	20 40	正北 西南	西
7	星期三	初十	丙子	辛丑年—牛 65歲	橄欖綠	深褐色	東南	正西	西南	庚午年—馬 36歲	暗金色	15 36	西北 正西	南
8	星期四	十一	丁丑	壬子年—鼠 54歲	粉綠色	咖啡色	正南	正西	正西	辛未年—羊 35歲	金黃色	01 39	西北 正西	東
9	星期五	十二	戊寅	癸亥年—豬 43歲	亮金色	水綠色	東南	正北	西南	壬申年—猴 34歲	天藍色	27 47	東北 西南	北
10	星期六	十三	己卯	甲戌年—狗 32歲	灰白色	楓綠色	正南	正北	正西	癸酉年—雞 33歲	湖水藍	02 28	正北 西南	西
11	星期日	十四	庚辰	乙酉年—雞 21 81歲	藍條紋	桃紅色	西南	正東	西北	甲戌年—狗 32歲	米黃色	06 39	東北 西南	南
12	星期一	十五	辛巳	丙申年—猴 70歲	寶藍色	火紅色	正西	正東	正北	乙亥年—豬 31歲	深棕色	14 26	正南 東北	東
13	星期二	十六	壬午	丁未年—羊 59歲	葡萄紫	金黃色	西北	正南	東北	丙子年—鼠 30歲	淺綠色	10 25	正東 東南	北
14	星期三	十七	癸未	戊午年—馬 48歲	深紅色	純白色	正北	正南	正東	丁丑年—牛 29歲	草青色	18 21	正東 東南	西
15	星期四	十八	甲申	己巳年—蛇 37歲	青翠色	咖啡色	東北	正中	東南	戊寅年—虎 28歲	銀白色	32 24	東北 西南	南

二〇二五年西元		太歲乙巳		幸運生肖	開運顏色	忌諱顏色	正財方位	偏財方位	文昌方位	正沖生肖	正沖生肖開運顏色	吉祥數字	貴人方位	煞方
4月16	星期三	三月十九	乙卯	庚戌年—狗 56歲	綠條紋	土黃色	正東	正中	正南	己酉年—雞 57歲	純白色	16 30	正北 西南	西
17	星期四	二十	丙辰	辛酉年—雞 45歲	金蔥色	草綠色	東南	正西	西南	庚戌年—狗 56歲	藍灰色	17 38	西北 正西	南
18	星期五	廿一	丁巳	壬申年—猴 34歲	雪白色	墨綠色	正南	正西	正西	辛亥年—豬 55歲	靛藍色	37 03	西北 正西	東
19	星期六	廿二	戊午	癸未年—羊 23歲	深咖啡	寶藍色	東南	正北	西南	壬子年—鼠 54歲	紅藍色	13 21	正東 東南	北
20	星期日	廿三	己未	甲午年—馬 12 72歲	稻草黃	深黑色	正南	正北	正西	癸丑年—牛 53歲	薰衣紫	01 16	正北 西南	西
21	星期一	廿四	庚申	乙巳年—蛇 61歲	粉紫色	銀白色	西南	正東	西北	甲寅年—虎 52歲	翠玉綠	29 33	東北 西南	南
22	星期二	廿五	辛酉	丙辰年—龍 50歲	深紫色	金黃色	正西	正東	正北	乙卯年—兔 51歲	翡翠綠	08 26	正南 東北	東
23	星期三	廿六	壬戌	丁卯年—兔 39歲	草綠色	淺棕色	西北	正南	東北	丙辰年—龍 50歲	金黃色	23 45	正東 東南	北
24	星期四	廿七	癸亥	戊寅年—虎 28歲	淺綠色	黃褐色	正北	正南	正東	丁巳年—蛇 49歲	銀白色	13 44	正東 東南	西
25	星期五	廿八	甲子	己丑年—牛 17 77歲	水藍色	紫紅色	東北	正中	東南	戊午年—馬 48歲	淡咖啡	02 47	東北 西南	南
26	星期六	廿九	乙丑	庚子年—鼠 66歲	深藍色	朱紅色	正東	正中	正南	己未年—羊 47歲	香檳黃	37 48	正北 西南	東
27	星期日	三十	丙寅	辛亥年—豬 55歲	墨綠色	寶藍色	東南	正西	西南	庚申年—猴 46歲	橘紅色	20 24	西北 正西	北
28	星期一	四月初一	丁卯	壬戌年—狗 44歲	咖啡色	藍灰色	正南	正西	正南	辛酉年—雞 45歲	粉紅色	07 49	西北 正西	西
29	星期二	初二	戊辰	癸酉年—雞 33歲	粉紅色	銀白色	東南	正北	西南	壬戌年—狗 44歲	嫩綠色	30 50	東北 西南	南
30	星期三	初三	己巳	甲申年—猴 22 82歲	橘紅色	粉金色	正南	正北	正西	癸亥年—豬 43歲	孔雀綠	25 08	正北 西南	東

西元二〇二五年		太歲乙巳		幸運辛丑	開運顏色	忌諱顏色	正財方位	偏財方位	文昌方位	正沖生肖	正沖生肖開運顏色	吉祥數字	貴人方位	煞方
4月1	星期二	三月初四	庚子	乙丑年—牛 41歲	銀白色	嫩綠色	西南	正東	西北	甲午年—馬 12歲	金白色	20 40	東北 西南	南
2	星期三	初五	辛丑	丙子年—鼠 30歲	乳白色	孔雀綠	正西	正東	正北	乙未年—羊 11歲	淺灰色	10 25	正南 東北	東
3	星期四	初六	壬寅	丁亥年—豬 19 79歲	道奇藍	山茶紅	西北	正南	東北	丙申年—猴 10 70歲	深黃色	14 26	正東 東南	北
4	星期五	初七	癸卯	戊戌年—狗 68歲	蔚藍色	粉紅色	正北	正南	正東	丁酉年—雞 9 69歲	鵝黃色	06 29	正東 東南	西
5	星期六	初八	甲辰	己酉年—雞 57歲	土黃色	水藍色	東北	正中	東南	戊戌年—狗 8 68歲	朱紅色	02 28	東北 西南	南
6	星期日	初九	乙巳	庚申年—猴 46歲	淺棕色	靛藍色	正東	正中	正南	己亥年—豬 7 67歲	蜜桃紅	27 47	正北 西南	東
7	星期一	初十	丙午	辛未年—羊 35歲	綠圖騰	淡咖啡	東南	正西	西南	庚子年—鼠 6 66歲	金蔥色	01 39	西北 正西	北
8	星期二	十一	丁未	壬午年—馬 24歲	碧綠色	香檳黃	正南	正西	正西	辛丑年—牛 5 65歲	金黃色	15 35	西北 正西	西
9	星期三	十二	戊申	癸巳年—蛇 13 73歲	金條紋	淺綠色	東南	正南	西南	壬寅年—虎 4 64歲	深藍色	36 31	東北 西南	南
10	星期四	十三	己酉	甲辰年—龍 62歲	乳白色	青綠色	正南	正北	正西	癸卯年—兔 63歲	天藍色	11 31	正北 西南	東
11	星期五	十四	庚戌	乙卯年—兔 51歲	淺藍色	亮紅色	西南	正東	正西	甲辰年—龍 62歲	鮮黃色	10 30	東北 西南	北
12	星期六	十五	辛亥	丙寅年—虎 40歲	深黑色	淺紫色	正西	正東	正北	乙巳年—蛇 61歲	深咖啡	25 05	正南 東北	西
13	星期日	十六	壬子	丁丑年—牛 29歲	鮮紅色	金黃色	西北	正南	東北	丙午年—馬 60歲	墨綠色	04 34	正東 東南	南
14	星期一	十七	癸丑	戊子年—鼠 18 78歲	深紫色	雪白色	正北	正南	正東	丁未年—羊 59歲	綠條紋	28 19	正東 東南	東
15	星期二	十八	甲寅	己亥年—豬 67歲	楓綠色	咖啡色	東北	正中	東南	戊申年—猴 58歲	金黃色	40 30	東北 西南	北

二〇二五年西元		太歲乙巳		幸運生肖	開運顏色	忌諱顏色	正財方位	偏財方位	文昌方位	正沖生肖	正沖生肖開運顏色	吉祥數字	貴人方位	煞方
3月17	星期一	二月十八	乙酉	庚辰年—龍 26歲	青碧綠	焦糖色	正東	正中	正南	己卯年—兔 27歲	雪白色	07 39	正北 西南	東
18	星期二	十九	丙戌	辛卯年—兔 15 75歲	金白色	青綠色	東南	正西	西南	庚辰年—龍 26歲	深黑色	15 27	西北 正西	北
19	星期三	二十	丁亥	壬寅年—虎 64歲	乳黃色	嫩綠色	正南	正西	正西	辛巳年—蛇 25歲	淺藍色	02 15	西北 正西	西
20	星期四	廿一	戊子	癸丑年—牛 53歲	淺黃色	淺土色	東南	正北	西南	壬午年—馬 24歲	深栗紫	18 32	東北 西南	南
21	星期五	廿二	己丑	甲子年—鼠 42歲	咖啡色	深藍色	正南	正北	正西	癸未年—羊 23歲	亮紅色	04 21	正北 西南	東
22	星期六	廿三	庚寅	乙亥年—豬 31歲	深藍色	金白色	西南	正東	西北	甲申年—猴 22歲	亮綠色	09 16	東北 西南	北
23	星期日	廿四	辛卯	丙戌年—狗 20 80歲	紅紫色	金黃色	正西	正東	正北	乙酉年—雞 21歲	楓綠色	11 31	正南 東北	西
24	星期一	廿五	壬辰	丁酉年—雞 69歲	墨綠色	深褐色	西北	正南	東北	丙戌年—狗 20歲	乳黃色	05 40	正東 東南	南
25	星期二	廿六	癸巳	戊申年—猴 58歲	粉綠色	咖啡色	正北	正南	正東	丁亥年—豬 19歲	檸檬黃	02 35	正東 東南	東
26	星期三	廿七	甲午	己未年—羊 47歲	藍灰色	粉紫色	東北	正中	東南	戊子年—鼠 18 78歲	深黃色	07 41	東北 西南	北
27	星期四	廿八	乙未	庚午年—馬 36歲	深黑色	橘紅色	正東	正中	正南	己丑年—牛 17歲	香檳黃	10 44	正北 西南	西
28	星期五	廿九	丙申	辛巳年—蛇 25歲	淡咖啡	水藍色	東南	正西	西南	庚寅年—虎 16歲	橘紅色	25 33	西北 正西	南
29	星期六	三月初一	丁酉	壬辰年—龍 14 74歲	土黃色	灰白色	正南	正西	正西	辛卯年—兔 15歲	桃紅色	30 42	西北 正西	東
30	星期日	初二	戊戌	癸卯年—兔 63歲	朱紅色	金白色	東南	正北	西南	壬辰年—龍 14歲	草綠色	29 36	東北 西南	北
31	星期一	初三	己亥	甲寅年—虎 52歲	粉紅色	金黃色	正南	正北	正西	癸巳年—蛇 13歲	碧綠色	14 28	正北 西南	西

西元二〇二五年	星期	太歲乙巳		幸運生肖	開運顏色	忌諱顏色	正財方位	偏財方位	文昌方位	正沖生肖	正沖生肖開運顏色	吉祥數字	貴人方位	煞方
3月2	星期日	二月初三	庚午	乙未年─羊 71歲	金黃色	草地綠	西南	正東	西北	甲子年─鼠 42歲	道奇藍	17 30	東北 西南	北
3	星期一	初四	辛未	丙午年─馬 60歲	乳白色	檸檬綠	正西	正東	正北	乙丑年─牛 41歲	蔚藍色	16 20	正南 東北	西
4	星期二	初五	壬申	丁巳年─蛇 49歲	銀白色	紫紅色	西北	正南	東北	丙寅年─虎 40歲	深咖啡	18 21	正東 東南	南
5	星期三	初六	癸酉	戊辰年─龍 38歲	水藍色	棗紅色	正北	正南	正東	丁卯年─兔 39歲	深棕色	05 39	正東 東南	東
6	星期四	初七	甲戌	己卯年─兔 27歲	可可色	淡藍色	東北	正中	東南	戊辰年─龍 38歲	棗紅色	06 18	東北 西南	北
7	星期五	初八	乙亥	庚寅年─虎 16 76歲	鵝黃色	丈青色	正東	正中	西南	己巳年─蛇 37歲	豔紅色	01 46	正北 西南	西
8	星期六	初九	丙子	辛丑年─牛 65歲	橄欖綠	深褐色	東南	正西	西南	庚午年─馬 36歲	暗金色	21 36	西北 正西	南
9	星期日	初十	丁丑	壬子年─鼠 54歲	粉綠色	咖啡色	正南	正西	正西	辛未年─羊 35歲	金黃色	01 06	西北 正西	東
10	星期一	十一	戊寅	癸亥年─豬 43歲	亮金色	水綠色	東南	正北	西南	壬申年─猴 34歲	天藍色	04 37	東北 西南	北
11	星期二	十二	己卯	甲戌年─狗 32歲	灰白色	楓綠色	正南	正北	正西	癸酉年─雞 33歲	湖水藍	14 24	正北 西南	西
12	星期三	十三	庚辰	乙酉年─雞 21 81歲	藍條紋	桃紅色	西南	正東	西北	甲戌年─狗 32歲	米黃色	05 39	東北 西南	南
13	星期四	十四	辛巳	丙申年─猴 70歲	寶藍色	火紅色	正西	正東	正北	乙亥年─豬 31歲	深棕色	14 30	正南 東北	東
14	星期五	十五	壬午	丁未年─羊 59歲	葡萄紫	金黃色	西北	正南	東北	丙子年─鼠 30歲	淺綠色	01 18	正東 東南	北
15	星期六	十六	癸未	戊午年─馬 48歲	深紅色	純白色	正北	正南	正東	丁丑年─牛 29歲	草青色	04 27	正東 東南	西
16	星期日	十七	甲申	己巳年─蛇 37歲	青翠色	咖啡色	東北	正中	東南	戊寅年─虎 28歲	銀白色	07 39	東北 西南	南

西元二〇二五年		太歲乙巳		幸運生肖	開運顏色	忌諱顏色	正財方位	偏財方位	文昌方位	正沖生肖	正沖生肖開運顏色	吉祥數字	貴人方位	煞方
2月15	星期六	一月十八	乙卯	庚戌年—狗 56歲	綠條紋	土黃色	正東	正中	正南	己酉年—雞 57歲	純白色	28 38	正北 西南	西
16	星期日	十九	丙辰	辛酉年—雞 45歲	金蔥色	草綠色	東南	正西	西南	庚戌年—狗 56歲	藍灰色	04 07	西北 正西	南
17	星期一	二十	丁巳	壬申年—猴 34歲	雪白色	墨綠色	正南	正西	正西	辛亥年—豬 55歲	靛藍色	06 37	西北 正西	東
18	星期二	廿一	戊午	癸未年—羊 23歲	深咖啡	寶藍色	東南	正北	西南	壬子年—鼠 54歲	紅藍色	25 06	正東 東南	北
19	星期三	廿二	己未	甲午年—馬 12 72歲	稻草黃	深黑色	正南	正北	正西	癸丑年—牛 53歲	薰衣紫	19 17	正北 西南	西
20	星期四	廿三	庚申	乙巳年—蛇 61歲	粉紫色	銀白色	西南	正東	西北	甲寅年—虎 52歲	翠玉綠	04 33	東北 西南	南
21	星期五	廿四	辛酉	丙辰年—龍 50歲	深紫色	金黃色	正西	正東	正北	乙卯年—兔 51歲	翡翠綠	16 41	正南 東北	東
22	星期六	廿五	壬戌	丁卯年—兔 39歲	草綠色	淺棕色	西北	正南	東北	丙辰年—龍 50歲	金黃色	24 01	正東 東南	北
23	星期日	廿六	癸亥	戊寅年—虎 28歲	淺綠色	黃褐色	正北	正南	正東	丁巳年—蛇 49歲	銀白色	25 20	正東 東南	西
24	星期一	廿七	甲子	己丑年—牛 17 77歲	水藍色	紫紅色	東北	正中	東南	戊午年—馬 48歲	淡咖啡	01 36	東北 西南	南
25	星期二	廿八	乙丑	庚子年—鼠 66歲	深藍色	朱紅色	正東	正中	正南	己未年—羊 47歲	香檳黃	13 16	正北 西南	東
26	星期三	廿九	丙寅	辛亥年—豬 55歲	墨綠色	寶藍色	東南	正西	西南	庚申年—猴 46歲	橘紅色	23 43	西北 正西	北
27	星期四	三十	丁卯	壬戌年—狗 44歲	咖啡色	藍灰色	正南	正西	正南	辛酉年—雞 45歲	粉紅色	04 39	西北 正西	西
28	星期五	二月初一	戊辰	癸酉年—雞 33歲	粉紅色	銀白色	東南	正北	西南	壬戌年—狗 44歲	嫩綠色	09 25	東北 西南	南
3月1	星期六	初二	己巳	甲申年—猴 22 82歲	橘紅色	粉金色	正南	正北	正西	癸亥年—豬 43歲	孔雀綠	02 17	正北 西南	東

西元二〇二五年	1月31	2月1	2	3	4	5	6	7	8	9	10	11	12	13	14
	星期五	星期六	星期日	星期一	星期二	星期三	星期四	星期五	星期六	星期日	星期一	星期二	星期三	星期四	星期五
太歲 乙	一月初三	初四	初五	初六	初七	初八	初九	初十	十一	十二	十三	十四	十五	十六	十七
巳	庚子	辛丑	壬寅	癸卯	甲辰	乙巳	丙午	丁未	戊申	己酉	庚戌	辛亥	壬子	癸丑	甲寅
幸運生肖	乙丑年—牛 41歲	丙子年—鼠 30歲	丁亥年—豬 19 79歲	戊戌年—狗 68歲	己酉年—雞 57歲	庚申年—猴 46歲	辛未年—羊 35歲	壬午年—馬 24歲	癸巳年—蛇 13 73歲	甲辰年—龍 62歲	乙卯年—兔 51歲	丙寅年—虎 40歲	丁丑年—牛 29歲	戊子年—鼠 18 78歲	己亥年—豬 67歲
開運顏色	銀白色	乳白色	道奇藍	蔚藍色	土黃色	淺棕色	綠圖騰	碧綠色	金條紋	乳白色	淺藍色	深黑色	鮮紅色	深紫色	楓綠色
忌諱顏色	嫩綠色	孔雀綠	山茶紅	粉紅色	水藍色	靛藍色	淡咖啡	香檳黃	淺綠色	青綠色	亮紅色	淺紫色	金黃色	雪白色	咖啡色
正財方位	西南	正西	西北	正北	東北	正東	東南	正南	東南	正南	西南	正西	西北	正北	東北
偏財方位	正東	正東	正南	正南	正中	正中	正西	正西	正南	正北	正東	正東	正南	正南	正中
文昌方位	西北	正北	東北	正東	東南	正南	西南	正西	西南	正西	正西	正北	東北	正東	東南
正沖生肖	甲午年—馬 12歲	乙未年—羊 11歲	丙申年—猴 10歲	丁酉年—雞 9歲	戊戌年—狗 8歲	己亥年—豬 7歲	庚子年—鼠 6歲	辛丑年—牛 5歲	壬寅年—虎 4歲	癸卯年—兔 3歲	甲辰年—龍 2歲	乙巳年—蛇 1歲	丙午年—馬 60歲	丁未年—羊 59歲	戊申年—猴 58歲
正沖生肖開運顏色	金白色	淺灰色	深黃色	鵝黃色	朱紅色	蜜桃紅	金蔥色	金黃色	深藍色	天藍色	鮮黃色	深咖啡	墨綠色	綠條紋	金黃色
吉祥數字	01 02	08 07	14 33	29 21	31 29	22 15	32 31	12 14	22 13	09 11	18 35	23 45	12 13	21 24	40 39
貴人方位	東北 西南	正南 東北	正東 東南	正東 東南	東北 西南	正北 西南	西北 正西	西北 正西	東北 西南	正北 西南	東北 西南	正南 東北	正東 東南	正東 東南	東北 西南
煞方	南	東	北	西	南	東	北	西	南	東	北	西	南	東	北

二〇二五年 西元	1月16	17	18	19	20	21	22	23	24	25	26	27	28	29	30
	星期四	星期五	星期六	星期日	星期一	星期二	星期三	星期四	星期五	星期六	星期日	星期一	星期二	星期三	星期四
太歲 甲辰	十二月十七	十八	十九	二十	廿一	廿二	廿三	廿四	廿五	廿六	廿七	廿八	廿九	一月初一	初二
	乙酉	丙戌	丁亥	戊子	己丑	庚寅	辛卯	壬辰	癸巳	甲午	乙未	丙申	丁酉	戊戌	己亥
幸運生肖	庚辰年—龍 25歲	辛卯年—兔 14 74歲	壬寅年—虎 63歲	癸丑年—牛 52歲	甲子年—鼠 41歲	乙亥年—豬 30歲	丙戌年—狗 19 79歲	丁酉年—雞 68歲	戊申年—猴 57歲	己未年—羊 46歲	庚午年—馬 35歲	辛巳年—蛇 24歲	壬辰年—龍 13 73歲	癸卯年—兔 63歲	甲寅年—虎 52歲
開運顏色	青碧綠	金白色	乳黃色	淺黃色	咖啡色	深藍色	紅紫色	墨綠色	粉綠色	藍灰色	深黑色	淡咖啡	土黃色	朱紅色	粉紅色
忌諱顏色	焦糖色	青綠色	嫩綠色	淺土色	深藍色	金白色	金黃色	深褐色	咖啡色	粉紫色	橘紅色	水藍色	灰白色	金白色	金黃色
正財方位	正東	東南	正南	東南	正南	西南	正西	西北	正北	東北	正東	東南	正南	東南	正南
偏財方位	正中	正西	正西	正北	正北	正東	正東	正南	正南	正中	正中	正西	正西	正北	正北
文昌方位	正南	西南	正西	西南	正西	西北	正北	東北	正東	東南	正南	西南	正西	西南	正西
正沖生肖	己卯年—兔 26歲	庚辰年—龍 25歲	辛巳年—蛇 24歲	壬午年—馬 23歲	癸未年—羊 22歲	甲申年—猴 21歲	乙酉年—雞 20歲	丙戌年—狗 19歲	丁亥年—豬 18歲	戊子年—鼠 77 17歲	己丑年—牛 16歲	庚寅年—虎 15 75歲	辛卯年—兔 14 74歲	壬辰年—龍 14歲	癸巳年—蛇 13歲
正沖生肖開運顏色	雪白色	深黑色	淺藍色	深栗紫	亮紅色	亮綠色	楓綠色	乳黃色	檸檬黃	深黃色	香檳黃	橘紅色	桃紅色	草綠色	碧綠色
吉祥數字	34 20	28 15	16 04	21 23	06 37	07 20	36 10	21 20	33 25	24 37	18 14	19 03	09 11	05 31	12 38
貴人方位	正北 西南	西北 正西	西北 正西	東北 西南	正北 西南	東北 西南	正南 東北	正東 東南	正東 東南	東北 西南	正北 西南	西北 正西	西北 正西	東北 西南	正北 西南
煞方	東	北	西	南	東	北	西	南	東	北	西	南	東	北	西

發財開運吉祥日課

二〇二五年 西元		太歲 甲辰		幸運生肖	開運顏色	忌諱顏色	正財方位	偏財方位	文昌方位	正沖生肖	正沖生肖開運顏色	吉祥數字	貴人方位	煞方
1月1	星期三	十二月初二	庚午	乙未年—羊 70歲	金黃色	草地綠	西南	正東	西北	甲子年—鼠 41歲	道奇藍	28 17	東北 西南	北
2	星期四	初三	辛未	丙午年—馬 59歲	乳白色	檸檬綠	正西	正東	正北	乙丑年—牛 40歲	蔚藍色	16 37	正南 東北	西
3	星期五	初四	壬申	丁巳年—蛇 48歲	銀白色	紫紅色	西北	正南	東北	丙寅年—虎 39歲	深咖啡	25 41	正東 東南	南
4	星期六	初五	癸酉	戊辰年—龍 37歲	水藍色	棗紅色	正北	正南	正東	丁卯年—兔 38歲	深棕色	02 42	正東 東南	東
5	星期日	初六	甲戌	己卯年—兔 26歲	可可色	淡藍色	東北	正中	東南	戊辰年—龍 37歲	棗紅色	05 13	東北 西南	北
6	星期一	初七	乙亥	庚寅年—虎 15 75歲	鵝黃色	丈青色	正東	正中	西南	己巳年—蛇 36歲	豔紅色	33 20	正北 西南	西
7	星期二	初八	丙子	辛丑年—牛 64歲	橄欖綠	深褐色	東南	正西	西南	庚午年—馬 35歲	暗金色	50 19	西北 正西	南
8	星期三	初九	丁丑	壬子年—鼠 53歲	粉綠色	咖啡色	正南	正西	正西	辛未年—羊 34歲	金黃色	20 07	西北 正西	東
9	星期四	初十	戊寅	癸亥年—豬 42歲	亮金色	水綠色	東南	正北	西南	壬申年—猴 33歲	天藍色	12 11	東北 西南	北
10	星期五	十一	己卯	甲戌年—狗 31歲	灰白色	楓綠色	正南	正北	正西	癸酉年—雞 32歲	湖水藍	30 38	正北 西南	西
11	星期六	十二	庚辰	乙酉年—雞 20 80歲	藍條紋	桃紅色	西南	正東	西北	甲戌年—狗 31歲	米黃色	32 22	東北 西南	南
12	星期日	十三	辛巳	丙申年—猴 69歲	寶藍色	火紅色	正西	正東	正北	乙亥年—豬 30歲	深棕色	21 14	正南 東北	東
13	星期一	十四	壬午	丁未年—羊 58歲	葡萄紫	金黃色	西北	正南	東北	丙子年—鼠 29歲	淺綠色	29 37	正東 東南	北
14	星期二	十五	癸未	戊午年—馬 47歲	深紅色	純白色	正北	正南	正東	丁丑年—牛 28歲	草青色	13 24	正東 東南	西
15	星期三	十六	甲申	己巳年—蛇 36歲	青翠色	咖啡色	東北	正中	東南	戊寅年—虎 27歲	銀白色	36 12	東北 西南	南

（斗指寅爲雨水，時東風解凍，冰雪皆散而爲水，化而爲雨，故名雨水。）

日	星期	神煞	紀事	農曆	干支	九星	建除	星宿	卦	宜忌	吉時	方位	沖煞	胎神
16	星期一	歲月德合	鳳凰	廿九	辛酉木	綠四	危	危	四八小過三 3八	宜 祭祀齋醮沐浴開生墳入殮成除服移柩破土安葬 忌 動土嫁娶作灶上樑 除夕○火盆暴	丑寅辰巳	西南 正東	沖兔5 歲煞東	廚灶門 外東南
17	星期二	天德合	●合朔戌正 20 02 32	正月初一	壬戌水	黃五	成	室	中五禽 4四	☆ 日逢受死日大凶吉事少取 天臘之辰 宜祭祀塞穴結網入殮成除服移柩破土安葬謝土	寅卯巳午	正南 正南	沖龍51 歲煞北	倉庫栖 外東南
18	星期三		獺祭雨 今日雨水	初二	癸亥水	碧三	收	壁	六八漸七 6六	宜 祭祀沐浴理髮作灶捕捉結網栽種(刀砧) 忌 嫁娶安葬開市造廟	子寅卯未	東南 正南	沖蛇50 歲煞西	占房床 外東南
19	星期四	二元一（刀砧）	時五福子 時入坤宮 四牛耕地	初三	甲子金	赤七	開	奎	七八蹇二 1一	宜 祭祀開光入學出行沐浴理髮嫁娶會親友動土安碓磨放水開市立券交易納財開渠開井栽種	卯辰未申	東北 東南	沖馬49 歲煞南	占門碓 外東南
20	星期五			初四	乙丑金	白八	閉	婁	八八艮一 6三	宜 祭祀祈福求嗣齋醮給由求醫治病結網斷蟻納畜入殮成除服啓攢謝土 忌 開光出行	寅卯巳申	西北 東南	沖羊48 歲煞東	碓磨廁 外東南
21	星期六	歲月德		初五	丙寅火	紫九	建	胃	九八謙六 4二	宜 開光問名納采裁衣會親友上樑安床開市立券交易納財開倉庫出貨財牧養入殮啓攢安葬	巳午酉戌	西南 正西	沖猴47 歲煞北	廚灶爐 外正南
22	星期日	天德	時五福酉 時入中宮	初六	丁卯火	白一	除	昴	一九否九 9六	宜 祭祀祈福出行納采裁衣嫁娶修造動土安床開市納財牧養納畜入殮 忌 作灶入宅出火	巳午未戌	正南 正西	沖雞46 歲煞西	倉庫門 外正南
23	星期一	人日瑞彩	天曹遷賞會	初七	戊辰木	黑二	滿	畢	二九萃四 6九	宜 祭祀祈福求嗣理髮冠笄會親友安床結網 候雁北 畋獵斷蟻牧養 忌 動土開市立券交易 七龍治水	巳未申酉	東南 正北	沖狗45 歲煞南	房床栖 外正南
24	星期二		◐上弦戌正 20 29 01	初八	己巳木	碧三	平	觜	三九晉三 2八	宜 作灶平治道塗 忌 開市祈福出行造廟	巳午申酉	東北 正北	沖豬44 歲煞東	占門床 外正南
25	星期三		玉皇大帝聖誕	初九	庚午土	綠四	定	參	四九豫八 9八	宜 祭祀開光祈福出行納采修造安床入宅開市納財結網畋獵牧養納畜入殮啓攢安葬(勿探病)	丑寅未申	西北 正東	沖鼠43 歲煞北	占碓磨 外正南
26	星期四	歲月德合	麒麟日 時午入乾	初十	辛未土	黃五	執	井	中五禽 3九	宜 祭祀祈福出行納采嫁娶出火修造動土起基上樑安床捕捉栽種牧養納畜入殮破土啓攢安葬	寅卯午申	西南 正東	沖牛42 歲煞西	廚灶廁 外西南
27	星期五	天德合		十一	壬申金	白六	破	鬼	六九觀二 7一	★ 日逢月破日大耗大凶不宜諸吉事 宜祭祀解除沐浴求醫治病破屋壞垣掃舍宇	子卯辰巳	正南 正南	沖虎41 歲煞南	倉庫爐 外西南
28	星期六	草木萌動		十二	癸酉金	赤七	危	柳	七九比七 7二	宜 祭祀開光祈福出行沐浴納采嫁娶出火修造動土上樑安門入宅開市栽種牧養取魚入殮破土安葬	子丑辰巳	東南 正南	沖兔40 歲煞東	房床門 外西南

雨水

日出：06時26分

台灣夜子23時53分16秒

台灣夜子初三刻08分16秒

日沒：17時51分

雙魚

330

蔬菜有益

北部：米豆、絲豆、烏豆、番椒、薤椒、結球、萵苣、石刁柏、白豆、紫蘇

中部：番石、白豆、絲瓜、紫蘇、烏豆

南部：白筍、蓮藕、絲瓜、紫蘇、石刁柏

漁我同在

新港：釘鯱

安平：白帶、沙魚、馬鮫

高雄：石鯽、釘鯱、沙魚、鰮

（斗指東北維爲立春，時春氣始至，四時之卒始，故名立春也。）

二〇二六FEB 陽曆二月平（28天）

陰曆正月大自乙巳年十二月十七日寅正
建庚寅室宿至丙午年正月十七日亥正

庚寅月（孟春端月）

元旦晴雲光霽天
雨雪霏霏是豐年
最喜立春晴一日
農夫不用力耕田

月煞（在北方）

三一有七

七	三	五
六	八	一
二	四	九

陽曆	星期	備註	陰曆	干支	九星	建除	星宿	卦	宜忌	每日吉時	每日喜神財神方位	每日沖肖年齡煞方	每日胎神占方
1	星期日		十四	丙午水	赤七	執	星	七六井六 3四	宜 沐浴理髮整手足甲捕捉畋獵進壽符開生墳入殮成除服移柩破土啓攢修墳立碑安葬謝土	巳未酉戌	西南 正西	沖鼠6 歲煞北	廚灶碓 房內東
2	星期一	○入望卯 正06 10 36	十五	丁未水	白八	破	張	八六蠱七 7六	☆ 逢月破日大耗大凶吉事少取 宜祭祀破屋壞垣	卯巳午酉	正南 正西	沖牛5 歲煞西	倉庫廁 房內東
3	星期二		十六	戊申土	紫九	危	翼	九六升二 6二	宜 祭祀理髮經絡立券交易納財出貨財開池牧養納畜入殮破土啓攢修墳安葬 忌嫁娶安床（刀砧）	丑辰巳午	東南 正北	沖虎4 歲煞南	房床爐 房內東
4	星期三	一元四子入中 東風解凍 今日立春	十七	己酉土	白一	危	軫	一七訟三 8三	宜 節前：逢受死日大凶吉事少取（刀砧） 節後：祭祀祈福齋醮裁衣造廟掛匾入殮破土	辰巳午申	東北 正北	沖兔3 歲煞東	占大門 外東北
5	星期四		十八	庚戌金	黑二	成	角	二七困八 9九	☆ 逢受死日大凶吉事少取 宜入學補垣塞穴結網入殮成除服移柩破土安葬	寅卯午未	西北 正東	沖龍2 歲煞北	碓磨栖 外東北
6	星期五	歲月德合 午未武曲 聖人登殿	十九	辛亥金	碧三	收	亢	三七未九 7七	宜 祭祀祈福出行納采修造動土起基上樑安床作灶開市納財教牛馬捕捉栽種牧養納畜（刀砧）	寅卯午未	西南 正東	沖蛇1 歲煞西	廚灶床 外東北
7	星期六	天德合 時五福酉 時入乾宮	二十	壬子木	綠四	開	氐	四七解四 1八	宜 祭祀開光祈福齋醮理髮納采裁衣嫁娶修造動土安床納財開池栽種牧養成除服破土啓攢（刀砧）	卯辰巳申	正南 正南	沖馬60 歲煞南	倉庫碓 外東北
8	星期日	午申二時 貴人登天	廿一	癸丑木	黃五	閉	房	中五禽六 8六	宜 祭祀給由裁衣合帳經絡伐木做樑開柱眼定磉安床作灶入殮成除服移柩啓攢 忌納采出火	子卯巳酉	東南 正南	沖羊59 歲煞東	房床廁 外東北
9	星期一	蟄蟲始振 ◑下弦戌 正20 44 33	廿二	甲寅水	白六	建	心	六七渙六 9七	宜 裁衣會親友伐木做樑造倉庫開市立券交易納財教牛馬納畜 忌嫁娶安葬（勿探病）	丑寅午未	東北 東南	沖猴58 歲煞北	占門爐 外東北
10	星期二		廿三	乙卯水	赤七	除	尾	七七坎一 4一	宜 祭祀祈福齋醮納采修造動土起基安床開市立券交易入殮破土啓攢安葬 忌栽種開井（勿探病）	卯未申戌	西北 東南	沖雞57 歲煞西	碓磨門 外正東
11	星期三	歲月德 時五福午 時入艮宮	廿四	丙辰土	白八	滿	箕	八七蒙二 1四	宜 祭祀開光祈福出行納采裁衣嫁娶會親友經絡修造拆卸起基安床入宅納財造倉庫牧養納畜	巳午申酉	西南 正西	沖狗56 歲煞南	廚灶栖 外正東
12	星期四	天德	廿五	丁巳土	紫九	平	斗	九七師七 8二	宜 祭祀修飾垣墻平治道塗 忌出行齋醮安門安葬	丑巳午申	正南 正西	沖豬55 歲煞東	倉庫床 外正東
13	星期五	辰戌二時 貴人登天	廿六	戊午火	白一	定	牛	一八遯四 4三	宜 祭祀開光祈福出行納采裁衣嫁娶修造起基安床入宅開市立券交易納財牧養納畜入殮啓攢安葬	寅巳午未	東南 正北	沖鼠54 歲煞北	房床碓 外正東
14	星期六	魚陟負冰	廿七	己未火	黑二	執	女	二八咸九 2一	宜 問名訂盟結婚姻納采嫁娶給由會親友進人口動土開廁捕捉牧養取魚入殮移柩破土安葬	子卯巳午	東北 正北	沖牛53 歲煞西	占門廁 外正東
15	星期日	時五福卯 時入巽宮	廿八	庚申木	碧三	破	虛	三八旅八 1七	★ 逢月破日大耗大凶凡事少取 宜求醫治病破屋壞垣	辰巳未申	西北 正東	沖虎52 歲煞南	碓磨爐 外東南

立春

日出：06時37分
台灣寅時04時03分17秒
台灣寅正初刻03分17秒
日沒：17時43分

寶瓶 315

蔬菜有益

北部：茄子、番茄、大蔥、牛蒡、分蔥
中部：白芋、西瓜、胡瓜、甜瓜、鵲豆
甕菜、幸菜、莿瓜、肉豆、蔥仔
南部：白芋、薑、越瓜、鵲豆、刀豆

漁我同在

淡水：鯧魚、鮑魚、釘鯃、沙魚
基隆：沙魚、梳齒、加蚋魚
蘇澳：狗母、龍蝦、花輝、沙魚
澎湖：梳齒、加蚋魚、釘鯃

（斗指丑為大寒，時大寒栗烈已極，故名大寒也。）

日期	16	17	18	19	20
神煞	歲天月德				一元三子入乾
星期	星期五	星期六	星期日	星期一	星期二
事項	時五福卯時入中宮	土王用事午11 04 10		●合朔寅初03 53 24	雞乳今日大寒
農曆	廿八	廿九	三十	十二月初一	初二
干支	庚寅木	辛卯木	壬辰水	癸巳水	甲午金
九星	紫九	白一	黑二	碧三	綠四
建除	除	滿	平	定	執
星宿	牛	女	虛	危	室
卦	九三夷三 1三	一四妄二 3二	二四隨七 4六	三四嗑六 6四	四四震一 1九
宜	宜	宜	宜	宜	宜
宜忌	開光出行沐浴理髮問名訂盟納采嫁娶動土開市納財牧養納畜入殮破土啓攢修墳安葬 忌 祭祀	祭祀出行理髮針灸裁衣嫁娶安床開市立券交易納財牧養入殮移柩啓攢修墳安葬 忌 入宅上樑	泥墻平治道塗 忌 作灶開井造廟造橋	祭祀訂盟納采裁衣會親友出火修造起基上樑安床移徙入宅納財牧養納畜 忌 出行造廟	祭祀開光祈福出行納采嫁娶起基上樑安床入宅捕捉牧養納畜入殮移柩破土修墳安葬
吉時	午未酉戌	寅午未申	卯巳申酉	子丑卯巳	寅卯未戌
方位	西北正東	西南正東	正南正南	東南正南	東北東南
沖煞	沖猴歲煞北22	沖雞歲煞西21	沖狗歲煞南20	沖豬歲煞東19	沖鼠歲煞北18
胎神	碓磨爐外正北	廚灶門外正北	倉庫栖外正北	占房床房內北	占門碓房內北

日期	21	22	23	24	25	26	27	28	29	30	31
神煞	歲天月德合				征鳥厲疾	歲天月德臘八				水澤腹堅	歲天月德合
星期	星期三	星期四	星期五	星期六	星期日	星期一	星期二	星期三	星期四	星期五	星期六
事項	麒麟		時五福酉時入艮宮		丑寅左輔聖人登殿	◐上弦午正12 48 51	時五福午時入巽宮		辰巳貪狼聖人登殿		時五福卯時入坤宮
農曆	初三	初四	初五	初六	初七	初八	初九	初十	十一	十二	十三
干支	乙未金	丙申火	丁酉火	戊戌木	己亥木	庚子土	辛丑土	壬寅金	癸卯金	甲辰火	乙巳火
九星	五黃	六白	七赤	八白	九紫	一白	二黑	三碧	四綠	五黃	六白
建除	破	危	成	收	開	閉	建	除	滿	平	定
星宿	壁	奎	婁	胃	昴	畢	觜	參	井	鬼	柳
卦	中五禽七 6七	六四益九 4八	七四屯四 9四	八四頤三 6一	九四復八 2二	一六姤八 9二	二六大過三 3一	三六鼎四 7九	四六恒九 7八	中五禽 2三	六六巽一 3七
宜	★	宜	☆	宜	宜	宜	◇	宜	宜	宜	宜
宜忌	日逢**月破日**大耗大凶不宜 宜祭祀破屋壞垣解除	祭祀齋醮出行納采嫁娶起基上樑入宅開市納財結網栽種牧養納畜入殮破土啓攢安葬(刀砧)	日逢**受死日**不宜諸吉事(刀砧) 宜祭祀齋醮入殮成除服破土啓攢修墳立碑安葬	祭祀納財捕捉畋獵 忌 造廟安床作灶造船	祭祀祈福求嗣設醮入學沐浴理髮問名訂盟納采會親友開渠開井牧養納畜造畜稠棲棧	祭祀祈福求嗣齋醮沐浴納采裁衣安床立券交易納財入殮移柩啓攢修墳安葬謝土 忌 開光鳳凰	日逢**正紅紗日**凡事少取 宜祭祀求嗣解除會親友教牛馬造畜稠棲棧	開光沐浴入學裁衣嫁娶出火拆卸修造起基上樑安床入宅開市入殮破土啓攢安葬(勿探病)	祭祀出行訂盟納采裁衣嫁娶會親友起基安床開市立券交易納財結網栽種入殮移柩啓攢安葬	結婚姻平治道塗 忌 造廟安門作灶栽種	祭祀開光納采裁衣嫁娶出火修造起基上樑安門安床作灶入宅納財牧養納畜 忌 出行開市
吉時	子寅卯午	辰巳午酉	辰巳午酉	卯巳午未	寅卯午未	辰未申酉	寅巳午申	子卯巳午	卯巳未戌	寅未申酉	寅卯申酉
方位	西北東南	西南正西	正南正西	東南正北	東北正北	西北正東	西南正東	正南正南	東南正南	東北東南	西北東南
沖煞	沖牛歲煞西17	沖虎歲煞南16	沖兔歲煞東15	沖龍歲煞北14	沖蛇歲煞西13	沖馬歲煞南12	沖羊歲煞東11	沖猴歲煞北10	沖雞歲煞西9	沖狗歲煞南8	沖豬歲煞東7
胎神	碓磨廁房內北	廚灶爐房內北	倉庫門房內北	房床栖房內南	占門床房內南	占碓磨房內南	廚灶廁房內南	倉庫爐房內南	房床門房內南	門雞栖房內東	碓磨床房內東

大寒

日出：06時42分

台灣巳時09時46分05秒

台灣巳初三刻01分05秒

日沒：17時32分

寶瓶

300

蔬菜有益

北部：紅菜頭、菜瓜、匏仔、萵蒿、東菠菜

中部：菠菜、菜瓜、小白菜、匏仔、紅菜頭、水芋

南部：白芋、蓮藕、絲瓜、扇浦、水芋、土白菜

漁我同在

新港：釘鮸、硼串

高雄：

東港：狗母、過仔魚

安平：馬鮫、沙魚、烏魚

（斗指癸為小寒，時天氣漸寒，尚未大冷，故名小寒。）

二〇二六 JAN 陽曆正月大（31天）

陰曆十一月大自十一月十七日申正建己丑危宿至十二月十七日寅正

己丑月（季臘冬月）

朔日西風六畜災　棉絲五穀總成堆　最喜大寒無雨雪　太平冬盡賀春來

（月煞在東方）　二二夬　六三

八	四	六
七	九	二
三	五	一

日期	星期	備註	農曆	干支	九星	建除	星宿	卦	宜忌	每日吉時	喜神	財神	沖肖/歲煞	胎神
1	星期四	歲德合；時五福卯時入乾宮	十三	乙亥火	碧三	閉	井	三二睽二 3三	宜 祭祀出行沐浴裁衣修造動土起基上樑安門作灶入宅納財築堤防斷蟻牧養造畜稠栖棧	寅卯未申	西北	東南	沖蛇37 歲煞西	碓磨床外西南
2	星期五		十四	丙子水	綠四	建	鬼	四二妹七 3六	宜 教牛馬造畜稠栖棧 忌 嫁娶作灶栽種	丑辰巳申	西南	正西	沖馬36 歲煞南	廚灶碓外西南
3	星期六	月德合；○入望酉正18 04 13	十五	丁丑水	黃五	除	柳	中五禽 7四	宜 祭祀出行沐浴納采裁衣出火修造動土安門安床入宅開市納財栽種牧養納畜 忌 齋醮安葬	巳午酉亥	正南	正西	沖羊35 歲煞東	倉庫廁外正西
4	星期日		十六	戊寅土	白六	滿	星	六二孚三 6八	宜 開光出行納采裁衣經絡修造起基上樑安門安床開市納財開渠牧養入殮啓攢修墳安葬	丑巳午未	東南	正北	沖猴34 歲煞北	房床爐外正西
5	星期一	一元二子入艮；雁北鄉 今日小寒	十七	己卯土	赤七	滿	張	七二節八 8七	節前 日逢**受死日**不宜諸吉事（勿探病） 節後 祭祀納采裁衣安床開市立券交易納財	子午未申	東北	正北	沖雞33 歲煞西	占大門外正西
6	星期二	歲天月德	十八	庚辰金	白八	平	翼	八二損九 9一	宜 祭祀裁衣冠笄嫁娶進人口安床修飾垣墻開市平治道塗入殮移柩安葬 忌 作灶造廟	丑未申酉	西北	正東	沖狗32 歲煞南	碓磨栖外正西
7	星期三	午戌二時貴人登天	十九	辛巳金	紫九	定	軫	九二臨四 7三	宜 祭祀祈福求嗣入學冠帶問名訂盟納采嫁娶會親友經絡動土起基納財牧養納畜開廁	寅午申酉	西南	正東	沖豬31 歲煞東	廚灶床外正西
8	星期四	時五福酉時入巽宮	二十	壬午木	白一	執	角	一三同七 1二	宜 祭祀祈福出行沐浴裁衣嫁娶修造動土起基上樑安床入宅捕捉畋獵入殮破土啓攢安葬（勿探病）	寅卯巳未	正南	正南	沖鼠30 歲煞北	倉庫碓外西北
9	星期五		廿一	癸未木	黑二	破	亢	二三革二 8四	★ 日逢**月破日**大耗大凶不宜諸吉事 宜 祭祀破屋壞垣	卯巳午未	東南	正南	沖牛29 歲煞西	房床廁外西北
10	星期六	鵲始巢；◑下弦夜子23 49 47	廿二	甲申水	碧三	危	氐	三三離一 9三	宜 祭祀求嗣出行納采嫁娶修造動土起基入宅結網栽種入殮破土啓攢安葬 忌 祈福設醮（刀砧）	卯辰巳未	東北	東南	沖虎28 歲煞南	占門爐外西北
11	星期日	歲天月德合	廿三	乙酉水	綠四	成	房	四三豐六 4九	☆ 日逢**受死日**不宜諸吉事（刀砧） 宜 祭祀祈福齋醮入殮成除服破土啓攢修墳安葬	丑寅辰巳	西北	東南	沖兔27 歲煞東	碓磨門外西北
12	星期一	時五福午時入坤宮	廿四	丙戌土	黃五	收	心	中五禽 1六	宜 祭祀冠笄嫁娶捕捉畋獵 忌 安床造廟開市作灶	卯巳午酉	西南	正西	沖龍26 歲煞北	廚灶栖外西北
13	星期二		廿五	丁亥土	白六	開	尾	六三家四 8八	宜 祭祀開光祈福齋醮納采裁衣修造動土起基上樑安門安床開市立券交易納財牧養納畜	寅卯午未	正南	正西	沖蛇25 歲煞西	倉庫床外西北
14	星期三		廿六	戊子火	赤七	閉	箕	七三既九 4七	宜 祭祀沐浴裁衣合帳作染安床立券交易入殮成除服移柩安葬 忌 開光嫁娶出行	丑辰巳未	東南	正北	沖馬24 歲煞南	房床碓外正北
15	星期四	雉雊	廿七	己丑火	白八	建	斗	八三賁八 2九	◇ 日逢**正紅紗日**大凶吉事少取 宜 祭祀解除交易教牛馬造畜稠栖棧	巳午申酉	東北	正北	沖羊23 歲煞東	占門廁外正北

小寒

日出：06時42分
台灣申時16時24分13秒
台灣申正一刻09分13秒
日沒：17時19分

摩羯 285

蔬菜有益

北部：菜豆、菜頭、蘿蔔、皇帝豆、石刁柏
中部：金瓜、冬瓜、南瓜、西瓜、石刁柏
南部：茄子菜、冬瓜、金瓜、石刁柏

漁我同在

蘇澳：梳齒、釘鯱、棘鬣魚
基隆：釘鯱、棘鬣魚(淡水)
澎湖：沙魚、狗母、龍蝦、棘鬣魚

（斗指子爲冬至，時陰極之至明，陽氣始至，日行至南，北半球晝最短而夜最長也。）

日期	16	17	18	19	20	21	22	23	24	25	26	27	28	29	30	31
神煞		荔挺出 歲德		月德		天赦 子入巽	歲德合		麒麟 月德合			歲德	午入中	鳳凰 月德		水泉動
星期	星期二	星期三	星期四	星期五	星期六	星期日	星期一	星期二	星期三	星期四	星期五	星期六	星期日	星期一	星期二	星期三
備註		時五福卯 時入艮宮			●合朔巳 初09 44 45	蚯蚓結 今日冬至	子辰二時 貴人登天		時五福酉 時入坤宮	申酉武曲 聖人登殿	麋角解		◐上弦寅 初03 11 15			寅卯左輔 聖人登殿
農曆	廿七	廿八	廿九	三十	十一月 初一	初二	初三	初四	初五	初六	初七	初八	初九	初十	十一	十二
干支	己未火	庚申木	辛酉木	壬戌水	癸亥水	甲子金	乙丑金	丙寅火	丁卯火	戊辰木	己巳木	庚午土	辛未土	壬申金	癸酉金	甲戌火
九星	五黃	四綠	三碧	二黑	一白	一白	二黑	三碧	四綠	五黃	六白	七赤	八白	九紫	一白	二黑
建除	危	成	收	開	閉	建	除	滿	平	定	執	破	危	成	收	開
星宿	尾	箕	斗	牛	女	虛	危	室	壁	奎	婁	胃	昴	畢	觜	參
卦	中五禽 2一	四一壯二 1七	三一有七 3八	二一夬六 4四	一一乾一 6六	一一乾一 1一	二一夬六 6三	三一有七 4二	四一壯二 9六	中五禽 6九	六一小畜八 2八	七一需三 9八	八一大畜四 3九	九一泰九 7一	一二履六 7二	二二兌一 2七
宜	宜	宜	宜	宜	宜	宜	宜	宜	☆	宜	宜	★	宜	宜	宜	宜
宜忌	祭祀祈福冠笄作染伐木動土安床放水作陂結網畋獵入殮移柩破土立碑 忌 作灶安門	開光祈福出行納采嫁娶出火修造起基上樑安門入宅納財牧養納畜入殮啟攢安葬(刀砧)	祭祀開光塑繪設醮沐浴理髮整手足甲裁衣安床作灶教牛馬掃舍宇捕捉結網畋獵(刀砧)	祭祀祈福納采裁衣會親友修造動土起基上樑安門安床作灶開市栽種牧養納畜移柩破土	沐浴裁衣合帳冠笄開柱眼安碓磨開廁作陂築堤防補垣塞穴斷蟻 忌 開光祈福嫁娶	祭祀赴舉給由沐浴作染交易捕捉入殮成除服移柩啟攢修墳安葬 忌 設醮移徙裁衣合帳	祭祀祈福出行納采裁衣修造動土起基上樑安門安床入宅開市納財出貨財牧養納畜	納采裁衣會親友經絡修造起基上樑安門安床立券交易牧養入殮啟攢安葬 忌 祭祀祈福	日逢**受死日**不宜諸吉事 宜祭祀平治道塗成除服安葬	祭祀祈福出行納采嫁娶修造動土起基上樑入宅立券交易納財納畜入殮移柩破土安葬	祭祀祈福設醮裁衣會親友修造動土起基上樑安門安床作灶結網 忌 出行安葬齋醮	日逢**月破日**大耗大凶不宜諸吉事 宜破屋壞垣(勿探病)	祭祀開光出行理髮冠笄伐木安床立券交易結網畋獵入殮成除服移柩破土啟攢修墳立碑	祭祀齋醮出行納采裁衣嫁娶修造起基上樑作灶入宅納財牧養納畜入殮啟攢安葬(刀砧)	祭祀沐浴理髮整手足甲進人口納財掃舍宇捕捉結網畋獵栽種 忌 移徙入宅出火作灶(刀砧)	祭祀祈福求嗣納采修造動土起基上樑安門安床作灶栽種移柩破土 忌 合帳冠笄嫁娶出火
吉時	子卯巳午	辰巳未申	丑寅辰巳	寅卯巳午	子寅卯未	卯辰未申	寅卯巳申	巳午酉戌	巳午未戌	巳未申酉	巳午申酉	丑寅未申	寅卯午申	子卯辰巳	子丑辰巳	寅卯午未
方位	東北 正北	西北 正東	西南 正東	正南 正南	東南 正南	東北 東南	西北 東南	西南 正西	正南 正西	東南 正北	東北 正北	西北 正東	西南 正東	正南 正南	東南 正南	東北 東南
沖煞	沖牛 歲煞西 5	沖虎 歲煞南 52	沖兔 歲煞東 51	沖龍 歲煞北 50	沖蛇 歲煞西 49	沖馬 歲煞南 48	沖羊 歲煞東 47	沖猴 歲煞北 46	沖雞 歲煞西 45	沖狗 歲煞南 44	沖豬 歲煞東 43	沖鼠 歲煞北 42	沖牛 歲煞西 41	沖虎 歲煞南 40	沖兔 歲煞東 39	沖龍 歲煞北 38
胎神	占門廁 外正東	碓磨爐 外東南	廚灶門 外東南	倉庫栖 外東南	占房床 外東南	占門碓 外東南	碓磨廁 外東南	廚灶爐 外正南	倉庫門 外正南	房床栖 外正南	占門床 外正南	占碓磨 外正南	廚灶廁 外西南	倉庫爐 外西南	房床門 外西南	門雞栖 外西南

冬至

日出：06時36分

台灣夜子23時04分07秒

台灣夜子初初刻04分07秒

日沒：17時10分

摩羯

270

蔬菜有益

北部：皇帝豆、菜豆、蘿蔔、石刁柏、蕪菁

中部：甘日羅蔔、石刁柏

南部：冬瓜、茄子、蕗蕎、蕹菜、蘿蔔、大蔥

漁我同在

高雄：硼串、過仔魚、沙魚

東港：過仔魚、沙魚、馬鮫、烏魚

安平：馬鮫、烏魚

（斗指壬，斯時積陰爲雪，至此栗烈而大，過於小雪，故名大雪也。）

二〇二五 DEC 陽曆十二月大（31天）

陰曆十月大自十月十八日卯初

建戊子虛宿至十一月十七日申正

戊子（仲葭）月（冬月）

初一西風盜賊多，更兼大雪有災魔，冬至天陰無日色，來年定唱太平歌

月煞（在南方）

一一乾 ☰

九	五	七
八	一	三
四	六	二

陽曆	星期	吉神	記事	陰曆	干支納音	九星	建除	宿	卦	宜忌	事項	每日吉時	每日喜神財神方位	每日沖肖年齡歲煞方	每日胎神占方
1	星期一	月德 鳳凰		十二	甲辰火	黑二	執	畢	二三革二 2三	宜	祭祀開光齋醮出行納采裁衣嫁娶修造起基上樑入宅納財捕捉結網牧養納畜入殮啓攢安葬	寅未申酉	東北 東南	沖狗 8 歲煞南	門雞栖 房內東
2	星期二	天德 歲德合	閉塞成冬 時卯入巽	十三	乙巳火	白一	破	觜	一三同七 3七	★	日逢**月破日**大凶大耗不宜諸吉事 宜祭祀解除求醫治病破屋壞垣	寅卯申酉	西北 東南	沖豬 7 歲煞東	碓磨床 房內東
3	星期三			十四	丙午水	紫九	危	參	九二臨四 3四	宜	祭祀沐浴掃舍宇畋獵入殮成除服移柩破土啓攢立碑安葬 忌入宅嫁娶修造動土	巳未酉戌	西南 正西	沖鼠 6 歲煞北	廚灶碓 房內東
4	星期四		下元〇 水官解厄	十五	丁未水	白八	成	井	八二損九 7六	宜	祭祀祈福納采裁衣經絡修造動土起基上樑安床納財牧養納畜入殮移柩破土安葬 忌嫁娶	卯巳午酉	正南 正西	沖牛 5 歲煞西	倉庫廁 房內東
5	星期五		〇入望辰 初07 15 24	十六	戊申土	赤七	收	鬼	七二節八 6二	☆	日逢**受死日**不宜諸吉事（刀砧） 宜祭祀沐浴掃舍宇捕捉結網畋獵	丑辰巳午	東南 正北	沖虎 4 歲煞南	房床爐 房內東
6	星期六	月德合 刀砧	七元四將 時子入坤	十七	己酉土	白六	開	柳	六二孚三 8三	宜	祭祀開光祈福求嗣齋醮出行沐浴裁衣動土起基安床開市納財栽種牧養移柩破土啓攢修墳	辰巳午申	東北 正北	沖兔 3 歲煞東	占大門 外東北
7	星期日	歲德	鶡鴠不鳴 今日大雪	十八	庚戌金	黃五	開	星	中五离 9九	宜	節前 祭祀斷蟻入殮成除服移柩破土立碑安葬 節後 祭祀設醮齋醮納采裁衣動土起基上樑	寅卯午未	西北 正東	沖龍 2 歲煞北	碓磨栖 外東北
8	星期一			十九	辛亥金	綠四	閉	張	四二妹七 7七	宜	沐浴裁衣合帳修造動土安門作灶開池作陂築堤防補垣塞穴栽種 忌祈福開光嫁娶	寅卯午未	西南 正東	沖蛇 1 歲煞西	廚灶床 外東北
9	星期二	月德	時五福酉 時入中宮	二十	壬子木	碧三	建	翼	三二睽二 1八	宜	開市令牌雷尺入殮成除服移柩啓攢安葬 忌嫁娶動土開渠栽種	卯辰巳申	正南 正南	沖馬 60 歲煞南	倉庫碓 外東北
10	星期三		申酉武曲 聖人登殿	廿一	癸丑木	黑二	除	軫	二二兑一 8六	宜	祭祀祈福出行沐浴裁衣嫁娶經絡出火修造動土起基上樑入宅開市納財栽種牧養納畜	子卯巳酉	東南 正南	沖羊 59 歲煞東	房床廁 外東北
11	星期四			廿二	甲寅水	白一	滿	角	一二履六 9七	宜	出行納采修造起基上樑安床開市立券交易納財栽種牧養入殮移柩（勿探病）	丑寅午未	東北 東南	沖猴 58 歲煞北	占門爐 外東北
12	星期五	歲德合	◑下弦寅 正04 53 01	廿三	乙卯水	紫九	平	亢	九一泰九 4一	☆	日逢**受死日**大凶不宜諸吉事（勿探病） 宜祭祀修飾垣墻平治道塗 虎始交	卯未申戌	西北 東南	沖雞 57 歲煞西	碓磨門 外正東
13	星期六		時五福午 時入乾宮	廿四	丙辰土	白八	定	氐	八一大畜四 1四	宜	祭祀開光祈福齋醮納采嫁娶修造動土起基上樑安門安床入宅納財納畜入殮移柩破土安葬	巳午申酉	西南 正西	沖狗 56 歲煞南	廚灶栖 外正東
14	星期日	月德合		廿五	丁巳土	赤七	執	房	七一需三 8二	宜	祭祀捕捉畋獵 忌嫁娶出行造廟開市	丑巳午申	正南 正西	沖豬 55 歲煞東	倉庫床 外正東
15	星期一			廿六	戊午火	白六	破	心	六一小畜八 4三	★	日逢**月破日**大凶大耗不宜諸吉事 宜祭祀沐浴破屋壞垣	寅巳午未	東南 正北	沖鼠 54 歲煞北	房床碓 外正東

大雪

日出：06時26分

台灣卯時05時05分46秒

台灣卯初初刻05分46秒

日沒：17時05分

人馬 255

蔬菜有益

北部：冬瓜、南瓜、扇蒲、卷心白菜、金瓜

中部：南瓜、扇蒲、蕹菜、款冬、蘿蔔、玉蜀黍

南部：西瓜、苦瓜、甜瓜、胡瓜、扇蒲、款冬、蕹菜、玉蜀黍

漁我同在

淡水：旗魚、棘鬣魚

基隆：梳齒、棘鬣魚

澎湖：梳齒

（斗指亥，斯時天一積陰，寒未深而雪未大，故名小雪也。）

小雪

日出：06時16分
台灣巳時09時36分35秒
台灣巳初二刻06分35秒
日沒：17時04分

人馬

240

蔬菜有益

北部：萵苣、芹菜、胡椒、莞、刈菜、朝鮮菜
中部：馬鈴薯、大蔥、玉蜀黍、甘日蘿蔔
南部：關刀豆、胡瓜、大蔥、甘日蘿蔔、玉蜀黍

漁我同在

蘇澳：旗魚
基隆：棘鬣魚、梳齒、目吼
淡水：旗魚、棘鬣魚、加蚋魚
澎湖：棘鬣魚、加蚋魚

日	星期	神煞	注記	農曆	干支	九星	建除	星宿	卦	宜忌	吉時	方位	沖煞	胎神
16	星期日	月德合		廿七	己丑火	八白	滿	房	八四頤三 2九	宜 祭祀開光塑繪沐浴理髮裁衣會親友經絡安門安床作陂塞穴結網 忌 祈福嫁娶	巳午申酉	東北 正北	沖羊23 歲煞東	占門廁 外正北
17	星期一	歲德 天德合	雉入大水爲蜃	廿八	庚寅木	七赤	平	心	七四屯四 1三	宜 開光出行納采裁衣嫁娶修造動土起基上樑入宅開市納財栽種牧養納畜入殮破土啓攢安葬	午未酉戌	西北 正東	沖猴22 歲煞北	碓磨爐 外正北
18	星期二		子申二時貴人登天	廿九	辛卯木	六白	定	尾	六四益九 3二	宜 祭祀祈福出行修造動土作灶入宅開市立券交易納財牧養入殮破土啓攢修墳安葬 忌 栽種	寅午未申	西南 正東	沖雞21 歲煞西	廚灶門 外正北
19	星期三	陽德		三十	壬辰水	五黃	執	箕	中五禽 4六	宜 祭祀入學赴舉解除沐浴理髮針灸整手足甲結婚姻納采嫁娶進人口捕捉結網畋獵 忌 動土	卯巳申酉	正南 正南	沖狗20 歲煞南	倉庫栖 外正北
20	星期四	民歲臘	●合朔未正 14 48 38	十一月初一	癸巳水	四綠	破	斗	四四震一 6四	★ 日逢**月破日**大耗大凶不宜諸吉事 宜求醫治病破屋壞垣	子丑卯巳	東南 正南	沖豬19 歲煞東	占房床 房內北
21	星期五	月德	七元三將時子入中	初二	甲午金	三碧	危	牛	三四嗑六 1九	宜 祭祀祈福出行納采嫁娶修造動土安床入宅開市納財栽種牧養納畜入殮移柩破土啓攢安葬	寅卯未戌	東北 東南	沖鼠18 歲煞北	占門碓 房內北
22	星期六	歲德合 天德	虹藏不見今日小雪	初三	乙未金	二黑	成	女	二四隨七 6七	宜 祭祀開光祈福齋醮納采裁衣修造起基上樑安床作灶牧養納畜入殮啓攢安葬謝土	子寅卯午	西北 東南	沖牛17 歲煞西	碓磨廁 房內北
23	星期日			初四	丙申火	一白	收	虛	一四妄二 4八	☆ 日逢**受死日**不宜諸吉事（刀砧） 宜沐浴掃舍宇捕捉畋獵	辰巳午酉	西南 正西	沖虎16 歲煞南	廚灶爐 房內北
24	星期一	（刀砧）	時五福西時入乾宮	初五	丁酉火	九紫	開	危	九三夷三 9四	宜 祭祀開光祈福齋醮出行沐浴裁衣嫁娶動土起基安床開市立券交易栽種破土啓攢修墳謝土	辰巳午酉	正南 正西	沖兔15 歲煞東	倉庫門 房內北
25	星期二		午未貪狼聖人登殿	初六	戊戌木	八白	閉	室	八三賁八 6一	宜 裁衣合帳冠笄嫁娶作染安床補垣塞穴造畜稠栖棧入殮成除服移柩破土立碑 忌 開光造廟	卯巳午未	東南 正北	沖龍14 歲煞北	房床栖 房內南
26	星期三	麒麟 月德合		初七	己亥木	七赤	建	壁	七三既九 2二	宜 出行冠笄 忌 作灶設醮嫁娶安葬	寅卯午未	東北 正北	沖蛇13 歲煞西	占門床 房內南
27	星期四	歲德 天德合	天氣上升地氣下降	初八	庚子土	六白	除	奎	六三家四 9二	宜 祭祀開光出行納采嫁娶修造動土起基上樑入宅開市栽種牧養納畜入殮破土啓攢安葬	辰未申酉	西北 正東	沖馬12 歲煞南	占碓磨 房內南
28	星期五	午入艮	◐上弦申初 15 00 11	初九	辛丑土	五黃	滿	婁	中五禽 3一	宜 祭祀開光塑繪理髮會親友開池作陂塞穴捕捉結網畋獵牧養造畜稠栖棧 忌 嫁娶入宅	寅巳午申	西南 正東	沖羊11 歲煞東	廚灶廁 房內南
29	星期六		（勿探病）	初十	壬寅金	四綠	平	胃	四三豐六 7九	宜 出行裁衣嫁娶會親友經絡出火修造動土起基上樑入宅開市立券交易納財栽種牧養納畜	子卯巳午	正南 正南	沖猴10 歲煞北	倉庫爐 房內南
30	星期日			十一	癸卯金	三碧	定	昴	三三離一 7八	宜 祭祀祈福出行納采嫁娶修造動土上樑作灶入宅開市納財牧養納畜入殮破土啓攢修墳安葬	卯巳未戌	東南 正南	沖雞9 歲煞西	房床門 房內南

玉玄門命理風水 Facebook‥Yu Xuan Men Feng Shui 玉玄門

（斗指西北維為立冬，冬者終也，立冬之時，萬物終成，故名立冬也。）

二〇二五 NOV 陽曆十一月小（30天）

陰曆九月大自九月十八日午正 建丁亥女宿至十月十八日卯初

丁亥月（孟冬 陽月）

立冬之日怕逢壬，來歲高田枉用心，此日更逢壬子日，人民又受病災臨

（月煞在西方） 九九坤 一 ☷

一	六	八
九	二	四
五	七	三

日	神煞	星期	節候	陰曆	干支	九星	建除	星宿	卦	宜忌	每日吉時	每日喜神財神方位	每日沖肖歲煞方年	每日胎神占方
1	鳳凰	星期六		十二	甲戌火	五黃	建	胃	中五禽 2七	宜 祭祀出行修造上樑蓋屋安門安床教牛馬造畜稠棲棧 忌 栽種安葬謝土	寅卯午未	東北 東南	沖龍38 歲煞北	門雞棲 外西南
2	歲德合	星期日	蟄蟲咸俯 時卯入中	十三	乙亥火	四綠	除	昴	四七解四 3三	宜 祭祀開光出行沐浴理髮訂盟納采裁衣會親友出火修造起基上樑安床入宅造畜稠棲棧	寅卯未申	西北 東南	沖蛇37 歲煞西	碓磨床 外西南
3	天月 德日	星期一		十四	丙子水	三碧	滿	畢	三七未九 3六	宜 祭祀祈福納采裁衣起基安床開市立券交易納財結網牧養納畜入殮啟攢安葬 忌 入宅設醮	丑辰巳申	西南 正西	沖馬36 歲煞南	廚灶碓 外西南
4		星期二		十五	丁丑水	二黑	平	觜	二七困八 7四	◇ 日逢正紅紗日凡事少取 宜祭祀平治道塗	巳午酉亥	正南 正西	沖羊35 歲煞東	倉庫廁 外正西
5		星期三	○入望亥 初21 20 38	十六	戊寅土	一白	定	參	一七訟三 6八	☆ 日逢受死日不宜諸吉事 宜捕捉結網畋獵	丑巳午未	東南 正北	沖猴34 歲煞北	房床爐 外正西
6	日入艮	星期四	七元二將 時子入乾	十七	己卯土	九紫	執	井	九六升二 8七	宜 祭祀捕捉入殮破土啟攢（勿探病） 忌 開市交易架馬開井	子午未申	東北 正北	沖雞33 歲煞西	占大門 外正西
7	歲德	星期五	水始冰 今日立冬	十八	庚辰金	八白	執	鬼	八六蠱七 9一	宜 節前 日逢月破日大耗大凶不宜諸吉事 節後 祭祀齋醮納畜入殮移柩啟攢安葬	丑未申酉	西北 正東	沖狗32 歲煞南	碓磨栖 外正西
8		星期六		十九	辛巳金	七赤	破	柳	七六井六 7三	★ 日逢月破日大耗大凶不宜諸吉事 宜求醫治病破屋壞垣	寅午申酉	西南 正東	沖豬31 歲煞東	廚灶床 外正西
9		星期日	時五福酉 時入艮宮	二十	壬午木	六白	危	星	六六巽一 1二	宜 祭祀開光祈福出行納采裁衣嫁娶修造動土上樑安床作灶入宅開市納財畋獵牧養納畜（勿探病）	寅卯巳未	東南 正南	沖鼠30 歲煞北	倉庫碓 外西北
10		星期一		廿一	癸未木	五黃	成	張	中五禽 8四	宜 祭祀開光祈福求嗣沐浴解除納采會親友起基納財築堤防栽種牧養納畜入殮啟攢修墳安葬	卯巳午未	東南 正南	沖牛29 歲煞西	房床廁 外西北
11	月德	星期二		廿二	甲申水	四綠	收	翼	四六恒九 9三	☆ 日逢受死日不宜諸吉事（刀砧） 宜祭祀解除掃舍宇結網畋獵入殮成除服移柩	卯辰巳未	東北 東南	沖虎28 歲煞南	占門爐 外西北
12	歲德合 天德	星期三	◑下弦未 初13 29 27	廿三	乙酉水	三碧	開	軫	三六鼎四 4九	宜 祭祀祈福出行納采修造動土起基安床開市納財牧養納畜移柩破土修墳謝土（刀砧） 地始凍	丑寅辰巳	西北 東南	沖兔27 歲煞東	碓磨門 外西北
13		星期四	時五福午 時入巽宮	廿四	丙戌土	二黑	閉	角	二六大過三 1六	宜 祭祀裁衣合帳嫁娶作染安床開池補垣塞穴捕捉結網畋獵入殮成除服移柩破土啟攢立碑	卯巳午酉	西南 正西	沖龍26 歲煞北	廚灶栖 外西北
14		星期五		廿五	丁亥土	一白	建	亢	一六姤八 8八	宜 祭祀求嗣沐浴 忌 齋醮理髮嫁娶作灶	寅卯午未	正南 正西	沖蛇25 歲煞西	倉庫床 外西北
15	忌作灶	星期六		廿六	戊子火	九紫	除	氐	九四復八 4七	宜 出行沐浴納采裁衣冠笄嫁娶出火動土起基上樑入宅造廟造畜稠棲棧入殮移柩破土安葬	丑辰巳未	東南 正北	沖馬24 歲煞南	房床碓 外正北

立冬

日出：06時06分

台灣午時12時05分11秒

台灣午正初刻05分11秒

日沒：17時11分

天蠍 225

蔬菜有益

北部：馬鈴薯、野蜀葵、茄子、皇帝豆、菜豆

中部：蕗蕎、百合、玉蜀黍、胡蘿蔔

南部：西瓜、苦瓜、石刁柏、球莖甘藍、大小麥

漁我同在

東港：馬鮫、沙魚、鯧仔

高雄：卓鰮、沙魚

（斗指戌爲霜降，氣嘯，露凝結爲霜而下降，故名霜降也。）

	16	17	18	19	20	21	22	23
			歲德 卯入乾	天月 德合				歲德合
	星期四	星期五	星期六	星期日	星期一	星期二	星期三	星期四
			菊有黃華	戌亥武曲 聖人登殿	土王用事 午11 30 02	●合朔戌 正20 26 27	七元一將 時子入艮	豺乃祭獸 今日霜降
	廿五	廿六	廿七	廿八	廿九	九月初一	初二	初三
	戊午 火	己未 火	庚申 木	辛酉 木	壬戌 水	癸亥 水	甲子 金	乙丑 金
	碧三	黑二	白一	紫九	白八	赤七	碧三	黃五
	成	收	開	閉	建	除	滿	平
	角	亢	氐	房	心	尾	箕	斗
	三九晉三 4三	二九萃四 2一	一九否九 1七	九八謙六 3八	八八艮一 4四	七八蹇二 6六	六八漸七 1一	中五禽 6三
	宜	宜	宜	宜	宜	宜	宜	◇
	祭祀出行納采雕刻經絡起基安床立券納財掛匾築堤防結網納畜 **忌**開市動土安葬（刀砧）	祭祀作灶納財捕捉畋獵 **忌**開市修墳立碑安葬	祭祀出行納采裁衣嫁娶修造動土起基上樑作灶開市納財栽種牧養移柩破土 **忌**齋醮安葬	祭祀祈福求嗣齋醮沐浴理髮裁衣嫁娶動土安床作灶開廁教牛馬栽種入殮移柩破土啓攢安葬	祭祀開光祈福求嗣出行問名訂盟納采嫁娶上樑安門安床入宅納財開倉庫牧養納畜造畜稠栖棧	祭祀開光設醮出行沐浴理髮裁衣冠笄會親友作染出火拆卸修造起基上樑安床造畜稠栖棧	祭祀沐浴理髮問名訂盟納采裁衣冠笄會親友作染安床結網開生墳入殮成除服移柩啓攢安葬	日逢**正紅紗日**凡事少取 宜祭祀修飾垣墻平治道塗造畜稠栖棧
	寅巳午未	子卯巳午	辰巳未申	丑寅辰巳	寅卯巳午	子寅卯未	卯辰未申	寅卯巳申
	東北 正北	東北 正北	西北 正東	西南 正東	正南 正南	東南 正南	東北 東南	西北 東南
	沖鼠54 歲煞北	沖牛53 歲煞西	沖虎52 歲煞南	沖兔51 歲煞東	沖龍50 歲煞北	沖蛇49 歲煞西	沖馬48 歲煞南	沖羊47 歲煞東
	房床碓 外正東	占門廁 外正東	碓磨爐 外東南	廚灶門 外東南	倉庫栖 外東南	占房床 外東南	占門碓 外東南	碓磨廁 外東南

霜降

日出：05時56分
台灣午時11時52分06秒
台灣午初三刻07分06秒
日沒：17時20分

天蠍 210

益有菜蔬

北部：馬鈴薯、卷心菜、胡椒草、皇帝豆角菜、刈菜
中部：番椒、火燄菜、蕪菁、番薯、蒜仔
南部：芹菜、番椒、蕃茄、蕪菁、火燄菜、蒿苣

在同我漁

淡水：鰮魚、棘鬣魚、龍蝦
高雄：硼串、卓鯤
東港：目賊

	24	25	26	27	28	29	30	31
	天月德 麒麟				草木 黃落	天月 德合		
	星期五	星期六	星期日	星期一	星期二	星期三	星期四	星期五
		時五福酉 時入巽宮			歲德 （勿探病）	時五福午 時入坤宮	◐上弦子 正00 22 07	
	初四	初五	初六	初七	初八	初九	初十	十一
	丙寅 火	丁卯 火	戊辰 木	己巳 木	庚午 土	辛未 土	壬申 金	癸酉 金
	綠四	碧三	黑二	白一	紫九	白八	赤七	白六
	定	執	破	危	成	收	開	閉
	牛	女	虛	危	室	壁	奎	婁
	四八小過三 4二	三八旅八 9六	二八咸九 6九	一八遯四 2八	九七師七 9八	八七蒙二 3九	七七坎一 7一	六七渙六 7二
	☆	宜	★	宜	宜	宜	宜	宜
	日逢**受死日**不宜諸吉事 宜入殮成除服移柩破土啓攢立碑安葬	祭祀祈福出行納采裁衣嫁娶經絡修造起基上樑安床捕捉畋獵入殮破土啓攢安葬 **忌**開市	日逢**月破日**大凶大耗不宜諸吉事 宜祭祀解除沐浴破屋壞垣	祭祀求嗣冠笄會親友進人口經絡安門安床納財畋獵牧養割蜜 **忌**祈福齋醮出行（刀砧）	祭祀開光祈福出行納采嫁娶修造起基入宅開市納財栽種牧養納畜入殮破土啓攢安葬（刀砧）	祭祀理髮冠笄會親友作灶納財捕捉 **忌**動土開井安葬修墳 重陽節	祭祀祈福求嗣齋醮出行嫁娶起基開市納財出貨財修置產室栽種牧養破土啓攢謝土	祭祀出行沐浴理髮裁衣嫁娶作染經絡安床作灶入宅補垣塞穴掃舍宇入殮移柩破土啓攢安葬
	巳午酉戌	巳午未戌	巳未申酉	巳午申酉	丑寅未申	寅卯午申	子卯辰巳	子丑辰巳
	西南 正西	正南 正西	東南 正北	東北 正北	西北 正東	西南 正東	正南 正南	東南 正南
	沖猴46 歲煞北	沖雞45 歲煞西	沖狗44 歲煞南	沖豬43 歲煞東	沖鼠42 歲煞北	沖牛41 歲煞西	沖虎40 歲煞南	沖兔39 歲煞東
	廚灶爐 外正南	倉庫門 外正南	房床栖 外正南	占門床 外正南	占碓磨 外正南	廚灶廁 外西南	倉庫爐 外西南	房床門 外西南

（斗指辛爲寒露，斯時露寒冷而將欲凝結，故名寒露也。）

二〇二五 OCT 陽曆十月大（31天）

陰曆八月小自八月十七日辰正　建丙戌牛宿至九月十八日午正

丙戌月（季菊）（秋月）

初一霜飛侵害民，重陽無雨一冬晴，月中紅色人多病，更遇雷鳴米價增。

月煞（在北方）　八九剝　六

二	七	九
一	三	五
六	八	四

陽曆	星期	神煞	記事	陰曆	干支	九星	建除	星宿	卦		宜忌	每日吉時	每日喜神財神方位	每日沖肖煞方年齡	每日胎神占方
1	星期三			初十	癸卯金	紫九	破	壁	九一泰九 7八	★	日逢月破日大耗大凶不宜諸吉事 宜求醫治病破屋壞垣	卯巳未戌	東南 正南	沖雞 歲煞西 9	房床門 房內南
2	星期四			十一	甲辰火	白八	危	奎	八一大畜四 2三	宜	祭祀出行納采裁衣嫁娶經絡作染出火拆卸修造動土上樑安床作灶結網畋獵破土 忌造廟	寅未申酉	東北 東南	沖狗 歲煞南 8	門雞棲 房內東
3	星期五	歲月德合	（刀砧）水始涸	十二	乙巳火	赤七	成	婁	七一需三 3七	宜	祭祀開光祈福納采裁衣嫁娶出火修造動土起基上樑安床作灶入宅開市納財築堤防牧養納畜	寅卯申酉	西北 東南	沖豬 歲煞東 7	碓磨床 房內東
4	星期六	鳳凰		十三	丙午水	白六	收	胃	六一小畜八 3四	宜	祭祀冠笄嫁娶捕捉（刀砧） 忌作灶伐木蓋屋合脊	巳未酉戌	西南 正西	沖鼠 歲煞北 6	廚灶碓 房內東
5	星期日			十四	丁未水	黃五	開	昴	中五離 7六	☆	日逢受死日不宜諸吉事 宜祭祀入學畋獵取魚成除服移柩啓攢修墳立碑	卯巳午酉	正南 正西	沖牛 歲煞西 5	倉庫廁 房內東
6	星期一	天赦	中秋節	十五	戊申土	綠四	閉	畢	四一壯二 6二	宜	祭祀出行動土起基上樑安門作灶入宅立券交易納財栽種牧養納畜入殮破土啓攢修墳安葬	丑辰巳午	東南 正北	沖虎 歲煞南 4	房床爐 房內東
7	星期二	六元四子入巽	○入望午初11 48 52	十六	己酉土	碧三	建	觜	三一有七 8三	宜	祭祀出行令牌雷尺受戒道牒 忌嫁娶移徙作灶入宅	辰巳午申	東北 正北	沖兔 歲煞東 3	占大門 外東北
8	星期三	歲德	鴻雁來賓 今日寒露	十七	庚戌金	黑二	建	參	二一夬六 9九	宜	節前 祭祀祈福設醮出行出火動土安床入宅 節後 祭祀出行裁衣雕刻豎柱上樑移徙納財	寅卯午未	西北 正東	沖龍 歲煞北 2	碓磨棲 外東北
9	星期四	天月德合	丑酉二時貴人登天	十八	辛亥金	白一	除	井	一一乾一 7七	宜	祭祀開光祈福求嗣設醮出行移徙沐浴理髮會親友修造起基安床牧養 忌訂盟納采嫁娶	寅卯午未	西南 正東	沖蛇 歲煞西 1	廚灶床 外東北
10	星期五		時五福西時入坤宮	十九	壬子木	紫九	滿	鬼	九九坤一 1八	宜	祭祀入學沐浴理髮冠笄會親友教牛馬入殮成除服移柩啓攢安葬 忌出行入宅祈福	卯辰巳申	正南 正南	沖馬 歲煞南 60	倉庫碓 外東北
11	星期六			二十	癸丑木	白八	平	柳	八九剝六 8六	◇	日逢正紅紗日大凶吉事少取 宜平治道塗造畜稠棲棧	子卯巳酉	東南 正南	沖羊 歲煞東 59	房床廁 外東北
12	星期日			廿一	甲寅水	赤七	定	星	七九比七 9七	☆	日逢受死日不宜諸吉事（勿探病） 宜結網畋獵取魚入殮成除服移柩立碑	丑寅午未	東北 東南	沖猴 歲煞北 58	占門爐 外東北
13	星期一	歲德合	雀入大水爲蛤	廿二	乙卯水	白六	執	張	六九觀二 4一	宜	祭祀齋醮針灸捕捉結網畋獵開生墳入殮成除服移柩破土啓攢立碑安葬（勿探病）	卯未申戌	西北 東南	沖雞 歲煞西 57	碓磨門 外正東
14	星期二	天月德	◑下弦丑正02 14 00	廿三	丙辰土	黃五	破	翼	中五離 1四	★	日逢月破日大耗大凶不宜諸吉事 宜祭祀解除沐浴破屋壞垣	巳午申酉	西南 正西	沖狗 歲煞南 56	廚灶棲 外正東
15	星期三			廿四	丁巳土	綠四	危	軫	四九豫八 8二	宜	祭祀求嗣問名訂盟結婚姻納采會親友進人口納財結網畋獵牧養納畜（刀砧）	丑巳午申	正南 正西	沖豬 歲煞東 55	倉庫床 外正東

寒露

日出：05時50分
台灣辰時08時42分10秒
台灣辰正二刻12分10秒
日沒：17時35分

天秤 195

蔬菜有益

北部：蕪菁、荷蘭豆、蘿蔔、馬鈴薯、碗豆、茄子
中部：茄子、碗豆、白菜、飛陵菜、馬鈴薯、荷蘭豆
南部：馬鈴薯、苦瓜、西瓜、花椰菜、荷蘭豆、甘薯

漁我同在

基隆：卓鯤、烏賊、棘鬣魚
蘇澳：加蚋魚、沙魚、硼串、目吼

（斗指酉為秋分，南北兩半球晝夜均分，又適當秋之半，故名也。）

秋分

日出：05時43分
台灣丑時02時20分20秒
台灣丑正一刻05分20秒
日沒：17時51分

天秤

180

16	17	18	19	20	21	22	23
		歲月德				六元三子入坤	歲月德合
星期二	星期三	星期四	星期五	星期六	星期日	星期一	星期二
	群鳥養羞	時五福卯時入巽宮				●合朔寅初03 55 19	雷始收聲今日秋分
廿五	廿六	廿七	廿八	廿九	三十	八月初一	初二
戊子火	己丑火	庚寅木	辛卯木	壬辰水	癸巳水	甲午金	乙未金
六白	五黃	四綠	三碧	二黑	一白	九紫	八白
平	定	執	破	危	成	收	開
翼	軫	角	亢	氐	房	心	尾
六三家四 4七	中五禽 2九	四三豐六 1三	三三离一 3二	二三革二 4六	一三同七 6四	九二臨四 1九	八二損九 6七
宜	宜	宜	★	宜	宜	宜	☆
祭祀沐浴修飾垣墻平治道塗 忌嫁娶出火作灶出行	祭祀齋醮出行納采嫁娶修造動土起基上樑作灶入宅開市納財牧養納畜入殮破土啓攢安葬	開光沐浴理髮訂盟納采裁衣會親友拆卸修造動土起基上樑捕捉入殮破土啓攢立碑安葬	日逢月破日大耗大凶不宜諸吉事 宜祭祀破屋壞垣	祭祀開光出行納采嫁娶修造動土上樑安門作灶立券交易納財入殮移柩破土	祭祀祈福求嗣納采嫁娶修造動土起基上樑作灶入宅開市立券交易納財栽種牧養納畜(刀砧)	祭祀理髮冠笄會親友捕捉成除服移柩(刀砧) 忌開市栽種安葬啓攢	日逢受死日不宜諸吉事 宜祭祀臨政親民解除成除服移柩啓攢修墳
丑辰巳未	巳午申酉	午未酉戌	寅午未申	卯巳申酉	子丑卯巳	寅卯未戌	子寅卯午
東南正北	東北正北	西北正東	西南正東	正南正南	東南正南	東北東南	西北東南
沖馬24歲煞南	沖羊23歲煞東	沖猴22歲煞北	沖雞21歲煞西	沖狗20歲煞南	沖豬19歲煞東	沖鼠18歲煞北	沖牛17歲煞西
房床碓外正北	占門廁外正北	碓磨爐外正北	廚灶門外正北	倉庫棲外正北	占房床房內北	占門碓房內北	碓磨廁房內北

蔬菜有益

北部：胡椒、蒲公英、馬鈴薯、蕹菜、萵苣、白菜、胡蘿蔔
中部：蘿蔔、牛蒡、甘薯、大蔥、蕪菁、茄子
南部：西瓜、苦瓜、蘿蔔、花椰菜、萵苣

漁我同在

澎湖：鰮魚
安平：鰮魚
淡水：烏格魚

24	25	26	27	28	29	30
		麒麟		歲月德		
星期三	星期四	星期五	星期六	星期日	星期一	星期二
	時五福酉時入中宮	秋社報穀之熟		蟄蟲壞戶	時五福午時入乾宮	◐上弦辰初07 55 00
初三	初四	初五	初六	初七	初八	初九
丙申火	丁酉火	戊戌木	己亥木	庚子土	辛丑土	壬寅金
七赤	六白	五黃	四綠	三碧	二黑	一白
閉	建	除	滿	平	定	執
箕	斗	牛	女	虛	危	室
七二節八 4八	六二孚三 9四	中五禽 6一	四二妹七 2二	三二睽二 9二	二二兌一 3一	一二履六 7九
宜	宜	宜	宜	宜	宜	宜
祭祀沐浴理髮裁衣合帳經絡伐木安門納財掃舍宇牧養納畜入殮移柩啓攢修墳立碑安葬	祭祀出行沐浴掃舍宇安葬 忌理髮作灶動土	祭祀納采冠笄嫁娶豎柱上樑安床掃舍宇栽種 忌作灶安門行喪安葬	祭祀開光祈福出行沐浴納采裁衣經絡出火修造起基上樑安門安床入宅開市納財捕捉結網	祭祀沐浴修飾垣墻平治道塗入殮安葬 忌嫁娶裁衣入宅作灶	開光祈福設醮納采嫁娶雕刻經絡修造動土安床移徙造廟納財修倉庫栽種牧養	沐浴理髮裁衣會親友修造動土起基捕捉結網牧養入殮移柩破土啓攢安葬(勿探病)
辰巳午酉	辰巳午酉	卯巳午未	寅卯午未	辰未申酉	寅巳午申	子卯巳午
西南正西	正南正西	東南正北	東北正北	西北正東	西南正東	正南正南
沖虎16歲煞南	沖兔15歲煞東	沖龍14歲煞北	沖蛇13歲煞西	沖馬12歲煞南	沖羊11歲煞東	沖猴10歲煞北
廚灶爐房內北	倉庫門房內北	房床棲房內南	占門床房內南	占碓磨房內南	廚灶廁房內南	倉庫爐房內南

玉玄門星相地理五術研究傳授服務中心　張清淵老師服務處：新北市板橋區中正路二一六巷一四八號

（斗指庚爲白露，陰氣漸重，露凝而白，故名白露也。）

二〇二五 SEP 陽曆九月小（30天）

陰曆七月大自七月十六日申正
建乙酉斗宿至八月十七日辰正

乙酉（仲桂）月（秋月）

秋分天氣白雲多
處處歡聲歌好禾
只怕此日雷電閃
冬來米貴價如何

月煞在東方（七九比）

七

三	八	一
二	四	六
七	九	五

白露

日出：05時38分
台灣申時16時53分03秒
台灣申正三刻08分03秒
日沒：18時07分

處女　165

蔬菜有益

北部：豆菜、花椰菜、胡瓜、菠菜、甘薯、恭菜、萵苣、番椒
中部：恭菜、花椰菜、菠菜、蕪菁、萵苣、番椒
南部：荷蘭豆、白菜、芥菜、落花生、大豆

漁我同在

基隆：加蚋魚、卓鯤、赤鯮、鰮魚、目吼
淡水：疏齋、髫魚
蘇澳：硼串

日	星期	神煞	記事	農曆	干支	九星	建除	宿	卦		宜忌	每日吉時	每日喜神財神方位	每日沖肖煞方年齡	每日胎神占方
1	星期一	天德		初十	癸酉金	碧三	除	危	三六鼎四 7二	宜	祭祀祈福求嗣訂盟納采裁衣修造動土起基上樑安床納財牧養納畜入殮破土啓攢安葬	子丑辰巳	東南 正南	沖兔 歲煞東 39	房床門外西南
2	星期二	禾乃登		十一	甲戌火	黑二	滿	室	二六大過三 2七	宜	開光塑繪沐浴理髮嫁娶會親友經絡補垣塞穴栽種牧養納畜 **忌** 祭祀祈福作灶安葬	寅卯午未	東北 東南	沖龍 歲煞北 38	門雞栖外西南
3	星期三	歲德合	時五福卯時入坤宮	十二	乙亥火	白一	平	壁	一六姤八 3三	宜	祭祀沐浴作灶修飾垣墻平治道塗 **忌** 祈福安葬	寅卯未申	西北 東南	沖蛇 歲煞西 37	碓磨床外西南
4	星期四		巳未二時貴人登天	十三	丙子水	紫九	定	奎	九四復八 3六	宜	祭祀祈福齋醮普度出行納采嫁娶修造動土起基入宅納財結網牧養納畜入殮破土啓攢安葬	丑辰巳申	西南 正西	沖馬 歲煞南 36	廚灶碓外西南
5	星期五	月德合		十四	丁丑水	白八	執	婁	八四頤三 7四	☆	日逢**受死日**不宜諸吉事 宜祭祀普度畋獵入殮成除服移柩破土立碑安葬	巳午酉亥	正南 正西	沖羊 歲煞東 35	倉庫廁外正西
6	星期六	天德合 鳳凰	中元節○ 地官赦罪	十五	戊寅土	赤七	破	胃	七四屯四 6八	★	日逢**月破日**大耗大凶不宜諸吉事 宜沐浴破屋壞垣	丑巳午未	東南 正北	沖猴 歲煞北 34	房床爐外正西
7	星期日	六元 二將	鴻雁來 今日白露	十六	己卯土	白六	破	昴	六四益九 8七	●	節前 節後；**月全食**．台灣能見按洪氏條例不宜諸吉事(勿探病)	子午未申	東北 正北	沖雞 歲煞西 33	占大門外正西
8	星期一	歲月德	○入望丑正02時10分08	十七	庚辰金	黃五	危	畢	中五禽 9一	●	**月全食**．台灣能見按洪氏條例不宜諸吉事	丑未申酉	西北 正東	沖狗 歲煞南 32	碓磨栖外正西
9	星期二			十八	辛巳金	綠四	成	觜	四四震一 7三	宜	祭祀祈福求嗣設醮納采嫁娶修造動土起基上樑入宅開市立券交易納財栽種牧養納畜(刀砧)	寅午申酉	西南 正東	沖豬 歲煞東 31	廚灶床外正西
10	星期三		時五福酉時入乾宮	十九	壬午木	碧三	收	參	三四嗑六 1二	宜	祭祀理髮針灸嫁娶會親友進人口教牛馬捕捉入殮成除服移柩(刀砧)(勿探病)	寅卯巳未	正南 正南	沖鼠 歲煞北 30	倉庫碓外西北
11	星期四			二十	癸未木	黑二	開	井	二四隨七 8四	☆	日逢**受死日**不宜諸吉事 宜祭祀祈福求嗣入學成除服移柩啓攢修墳立碑	卯巳午未	東南 正南	沖牛 歲煞西 29	房床廁外西北
12	星期五		玄鳥歸	廿一	甲申水	白一	閉	鬼	一四妄二 9三	宜	祭祀出行沐浴裁衣嫁娶出火修造動土起基作灶納財栽種牧養納畜入殮破土啓攢安葬	卯辰巳未	東北 東南	沖虎 歲煞南 28	占門爐外西北
13	星期六	歲月德合		廿二	乙酉水	紫九	建	柳	九三夷三 4九	宜	祭祀出行沐浴結婚姻嫁娶掃舍宇入殮成除服安葬 **忌** 設醮開井動土栽種	丑寅辰巳	西北 東南	沖兔 歲煞東 27	碓磨門外西北
14	星期日	午入艮	◑下弦酉正18時34分18	廿三	丙戌土	白八	除	星	八三賁八 1六	宜	祭祀設醮上官赴任出行沐浴理髮納采裁衣雕刻動土起基安床開池作陂掃舍宇栽種 **忌** 安葬	卯巳午酉	西南 正西	沖龍 歲煞北 26	廚灶栖外西北
15	星期一		申酉貪狼聖人登殿	廿四	丁亥土	赤七	滿	張	七三既九 8八	宜	祭祀開光祈福設醮出行沐浴裁衣會親友雕刻經絡修造起基上樑安床入宅開市立券交易納財結網	寅卯午未	正南 正西	沖蛇 歲煞西 25	倉庫床外西北

（斗指申爲處暑，暑將退，伏而潛處，故名也。）

處暑

日出：05時31分
台灣寅時04時35分00秒
台灣寅正二刻05分00秒
日沒：18時22分

處女

150

日期	星期	神煞	註記	農曆	干支	九星	建除	宿	卦	宜/忌	事項	吉時	方位	沖煞	胎神
16	星期六	月德合	◑下弦未 初13 13 34	廿三	丁巳 土	白一	收	柳	一八遯四 8二	宜	祭祀祈福納采會親友經絡移徙開市立券交易納財出貨財捕捉牧養納畜 忌入學出行(刀砧)	丑巳午申	正南 正西	沖豬 歲煞東 55	倉庫床 外正東
17	星期日	天德合(刀砧)	寒蟬鳴	廿四	戊午 火	紫九	開	星	九七師七 4三	宜	祭祀開光祈福普度出行訂盟納采嫁娶會親友修造起基安床開市修置產室栽種牧養納畜移柩	寅巳午未	東南 正北	沖鼠 歲煞北 54	房床碓 外正東
18	星期一			廿五	己未 火	白八	閉	張	八七蒙二 2一	宜	祭祀普度會親友動土放水開池築堤防補垣塞穴斷蟻入殮成除服移柩破土立碑 忌入宅開光	子卯巳午	東北 正北	沖牛 歲煞西 53	占門廁 外正東
19	星期二	歲德	時五福卯時入中宮	廿六	庚申 木	赤七	建	翼	七七坎一 1七	宜	祭祀上官赴任出行沐浴裁衣冠笄嫁娶進人口安門作灶納財掃舍宇納畜造畜稠栖棧 忌設齋醮	辰巳未申	西北 正東	沖虎 歲煞南 52	碓磨爐 外東南
20	星期三			廿七	辛酉 木	白六	除	軫	六七渙六 3八	宜	祭祀沐浴理髮裁衣修造動土起基上樑蓋屋安門安床開渠開池掃舍宇入殮破土啓攢立碑安葬	丑寅辰巳	西南 正東	沖兔 歲煞東 51	廚灶門 外東南
21	星期四	月德	子寅二時貴人登天	廿八	壬戌 水	黃五	滿	角	中五禽 4四	宜	開光出行納采裁衣嫁娶出火修造起基上樑安門安床入宅開市立券交易納財栽種牧養納畜	寅卯巳午	正南 正南	沖龍 歲煞北 50	倉庫栖 外東南
22	星期五	天德		廿九	癸亥 水	綠四	平	亢	四七解四 6六	宜	祭祀沐浴作灶修飾垣墻平治道塗 忌祈福嫁娶造廟安葬	子寅卯未	東南 正南	沖蛇 歲煞西 49	占房床 外東南
23	星期六	●朔未 14 07 46	鷹祭鳥 今日處暑	七月初一	甲子 金	碧三	定	氐	三七未九 1一	宜	祭祀祈福普度出行納采修造動土起基上樑安床納財牧養納畜入殮破土啓攢安葬 忌齋醮	卯辰未申	東北 東南	沖馬 歲煞南 48	占門碓 外東南
24	星期日	歲德合		初二	乙丑 金	黑二	執	房	二七困八 6三	☆	日逢**受死日**不宜諸吉事 宜捕捉牧養入殮成除服移柩破土立碑安葬	寅卯巳申	西北 東南	沖羊 歲煞東 47	碓磨廁 外東南
25	星期一			初三	丙寅 火	白一	破	心	一七訟三 4二	★	日逢**月破日**大耗大凶不宜諸吉事 宜治病破屋壞垣	巳午酉戌	西南 正西	沖猴 歲煞北 46	廚灶爐 外正南
26	星期二	月德合	時五福酉時入艮宮	初四	丁卯 火	紫九	危	尾	九六升二 9六	宜	祭祀開光齋醮納采嫁娶上樑入宅立券交易牧養納畜入殮移柩啓攢安葬	巳午未戌	正南 正西	沖雞 歲煞西 45	倉庫門 外正南
27	星期三	天德合 神在	申時三奇卯酉登貴	初五	戊辰 木	白八	成	箕	八六蠱七 6九	宜	祭祀開光設醮出行納采嫁娶修造動土起基入宅開市納財結網牧養取魚入殮破土安葬	巳未申酉	東南 正北	沖狗 歲煞南 44	房床栖 外正南
28	星期四		天地始肅	初六	己巳 木	赤七	收	斗	七六井六 2八	宜	祭祀祈福裁衣嫁娶經絡修造動土上樑安床作灶開市交易納財出貨財捕捉栽種牧養納畜(刀砧)	巳午申酉	東北 正北	沖豬 歲煞東 43	占門床 外正南
29	星期五	麒麟 歲德	七夕○ 道德臘	初七	庚午 土	白六	開	牛	六六巽一 9八	宜	祭祀設醮出行理髮訂盟納采裁衣會親友動土安床安碓磨開渠開井栽種(刀砧)(勿探病)	丑寅未申	西北 正東	沖鼠 歲煞北 42	占碓磨 外正南
30	星期六		時五福午時入巽宮	初八	辛未 土	黃五	閉	女	中五禽 3九	宜	祭祀普度出行合帳嫁娶出火修造動土起基安床作灶入宅造畜稠栖棧入殮破土立碑 忌開光	寅卯午申	西南 正東	沖牛 歲煞西 41	廚灶廁 外西南
31	星期日	月德	◐上弦未 正14 26 22	初九	壬申 金	綠四	建	虛	四六恒九 7一	◉	弦日逢虛宿係**真滅沒**大凶宜事不取	子卯辰巳	正南 正南	沖虎 歲煞南 40	倉庫爐 外西南

蔬菜有益

北部：芥藍菜、菜豆、八月豆、甘薯、高麗菜

中部：蕃茄、蕃薯、八月豆、落花生、大豆、花椰菜

南部：甘藍、花椰菜、落花生、大豆、萵苣、甘薯

漁我同在

安平：烏鰡、虱目魚苗

高雄：虱目魚苗

東港：虱目魚苗

（斗指西南維爲立秋，陰意出地始殺萬物，按秋訓禾，穀熟也。）

二〇二五 AUG 陽曆八月大（31天）

陰曆閏六月小 建甲申箕宿至

自閏六月十四日未初 七月十六日申正

甲申月（孟秋 瓜月）

立秋無雨最堪愁，萬物從來只半收，處暑若逢天下雨，縱然結實也悲憂。

月煞在南方

六九觀 ☴☷

四	九	二
三	五	七
八	一	六

神煞	日	星期	節令	農曆	干支	九星	建除	宿	卦	宜忌	每日吉時	每日喜神財神方位	每日沖肖煞年方	每日胎神占方
大雨時行	1	星期五	◐上弦 戌正 20 42 35	初八	壬寅金	七赤	危	牛	七九 比七 7九	宜：開光出行嫁娶修造起基安床入宅開市立券交易納財栽種入殮破土啓攢安葬（刀砧）（勿探病）	子卯巳午	喜神正南 財神正南	沖猴10 歲煞北	倉庫爐 房內南
	2	星期六		初九	癸卯金	六白	成	女	六九 觀二 7八	宜：祭祀祈福出行納采修造起基安床入宅開市納財栽種牧養納畜入殮破土啓攢安葬（刀砧）	卯巳未戌	喜神東南 財神正南	沖雞9 歲煞西	房床門 房內南
天月德	3	星期日	未申左輔 聖人登殿	初十	甲辰火	五黃	收	虛	中五 禽 2三	宜：祭祀開光求嗣出行沐浴納采嫁娶修造起基入宅栽種牧養入殮移柩 忌：破土開市安葬	寅未申酉	喜神東北 財神東南	沖狗8 歲煞南	門雞栖 房內東
歲德合	4	星期一	時五福卯 時入乾宮	十一	乙巳火	四綠	開	危	四九 豫八 3七	宜：祭祀沐浴理髮訂盟納采裁衣嫁娶會親友出火修造起基上樑安床作灶掛匾 忌：出行安葬	寅卯申酉	喜神西北 財神東南	沖豬7 歲煞東	碓磨床 房內東
	5	星期二		十二	丙午水	三碧	閉	室	三九 晉三 3四	☆ 日逢受死日不宜諸吉事 宜祭祀入殮成除服移柩破土啓攢立碑安葬	巳未酉戌	喜神西南 財神正西	沖鼠6 歲煞北	廚灶碓 房內東
聖心 守日	6	星期三	午時三奇 午申登貴	十三	丁未水	二黑	建	壁	二九 萃四 7六	宜：祭祀臨政親民教牛馬割蜜造畜稠棲棧 忌：動土破土作灶造船	卯巳午酉	喜神正南 財神正西	沖牛5 歲煞西	倉庫廁 房內東
天赦 天德合	7	星期四	涼風至 今日立秋	十四	戊申土	一白	建	奎	一九 否九 6二	宜：節前 祭祀開光入學解除沐浴開池掃舍宇牧養；節後 祭祀祈福裁衣納財入殮移柩啓攢安葬	丑辰巳午	喜神東南 財神正北	沖虎4 歲煞南	房床爐 房內東
日入中	8	星期五	五元四將 時子入艮	十五	己酉土	九紫	除	婁	九八 謙六 8三	宜：祭祀解除沐浴理髮整手足甲冠笄掃舍宇入殮移柩破土啓攢立碑安葬 忌：齋醮移徙入宅	辰巳午申	喜神東北 財神正北	沖兔3 歲煞東	占大門 外東北
歲德 鳳凰	9	星期六	○入望申 初15 56 21	十六	庚戌金	八白	滿	胃	八八 艮一 9九	宜：開光塑繪嫁娶會親友進人口補垣塞穴捕捉栽種牧養納畜 忌：祈福上樑裁衣（末伏）	寅卯午未	喜神西北 財神正東	沖龍2 歲煞北	碓磨栖 外東北
	10	星期日		十七	辛亥金	七赤	平	昴	七八 蹇二 7七	宜：祭祀沐浴作灶修飾垣墻平治道塗 忌：祈福造廟嫁娶安葬	寅卯午未	喜神西南 財神正東	沖蛇1 歲煞西	廚灶床 外東北
月德	11	星期一	時五福酉 時入巽宮	十八	壬子木	六白	定	畢	六八 漸七 1八	宜：祭祀開光祈福普度出行納采嫁娶修造動土上樑入宅納財栽種牧養納畜入殮破土啓攢安葬	卯辰巳申	喜神正南 財神正南	沖馬60 歲煞南	倉庫碓 外東北
天德	12	星期二	白露降	十九	癸丑木	五黃	執	觜	中五 禽 8六	☆ 日逢受死日不宜諸吉事 宜祭祀祈福普度入殮成除服移柩破土立碑安葬	子卯巳酉	喜神東南 財神正南	沖羊59 歲煞東	房床廁 外東北
	13	星期三		二十	甲寅水	四綠	破	參	四八 小過三 9七	★ 日逢月破日大耗大凶不宜諸吉事 宜破屋壞垣（勿探病）	丑寅午未	喜神東北 財神東南	沖猴58 歲煞北	占門爐 外東北
歲德合	14	星期四		廿一	乙卯水	三碧	危	井	三八 旅八 4一	宜：祭祀結網畋獵取魚入殮成除服移柩啓攢安葬 忌：安床動土作灶開井（勿探病）	卯未申戌	喜神西北 財神東南	沖雞57 歲煞西	碓磨門 外正東
	15	星期五	時五福午 時入坤宮	廿二	丙辰土	二黑	成	鬼	二八 咸九 1四	宜：祭祀祈福齋醮普度納采修造動土起基上樑安床開市立券交易納財入殮破土安葬	巳午申酉	喜神西南 財神正西	沖狗56 歲煞南	廚灶栖 外正東

立秋

日出：05時24分

台灣未時13時52分48秒

台灣未初三刻07分48秒

日沒：18時36分

獅子 135

蔬菜有益

北部：烏豆、白豆、大蔥、大豆、早芹菜、花椰菜、甘藍

中部：茄子、蕃茄、芹菜、芥藍菜、甘薯

南部：芹菜、甘藍、玉蜀黍、甘薯、菴瓜

漁我同在

基隆：棘鬣魚、卓鯤、目吼、鰛魚

淡水：鰛魚

澎湖：沙魚、龍尖、鰛魚

（斗指未爲大暑，斯時天氣甚熱於小暑，故名大暑。）

大暑

日出：05時17分
日沒：18時44分
台灣亥時21時30分39秒
台灣亥初二刻00分39秒

獅子

120

蔬菜有益

北部：花椰菜、土白菜、高腳白菜、甘藍
中部：抱子甘藍、芥藍菜、冬瓜、甘薯
南部：冬瓜、菜豆、黃秋葵、玉蜀黍、茼蒿、土白菜

漁我同在

東港：龍蝦、鯃魚、虱目魚苗
安平：烏鯃、鯃魚、虱目魚苗
澎湖：龍蝦、鰮魚、龍尖、烟仔魚、虱目魚苗
高雄：飛烏、虱目魚、鯃魚

日	星期	節令	註記	農曆	干支	九星	建除	星宿	卦	宜/★	宜忌	吉時	方位	沖煞	胎神
16	星期三		時五福午 時入乾宮	廿二	丙戌土	五黃	平	參	中五離 1六	宜	祭祀祈福結網畋獵取魚 忌作灶造廟動土開井	卯巳午酉	西南正西	沖龍26 歲煞北	廚灶栖 外西北
17	星期四	鷹始摯		廿三	丁亥土	四綠	定	井	四二妹七 8八	宜	祭祀祈福設醮沐浴裁衣會親友經絡出火修造動土起基上樑安床入宅牧養納畜 忌嫁娶理髮	寅卯午未	正南正西	沖蛇25 歲煞西	倉庫床 外西北
18	星期五		◑下弦辰 正08 38 57	廿四	戊子火	三碧	執	鬼	三二睽二 4七	宜	祭祀解除沐浴理髮整手足甲裁衣教牛馬捕捉結網取魚入殮移柩破土啓攢立碑安葬	丑辰巳未	東南正北	沖馬24 歲煞南	房床碓 外正北
19	星期六	天德合 月德合	土王用事 西18 06 26	廿五	己丑火	二黑	破	柳	二二兌一 2九	★	日逢月破日大耗大凶不宜諸吉事 宜祭祀 忌破屋壞垣	巳午申酉	東北正北	沖羊23 歲煞東	占門廁 外正北
20	星期日	歲德 初伏	時五福卯 時入艮宮	廿六	庚寅木	一白	危	星	一二履六 1三	宜	出行訂盟納采嫁娶會親友開市立券交易納財栽種牧養納畜入殮破土啓攢安葬(刀砧)	午未酉戌	西北正東	沖猴22 歲煞北	碓磨爐 外正北
21	星期一			廿七	辛卯木	九紫	成	張	九一泰九 3二	宜	祭祀開光祈福齋醮出行嫁娶修造起基入宅開市納財栽種牧養納畜入殮破土啓攢安葬(刀砧)	寅午未申	西南正東	沖雞21 歲煞西	廚灶門 外正北
22	星期二		腐草爲螢 今日大暑	廿八	壬辰水	八白	收	翼	八一大畜四 4六	宜	祭祀冠笄進人口作灶交易納財捕捉結網栽種牧養納畜 忌安床出行造廟造船	卯巳申酉	正南正南	沖狗20 歲煞南	倉庫栖 外正北
23	星期三			廿九	癸巳水	七赤	開	軫	七一需三 6四	宜	祭祀開光祈福求嗣納采裁衣冠笄嫁娶會親友修造起基上樑蓋屋安門安床作灶牧養 忌出行	子丑卯巳	東南正南	沖豬19 歲煞東	占房床 房內北
24	星期四	天赦 天月德	五元三將 時子入巽	三十	甲午金	六白	閉	角	六一小畜八 1九	☆	日逢受死日大凶不宜諸吉事 宜祭祀補垣塞穴入殮移柩破土啓攢立碑安葬	寅卯未戌	東北東南	沖鼠18 歲煞北	占門碓 房內北
25	星期五	歲德合	●合朔寅 初03 12 25	閏六月 初一	乙未金	五黃	建	亢	中五離 6七	宜	祭祀上官赴任臨政親民出行裁衣冠笄雕刻交易納財教牛馬造畜稠棲棧 忌栽種做樑開井	子寅卯午	西北東南	沖牛17 歲煞西	碓磨廁 房內北
26	星期六			初二	丙申火	四綠	除	氐	四一壯二 4八	宜	祭祀開光沐浴裁衣嫁娶經絡出火修造起基入宅開市栽種造畜稠棲棧入殮破土啓攢安葬	辰巳午酉	西南正西	沖虎16 歲煞南	廚灶爐 房內北
27	星期日	土潤溽暑	時五福酉 時入坤宮	初三	丁酉火	三碧	滿	房	三一有七 9四	宜	祭祀沐浴納采裁衣冠笄嫁娶起基安床立券交易栽種牧養入殮啓攢安葬 忌祈福入宅作灶	辰巳午酉	正南正西	沖兔15 歲煞東	倉庫門 房內北
28	星期一			初四	戊戌木	二黑	平	心	二一夬六 6一	宜	祭祀嫁娶結網畋獵 忌造廟作灶開渠造船	卯巳午未	東南正北	沖龍14 歲煞北	房床栖 房內南
29	星期二	麒麟	天月德合	初五	己亥木	一白	定	尾	一一乾一 2二	宜	祭祀開光祈福出行沐浴理髮訂盟納采經絡開市立券交易納財出貨財栽種牧養納畜	寅卯午未	東北正北	沖蛇13 歲煞西	占門床 房內南
30	星期三	歲德	中伏	初六	庚子土	九紫	執	箕	九九坤一 9二	宜	祭祀祈福入學解除整手足甲安床入殮移柩破土啓攢立碑安葬謝土 忌嫁娶齋醮	辰未申酉	西北正東	沖馬12 歲煞南	占碓磨 房內南
31	星期四		時五福午 時入中宮	初七	辛丑土	八白	破	斗	八九剝六 3一	★	日逢月破日大耗大凶不宜諸吉事 宜求醫治病破屋壞垣	寅巳午申	西南正東	沖羊11 歲煞東	廚灶廁 房內南

（斗指丁爲小暑，斯時天氣已熱，尚未達於極點，故名小暑也。）

二〇二五 JUL 陽曆七月大（31天）

陰曆六月大自六月十三日寅正 建癸未尾宿至閏六月十四日未初

癸未月（夏季荔月）

三伏之中逢酷熱
五穀田中秋下結
此時若不逢災厄
定是三冬多雨雪

月煞（在西方）

中五禽

五	一	三
四	六	八
九	二	七

小暑　巨蟹

日出：05時09分
台灣寅時04時06分14秒
台灣寅正初刻06分14秒
日沒：18時48分

105

日期	星期	神煞	備註	農曆	干支	九星	建除	宿	卦		宜忌	每日吉時	每日喜神財神方位	每日沖肖煞方年齡	每日胎神占方
1	星期二	麒麟月德合	半夏生22 14 26	初七	辛未土	黑二	除	尾	二四隨七 3九	宜	祭祀祈福求嗣出行沐浴納采裁衣會親友修造動土起基安床入宅開市納財栽種牧養納畜	寅卯午申	西南 正東	沖牛41 歲煞西	廚灶廁 外西南
2	星期三			初八	壬申金	白一	滿	箕	一四妄二 7一	宜	祭祀開光祈福求嗣出行沐浴裁衣嫁娶經絡出火修造起基入宅開市納財入殮啓攢安葬謝土	子卯辰巳	正南 正東	沖虎40 歲煞南	倉庫爐 外西南
3	星期四		◐上弦寅 初03 31 31	初九	癸酉金	紫九	平	斗	九三夷三 7二	宜	祭祀沐浴理髮整手足甲修飾垣墻平治道塗掃舍宇 忌 裁衣入宅上樑出行	子丑辰巳	東南 正南	沖兔39 歲煞東	房床門 外西南
4	星期五			初十	甲戌火	白八	定	牛	八三賁八 2七	宜	祭祀出行納采嫁娶修造動土起基安床入宅牧養入殮破土安葬 忌 造廟作灶修置產室	寅卯午未	東北 東南	沖龍38 歲煞北	門雞栖 外西南
5	星期六	歲德合	時五福卯 時入巽宮	十一	乙亥火	赤七	執	女	七三既九 3三	宜	祭祀開光祈福設醮出行沐浴納采裁衣出火修造動土起基上樑安床作灶入宅捕捉結網牧養	寅卯未申	西北 東南	沖蛇37 歲煞西	碓磨床 外西南
6	星期日	月德		十二	丙子水	白六	破	虛	六三家四 3六	★	日逢**月破日**大耗大凶不宜諸吉事 宜祭祀沐浴破屋壞垣	丑辰巳申	西南 正西	沖馬36 歲煞南	廚灶碓 外西南
7	星期一		溫風至 今日小暑	十三	丁丑水	黃五	破	危	中五禽 7四	★	節前 祭祀開光祈福設醮出行裁衣嫁娶安床 節後 日逢**月破日**大耗大凶不宜諸吉事	巳午酉亥	正南 正西	沖羊35 歲煞東	倉庫廁 外正西
8	星期二			十四	戊寅土	綠四	危	室	四三豐六 6八	宜	出行納采嫁娶修造動土上樑作灶入宅開市納財捕捉栽種牧養納畜入殮破土啓攢安葬（刀砧）	丑巳午未	東南 正北	沖猴34 歲煞北	房床爐 外正西
9	星期三	天月德合	五元二將（勿探病）	十五	己卯土	碧三	成	壁	三三離一 8七	宜	祭祀祈福出行納采修造動土起基上樑安床作灶入宅開市立券交易納財栽種牧養納畜（刀砧）	子午未申	東北 正北	沖雞33 歲煞西	占大門 外正西
10	星期四	歲德		十六	庚辰金	黑二	收	奎	二三革二 9一	宜	祭祀進人口作灶納財捕捉栽種牧養納畜 忌 安床造廟開市	丑未申酉	西北 正東	沖狗32 歲煞南	碓磨栖 外正西
11	星期五		○入望寅 正04 34 03	十七	辛巳金	白一	開	婁	一三同七 7三	宜	祭祀開光塑繪祈福求嗣入學習藝理髮求醫治病問名訂盟結婚姻納采開市牧養 忌 出行入宅	寅午申酉	西南 正東	沖豬31 歲煞東	廚灶床 外正西
12	星期六	蟋蟀居壁	時五福酉 時入中宮	十八	壬午木	紫九	閉	胃	九二臨四 1二	☆	日逢**受死日**大凶不宜諸吉事（勿探病） 宜祭祀入殮成除服移柩破土啓攢立碑安葬謝土	寅卯巳未	正南 正南	沖鼠30 歲煞北	倉庫碓 外西北
13	星期日	鳳凰	出霉	十九	癸未木	白八	建	昴	八二損九 8四	宜	祭祀上官赴任出行裁衣冠笄嫁娶會親友交易割蜜造畜稠棲棧 忌 動土作灶開井謝土	卯巳午未	東南 正南	沖牛29 歲煞西	房床廁 外西北
14	星期一	天月德	巳亥二時 貴人登天	二十	甲申水	赤七	除	畢	七二節八 9三	宜	祭祀開光祈福出行納采嫁娶修造動土起基入宅栽種牧養入殮移柩破土啓攢安葬 忌 作灶造廟	卯辰巳未	東北 東南	沖虎28 歲煞南	占門爐 外西北
15	星期二	歲德合		廿一	乙酉水	白六	滿	觜	六二孚三 4九	宜	祭祀開光沐浴理髮裁衣冠笄嫁娶安床造倉庫開市掃舍宇牧養入殮成除服移柩啓攢安葬	丑寅辰巳	西北 東南	沖兔27 歲煞東	碓磨門 外西北

蔬菜有益

北部：蕹菜、芹菜、越瓜、甘薯、天王寺蕪
中部：胡瓜、菜豆、芥藍菜、玉蜀黍、夏蕪
南部：天王寺蕪、夏蕪、番椒、蕃茄、土白菜

漁我同在

基隆：飛烏、烟仔魚
澎湖：龍蝦、鰮魚、龍尖、烟仔魚
高雄：飛烏、虱目魚

（斗指午爲夏至，萬物於此皆假大而極至，時夏將至，故名也。）

夏至

日出：05時04分
台灣巳時10時43分24秒
台灣巳正二刻13分24秒
日沒：18時47分

巨蟹

90

日	神煞	星期	節氣／時	農曆	干支	九星	建除	星宿	卦		宜／忌	吉時	方位	沖煞	胎神
16	月德	星期一	時五福午 時入巽宮	廿一	丙辰 土	黑二	開	畢	八六蠱七 1四	宜	祭祀祈福出行納采嫁娶出火修造動土起基上樑 安床入宅開市納財出貨財栽種牧養納畜破土	巳午 申酉	西南 正西	沖狗 歲煞南 56	廚灶栖 外正東
17		星期二		廿二	丁巳 土	碧三	閉	觜	七六井六 8二	宜	裁衣合帳冠笄嫁娶伐木修造動土起基定磉放水 移徙開池築堤防補垣塞穴造畜稠棲棧	丑巳 午申	正南 正西	沖豬 歲煞東 55	倉庫床 外正東
18		星期三		廿三	戊午 火	綠四	建	參	六六巽一 4三	宜	祭祀教牛馬斷蟻 忌 入宅上樑開光齋醮	寅巳 午未	東南 正北	沖鼠 歲煞北 54	房床碓 外正東
19		星期四	◑下弦寅 初03 20 22	廿四	己未 火	黃五	除	井	中五禽 2一	宜	祭祀開光出行納采裁衣嫁娶修造動土起基上樑 安床入宅開市立券交易納財栽種牧養納畜	子卯 巳午	東北 正北	沖牛 歲煞西 53	占門廁 外正東
20	歲德	星期五	時五福卯 時入坤宮	廿五	庚申 木	白六	滿	鬼	四六恒九 1七	宜	祭祀栽種造畜稠棲棧入殮移柩啓攢安葬 忌 安床作灶設醮造廟	辰巳 未申	西北 正東	沖虎 歲煞南 52	碓磨爐 外東南
21	月德合	星期六	鹿角解 今日夏至	廿六	辛酉 木	白六	平	柳	三六鼎四 3八	宜	祭祀沐浴理髮整手足甲冠笄修飾垣墻平治道塗 掃舍宇安葬 忌 醞釀鑄鎔栽種	丑寅 辰巳	西南 正東	沖兔 歲煞東 51	廚灶門 外東南
22		星期日		廿七	壬戌 水	黃五	定	星	二六大過三 4四	宜	祭祀祈福出行納采裁衣嫁娶修造起基安床入宅 立券交易納財牧養納畜入殮啓攢安葬	寅卯 巳午	正南 正南	沖龍 歲煞北 50	倉庫栖 外東南
23		星期一		廿八	癸亥 水	綠四	執	張	一六姤八 6六	宜	祭祀沐浴捕捉結網畋獵取魚 忌 嫁娶開市訂盟納采	子寅 卯未	東南 正南	沖蛇 歲煞西 49	占房床 外東南
24	日入坤	星期二	五元一將 時子入中	廿九	甲子 金	紫九	破	翼	九四復八 1一	★	日逢月破日大耗大凶不宜諸吉事 宜祭祀破屋壞垣	卯辰 未申	東北 東南	沖馬 歲煞南 48	占門碓 外東南
25	歲德合	星期三	●合朔酉 正18 32 49	六月初一	乙丑 金	白八	危	軫	八四頤三 6三	宜	祭祀開光齋醮出行裁衣作染修造動土安床開池 開廁放水結網入殮移柩破土立碑安葬	寅卯 巳申	西北 東南	沖羊 歲煞東 47	碓磨廁 外東南
26	月德	星期四	蜩始鳴	初二	丙寅 火	赤七	成	角	七四屯四 4二	宜	出行納采裁衣修造動土起基安床開市立券交易 納財栽種牧養納畜入殮移柩破土安葬（刀砧）	巳午 酉戌	西南 正西	沖猴 歲煞北 46	廚灶爐 外正南
27		星期五	時五福酉 時入乾宮	初三	丁卯 火	白六	收	亢	六四益九 9六	宜	祭祀結網（刀砧） 忌 嫁娶出行入宅安葬	巳午 未戌	正南 正西	沖雞 歲煞西 45	倉庫門 外正南
28		星期六		初四	戊辰 木	黃五	開	氐	中五禽 6九	宜	祭祀開光求嗣出行納采裁衣嫁娶修造動土起基 上樑安門安床作灶入宅栽種牧養移柩破土	巳未 申酉	東南 正北	沖狗 歲煞南 44	房床栖 外正南
29		星期日	申酉左輔 聖人登殿	初五	己巳 木	綠四	閉	房	四四震一 2八	宜	祭祀裁衣冠笄嫁娶出火修造動土起基安門作灶 移徙納財修倉庫築堤防補垣塞穴栽種牧養	巳午 申酉	東北 正北	沖豬 歲煞東 43	占門床 外正南
30	歲德	星期一		初六	庚午 土	碧三	建	心	三四噬六 9八	宜	出行教牛馬割蜜（勿探病） 忌 齋醮動土修造	丑寅 未申	西北 正東	沖鼠 歲煞北 42	占碓磨 外正南

蔬菜有益

北部：小白菜、櫻桃、蘿蔔、恭菜、金針菜
中部：金針菜、土白菜、水芹菜、胡豆、豆仔
南部：水芹菜、越瓜、金針菜、胡瓜

漁我同在

基隆：飛烏
東港：龍蝦、飛烏、虱目魚苗
安平：烏鰷、鯢魚、虱目魚苗
高雄：虱目魚苗

（斗指丙為芒種，此時可有種芒之穀，過此即失效，故名芒種也。）

二〇二五 JUN 陽曆六月小（30天）

陰曆五月小自五月初十日酉初 建壬午心宿至六月十三日寅正

壬午月（仲夏月）

端陽有雨是豐年 芒種逢雷美亦然 夏至風從西北起 瓜蔬園內受煎熬

月煞（在北方） 四九豫 八 ☳

四	二	六
九	七	五
八	三	一

陽曆	星期	神煞	節氣/記事	陰曆	干支	九星	建除	宿	卦	宜忌	每日吉時	每日喜神財神方位	每日沖肖煞年齡方	每日胎神占方
1	星期日	天德	時五福午 時入坤宮	初六	辛丑土	黃五	成	房	中五禽 3一	宜 祭祀開光祈福出行訂盟納采動土起基開市納財築堤防栽種牧養納畜移柩破土啓攢安葬	寅巳午申	西南 正東	沖羊11 歲煞東	廚灶廁 房內南
2	星期一			初七	壬寅金	白六	收	心	四八小過三 7九	宜 沐浴捕捉結網（刀砧）（勿探病） 忌 祭祀祈福設醮作灶	子卯巳午	正南 正南	沖猴10 歲煞北	倉庫爐 房內南
3	星期二	（刀砧）麒麟	◐上弦午 初11 42 19	初八	癸卯金	赤七	開	尾	三八旅八 7八	宜 祭祀開光祈福出行沐浴訂盟納采裁衣嫁娶會親友動土起基安床開池栽種移柩破土啓攢修墳	卯巳未戌	東南 正南	沖雞9 歲煞西	房床門 房內南
4	星期三			初九	甲辰火	白八	閉	箕	二八咸九 2三	宜 祭祀出行裁衣作染安床作灶移徙交易作陂補垣塞穴入殮成除服移柩破土啓攢立碑 忌 開光	寅未申酉	東北 東南	沖狗8 歲煞南	門雞栖 房內東
5	星期四	歲德合 卯入中	螳螂生 今日芒種	初十	乙巳火	紫九	閉	斗	一八遯四 3七	☆ 節前 日逢受死日大凶不宜諸吉事 節後 納采嫁娶修造動土起基上樑開池築堤防	寅卯申酉	西北 東南	沖豬7 歲煞東	碓磨床 房內東
6	星期五	月德	入霉	十一	丙午水	白一	建	牛	九七師七 3四	宜 祭祀入殮移柩安葬 忌 嫁娶安床作灶動土	巳未酉戌	西南 正西	沖鼠6 歲煞北	廚灶碓 房內東
7	星期六			十二	丁未水	黑二	除	女	八七蒙二 7六	宜 祭祀開光祈福出行納采裁衣嫁娶修造動土起基上樑入宅開市納財捕捉栽種牧養造畜稠栖棧	卯巳午酉	正南 正西	沖牛5 歲煞西	倉庫廁 房內東
8	星期日			十三	戊申土	碧三	滿	虛	七七坎一 6二	宜 祭祀祈福出行經絡出火拆卸修造起基上樑入宅開市納財栽種牧養入殮移柩啓攢安葬	丑辰巳午	東南 正北	沖虎4 歲煞南	房床爐 房內東
9	星期一		四元四將 時子入乾	十四	己酉土	綠四	平	危	六七渙六 8三	宜 祭祀沐浴理髮整手足甲修飾垣墻平治道塗掃舍宇 忌 嫁娶入宅出行	辰巳午申	東北 正北	沖兔3 歲煞東	占大門 外東北
10	星期二	歲德	鵙始鳴	十五	庚戌金	黃五	定	室	中五禽 9九	宜 祭祀祈福齋醮出行納采修造動土起基安床入宅牧養入殮破土安葬 忌 伐木造廟 入梅 22 25 16	寅卯午未	西北 正東	沖龍2 歲煞北	碓磨栖 外東北
11	星期三	月德合	○入望申 初15 45 08	十六	辛亥金	白六	執	壁	四七解四 7七	宜 祭祀開光祈福設醮出行沐浴納采裁衣會親友出火修造動土起基上樑安門安床作灶入宅捕捉	寅卯午未	西南 正東	沖蛇1 歲煞西	廚灶床 外東北
12	星期四		時五福酉 時入艮宮	十七	壬子木	赤七	破	奎	三七未九 1八	★ 日逢月破日大耗大凶不宜諸吉事 宜破屋壞垣	卯辰巳申	正南 正南	沖馬60 歲煞南	倉庫碓 外東北
13	星期五			十八	癸丑木	白八	危	婁	二七困八 8六	宜 祭祀嫁娶經絡修造動土安床放水開市立券交易納財開池結網入殮成除服移柩破土立碑	子卯巳酉	東南 正南	沖羊59 歲煞東	房床廁 外東北
14	星期六			十九	甲寅水	紫九	成	胃	一七訟三 9七	宜 出行納采經絡修造動土起基上樑安床作灶開市納財栽種牧養納畜入殮移柩（刀砧）（勿探病）	丑寅午未	東北 東南	沖猴58 歲煞北	占門爐 外東北
15	星期日	歲德合 鳳凰	反舌無聲	二十	乙卯水	白一	收	昴	九六升二 4一	宜 祭祀作灶（刀砧）（勿探病） 忌 嫁娶栽種出行開市	卯未申戌	西北 東南	沖雞57 歲煞西	碓磨門 外正東

芒種

日出：05時03分
台灣酉時17時57分34秒
台灣酉初三刻12分34秒
日沒：18時42分

雙子 75

蔬菜有益

北部：分蔥(移種)、蔥仔、胡瓜
中部：茄子、菜豆、土白菜、蕹菜、蕃薯
南部：蕹菜、小白菜、越瓜、大豆

漁我同在

淡水：鯔魚、龍尖
基隆：卓鯤、棘鬣魚、鯔魚
安平：鯱魚、烟仔魚
高雄：飛魚、棘鬣魚
東港：烏鰦、龍蝦、沙魚

（斗指巳爲小滿，萬物長於此少得盈滿，麥至此方，小滿而未全熟，故名也。）

小滿

日出：05時07分
台灣丑時02時55分48秒
台灣丑正三刻10分48秒
日沒：18時34分

雙子

60

16	星期五	歲月德合		十九	乙酉水	七赤	定	婁	三一有七 4九	宜	祭祀祈福出行納采嫁娶修造動土起基上樑入宅開市納財牧養納畜入殮破土修墳安葬	丑寅辰巳	西北 東南	沖兔27歲煞東	碓磨門外西北
17	星期六	天德合	時五福午時入中宮	二十	丙戌土	八白	執	胃	二一夬六 1六	宜	祭祀祈福求嗣設醮訂盟納采裁衣合帳嫁娶會親友修造動土起基上樑安床入宅捕捉 忌安葬	卯巳午酉	西南 正西	沖龍26歲煞北	廚灶棲外西北
18	星期日	鳳凰	子丑貪狼聖人登殿	廿一	丁亥土	九紫	破	昴	一一乾一 8八	★	日逢月破日大耗大凶不宜諸吉事宜祭祀解除沐浴破屋壞垣	寅卯午未	正南 正西	沖蛇25歲煞西	倉庫床外西北
19	星期一			廿二	戊子火	一白	危	畢	九九坤一 4七	宜	祭祀設醮出行納采裁衣嫁娶修造動土安床作灶入宅開市栽種牧養入殮移柩破土安葬	丑辰巳未	東南 正北	沖馬24歲煞南	房床碓外正北
20	星期二		◑下弦戌正20 00 03	廿三	己丑火	二黑	成	觜	八九剝六 2九	宜	祭祀祈福出行納采修造動土起基安床作灶開市納財栽種牧養納畜入殮移柩破土啓攢安葬	巳午申酉	東北 正北	沖羊23歲煞東	占門廁外正北
21	星期三	歲月德卯入乾	苦菜秀今日小滿	廿四	庚寅木	三碧	收	參	七九比七 1三	宜	出行問名訂盟納采裁衣冠笄嫁娶會親友上樑作灶開市立券交易納財捕捉結網牧養納畜(刀砧)	午未酉戌	西北 正東	沖猴22歲煞北	碓磨爐外正北
22	星期四	天德		廿五	辛卯木	四綠	開	井	六九觀二 3二	宜	祭祀求嗣齋醮出行動土起基安床栽種牧養破土啓攢 忌訂盟入宅入殮(刀砧)	寅午未申	西南 正東	沖雞21歲煞西	廚灶門外正北
23	星期五		寅辰二時貴人登天	廿六	壬辰水	五黃	閉	鬼	中五禽 4六	宜	嫁娶交易開廁補垣塞穴結網 忌上樑入宅開光	卯巳申酉	正南 正南	沖狗20歲煞南	倉庫棲外正北
24	星期六			廿七	癸巳水	六白	建	柳	四九豫八 6四	☆	日逢受死日大凶不宜諸吉事宜會親友結網畋獵斷蟻	子丑卯巳	東南 正南	沖豬19歲煞東	占房床房內北
25	星期日	天赦	四元三將時子入艮	廿八	甲午金	七赤	除	星	三九晉三 1九	宜	祭祀祈福齋醮出行沐浴納采嫁娶修造動土起基入宅栽種牧養納畜入殮破土啓攢修墳安葬	寅卯未戌	東北 東南	沖鼠18歲煞北	占門碓房內北
26	星期一	歲月德合	靡草死	廿九	乙未金	八白	滿	張	二九革四 6七	宜	祭祀開光塑繪訂盟結婚姻納采裁衣冠笄嫁娶進人口安床作灶塞穴結網 忌修造動土安葬	子寅卯午	西北 東南	沖牛17歲煞西	碓磨廁房內北
27	星期二	天德合	●合朔午初11 03 38	五月初一	丙申火	九紫	平	翼	一九否九 4八	宜	祭祀出行移徙納采裁衣修造動土上樑入宅開市立券交易納財平治道塗栽種牧養納畜	辰巳午酉	西南 正西	沖虎16歲煞南	廚灶爐房內北
28	星期三		時五福酉時入巽宮	初二	丁酉火	一白	定	軫	九八謙六 9四	宜	祭祀祈福齋醮納采嫁娶修造動土起基上樑安床入宅牧養納畜入殮破土啓攢安葬 忌理髮作灶	辰巳午酉	正南 正西	沖兔15歲煞東	倉庫門房內北
29	星期四			初三	戊戌木	二黑	執	角	八八艮一 6一	宜	祭祀祈福沐浴納采裁衣嫁娶出火修造動土安床入宅捕捉栽種牧養入殮移柩破土安葬	卯巳午未	東南 正北	沖龍14歲煞北	房床棲房內南
30	星期五			初四	己亥木	三碧	破	亢	七八蹇二 2二	★	日逢月破日大耗大凶不宜諸吉事宜祭祀解除沐浴破屋壞垣	寅卯午未	東北 正北	沖蛇13歲煞西	占門床房內南
31	星期六	歲月德麥秋至	端午節地臘之辰	初五	庚子土	四綠	危	氐	六八漸七 9二	宜	祭祀開光祈福齋醮出行納采嫁娶開市栽種牧養納畜入殮破土修墳安葬 忌作灶經絡	辰未申酉	西北 正東	沖馬12歲煞南	占碓磨房內南

蔬菜有益

北部：大蔥、分蔥、胡瓜、茄子、菜豆、甘薯
中部：甕菜、土白菜、蕹菜、蒜子、白豆
南部：甘日小蘿蔔、小白菜、甕菜、越瓜、大豆

漁我同在

安平：鯰魚、虱目魚苗
高雄：飛魚、加蚋魚、棘鬣魚、虱目魚
東港：沙魚、烏鰗、龍蝦

（斗指東南維爲立夏，萬物至此皆已長大，故名立夏也。）

二〇二五 MAY 陽曆五月大（31天）

陰曆四月小自建辛巳房宿至

四月初八日未初
五月初十日酉初

辛巳月（孟夏 梅月）

立夏東風熟稻禾，時逢初八果成多，雷鳴甲子庚辰日，定主蝗蟲損稻禾。

月煞在東方　三九晉

五	三	七
一	八	六
九	四	二

陽曆	星期	神煞	備註	陰曆	干支	九星	建除	星宿	卦	宜	宜忌事項	每日吉時	每日喜神	每日財神	每日沖肖年齡煞方	每日胎神占方
1	星期四	歲德	（勿探病）	初四	庚午土	白一	滿	角	九二臨四 9八	宜	祭祀開光出行理髮針灸納采嫁娶會親友安床開市教牛馬結網入殮成除服移柩啓攢修墳安葬	丑寅未申	西北	正東	沖鼠42 歲煞北	占碓磨外正南
2	星期五		時五福午 時入乾宮	初五	辛未土	黑二	平	亢	八二損九 3九	宜	祭祀作灶平治道塗 忌安床醞釀栽種	寅卯午申	西南	正東	沖牛41 歲煞西	廚灶廁外西南
3	星期六	天月德		初六	壬申金	碧三	定	氐	七二節八 7一	宜	祭祀祈福求嗣齋醮沐浴伐木開市掃舍宇納畜開生墳入殮移柩破土啓攢立碑安葬謝土	子卯辰巳	正南	正東	沖虎40 歲煞南	倉庫爐外西南
4	星期日		◐上弦亥初21 53 03	初七	癸酉金	綠四	執	房	六二孚三 7二	宜	祭祀祈福齋醮沐浴裁衣捕捉結網納畜入殮啓攢安葬謝土 忌開市交易動土	子丑辰巳	東南	正南	沖兔39 歲煞東	房床門外西南
5	星期一		螻蟈鳴 今日立夏	初八	甲戌火	黃五	執	心	中五离 2七	★	節前 日逢**月破日**大凶不宜諸吉事 節後 祭祀開光祈福齋醮入殮啓攢安葬謝土	寅卯午未	東北	東南	沖龍38 歲煞北	門雞栖外西南
6	星期二	歲月德合	時五福卯 時入艮宮	初九	乙亥火	白六	破	尾	四二妹七 3三	★	日逢**月破日**大耗大凶不宜諸吉事 麒麟 宜祭祀解除沐浴破屋壞垣	寅卯未申	西北	東南	沖蛇37 歲煞西	碓磨床外西南
7	星期三	天德合		初十	丙子水	赤七	危	箕	三二睽二 3六	宜	祭祀祈福設醮出行裁衣嫁娶修造動土起基上樑安床入宅開市立券交易納財栽種牧養納畜	丑辰巳申	西南	正西	沖馬36 歲煞南	廚灶碓外西南
8	星期四		酉戌左輔 聖人登殿	十一	丁丑水	白八	成	斗	二二兑一 7四	宜	祭祀納采裁衣修造動土起基安床開市立券交易納財牧養納畜入殮破土安葬謝土 忌嫁娶入宅	巳午酉亥	正南	正西	沖羊35 歲煞東	倉庫廁外正西
9	星期五			十二	戊寅土	紫九	收	牛	一二覆六 6八	宜	捕捉結網畋獵取魚（刀砧） 忌祭祀設醮祈福修造	丑巳午未	東南	正北	沖猴34 歲煞北	房床爐外正西
10	星期六	蚯蚓出 勿探病	四元二將 時子入巽	十三	己卯土	白一	開	女	九一泰九 8七	宜	祭祀開光祈福齋醮出行訂盟納采裁衣嫁娶會親友起基安床開市立券交易納財啓攢修墳（刀砧）	子午未申	東北	正北	沖雞33 歲煞西	占大門外正西
11	星期日	歲月德		十四	庚辰金	黑二	閉	虛	八一大畜四 9一	宜	祭祀祈福出行裁衣嫁娶出火修造動土上樑安床作灶入宅立券交易結網入殮移柩破土安葬	丑未申酉	西北	正東	沖狗32 歲煞南	碓磨栖外正西
12	星期一	天德		十五	辛巳金	碧三	建	危	七一需三 7三	☆	日逢**受死日**大凶不宜諸吉事 祭祀解除會親友結網斷蟻	寅午申酉	西南	正東	沖豬31 歲煞東	廚灶床外正西
13	星期二	勿探病 酉入坤	○入望子正00 57 20	十六	壬午木	綠四	除	室	六一小畜八 1二	宜	祭祀祈福齋醮出行嫁娶修造動土起基入宅開市立券交易納財入殮移柩破土啓攢修墳安葬	寅卯巳未	正南	正南	沖鼠30 歲煞北	倉庫碓外西北
14	星期三			十七	癸未木	黃五	滿	壁	中五离 8四	宜	祭祀會親友進人口塞穴結網 忌入宅栽種上樑動土	卯巳午未	東南	正南	沖牛29 歲煞西	房床廁外西北
15	星期四	王瓜生	丑未二時 貴人登天	十八	甲申水	白六	平	奎	四一壯二 9三	宜	祭祀沐浴裁衣冠笄嫁娶平治道塗掃舍宇入殮成除服移柩破土立碑安葬 忌祈福安床	卯辰巳未	東北	東南	沖虎28 歲煞南	占門爐外西北

立夏

日出：05時16分
台灣未時13時58分27秒
台灣未初三刻13分27秒
日沒：18時27分

金牛

45

蔬菜有益

北部：紅豆、芥菜、黃秋葵、甘薯
中部：菜瓜、大蔥、大豆、菴瓜、甘薯
南部：白豆、烏豆、蘿蔔

漁我同在

蘇澳：飛魚、烟仔魚
澎湖：白鯧、龍尖、沙魚、烟仔魚
淡水：鰮魚、沙魚
基隆：沙魚、棘鬣魚、鯧魚

（斗指辰爲穀雨，言雨生百穀也。時必雨不降，百穀滋長之意，蓋本於此。）

日	星期	神煞	節令	農曆	干支	九星	建除	星宿	卦		宜忌	吉時	方位	沖煞	胎神
16	星期三	歲德合	（勿探病）	十九	乙卯水	四綠	閉	壁	六四益九 4一	宜	祭祀齋醮裁衣合帳嫁娶安床作灶立券交易補垣塞穴造畜稠棲棧入殮移柩破土啓攢安葬謝土	卯未申戌	西北 東南	沖雞57 歲煞西	碓磨門 外正東
17	星期四	午入艮	土王用事 丑02 16 58	二十	丙辰土	五黃	建	奎	中五禽 1四	宜	祭祀出行開市教牛馬掃舍宇 忌 作灶動土開光安葬	巳午申酉	西南 正西	沖狗56 歲煞南	廚灶棲 外正東
18	星期五	天月德合		廿一	丁巳土	六白	除	婁	四四震一 8二	宜	祭祀開光祈福問名訂盟納采嫁娶會親友經絡開市立券交易納財出貨財栽種牧養納畜	丑巳午申	正南 正西	沖豬55 歲煞東	倉庫床 外正東
19	星期六			廿二	戊午火	七赤	滿	胃	三四嗑六 4三	宜	祭祀出行沐浴理髮嫁娶會親友安床開市交易塞穴結網 忌 動土入宅祈福	寅巳午未	東南 正北	沖鼠54 歲煞北	房床碓 外正東
20	星期日		萍始生 今日穀雨	廿三	己未火	五黃	平	昴	二四隨七 2一	宜	祭祀作灶修飾垣墻開市平治道塗捕捉結網畋獵取魚 忌 安床安葬修墳	子卯巳午	東北 正北	沖牛53 歲煞西	占門廁 外正東
21	星期一	歲德 卯入巽	◑下弦巳 初09 36 54	廿四	庚申木	六白	定	畢	一四妄二 1七	宜	祭祀解除沐浴掃舍宇進壽符開生墳入殮成除服移柩破土啓攢立碑安葬謝土 忌 嫁娶安床	辰巳未申	西北 正東	沖虎52 歲煞南	碓磨爐 外東南
22	星期二			廿五	辛酉木	七赤	執	觜	九三夷三 3八	宜	祭祀齋醮解除沐浴理髮掃舍宇捕捉畋獵取魚入殮成除服移柩啓攢安葬謝土 忌 出火動土	丑寅辰巳	西南 正東	沖兔51 歲煞東	廚灶門 外東南
23	星期三	天德 月德		廿六	壬戌水	八白	破	參	八三賁八 4四	★	日逢**月破日**大耗大凶不宜諸吉事 宜祭祀解除沐浴求醫治病破屋壞垣	寅卯巳午	正南 正南	沖龍50 歲煞北	倉庫棲 外東南
24	星期四	麒麟		廿七	癸亥水	九紫	危	井	七三既九 6六	☆	日逢**受死日**不宜諸吉事 宜沐浴掃舍宇結網斷蟻（刀砧）	子寅卯未	東南 正南	沖蛇49 歲煞西	占房床 外東南
25	星期五	（刀砧）四元一	鳴鳩拂其羽	廿八	甲子金	四綠	成	鬼	六三家四 1一	宜	祭祀開光祈福出行修造起基上樑安床作灶開市立券交易納財牧養納畜入殮移柩啓攢安葬	卯辰未申	東北 東南	沖馬48 歲煞南	占門碓 外東南
26	星期六	歲德合		廿九	乙丑金	五黃	收	柳	中五禽 6三	◇	日逢**正紅紗日**大凶吉事少取 宜祭祀進人口納財捕捉取魚	寅卯巳申	西北 東南	沖羊47 歲煞東	碓磨廁 外東南
27	星期日		酉時三奇 亥酉登貴	三十	丙寅火	六白	開	星	四三豐六 4二	宜	出行納采裁衣嫁娶修造起基上樑安床入宅開市納財栽種牧養移柩破土啓攢 忌 祭祀入殮安葬	巳午酉戌	西南 正西	沖猴46 歲煞北	廚灶爐 外正南
28	星期一	天德合 月德合	●合朔寅 初03 32 27	四月初一	丁卯火	七赤	閉	張	三三離一 9六	宜	祭祀出行納采裁衣合帳修造安床入宅補垣塞穴造畜稠棲棧入殮破土啓攢安葬 忌 開光安門	巳午未戌	正南 正西	沖雞45 歲煞西	倉庫門 外正南
29	星期二			初二	戊辰木	八白	建	翼	二三革二 6九	宜	祭祀裁衣修飾垣墻開市 忌 造廟齋醮安葬動土	巳未申酉	東南 正北	沖狗44 歲煞南	房床棲 外正南
30	星期三		戴勝降於桑	初三	己巳木	九紫	除	軫	一三同七 2八	宜	祭祀祈福設醮嫁娶會親友出火修造上樑安床入宅結網畋獵栽種造畜稠棲棧 忌 安葬納采開市	巳午申酉	東北 正北	沖豬43 歲煞東	占門床 外正南

穀雨

日出：05時27分

台灣寅時03時57分08秒

台灣寅初三刻12分08秒

日沒：18時19分

金牛

30

蔬菜有益

北部：胡瓜、西瓜、甕菜、大蔥、韭菜、白芋、落花生、甘薯、菜瓜

中部：番椒、菜谷、蔥仔、甕菜、大蔥、黃麻

南部：大蔥、豇豆、芥菜、蔥仔、甕菜、黃麻、菜豆

漁我同在

安平：鯇魚、棘鬣魚、虱目魚苗

東港：沙魚、目吼、虱目魚苗

高雄：沙魚、鰛魚、烏鰡、白帶魚

中華星相王：http://www.ccy227223095.com.tw Facebook：張清淵—易經五術生活研究網

（斗指乙爲清明，時萬物潔顯而清明，蓋時當氣清景明，萬物皆齊，故名也。）

二〇二五 APR 陽曆四月小（30天）

陰曆三月大自三月初七日戌正 四月初八日未初

建庚辰 氐宿至

庚辰月 季春 桐月

風雨相逢初一頭 只恐人民疾病愁 清明風若從南起 定主田禾大有收

月煞在南方

二九萃 四

六	四	八
二	九	七
一	五	三

陽曆	1	2	3	4	5	6	7	8	9	10	11	12	13	14	15
神煞	歲德					歲德合		月德合 天德合		三元 四將	歲德		月德 天德	鳳凰	
星期	星期二	星期三	星期四	星期五	星期六	星期日	星期一	星期二	星期三	星期四	星期五	星期六	星期日	星期一	星期二
註		時五福午 時入巽宮		桐始華 今日清明	◐上弦巳 正10 15 56	時五福卯 時入坤宮	辰巳武曲 聖人登殿		田鼠化爲 鴽	時五福子 時入中宮		未卯二時 貴人登天	○入望辰 正08 23 35	虹始見	
陰曆	初四	初五	初六	初七	初八	初九	初十	十一	十二	十三	十四	十五	十六	十七	十八
干支	庚子土	辛丑土	壬寅金	癸卯金	甲辰火	乙巳火	丙午水	丁未水	戊申土	己酉土	庚戌金	辛亥金	壬子木	癸丑木	甲寅水
九星	赤七	白八	紫九	白一	黑二	碧三	綠四	黃五	白六	赤七	白八	紫九	白一	黑二	碧三
建除	收	開	閉	閉	建	除	滿	平	定	執	破	危	成	收	開
宿	翼	軫	角	亢	氐	房	心	尾	箕	斗	牛	女	虛	危	室
卦	三七未九 9二	二七困八 3一	一七訟三 7九	九六升二 7八	八六蠱七 2三	七六井六 3七	六六巽一 3四	中五禽 7六	四六恒九 6二	三六鼎四 8三	二六大過三 9九	一六姤八 7七	九四復八 1八	八四頤三 8六	七四屯四 9七
	宜	宜	宜	宜	宜	宜	宜	宜	宜	宜	★	☆	宜	◇	宜
宜忌	理髮嫁娶進人口立券交易教牛馬捕捉結網栽種取魚 忌 作灶入宅上樑修造(刀砧)	祭祀祈福設醮出行移徙訂盟納采嫁娶出火修造動土起基上樑安床入宅牧養移柩破土 忌 開市	裁衣合帳上樑安床立券交易納財築堤防栽種牧養納畜入殮破土啓攢安葬 忌 祭祀入宅(勿探病)	節前：祭祀出行會親友開市立券交易納財 節後：出行裁衣安床作灶入殮破土立碑安葬	出行修飾垣墻開市教牛馬造畜稠棲棧 忌 安床造廟破土安葬	祭祀開光祈福設醮納采裁衣修造動土起基安床結網造畜稠棲棧 忌 栽種出行安葬開市	祭祀出行理髮訂盟納采嫁娶會親友安床開市結網栽種牧養入殮成除服移柩啓攢安葬	祭祀修飾垣墻開市平治道塗入殮成除服移柩破土立碑安葬 忌 作灶安床理髮謝土	祭祀開光塑繪祈福設醮給由解除沐浴動土開市交易納財作陂塞穴掃舍宇納畜 忌 訂盟嫁娶	祭祀開光祈福設醮裁衣出火修造起基上樑安床作灶入宅捕捉納畜造畜稠棲棧入殮啓攢安葬	日逢**月破日**大凶不宜諸吉事 宜祭祀解除沐浴理髮求醫治病破屋壞垣	日逢**受死日**不宜諸吉事(刀砧) 沐浴會親友納財掃舍宇捕捉結網栽種牧養取魚	祭祀開光祈福出行納采修造動土起基上樑築堤防栽種牧養入殮破土啓攢安葬(刀砧)	日逢**正紅紗日**大凶吉事少取 宜祭祀進人口納財捕捉	出行訂盟納采裁衣嫁娶修造動土起基上樑安床作灶入宅開市立券交易栽種牧養(勿探病)
每日吉時	辰未 申酉	寅巳 午申	子卯 巳午	卯巳 未戌	寅未 申酉	寅卯 申酉	巳未 酉戌	卯巳 午酉	丑辰 巳午	辰巳 午申	寅卯 午未	寅卯 午未	卯辰 巳申	子卯 巳酉	丑寅 午未
每日喜神財神方位	西北 正東	西南 正東	正南 正南	東南 正南	東北 東南	西北 東南	西南 正西	正南 正西	東南 正北	東北 正北	西北 正東	西南 正東	正南 正南	東南 正南	東北 東南
每日沖肖煞方年齡	沖馬 歲煞南 12	沖羊 歲煞東 11	沖猴 歲煞北 10	沖雞 歲煞西 9	沖狗 歲煞南 8	沖豬 歲煞東 7	沖鼠 歲煞北 6	沖牛 歲煞西 5	沖虎 歲煞南 4	沖兔 歲煞東 3	沖龍 歲煞北 2	沖蛇 歲煞西 1	沖馬 歲煞南 60	沖羊 歲煞東 59	沖猴 歲煞北 58
每日胎神占方	占碓磨 房內南	廚灶廁 房內南	倉庫爐 房內南	房床門 房內南	門雞栖 房內東	碓磨床 房內東	廚灶碓 房內東	倉庫廁 房內東	房床爐 房內東	占大門 外東北	碓磨栖 外東北	廚灶床 外東北	倉庫碓 外東北	房床廁 外東北	占門爐 外東北

清明

日出：05時42分

台灣戌時20時49分44秒

台灣戌正三刻04分44秒

日沒：18時12分

白羊

15

蔬菜有益

北部：刈薯、荇菜、荳蘺、莧菜、萵苣、筊白筍、落花生、甘薯

中部：萵苣、筊白筍、番薯、鍋仔菜、大豆、黃麻

南部：烏豆、黃帝豆、芥菜、大豆、黃麻、白豆、筊白筍

漁我同在

基隆：梳齒、加蚋魚、鰮魚、沙魚、烟仔魚

澎湖：白昌、加蚋魚、鰮魚、沙魚、烟仔魚

蘇澳：飛魚、目吼、鰮魚、沙魚

（斗指卯爲春分，日行周天，南北兩半球晝夜均分，又適當春之半，故名也。）

日	星期	吉神	節令	農曆	干支	九星	建除	星宿	卦		宜忌	吉時	方位	沖煞	胎神
16	星期日	月德	巳午武曲 聖人登殿	十七	甲申 水	紫九	執	虛	一九否九 9三	宜	祭祀祈福求嗣齋醮出行出火拆卸修造動土起基 安門入宅捕捉入殮破土啓攢 忌 作灶造廟	卯辰 巳未	東北 東南	沖虎28 歲煞南	占門爐 外西北
17	星期一	歲德合 鳳凰		十八	乙酉 水	白一	破	危	九八謙六 4九	★	日逢**月破日**大耗大凶不宜諸吉事 宜祭祀求醫治病破屋壞垣	丑寅 辰巳	西北 東南	沖兔27 歲煞東	碓磨門 外西北
18	星期二		時五福午 時入坤宮	十九	丙戌 土	黑二	危	室	八八艮一 1六	宜	祭祀冠笄修造動土安門安床結網入殮移柩破土 忌 作灶齋醮造廟開光	卯巳 午酉	西南 正西	沖龍26 歲煞北	廚灶栖 外西北
19	星期三			二十	丁亥 土	碧三	成	壁	七八蹇二 8八	宜	祭祀開光祈福裁衣納財開渠栽種牧養（刀砧） 忌 嫁娶齋醮安葬	寅卯 午未	正南 正西	沖蛇25 歲煞西	倉庫床 外西北
20	星期四	春社〇 祈穀生	元鳥至 今日春分	廿一	戊子 火	綠四	收	奎	六八漸七 4七	宜	冠笄捕捉取魚（刀砧） 忌 開市破土啓攢安葬	丑辰 巳未	東南 正北	沖馬24 歲煞南	房床碓 外正北
21	星期五	月德合		廿二	己丑 火	黃五	開	婁	中五禽 2九	宜	祭祀開光祈福齋醮出行問名訂盟納采嫁娶出火 修造動土起基安床作灶入宅牧養納畜移柩破土	巳午 申酉	東北 正北	沖羊23 歲煞東	占門廁 外正北
22	星期六	歲德 卯入中	◑下弦戌 初19 30 53	廿三	庚寅 木	白六	閉	胃	四八小過三 1三	宜	裁衣立券交易納采修造動土起基安床作灶納財 築堤防栽種牧養納畜入殮破土啓攢修墳安葬	午未 酉戌	西北 正東	沖猴22 歲煞北	碓磨爐 外正北
23	星期日			廿四	辛卯 木	赤七	建	昴	三八旅八 3二	宜	祭祀上官赴任出行嫁娶會親友進人口開市立券 交易教牛馬栽種牧養入殮成除服移柩啓攢安葬	寅午 未申	西南 正東	沖雞21 歲煞西	廚灶門 外正北
24	星期一			廿五	壬辰 水	白八	除	畢	二八咸九 4六	☆	逢**受死日**大凶吉事少取 出行理髮整手足甲塞穴掃舍宇捕捉結網畋獵	卯巳 申酉	正南 正南	沖狗20 歲煞南	倉庫栖 外正北
25	星期二		雷乃發聲	廿六	癸巳 水	紫九	滿	觜	一八遯四 6四	宜	祭祀開光祈福理髮裁衣會親友雕刻伐木修造起 基上樑安門安床作灶開市立券交易納財結網	子丑 卯巳	東南 正南	沖豬19 歲煞東	占房床 房內北
26	星期三	月德 日入艮	三元三將 時子入乾	廿七	甲午 金	白一	平	參	九七師七 1九	宜	祭祀祈福冠笄嫁娶進人口修飾垣墻修置產室平 治道塗 忌 開市作灶蓋屋栽種	寅卯 未戌	東北 東南	沖鼠18 歲煞北	占門碓 房內北
27	星期四	麒麟 歲德合		廿八	乙未 金	黑二	定	井	八七蒙二 6七	宜	祭祀開光祈福設醮出行問名訂盟納采裁衣嫁娶 雕刻修造上樑安床作灶入宅開市納財納畜	子寅 卯午	西北 東南	沖牛17 歲煞西	碓磨廁 房內北
28	星期五			廿九	丙申 火	碧三	執	鬼	七七坎一 4八	◉	日逢**真滅沒日**大凶宜事不取	辰巳 午酉	西南 正西	沖虎16 歲煞南	廚灶爐 房內北
29	星期六	酉入艮	●合朔酉 正18 59 01	三月初一	丁酉 火	綠四	破	柳	六七渙六 9四	★	日逢**月破日**大耗大凶不宜諸吉事 宜求醫治病破屋壞垣	辰巳 午酉	正南 正西	沖兔15 歲煞東	倉庫門 房內北
30	星期日		始電	初二	戊戌 木	黃五	危	星	中五禽 6一	宜	入學出行納采裁衣冠笄嫁娶經絡進人口安床移 徙開市立券交易結網畋獵取魚入殮破土立碑	卯巳 午未	東南 正北	沖龍14 歲煞北	房床栖 房內南
31	星期一	月德合	（刀砧）	初三	己亥 木	白六	成	張	四七解四 2二	宜	祭祀開光祈福出行納采經絡理髮出火修造動土 起基上樑安門安床入宅開市納財栽種牧養納畜	寅卯 午未	東北 正北	沖蛇13 歲煞西	占門床 房內南

春分

日出：05時59分

台灣酉時17時02分40秒

台灣酉初初刻02分40秒

日沒：18時06分

白羊

0 360

蔬菜有益

北部：苦瓜、甕菜、萵菜、肉豆、田薯、薤菜、蓮藕、水芋、山藥

中部：甘薯、田薯、薑仔、幸菜、水芋、蔥仔、胡瓜、蓮藕、落花生、肉豆

南部：荳薯、莧菜、落花生、莿瓜、肉豆

漁我同在

澎湖：棘鬣魚、鬮北、沙魚

東港：白帶魚、鯧魚、烏鮸、虱目魚苗

高雄：釘鮸、沙魚、虱目魚苗

（斗指甲爲驚蟄，雷鳴動，蟄蟲皆震起而出，故名驚蟄也。）

二〇二五 MAR 陽曆三月大（31天）

陰曆二月小 自二月初六日申正 建己卯亢宿 至三月初七日戌正

己卯月（仲春月） 驚蟄雷鳴未足奇，春分有雨病人稀，月內相逢三卯日，豆麥田蠶處處宜 煞西（在方） 一九否 九☰

七	五	九
三	一	八
二	六	四

日	神煞	星期	節令	農曆	干支	九星	建除	宿	卦	宜忌	每日吉時	每日喜神財神方位	每日沖肖煞方年齡	每日胎神占方
1		星期六	子丑左輔 聖人登殿	初二	己巳 木	碧三	平	柳	七一 需三 2八	宜 作灶平治道塗 忌開市祈福出行造廟	巳午 申酉	東北 正北	沖豬 歲煞東 43	占門床 外正南
2	歲德	星期日		初三	庚午 土	綠四	定	星	六一 小畜八 9八	宜 祭祀祈福納采嫁娶修造上樑安門安床入宅結網畋獵牧養納畜入殮啓攢安葬 忌動土（勿探病）	丑寅 未申	西北 正東	沖鼠 歲煞北 42	占碓磨 外正南
3	月德合	星期一	時五福午 時入中宮	初四	辛未 土	黃五	執	張	中五 禽 3九	宜 祭祀祈福出行納采嫁娶出火修造動土起基上樑安門安床捕捉栽種牧養入殮破土啓攢安葬	寅卯 午申	西南 正東	沖牛 歲煞西 41	廚灶廁 外西南
4	天德合	星期二		初五	壬申 金	白六	破	翼	四一 壯二 7一	★ 日逢**月破日**大耗大凶不宜諸吉事 宜祭祀解除沐浴求醫治病破屋壞垣掃舍宇	子卯 辰巳	正南 正南	沖虎 歲煞南 40	倉庫爐 外西南
5		星期三	桃始華 今日驚蟄	初六	癸酉 金	赤七	破	軫	三一 有七 7二	★ 節前 祭祀祈福出行入宅開市栽種安葬 節後 日逢**月破日**大耗大凶不宜諸吉事	子丑 辰巳	東南 正南	沖兔 歲煞東 39	房床門 外西南

驚蟄

日出：06時13分
台灣申時16時08分23秒
台灣申正初刻08分23秒
日沒：17時59分

雙魚 345

蔬菜有益

北部：胡瓜、西瓜、甜瓜、白芋、筊白筍、薑、落花生
中部：薑、刀豆、菜豆、筊白筍、落花生
南部：烏豆、菜豆、筊白筍、落花生

漁我同在

蘇澳：花輝、目吼、釘鮸、沙魚
基隆：加蚋魚、釘鮸、鰛魚、沙魚
澎湖：鮸魚、青

日	神煞	星期	節令	農曆	干支	九星	建除	宿	卦	宜忌	每日吉時	每日喜神財神方位	每日沖肖煞方年齡	每日胎神占方
6	月德	星期四		初七	甲戌 火	白八	危	角	二一 夬六 2七	宜 祭祀祈福出行納采裁衣修造動土起基上樑安床作灶入宅開市納財結網牧養納畜入殮破土安葬	寅卯 午未	東北 東南	沖龍 歲煞北 38	門雞栖 外西南
7	歲德合 卯入乾	星期五	◐上弦子正 00 32 55	初八	乙亥 火	紫九	成	亢	一一 乾一 3三	宜 開光出行裁衣出火安床入宅開市立券交易納財築堤防結網牧養 忌嫁娶納采安葬（刀砧）	寅卯 未申	西北 東南	沖蛇 歲煞西 37	碓磨床 外西南
8		星期六		初九	丙子 水	白一	收	氐	九九 坤一 3六	宜 裁衣冠笄進人口安床捕捉結網畋獵栽種（刀砧） 忌作灶開市造橋	丑辰 巳申	西南 正西	沖馬 歲煞南 36	廚灶碓 外西南
9		星期日		初十	丁丑 水	黑二	開	房	八九 剝六 7四	宜 祭祀開光祈福齋醮出行納采裁衣嫁娶出火修造動土起基上樑入宅牧養納畜移柩破土謝土	巳午 酉亥	正南 正西	沖羊 歲煞東 35	倉庫廁 外正西
10	天赦	星期一	倉庚鳴	十一	戊寅 土	碧三	閉	心	七九 比七 6八	宜 納采修造動土起基上樑安門安床作灶立券交易納財栽種牧養納畜入殮移柩破土修墳安葬	丑巳 午未	東南 正北	沖猴 歲煞北 34	房床爐 外正西
11	月德合	星期二	三元二將 時子入艮	十二	己卯 土	綠四	建	尾	六九 觀二 8七	宜 祭祀出行訂盟冠笄嫁娶進人口作染開市 忌開井修造動土（勿探病）	子午 未申	東北 正北	沖雞 歲煞西 33	占大門 外正西
12	歲德	星期三		十三	庚辰 金	黃五	除	箕	中五 禽 9一	☆ 日逢**受死日**不宜諸吉事 宜祭祀解除沐浴理髮整手足甲塞穴掃舍宇	丑未 申酉	西北 正東	沖狗 歲煞南 32	碓磨栖 外正西
13		星期四		十四	辛巳 金	白六	滿	斗	四九 豫八 7三	宜 祭祀開光祈福求嗣入學理髮冠笄納采裁衣會親友經絡安門安床作灶造倉庫開市立券交易納財	寅午 申酉	西南 正東	沖豬 歲煞東 31	廚灶床 外正西
14	酉入巽	星期五	○入望未正 14 55 55	十五	壬午 木	赤七	平	牛	三九 晉三 1二	◉ 逢**真滅沒日**大凶宜事不取（勿探病）	寅卯 巳未	正南 正南	沖鼠 歲煞北 30	倉庫碓 外西北
15		星期六	鷹化爲鳩	十六	癸未 木	白八	定	女	二九 萃四 8四	宜 祭祀開光祈福出行納采裁衣嫁娶修造起基安床作灶入宅開市納財納畜造畜稠栖棧入殮安葬	卯巳 午未	東南 正南	沖牛 歲煞西 29	房床廁 外西北

（斗指寅爲雨水，時東風解凍，冰雪皆散而爲水，化而爲雨，故名雨水。）

日期	16	17	18	19	20	21	22	23	24	25	26	27	28
神煞	月德	天德 鳳凰			歲德	月德合	天德合	候雁北	三元 一將	歲德合	月德	麒麟 天德	草木萌動
星期	星期日	星期一	星期二	星期三	星期四	星期五	星期六	星期日	星期一	星期二	星期三	星期四	星期五
備註	時五福午 時入乾宮		獺祭雨 今日雨水		時五福卯 時入艮宮	◑下弦丑 初01 33 56		卯辰貪狼 聖人登殿	時五福子 時入巽宮			時五福酉 時入坤宮	●合朔辰 正08 46 02
農曆	十九	二十	廿一	廿二	廿三	廿四	廿五	廿六	廿七	廿八	廿九	三十	二月初一
干支	丙辰土	丁巳土	戊午火	己未火	庚申木	辛酉木	壬戌水	癸亥水	甲子金	乙丑金	丙寅火	丁卯火	戊辰木
九星	八白	九紫	七赤	八白	九紫	一白	二黑	三碧	七赤	八白	九紫	一白	二黑
建除	滿	平	定	執	破	危	成	收	開	閉	建	除	滿
星宿	虛	危	室	壁	奎	婁	胃	昴	畢	觜	參	井	鬼
卦	二三革二 1四	一三同七 8二	九二臨四 4三	八二損九 2一	七二節八 1七	六二孚三 3八	中五禽 4四	四二妹七 6六	三二睽二 1一	二二兑一 6三	一二履六 4二	九一泰九 9六	八一大畜四 6九
	宜	宜	宜	宜	★	宜	☆	宜	宜	宜	宜	宜	宜
宜忌	祭祀開光祈福出行納采裁衣嫁娶會親友經絡修造拆卸起基安床入宅納財造倉庫牧養納畜	祭祀修飾垣墻平治道塗 忌 出行齋醮安門安葬	祭祀開光祈福出行納采嫁娶修造起基安床入宅牧養入殮啓攢安葬 忌 栽種作灶動土破土	問名訂盟結婚姻納采嫁娶會親友進人口動土開廟捕捉牧養取魚入殮移柩破土安葬 忌 入宅開市	日逢月破日大耗大凶不宜諸吉事 宜求醫治病破屋壞垣	祭祀齋醮沐浴開生墳入殮成除服移柩破土安葬 忌 動土嫁娶作灶上樑	日逢受死日大凶吉事少取 宜祭祀塞穴結網入殮成除服移柩破土安葬謝土	祭祀沐浴理髮作灶捕捉結網栽種(刀砧) 忌 嫁娶安葬開市造廟	祭祀開光祈福入學出行沐浴理髮嫁娶會親友動土安碓磨放水開市納財開渠開井栽種(刀砧)	祭祀祈福求嗣齋醮給由求醫治病結網斷蟻納畜入殮成除服啓攢安葬謝土 忌 栽種入學開光出行	開光問名納采裁衣會親友上樑安床開市立券交易納財開倉庫出貨財牧養入殮啓攢安葬	祭祀祈福出行納采裁衣嫁娶修造動土安床開市立券納財牧養納畜入殮破土啓攢安葬 忌 入宅	祭祀祈福求嗣理髮裁衣經絡冠笄會親友進人口安床結網畋獵斷蟻牧養
吉時	巳午申酉	丑巳午申	寅巳午未	子卯巳午	辰巳未申	丑寅辰巳	寅卯巳午	子寅卯未	卯辰未申	寅卯巳申	巳午酉戌	巳午未戌	巳未申酉
方位	西南 正西	正南 正西	東南 正北	東北 正北	西北 正東	西南 正東	正南 正南	東南 正南	東北 東南	西北 東南	西南 正西	正南 正西	東南 正北
沖煞	沖狗56 歲煞南	沖豬55 歲煞東	沖鼠54 歲煞北	沖牛53 歲煞西	沖虎52 歲煞南	沖兔51 歲煞東	沖龍50 歲煞北	沖蛇49 歲煞西	沖馬48 歲煞南	沖羊47 歲煞東	沖猴46 歲煞北	沖雞45 歲煞西	沖狗44 歲煞南
胎神	廚灶栖 外正東	倉庫床 外正東	房床碓 外正東	占門廁 外正東	碓磨爐 外東南	廚灶門 外東南	倉庫栖 外東南	占房床 外東南	占門碓 外東南	碓磨廁 外東南	廚灶爐 外正南	倉庫門 外正南	房床栖 外正南

雨水

日出：06時26分

台灣西時18時07分44秒

台灣西正初刻07分44秒

日沒：17時51分

雙魚

330

蔬菜有益

北部：米豆、絲豆、烏豆、番椒、蕹椒、結球、萵苣、石刁柏、白豆、紫蘇

中部：番石、白豆、絲瓜、紫蘇、烏豆

南部：白筍、蓮藕、絲瓜、紫蘇、石刁柏

漁我同在

新港：釘鯱

安平：白帶、沙魚、馬鮫

高雄：石鯽、釘鯱、沙魚、鰮魚

（斗指東北維爲立春，時春氣始至，四時之卒始，故名立春也。）

二〇二五FEB 陽曆二月平（28天）

陰曆正月大自正月初六日亥正 建戊寅角宿至二月初六日申正

戊寅月（孟春端月）

元旦晴雲光霽天 雨雪霏霏是豐年 最喜立春晴一日 農夫不用力耕田

（月煞在北方） 六 ☷☶ 九八謙

八	六	一
四	二	九
三	七	五

陽曆	1	2	3	4	5	6	7	8	9	10	11	12	13	14	15
	四牛耕地			人日瑞彩	歲德合 卯入巽	月德	天德		二元 四將	歲德	月德合	天德合 酉入中			歲德合
星期	星期六	星期日	星期一	星期二	星期三	星期四	星期五	星期六	星期日	星期一	星期二	星期三	星期四	星期五	星期六
	時五福午 時入艮宮		東風解凍 今日立春	天曹遷賞會	◐上弦申正 16 03 27	玉皇大帝聖誕		蟄蟲始振	日入乾宮 時子入坤			○入望亥初 21 54 42	魚陟負冰		午未武曲 聖人登殿
陰曆	初四	初五	初六	初七	初八	初九	初十	十一	十二	十三	十四	十五	十六	十七	十八
干支	辛丑土	壬寅金	癸卯金	甲辰火	乙巳火	丙午水	丁未水	戊申土	己酉土	庚戌金	辛亥金	壬子木	癸丑木	甲寅水	乙卯水
九星	黑二	碧三	綠四	黃五	白六	赤七	白八	紫九	白一	黑二	碧三	綠四	黃五	白六	赤七
建除	建	除	除	滿	平	定	執	破	危	成	收	開	閉	建	除
宿	柳	星	張	翼	軫	角	亢	氐	房	心	尾	箕	斗	牛	女
卦	八四頤三 3一	七四屯四 7九	六四益九 7八	中五禽 2三	四四震一 3七	三四噬六 3四	二四隨七 7六	一四妄二 6二	九三夷三 8三	八三賁八 9九	七三既九 7七	六三家四 1八	中五禽 8六	四三豐六 9七	三三離一 4一
	◇	宜	宜	宜	宜	宜	宜	★	宜	☆	宜	宜	宜	宜	宜
	日值**正紅紗日**凡事少取 農人得辛祈穀於上帝 宜祭祀求嗣解除會親友教牛馬造畜稠棲棧	開光沐浴入學裁衣拆卸入殮破土啓攢安葬 忌祭祀問名訂盟納采（勿探病）	節前祭祀裁衣會親友納財結網入殮啓攢安葬 節後祭祀祈福納財入殮破土啓攢安葬	祭祀祈福求嗣針灸冠笄會親友安床牧養 忌造廟設醮開市安門 七龍治水	作灶平治道塗 忌栽種出行造廟安葬	祭祀開光祈福出行納采修造動土起基安床入宅開市納財栽種牧養納畜入殮移柩破土安葬	祭祀祈福出行納采裁衣嫁娶修造動土拆卸起基安床入宅納財栽種牧養納畜入殮破土啓攢安葬	日逢**月破日**大耗大凶不宜諸吉事 宜祭祀解除沐浴求醫治病破屋壞垣掃舍宇	祭祀開光祈福齋醮裁衣修造動土拆卸起基上樑造廟開市掛匾入殮破土啓攢安葬 忌納采嫁娶	日逢**受死日**不宜諸吉事 宜入學補垣塞穴結網入殮成除服移柩破土安葬	祭祀祈福出行納采修造動土起基上樑安床作灶入宅開市納財教牛馬捕捉栽種牧養納畜（刀砧）	祭祀祈福齋醮理髮納采裁衣修造動土安床納財開池栽種牧養納畜破土啓攢 上元天官賜福	祭祀給由裁衣合帳經絡伐木做樑開柱眼定磉床作灶入殮成除服移柩啓攢 忌納采入宅	裁衣會親友伐木做樑造倉庫開市立券交易納財教牛馬 忌祭祀祈福嫁娶安葬（勿探病）	祭祀祈福齋醮出行納采嫁娶修造動土起基安床入宅開市立券交易入殮破土啓攢安葬（勿探病）
每日吉時	寅巳午申	子卯巳午	卯巳未戌	寅未申酉	寅卯申酉	巳未酉戌	卯巳午酉	丑辰巳午	辰巳午申	寅卯午未	寅卯午未	卯辰巳申	子卯巳酉	丑寅午未	卯未申戌
每日喜神財神方位	西南 正東	正南 正南	東南 正南	東北 東南	西北 東南	西南 正西	正南 正西	東南 正北	東北 正北	西北 正東	西南 正東	正南 正南	東南 正南	東北 東南	西北 東南
每日沖肖煞年齡方	沖羊11 歲煞東	沖猴10 歲煞北	沖雞9 歲煞西	沖狗8 歲煞南	沖豬7 歲煞東	沖鼠6 歲煞北	沖牛5 歲煞西	沖虎4 歲煞南	沖兔3 歲煞東	沖龍2 歲煞北	沖蛇1 歲煞西	沖馬60 歲煞南	沖羊59 歲煞東	沖猴58 歲煞北	沖雞57 歲煞西
每日胎神占方	廚灶廁 房內南	倉庫爐 房內南	房床門 房內南	門雞栖 房內東	碓磨床 房內東	廚灶碓 房內東	倉庫廁 房內東	房床爐 房內東	占大門 外東北	碓磨栖 外東北	廚灶床 外東北	倉庫碓 外東北	房床廁 外東北	占門爐 外東北	碓磨門 外正東

立春

日出：06時37分

台灣亥時22時11分42秒

台灣亥正初刻11分42秒

日沒：17時42分

寶瓶 315

蔬菜有益

北部：茄子、番茄、大蔥、牛蒡、分蔥

中部：白芋、西瓜、胡瓜、甜瓜、鵲豆、甕菜、幸菜、薊瓜、肉豆、蔥仔

南部：白芋、薑、越瓜、鵲豆、刁豆

漁我同在

淡水：鯧魚、鮑魚、釘鯢、沙魚

基隆：沙魚、梳齒、加蚋魚

蘇澳：狗母、龍蝦、花輝、沙魚

澎湖：梳齒、加蚋魚、釘鯢

（斗指丑爲大寒，時大寒栗烈已極，故名大寒也。）

大寒

日出：06時42分 台灣寅時04時01分23秒 台灣寅正初刻01分23秒 日沒：17時30分

寶瓶 300

蔬菜有益

北部：紅菜頭、菾瓜、匏仔、萵蒿、東菠菜
中部：菠菜、菜瓜、小白菜、匏仔、紅菜頭、水芋
南部：白芋、蓮藕、絲瓜、扁浦、水芋、土白菜

漁我同在

新港 高雄：釘鮸、硼串
東港：狗母、過仔魚
安平：馬鮫、沙魚、烏魚

日期	神煞	星期	節令	農曆	干支	九星	建除 星宿	卦	吉凶	宜忌	吉時	方位	沖煞	胎神
16	天月德合	星期四		十七	乙酉水	綠四	成 斗	六七渙六 4九	☆	日逢**受死日**不宜諸吉事（刀砧）宜祭祀沐浴掃舍宇入殮成除服破土啓攢修墳	丑寅辰巳	西北 東南	沖兔26 歲煞東	碓磨門 外西北
17		星期五	時五福午 時入巽宮	十八	丙戌土	黃五	收 牛	中五禽 1六	宜	祭祀冠笄捕捉畋獵 忌安床造廟開市作灶	卯巳午酉	西南 正西	沖龍25 歲煞北	廚灶棲 外西北
18		星期六		十九	丁亥土	白六	開 女	四七解四 8八	宜	祭祀祈福齋醮納采裁衣修造起基上樑安門安床開市立券交易納財牧養納畜 忌嫁娶作灶栽種	寅卯午未	正南 正西	沖蛇24 歲煞西	倉庫床 外西北
19		星期日		二十	戊子火	赤七	閉 虛	三七未九 4七	宜	祭祀沐浴裁衣合帳作染安床立券交易入殮成除服移柩安葬 忌開光嫁娶出行破土	丑辰巳未	東南 正北	沖馬23 歲煞南	房床碓 外正北
20	歲德合	星期一	雞乳 今日大寒	廿一	己丑火	白八	建 危	二七困八 2九	◇	日逢**正紅紗日**凡事少取 宜祭祀解除交易教牛馬造畜稠棲棧	巳午申酉	東北 正北	沖羊22 歲煞東	占門廁 外正北
21	天月德	星期二	時五福卯 時入坤宮	廿二	庚寅木	紫九	除 室	一七訟三 1三	宜	開光出行沐浴理髮問名訂盟納采嫁娶開市納財栽種牧養納畜入殮破土啓攢修墳安葬 忌設醮	午未酉戌	西北 正東	沖猴21 歲煞北	碓磨爐 外正北
22	麒麟	星期三	◑下弦寅 正042303	廿三	辛卯木	白一	滿 壁	九六升二 3二	宜	祭祀出行理髮針灸裁衣安床開市立券交易納財牧養入殮移柩啓攢修墳安葬 忌入宅上樑祈福	寅午未申	西南 正東	沖雞20 歲煞西	廚灶門 外正北
23		星期四		廿四	壬辰水	黑二	平 奎	八六蠱七 4六	宜	泥墻平治道塗 忌作灶開井造廟造橋	卯巳申酉	正南 正南	沖狗19 歲煞南	倉庫棲 外正北
24		星期五		廿五	癸巳水	碧三	定 婁	七六井六 6四	宜	祭祀訂盟納采會親友修造起基安床牧養 忌出行造廟安葬破土	子丑卯巳	東南 正南	沖豬18 歲煞東	占房床 房內北
25	歲德 二元三	星期六	征鳥厲疾 時子入中	廿六	甲午金	綠四	執 胃	六六巽一 1九	宜	祭祀開光祈福出行納采嫁娶起基上樑安床入宅捕捉牧養納畜入殮移柩破土修墳安葬 忌作灶	寅卯未戌	東北 東南	沖鼠17 歲煞北	占門碓 房內北
26	天月德合	星期日		廿七	乙未金	黃五	破 昴	中五禽 6七	★	日逢**月破日**大耗大凶不宜諸吉事 宜祭祀解除破屋壞垣	子寅卯午	西北 東南	沖牛16 歲煞西	碓磨廁 房內北
27	鳳凰	星期一		廿八	丙申火	白六	危 畢	四六恒九 4八	宜	祭祀齋醮出行納采嫁娶起基上樑入宅開市納財結網栽種牧養納畜入殮破土啓攢安葬（刀砧）	辰巳午酉	西南 正西	沖虎15 歲煞南	廚灶爐 房內北
28	除夕◯ 火盆暴	星期二	時五福酉 時入乾宮	廿九	丁酉火	赤七	成 觜	三六鼎四 9四	☆	日逢**受死日**不宜諸吉事（刀砧）宜祭祀齋醮結網畋獵入殮破土啓攢立碑安葬	辰巳午酉	正南 正西	沖兔14 歲煞東	倉庫門 房內北
29	天臘之辰	星期三	●合朔戌 正203716	正月初一	戊戌木	白八	收 參	二六大過三 6一	宜	祭祀納財捕捉畋獵 忌造廟安床作灶造船 大姑把蠶 蠶食一葉	卯巳午未	東南 正北	沖龍14 歲煞北	房床棲 房內南
30	歲德合	星期四	水澤腹堅	初二	己亥木	紫九	開 井	一六姤八 2二	宜	祭祀求嗣入學沐浴理髮問名訂盟納采會親友開渠開井牧養納畜造畜稠棲棧 忌嫁娶裁衣上樑	寅卯午未	東北 正北	沖蛇13 歲煞西	占門床 房內南
31	天月德	星期五		初三	庚子土	白一	閉 鬼	九四復八 9二	宜	祭祀祈福求嗣齋醮沐浴納采裁衣安床立券交易納財入殮移柩啓攢修墳安葬謝土 忌嫁娶開市	辰未申酉	西北 正東	沖馬12 歲煞南	占碓磨 房內南

（斗指癸爲小寒，時天氣漸寒，尚未大冷，故名小寒。）

二〇二五 JAN 陽曆正月大 (31天)

陰曆十二月小自甲辰年十二月初六日巳正
建丁丑軫宿至乙巳年正月初六日亥正
丁丑月（季冬臘月）

朔日西風六畜災　棉絲五穀總成堆
最喜大寒無雨雪　太平冬盡賀春來

月煞在東（方）　八八艮 ䷳

二	七	九
一	三	五
六	八	四

日	星期	註記	時事	農曆	干支	九星	建除	宿	卦	宜忌	每日吉時	每日喜神財神方位	每日沖肖煞年齡方	每日胎神占方
1	星期三			初二	庚午土	七赤	破	參	三九晉三 9八	★ 日逢月破日大耗大凶不宜諸吉事 宜破屋壞垣（勿探病）	丑寅未申	西北 正東	沖鼠 歲煞北 41	占碓磨 外正南
2	星期四		時五福午 時入坤宮	初三	辛未土	八白	危	井	二九萃四 3九	宜 祭祀出行理髮冠笄伐木安床立券交易結網畋獵入殮成除服移柩破土啓攢修墳立碑 忌作灶安門	寅卯午申	西南 正東	沖牛 歲煞西 40	廚灶廁 外西南
3	星期五	月德		初四	壬申金	九紫	成	鬼	一九否九 7一	宜 祭祀開光齋醮出行納采裁衣嫁娶修造起基上樑安門作灶入宅納財牧養入殮啓攢安葬（刀砧）	子卯辰巳	正南 正南	沖虎 歲煞南 39	倉庫爐 外西南
4	星期六			初五	癸酉金	一白	收	柳	九八謙六 7二	宜 祭祀沐浴理髮整手足甲掃舍宇捕捉結網畋獵 忌移徙入宅出火作灶（刀砧）	子丑辰巳	東南 正南	沖兔 歲煞東 38	房床門 外西南
5	星期日	歲德	雁北鄉 今日小寒	初六	甲戌火	二黑	收	星	八八艮一 2七	宜 節前 祭祀祈福納采裁衣動土起基上樑安門 節後 祭祀開光祈福設醮裁衣作灶納財栽種	寅卯午未	東北 東南	沖龍 歲煞北 37	門雞栖 外西南
6	星期一	天月德合	時五福卯 時入中宮	初七	乙亥火	三碧	開	張	七八蹇二 3三	宜 祭祀祈福設醮納采裁衣修造動土起基上樑安床作灶入宅開市立券交易納財牧養納畜 忌栽種	寅卯未申	西北 東南	沖蛇 歲煞西 36	碓磨床 外西南
7	星期二	臘八	◐上弦辰 初07 57 41	初八	丙子水	四綠	閉	翼	六八漸七 3六	宜 祭祀齋醮沐浴裁衣合帳經絡安床立券交易納財造車器入殮成除服移柩啓攢修墳立碑安葬	丑辰巳申	西南 正西	沖馬 歲煞南 35	廚灶碓 外西南
8	星期三			初九	丁丑水	五黃	建	軫	中五禽 7四	◇ 日逢正紅紗日大凶吉事少取 宜祭祀解除針灸教牛馬	巳午酉亥	正南 正西	沖羊 歲煞東 34	倉庫廁 外正西
9	星期四		巳亥二時 貴人登天	初十	戊寅土	六白	除	角	四八小過三 6八	宜 開光納采裁衣嫁娶修造動土上樑安床入宅開市立券交易納財牧養納畜入殮破土啓攢安葬	丑巳午未	東南 正北	沖猴 歲煞北 33	房床爐 外正西
10	星期五	歲德合 鵲始巢	二元二將 時子入乾	十一	己卯土	七赤	滿	亢	三八旅八 8七	宜 祭祀納采裁衣嫁娶會親友進人口安床開市立券交易納財造倉庫開池補垣塞穴結網（勿探病）	子午未申	東北 正北	沖雞 歲煞西 32	占大門 外正西
11	星期六	天月德		十二	庚辰金	八白	平	氐	二八咸九 9一	宜 祭祀裁衣冠笄嫁娶進人口安床修飾垣墻開市平治道塗入殮移柩安葬 忌作灶造廟栽種造橋	丑未申酉	西北 正東	沖狗 歲煞南 31	碓磨栖 外正西
12	星期日			十三	辛巳金	九紫	定	房	一八遯四 7三	宜 祭祀求嗣入學冠帶問名訂盟納采嫁娶會親友經絡動土起基納財牧養納畜開廁 忌出行入宅開市	寅午申酉	西南 正東	沖豬 歲煞東 30	廚灶床 外正西
13	星期一		時五福酉 時入艮宮	十四	壬午木	一白	執	心	九七師七 1二	宜 祭祀祈福出行沐浴裁衣嫁娶修造動土起基上樑安床入宅捕捉畋獵入殮破土啓攢安葬（勿探病）	寅卯巳未	正南 正南	沖鼠 歲煞北 29	倉庫碓 外西北
14	星期二		○入望卯 正06 28 13	十五	癸未木	二黑	破	尾	八七蒙二 8四	★ 日逢月破日大耗大凶不宜諸吉事 宜祭祀破屋壞垣	卯巳午未	東南 正南	沖牛 歲煞西 28	房床廁 外西北
15	星期三	（刀砧） 歲德	雉始雊	十六	甲申水	三碧	危	箕	七七坎一 9三	宜 祭祀開光求嗣出行納采嫁娶修造動土起基入宅開市納財結網栽種納畜入殮破土啓攢安葬	卯辰巳未	東北 東南	沖虎 歲煞南 27	占門爐 外西北

小寒

日出：06時42分
台灣巳時10時33分51秒
台灣巳正二刻03分51秒
日沒：17時19分

摩羯 285

蔬菜有益

北部：菜豆、菜頭、蘿蔔、皇帝豆、石刁柏
中部：金瓜、冬瓜、南瓜、西瓜、石刁柏
南部：茄子菜、冬瓜、金瓜、石刁柏

漁我同在

蘇澳：梳齒、釘鯢、棘鬣魚
基隆：釘鯢、棘鬣魚(淡水)
澎湖：沙魚、狗母、龍蝦、棘鬣魚

民國一一四年 太歲乙巳年 西曆二〇二五年
九七七師 九紫火
干木支火 納音屬火
歲干旃蒙 歲支名大荒落
歲名吳遂 歲德庚 歲合乙
宜修造取土吉
柳土獐 值年 翼火蛇
管局 遇戊胃 卯女 為暗金伏斷

道曆四七二二年佛曆二五六九年

乙巳年大利南北不利東方小利西方

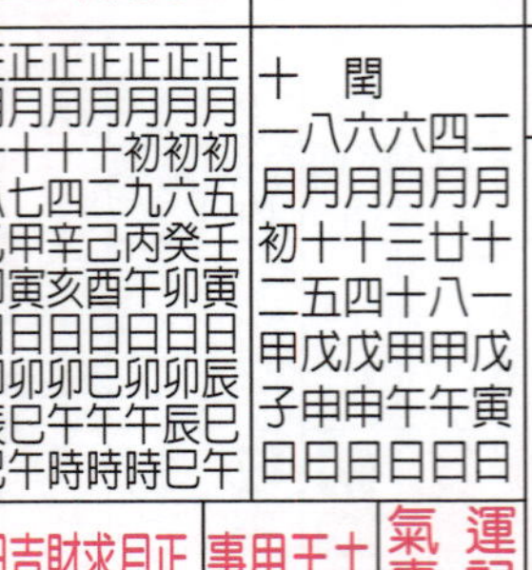

正月開市吉日

正月初五壬寅日辰巳午
正月初六癸卯日卯辰巳
正月初九丙午日卯午時
正月十二己酉日巳午時
正月十四辛亥日卯午時
正月十七甲寅日卯巳午
正月十八乙卯日卯辰巳

天赦吉日

二月十一戊寅日
四月廿八甲午日
六月三十甲午日
閏六月十四戊申日
八月十五戊申日
十一月初二甲子日

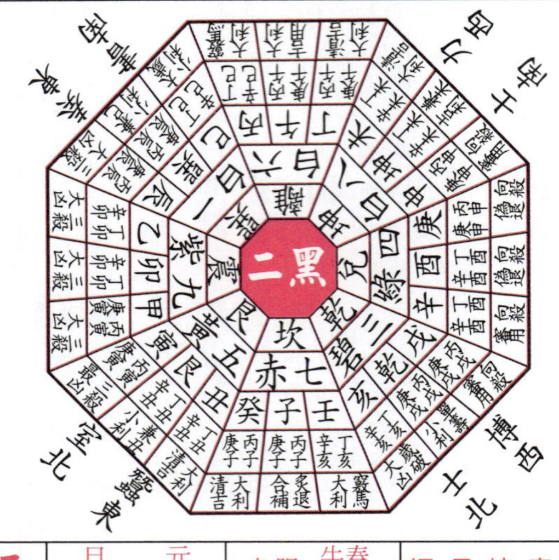

正月求財吉日

正月初一戊戌日卯巳時
正月初三庚子日卯辰巳
正月初九丙午日卯午時
正月初十丁未日辰巳午
正月十四辛亥日卯午時

土王用事

三月二十丙辰日 02 16 58
六月廿五己丑日 18 06 26
八月廿九壬戌日 11 30 02
十一月廿九辛卯日 11 04 10

運氣記事

七龍治水◯大姑把蠶◯蠶食一葉◯四牛耕地◯四日得辛

張清淵著

黃帝地母經

太歲乙巳年
高下禾苗翠
春夏多漂流
秋冬五穀豐
豆麥美燕齊
◎◎◎◎◎
桑柘益吳楚
天蟲筐內走
蠶娘哭葉空
絲綿不上秤
匹帛價更高
◎◎◎◎◎

地母曰

蛇頭值歲初
穀食盈有餘
早禾莫令晚
蠶亦莫令遲
夏季麥苗秀
三冬成實肥

春社三伏日

春社二月廿一戊子日
秋社八月初五戊戌日
初伏六月廿六庚寅日
中伏閏六月初六庚子日
末伏閏六月十六庚戌日
入霉五月十一丙午日
出霉六月十九癸未日

春牛芒神服色

春牛身高四尺，長八尺，尾一尺二寸。頭青色，身紅色，腹紅色，牛角、耳、尾黑色，脛青色，牛蹄白色，牛口合，尾右繳，牛籠頭用苧繩拘子俱用桑柘木，結黃色，牛踏板用縣門右扇，⊙芒神身高三尺六寸五分，面如老年像，白衣繫紅腰帶，平梳兩髻在耳前，罨耳全戴揭起右邊，行纏鞋褲俱全，左行纏懸於左腰，鞭杖用柳枝長二尺四寸用苧結，俱用五綵色醮染，芒神晚閒立於牛後右邊。

元旦焚香開門

●子丑二時均犯截路空亡忌焚香◯寅時司命鳳輦長生三合◯卯時勾陳太陽天官六合●辰時犯日破大凶忌焚香◯巳時明堂貴人天赦日德日祿◑午時犯六戊忌焚香◯未時木星右弼河魁日貴◯申時金匱福德福星文昌◯酉時天德寶光土星●戊亥二時均犯截路空亡忌焚香◎取寅卯時焚香開門大吉◯取卯時向東南休門方或巳時向西方天月德並喜神方啓行大吉◎取酉時天德寶光土星焚香關門吉

運算人生19

張清淵2025發財開運寶典

國家圖書館出版品預行編目資料

張清淵發財開運寶典. 2025 / 張清淵著. -- 一版.
-- [新北市]：上優文化事業有限公司, 2024.11
256面；15x21公分. -- (運算人生；19)

ISBN 978-626-98932-5-6(平裝)

1.CST: 改運法

295.7　　113016066

作　　者　張清淵
企劃編輯　玉宸齋有限公司
校　　對　張瑞蘭、張瑞珍、張家瑜、張瑞麟、郭德言
文字編輯　蔡欣容
美術總監　馬慧琪
英文翻譯　新加坡陳鳳如
出 版 者　上優文化事業有限公司
電話：(02)8521-3848
傳真：(02)8521-6206
Email：8521book@gmail.com
（如有任何疑問請聯絡此信箱洽詢）
網站：www.8521book.com.tw
印　　刷　鴻嘉彩藝印刷股份有限公司
業務副總　林啟瑞0988-558-575
總 經 銷　紅螞蟻圖書有限公司
台北市內湖區舊宗路二段121巷19號
電話：(02)2795-3656
傳真：(02)2795-4100
網路書店　www.books.com.tw博客來網路書店
出版日期　2024年11月
版　　次　一版一刷
定　　價　288元

上優好書網

Facebook
粉絲專頁

LINE
官方帳號

YouTube
頻道

一本萬利通曆

二〇二五乙巳蛇年

張清淵 著